THIS BOOK IS THE PROPERTY OF:

STATE _____
PROVINCE _____
COUNTY _____
PARISH _____
SCHOOL DISTRICT_____
OTHER _____

Book No. _____
Enter information
in spaces
to the left as
instructed

ISSUED TO	Year Used	CONDITION	
		ISSUED	RETURNED
....	....	....	....
....	....	....	....
....	....	....	....
....	....	....	....
....	....	....	....
....	....	....	....
....	....	....	....
....	....	....	....
....	....	....	....

PUPILS to whom this textbook is issued must not write on any page
or mark any part of it in any way, consumable textbooks excepted.

1. Teachers should see that the pupil's name is clearly written in ink in the spaces above in every book issued.
2. The following terms should be used in recording the condition of the book: New; Good; Fair; Poor; Bad.

SUCCEEDING
in the
World
of Work

SIXTH EDITION

Grady Kimbrell
Educational Consultant
Santa Barbara, California

Ben S. Vineyard
Professor and
    Chairman Emeritus
Vocational and
    Technical Education
Pittsburg State University
Pittsburg, Kansas

 **Glencoe**
McGraw-Hill

New York, New York   Columbus, Ohio   Woodland Hills, California   Peoria, Illinois

Glencoe/McGraw-Hill

A Division of The **McGraw·Hill** *Companies*

Send all inquiries to:
Glencoe/McGraw-Hill
21600 Oxnard Street, Suite 500
Woodland Hills, California 91367

ISBN 0-02-814219-5 (Student Text)
ISBN 0-02-814221-7 (Teacher's Wraparound Edition)

6 7 8 9   004   01 00

Advisory Board

To best research and address the needs of today's workplace, Glencoe/McGraw-Hill assembled an advisory board of industry leaders and educators. The board lent its expertise and experience to establish the foundation for this innovative, real-world, career education program. Glencoe/McGraw-Hill would like to acknowledge the following companies and individuals for their support and commitment to this project:

Reviewers

Debra Brewster
Local Vocation Educator/Coordinator
DeForest High School
DeForrest, WI

Annie Hunter Clasen
Diversified Cooperative Training
    Coordinator
Bloomingdale Senior High School
Valrico, FL

Robert P. Dasco
Occupational Work Experience
    Coordinator
McKinley Senior High School
Canton, OH

Karen Ann Altfilisch Ellis
School-to-Career Program Director
Manual High School
Denver, CO

James R. Flanigan
English Teacher
McGuffey High School
Claysville, PA

Anthony M. Kemps
Technology Education Supervisor
Ramsey Public Schools
Ramsey, NJ

Albert A. Kennedy, Jr.
Industrial Cooperative Training
    Coordinator
Stephen F. Austin High School
Houston, TX

LouGene McKinney
Teacher/Coordinator Business and
    Marketing
Laramie High School
Laramie, WY

Lyn Flammia McMillan
Industrial Cooperative Training Teacher
Millbrook High School
Raleigh, NC

Mary Ann Carey-Nelson
Business Teacher
Ken-Ton School District
Kenmore West High School
Kenmore, NY

Ted Pietrzak
Marketing/Management Coordinator
Hayward High School
Hayward, CA

David E. Renkenberger
Construction Trades Department Head,
    Co-op Coordinator
Anthis Career Center
Fort Wayne, IN

Pam Schaffer
Vocational Education Coordinator
Utic Schools
Sterling Heights, MI

Jay L. Smith
I.C.E. Director
Lakeland High School
La Grange, IN

Table of Contents

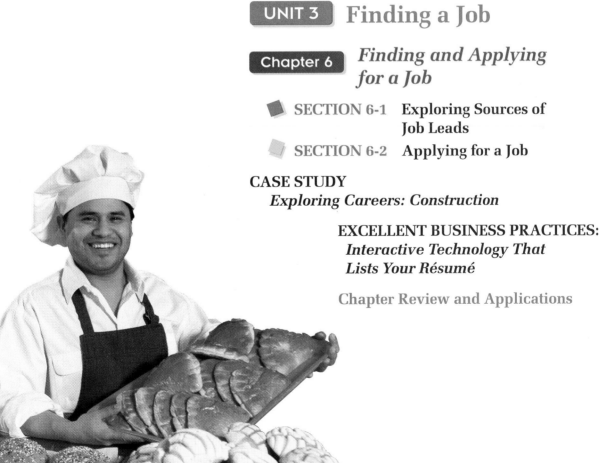

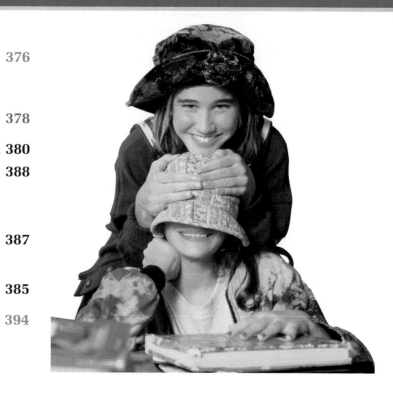

Welcome to *Succeeding in the World of Work*!

What do you want to do with your life? What do you dream of becoming? What are you good at? What do you enjoy? This book will help you find the answers to these questions.

If you really think about it, there is at least one thing, if not several things, you really enjoy—things that make the time fly and make you feel good about yourself. Maybe you love playing sports or acting in plays. Maybe you like working with computers or writing stories. Throughout this course, your challenge is to convert the things that interest you into a satisfying career. This book will help you do just that.

First, you'll take a look at yourself. You'll determine your interests, values, and ideal life-style and consider how they will influence your career choice. You'll then explore the many career areas and decide which careers best suit you. For example, if you love animals and value education, you may decide a career working as an exhibit interpreter at a zoo or aquarium is right for you.

Next, you will develop your individual career plan. You will look at the type of education you will need, and how to find, apply, and interview for a job.

From there, you'll take a good look at the skills you'll need on the job and gain valuable insight into how to develop these professional skills.

You'll also take an in-depth look at what to expect once you're living on your own. You'll learn how to manage your money,

make wise consumer purchases, and meet your adult responsibilities.

Finally, you'll focus on the importance of lifelong learning. You'll receive valuable advice on how to get ahead on the job and how to put your career on the fast track. You'll also learn tips on how to balance your work and personal life to achieve career and personal success.

Understanding the Text Structure

You'll find the structure of *Succeeding in the World of Work* easy to read and comprehend. The text is divided into seven units. Each unit covers a distinct area of career exploration: Self-Assessment, Exploring Careers, Finding a Job, Joining the Workforce, Professional Development, Life Skills, and Lifelong Learning.

Within each unit there are chapters. Each chapter is broken down into two or three short sections. The sections begin with a list of **Objectives** that tell you the skills and knowledge you will have mastered once you complete the section. The section's **Key Terms** are also listed. Each section concludes with a **Section Review** that helps to reinforce your understanding of section concepts.

At the end of the chapter, a **Highlights** page summarizes the chapter information. You can use this summary to review chapter content. A two-page **Chapter Review**

and journal writing as you apply chapter content to your own career explorations. This activity appears on the opening pages of each chapter.

• **Exploring Careers** presents information about various careers and individuals who work in them.

• **Excellent Business Practices** highlights unusually effective business practices of specific business organizations.

• **Career Do's and Don'ts** provides helpful tips to use in real-life situations.

follows the Highlights page. The review provides extensive questions and activities designed to help you check your understanding of the chapter.

Chapter Features

Text features provide further insight into career topics and challenge your creativity and imagination.

• The **Workforce 2000 Video** explores career material related to the chapter content. There is a video segment for every chapter. A scene from the chapter video segment appears on the chapter opener pages.

• The **Unit Quiz** gives you a chance to pretest your familiarity with the unit material you are about to explore.

• The **Unit Lab** gives you an opportunity to research all aspects of industry.

• **Journal: Personal Career Plan** gives you an opportunity to do some creative thinking

• **Attitude Counts** stresses the importance of adopting a positive viewpoint at work.

• **Ethics in Action** gives you the opportunity to consider what ethical decision you would make given specific real-life situations.

• **You're the Boss: Solving Workplace Problems** invites you to make managerial decisions about challenging workplace situations.

• The **Glossary** and **Index** allow you to quickly access definitions to terms and locate career subjects. The **Glossary** provides definitions for more than 200 terms. Following each definition in parentheses is the chapter page number on which the term is explained. The **Index** lists key terms and concepts along with important graphs, charts, and other chapter illustrations.

Get ready for an exciting career exploration adventure with *Succeeding in the World of Work*. An adventure that will prepare you for a lifetime!

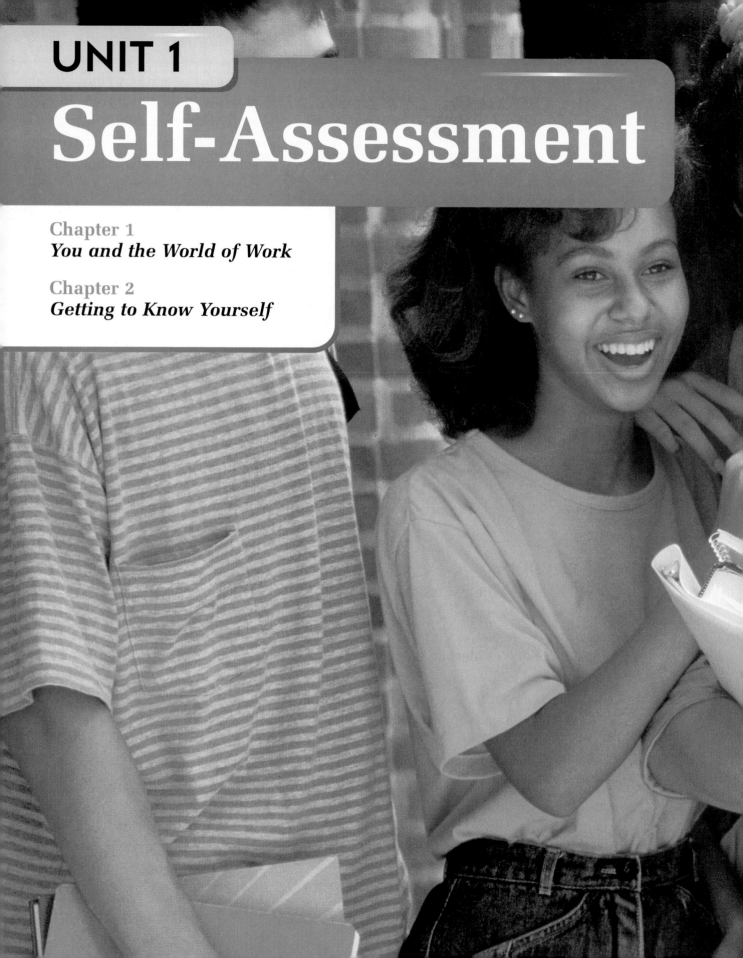

UNIT 1

Self-Assessment

Chapter 1
You and the World of Work

Chapter 2
Getting to Know Yourself

UNIT 1 QUIZ:

What Do You Know About Self-Assessment?

- How is a job different from a career?
- Why do people work?
- How has the workplace changed in the last ten years?
- Picture yourself in five years. What will your life be like?
- What things are important to you?
- What do you want from a career?

You and the World of Work

Section 1-1
Exploring the World of Work

Section 1-2
The Changing Workplace

In this video segment, find out why success means something different to everyone.

Journal
Personal Career Plan

Take a look into your future—it's the day of your retirement party. As you look back on your career, what are you most proud of? What will you say to the friends and coworkers who have gathered to celebrate with you? What do you hope to hear them say about you and your work? Write a journal entry about your feelings and ideas.

Exploring the World of Work

OBJECTIVES

After studying this section, you will be able to:

- **Distinguish between a job and a career.**
- **Explain the different reasons why people work.**

KEY TERMS

job
career
lifestyle

Are you nervous about the thought of graduating from high school and wondering what you're going to do afterward? Well, maybe that nervousness is a good sign. Maybe it's time to think about your options and to prepare for them. Will you go to trade school or college? Will you go to work? What kind of work will you do?

You probably won't be surprised to learn that most people prefer to do work that uses their interests and talents. After all, work takes up a lot of time. With a full-time job, you could spend more than 2,000 hours a year at work. (That's more time than you spend doing anything else except sleeping!)

What kind of job would be right for you? Think about what skills you have and what interests you. To get an idea of what work you'd like to do, make two lists.

- Write down your *skills*—the things you feel you're good at—such as drawing, being organized, solving math problems, or dancing.
- Then write down your *interests*, or favorite activities. You may like to listen to music, play basketball, or work with computers.

What jobs can you think of that might suit your skills and interests?

What Is Work?

Is work something people do simply to earn money, or is it something much more? Here's what Robert Lombardi, a graphic production artist, has to say about the meaning of work.

"I've found that work can be an enjoyable experience, not just the thing you do to make money. If you have a job you like, work means much more than just paying your bills. It means using your talents, being with people who have similar interests, making a contribution, and getting a real sense of satisfaction from doing a good job."

Robert uses a computer to arrange the words and artwork in magazines, books, and print advertisements. He finds his work satisfying because it suits his interests, skills, and talents.

Jobs and Careers

Is a job the same thing as a career? What's the difference between the two?

A **job** is work that people do for pay. The work usually consists of certain tasks. Often a job is a position with a company. For example, Robert has had jobs with advertising agencies and publishing companies. Sometimes jobs lead to careers.

A **career** is a series of related jobs built on a foundation of interest, knowledge, training, and experience. Robert developed his career by working at different graphic production jobs. As he gained experience, he found more challenging—and better-paying—work with each new job.

Like Robert, many people work at several jobs during their careers. According to the U.S. Department of Labor, the average American has at least seven jobs, including

Robert wanted to be a graphic production artist because he had a talent for visual arts. *Why is following your skills and interests so important in choosing a career?*

part-time jobs as teenagers, before age 30. Other recent reports show that those beginning their first jobs in the mid-1990s will change employers six or seven times before retirement.

Impact on Lifestyle

Your **lifestyle** is the way you use your time, energy, and resources. Many people use much of their time and energy and many of their resources at work. The work you do affects other parts of your life. It can determine how much time you have to spend with friends and family and how much money and energy you have to pursue your favorite activities. Your lifestyle may vary according to changes in your career.

To see how work affects lifestyle, read about Amelia. Amelia Sanchez is studying for her associate degree in early childhood education. Her goal is to work at a day care center, but for now she baby-sits for two elementary school children in the afternoons and on weekends.

Amelia's baby-sitting schedule frees her to take classes in the morning. She also is gaining experience working with children. Between going to school and working, though, she

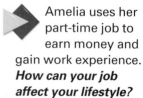
Amelia uses her part-time job to earn money and gain work experience. *How can your job affect your lifestyle?*

doesn't have much free time to spend with her friends and family. In addition, she spends most of her income and energy on getting her training. However, Amelia knows that she'll soon have the career she wants. She's willing to make sacrifices now. She knows that they are only temporary.

What kind of lifestyle do *you* want in the future? What things are important to you? Make a list of how you'd like to spend your time, resources, and energy. Look back at the lists you made earlier about your skills and interests. These lists can help you find out the kind of work you'd like to do and the kind of lifestyle you'd like to have.

Why People Work

Why do people work? Why do your family members work? Why do your friends work? If you have an after-school job, why do *you* work?

That's a no-brainer, you say—to make money! That's the most basic reason, of course, but can you think of other reasons for having a job? Here's a short list of why people work:

- People work to earn money to pay for housing, transportation, food, and clothes. There are other expenses, too, such as health care, insurance, education, and taxes. That's not all. Most people want money to pay for movies, gifts, travel, and other extras. Look at **Figure 1-1** below to see how consumers spend their money.

- People also work because they want to be with other people. They may enjoy working with a group of people, helping others, or just being in an environment with people who have similar interests.

- Self-fulfillment is another reason why people work. They feel good about

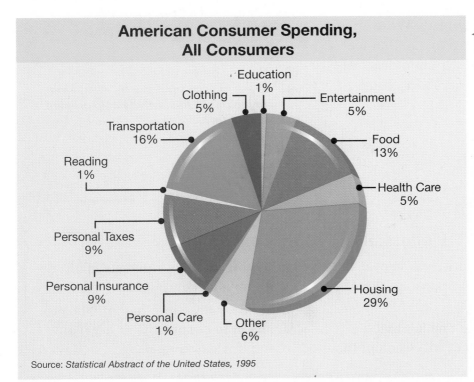

American Consumer Spending, All Consumers

Education 1%
Clothing 5%
Entertainment 5%
Transportation 16%
Food 13%
Reading 1%
Health Care 5%
Personal Taxes 9%
Personal Insurance 9%
Personal Care 1%
Other 6%
Housing 29%

Source: *Statistical Abstract of the United States, 1995*

 **Figure 1-1**

American consumers spend more than half their money in three areas. What are they? Why do you think this fact is a real eye-opener to people just starting out on their own?

themselves when they do a job well. Working at a job that suits them gives them a feeling of accomplishment.

If people do their work well, others repect them. When this happens they feel proud and respect themselves. For most people the chief source of self-fulfillment is success in the world of work.

People can find satisfaction in their jobs for many reasons. Herminio Fernandez, a video-game programmer, loves to create video games and figure out ways to make them work. He gets a real sense of satisfaction when he writes programs that help artists assemble the pictures for video games.

What task or job have you done recently that gave you a feeling of accomplishment? Perhaps it was illustrating a poster for a school fund-raising project or coaching basketball to younger children in your neighborhood. Write a brief entry in your journal describing the task and how you felt after completing it. What else could you do that might give you that feeling again? Finding self-fulfillment has lasting effects. You feel good about yourself and about what you do.

 Helping others gives some people a sense of accomplishment. *What kind of job might this activity help prepare this student for?*

SECTION 1-1 *Review*

Understanding Key Concepts

Using complete sentences, answer the following questions on a separate sheet of paper.

1. Give an example of one job that a high school graduate with each of the following skills or interests might do: math, music, computers.

2. Describe a situation that might cause a person to change his or her main reason for working.

Exploring Careers: Public Service

Lt. Commander Sally de Gozzaldi
Helicopter Pilot, US Navy

Q: Were you always interested in the military?

A: If anyone had told me, when I was a senior in high school, that I would be doing this, I would have said he or she was crazy. I studied geology in college. I didn't know anything about the military, but I always wanted to be a pilot. I heard about the Navy's pilot program from a woman I met at college.

Q: What was the training like?

A: You're trained very carefully, but it's tough. They try to weed out those who are not doing well. I didn't meet anyone who made it through who didn't really want to make it.

Q: Why did you choose helicopters?

A: There were three choices for flight training: the jet program, the multi-engine program, or helicopters. Helicopters was the only program that allowed women to be completely competitive with men. Other programs are open to women now.

Q: What's the most difficult part of your job?

A: I love to fly and I like to be out at sea, because that's when I fly the most and do what I was trained to do, but that's also when I'm away from my husband and baby. The ship is loud, and I usually share a room and a bathroom.

Q: Why did you make the Navy your career?

A: I was pleasantly surprised with the people I met. I realized I was doing what I wanted to do. Why get out when I'm having fun?

Thinking Critically

Would a career in the Navy be appropriate for you? Why or why not?

CAREER FACTS

Nature of the Work:
    May include deployments at sea or nonflying onshore assignments.

Training or Education Needed:
    Bachelor's degree; 13 weeks at Officer's Candidate School; 1½ years of flight training; 6 months of readiness training.

Aptitudes, Abilities, and Skills:
    Responsibility; self-esteem; desire to fly; excellent physical and emotional health.

Salary Range:
    Varies with time in the Navy and rank; $27,400 to $59,500, plus benefits and bonuses.

Career Path:
    Advance through the ranks, depending on abilities; after service in the Navy, work in corporate industry or in medical or rescue positions.

The Changing Workplace

OBJECTIVES

After studying this section, you will be able to:

- Describe how the global economy affects jobs in the United States.
- Explain how technology is changing the workplace.
- Explain how the job outlook will affect your career plans.

KEY TERMS

economy
global economy
job market
team
outsourcing
telecommute

Your place in the world of work will influence every aspect of your life. This is why choosing the kind of work you will do is one of the most important decisions you will ever make. So far, you've been thinking about the kind of work that might fit your interests and skills. You've also been thinking about the kind of lifestyle you'd like to have and how your work would affect it. What else might be important to consider when thinking about the work you'd like to do?

Well, there's the workplace itself. Today, however, the workplace is constantly changing. Changes in the world affect what work is available for people to do and the way in which they do it. Knowing about these changes can help you make sound decisions about your job, your career, and your future. How can you keep up with all these changes?

You can follow trends in the world of work the same way you keep up with what's happening in music, fashion, sports, and entertainment. Which are the up-and-coming industries and occupations? Which ones are on the way out? To find out, read newspapers and magazines and watch the news on television. Talk to people who work in the field that you're interested in and ask them questions about the changes and opportunities in their workplace.

The Global Economy and the Job Market

Look at a few of the things you own—a pair of pants, a book, a CD, a bicycle—and check their labels or packaging. Where were the objects made? At least some of your possessions were probably made in other countries. Because of what you buy, you are part of the global economy. The term **economy** refers to the ways in which a group produces, distributes, and consumes its goods and services. *Goods* are the items that people buy. *Services* are activities done for others for a fee. The term **global economy** refers to the ways in which the world's economies are linked.

The global economy has a direct impact on the **job market**, or the demand for particular jobs, in each country. How does the global economy affect the job market in the United States—the job market you will probably be entering?

Some critics say that the global economy is bad for this country. Trade with foreign countries, they argue, can lead to American workers losing their jobs to workers overseas. For instance, some American computer software companies hire workers in India and Pakistan—where labor costs are cheaper—to do basic programming.

On the other hand, many people believe that the global economy is good for the United States. Many American businesses export goods (sell goods to other countries), and these exports create jobs. In fact, the export business accounted for one of every six new manufacturing jobs in this country in a recent year. Also, foreign firms employ more than 10 million Americans in their U.S.-based offices.

Keeping abreast of the global economy can help you learn more about the worldwide job market. For example, which jobs

As a part of the global economy, consumers can buy products from around the world. *What are the advantages?*

Career Do's & Don'ts

When Entering the Workplace...

Do:
- define your goals.
- be informed.
- expect the best.
- learn from others.

Don't:
- be influenced by negative people.
- let failure stop you.
- be self-critical.
- limit your thinking.

will be sent abroad? Which jobs will be created because of the changing economy? Which jobs will involve trade with foreign countries? Which jobs will be available to American workers in foreign countries?

Impact on Today's Workers

The global economy creates stiff competition for businesses. Just as you want to do well in your career, an employer wants his or her business to do well. As a result,

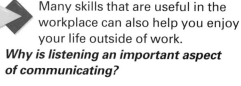

Many skills that are useful in the workplace can also help you enjoy your life outside of work. *Why is listening an important aspect of communicating?*

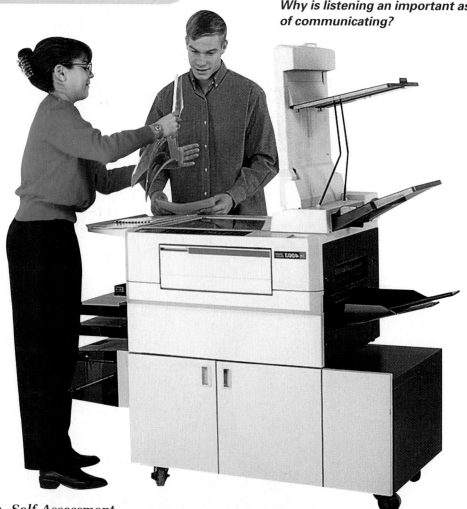

the employer will need employees who can do a variety of tasks and who possess a variety of skills.

How can you meet the demands put on workers in a global economy? You can develop skills—many of which you are already learning—and apply them in your job. The U.S. Labor Department Secretary's Commission on Achieving Necessary Skills (SCANS) has identified the following workplace skills:

- *basic skills*, such as reading, writing, mathematics, listening, and speaking;
- *thinking skills*, such as creative thinking, decision making, problem solving, seeing things in the mind's eye (picturing things in your mind), knowing how to learn, and reasoning; and
- *personal qualities*, such as responsibility, self-esteem, sociability, self-management, integrity, and honesty.

EXCELLENT BUSINESS PRACTICES

Seattle Times Company Focuses on Diversity

The Seattle Times Company of Seattle, Washington, has established programs that address the need to serve a diverse population.

Periodically, staff editors review photographs in the paper for an accurate representation of people of color and women. Editors also critique articles to make sure they accurately represent ethnicity, lifestyles, and family situations of people of different backgrounds.

The paper takes a strong stance on maintaining a diverse workforce. For instance, 21 percent of employees, including reporters and editors, are minorities, well over the average of 13 percent of the local population. Women make up 44 percent of the newsroom employees and 33 percent of the overall company.

Even so, the Seattle Times Company realizes that it is not enough to just hire minorities. It also conducts a two-day diversity training program. The program provides

workers with an opportunity to talk about their experiences with stereotyping, prejudice, and lack of awareness of other cultures.

The Seattle Times also has a diversity council of volunteers who evaluate the workforce, an employee mentoring program, internships, career planning, and a library. The company even conducts an anonymous survey of how effective it has been in creating a nurturing environment for people of diverse backgrounds.

Thinking Critically

Why is it especially important for a newspaper to employ people from diverse backgrounds? How does a diverse workforce affect coworkers?

Changing Technology

Not long ago, floppy disks were still floppy, laptops had not been invented, there were no CD-ROMs, and the Internet did not exist. Desktop personal computers were just coming into common use. Such advances in technology are constantly—and rapidly—changing how people work. As *Figure 1-2* shows, people working in very different fields use a wide range of technology to help them do their work more quickly and efficiently.

▶ Figure 1-2

Technology in the Workplace

Modern technology enables a variety of workers to do their jobs quickly and efficiently.

A Sales workers in stores wave wands over goods so that lasers can read prices. The sale is instantly fed into a computerized database that tracks the store's inventory. Sales workers can help customers complete their shopping more quickly. Stores keep better track of how each item sells and when they need to reorder.

B Repair workers out on calls communicate with the home office via cellular phones. In this way they can quickly learn of homes or offices they must visit to make repairs. The company saves time. Customers get faster service.

Today's Workplace

Modern technology affects not only what work you do but how and where you do it. Trends that you'll probably encounter in the workplace include the use of teams, outsourcing, and telecommuting.

- A **team** is an organized group that sets goals, makes decisions, and implements actions within a company. As companies increase their use of technology, some new jobs are created (such as technical jobs), and others

A business team may have a facilitator rather than a leader. ***How can you develop teamwork skills?***

The most widespread technology, though, is the computer. Millions of workers now use computers. Office workers use them to prepare letters and reports. Manufacturing workers use them to run robots and to test products. Farmworkers use them to test the soil and to keep track of livestock.

are eliminated. Many companies have eliminated the position of middle manager—a job that involves directing other workers. As a result, workers are collaborating on projects rather than just doing what a manager tells them to do.

- Another practice is **outsourcing**. In this practice, businesses hire other companies or individuals to produce their services or goods. For example, airline companies often contract with individuals or other companies to provide baggage handling and meals for their customers.

- More than 24 million workers do not work at a company's work site. Instead they **telecommute**, or work at home, using a computer, fax (facsimile), and telephone to perform their jobs.

Impact on Today's Workers

The workplace may be changing, but one thing is certain. You'll be involved with technology in some form—especially computers—in whatever career you choose. Does that mean you need to know what goes on inside a computer? No, says one expert: "After all, you don't have to know how to design a car to drive one." You will need to know how to *use* one, though.

You'll also probably continue learning for as long as you work—not just about new technologies but also about new ways of working. While advanced technology offers you many different opportunities for work, it also means you'll need to keep up with the changes.

The Job Outlook

What can you expect jobwise when you graduate from high school? The good news is that nearly 25 million new jobs are predicted to be created by the year 2005. However, these jobs will not be evenly distributed across industries. Most of the work will be in the service-producing

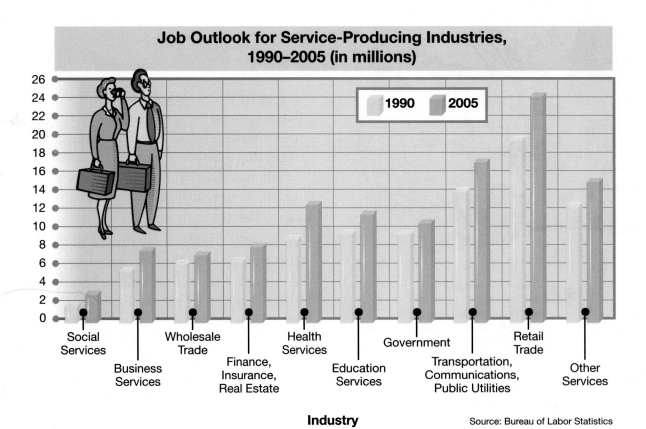

Job Outlook for Service-Producing Industries, 1990–2005 (in millions)

1990 2005

Social Services · Business Services · Wholesale Trade · Finance, Insurance, Real Estate · Health Services · Education Services · Government · Transportation, Communications, Public Utilities · Retail Trade · Other Services

Industry

Source: Bureau of Labor Statistics

▲ Figure 1-3 Why do you think the service sector—health, business, education, social services—is creating so many jobs?

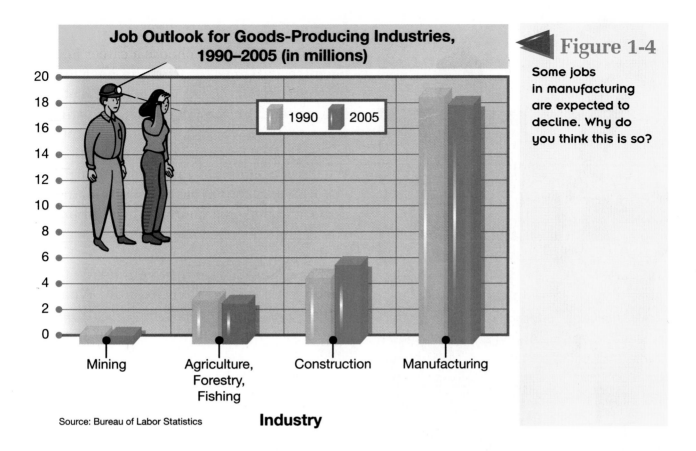

Job Outlook for Goods-Producing Industries, 1990–2005 (in millions)

1990 | 2005

Mining — Agriculture, Forestry, Fishing — Construction — Manufacturing

Industry

Source: Bureau of Labor Statistics

Figure 1-4

Some jobs in manufacturing are expected to decline. Why do you think this is so?

industries. *Service-producing industries* provide services for a fee. These include medical care, travel accommodations, and education. Fewer jobs are expected in the *goods-producing industries*, which provide goods such as stereo systems, cars, and buildings.

Figure 1-3 and ***Figure 1-4*** identify these different industries and show expectations for their growth or decline. Read the graphs to find out which industries are growing and which are declining. How does this information affect your ideas about a career? Think about your skills and interests. Which industries do you think would be appropriate for you?

YOU'RE THE BOSS!

Solving Workplace Problems

You own and manage a bagel bakery. Since you spend most of your time in the office, you've hired several clerks to sell directly to the customers. Lately you've noticed that your morning clerk is efficient —but not very friendly. She rushes on, even when customers want to chat for a minute. What should you do?

Impact on Today's Workers

You don't have to choose a career just because it seems to offer the best job prospects. Even though you're learning to follow trends in the job market, you still want to find work that matches your interests, skills, personality, and abilities. Whatever occupation you choose, though, you *will* need certain basic skills, thinking skills, and personal qualities. In addition, you'll probably need specific task-related skills.

For example, suppose you decide to become a physical therapy aide. What interests, skills, and personal qualities would you need for this occupation? Here are a few:

- a desire to help and motivate people,
- good listening skills in order to learn what your patients' needs are,
- good speaking skills in order to explain the exercises to your patients, and
- the ability to work under the supervision of a physical therapist.

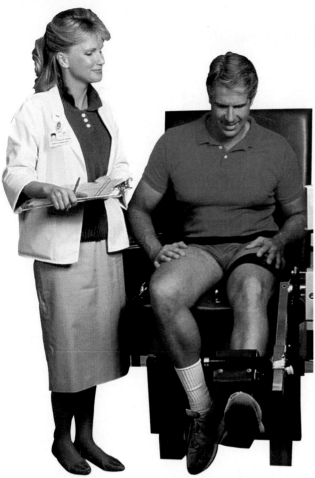

A physical therapy aide helps people recover their strength after orthopedic surgery. *Why does a physical therapy aide need to have a sense of responsibility and self-esteem?*

SECTION 1-2 *Review*

Understanding Key Concepts

Using complete sentences, answer the following questions on a separate sheet of paper.

1. How does the global economy affect the job market?

2. Choose a career you're interested in, and describe how technology may affect it.

3. Which do you consider more important in choosing a career—following your own interests or following the job outlook? Why?

Highlights

SECTION 1-1 Summary

- Consider your interests and skills when planning the kind of work you'd like to do.

- A job is work that people do for pay. The work usually consists of certain tasks. A career is a series of related jobs built on a person's interests, knowledge, training, and experience.

- Your lifestyle is the way you use your time, energy, and resources.

- Three important reasons why people work are (1) to earn money to pay expenses, (2) to fulfill their need to be with other people, and (3) to receive satisfaction from doing a job well.

Key Terms

job *(p. 5)*
career *(p. 5)*
lifestyle *(p. 6)*

Key Terms

economy *(p. 11)*
global economy *(p. 11)*
job market *(p. 11)*
team *(p. 15)*
outsourcing *(p. 15)*
telecommute *(p. 16)*

SECTION 1-2 Summary

- The global economy has a direct impact on the job market. You need basic skills, thinking skills, and personal qualities to meet the demands of the job market.

- Rapidly advancing technology has changed the workplace. Trends in the workplace include the use of teams, outsourcing, and telecommuting.

- Most of the new jobs predicted for 1990 through 2005 will fall in the service-producing sector. While you need to be aware of trends, seeking job satisfaction is also very important.

Reviewing Key Terms

Write a short paragraph about the world of work, using the terms below.

job	job market
career	team
lifestyle	outsourcing
economy	telecommute
global economy	

Recalling Key Concepts

Choose the correct answer for each item below.

1. Work that you do for pay is ____.

   (a) a career (b) an industry (c) a job

2. American consumers spend the most money on ____.

   (a) food (b) housing (c) health care

3. Why do some people think the global economy is good for the United States?

   (a) Some jobs go to workers overseas.

   (b) Foreign products are of a higher quality.

   (c) The U.S. export business creates new jobs here at home.

4. Telecommuting means ____.

   (a) working at home, using a computer, fax, and telephone

   (b) transporting manufactured goods

   (c) communicating by television

5. By 2005, most new jobs will be in ____.

   (a) manufacturing (b) entertainment

   (c) services

Thinking Critically

Using complete sentences, answer each of the questions below on a separate sheet of paper.

1. Why is it an advantage to have several jobs while you are building your career?

2. How does your job's income affect other aspects of your lifestyle?

3. Do you agree that the global economy makes businesses more competitive? Explain.

4. What is the danger of limiting your career opportunities to only those you have heard about or been trained for?

5. Why do people who telecommute need good organizational and management skills?

SCANS Foundation Skills and Workplace Competencies

Basic Skills: *Math*

1. Your clothing store is open seven days a week from 9 a.m. to 9 p.m. You are the manager of three employees, each of whom wants to work at least 24 hours a week. Each employee can work the 9:00 a.m. to 3:00 p.m. shift or the 3:00 p.m. to 9:00 p.m. shift and at least one weekend day. No one can work both shifts on the same day. Make up a schedule that will meet these requirements.

Interpersonal Skills: *Teaching Others*

2. Sherry works as an administrative assistant for a small law firm. Today she needs to explain to a new lawyer how to use the office's voice mail

system. Prepare an outline of one good way for Sherry to teach the lawyer the system so that he fully understands it.

Connecting Academics to the Workplace

Health

1. Anita works as a bookkeeper for an insurance company. One day, she notices a loose telephone wire on the floor. Research workplace safety in the library, via the Internet, or by speaking to an employer. Is there a safety law that protects workers? Then explain what you think Anita should do.

Math

2. Rick is an intern in a restaurant. He wants to become a chef. It takes three workers 20 minutes each to prepare the vegetables for the salad bar. If the salad bar is filled four times a night, on average, how much worker time is required to keep it filled?

Social Studies

3. Sarah is a hot-line computer trouble-shooter for a manufacturer in the United States. She is interested in living and working in Japan. Research the current job outlook in Japan. Which industries and occupations are growing and which are declining? What openings are there for foreigners?

Developing Teamwork and Leadership Skills

Divide into teams of four. Select one member as the facilitator to keep the team organized. Assume that you all work in the personnel department of a publishing company. There is an opening for a receptionist. First, work together to write a job description. Then write a classified ad.

Real-World Workshop

Develop a list of jobs that you've had—volunteer and for pay. For each job, list the tasks you had to complete. Then list the skills you used to perform each task.

School-to-Work Connection

Think of an industry that you are interested in. Identify someone who works in that industry, and discuss with that person the impact of the global economy and technological changes on that industry. Ask what impact these changes have had—and are expected to have—on the training needed by workers in that industry. Prepare a brief report on your findings.

Individual Career Plan

Select an industry that you are interested in working in. Locate the most recent Bureau of Labor Statistics report analyzing future employment trends. Find your industry in the report, and note how much jobs in that industry are expected to grow or decline in the future. Explain in a paragraph how the trends you read about affect your interest in that industry. Keep this and other information about the industry in order to maintain a personal update on your future career.

Getting to Know Yourself

Section 2-1
Decision Making

Section 2-2
Setting Lifestyle Goals

Section 2-3
Are Your Goals Realistic?

In this video segment, explore why it's important to consider your personality, interests, and abilities, when choosing a career.

Journal
Personal Career Plan

Think about all your activities during a typical week—at school and work, with your friends, with your family, and alone. Which particular activity do you find most satisfying? What makes that activity especially satisfying for you? What does this tell you about your values and your interests? Record your ideas in your journal.

Decision Making

SECTION 2-1

OBJECTIVES

After studying this section, you will be able to:

- Follow the seven steps in the decision-making process.
- Follow an effective strategy for choosing a career.

KEY TERM

decision-making process

How do you make decisions? Do you flip a coin? Consult friends? Make lists of pros and cons? If you're the kind of person who waits for someone else to make decisions for you, you may not be very happy with the outcome.

Maybe you've been putting off deciding what to do after graduation. If so, keep the following fact in mind: Most people don't plan to fail; they just fail to plan. The truth is, half of all employed people simply fall into their jobs—out of laziness or luck or from being unaware of other options. If you'd rather have a say in your future, it's time to take control of your own life.

A Seven-Step Process

If you've ever made an important decision, you know that good decision making doesn't just happen. The longer a decision will affect your life, the more time you need to think about possible consequences. Decisions that will affect your life for many years should be made carefully and logically. One of the biggest decisions in your life—your career choice—will require serious planning. This will be easier if you follow a **decision-making process**—a logical series of steps to identify and evaluate possibilities and to arrive at a good choice.

Some decisions are more important than others. *Why might these newlyweds take a long time to decide which house to buy?*

Breaking It Down

Like learning a new dance, following a decision-making process may feel awkward at first as you work through the basic steps. Once you have learned them, however, you can add variations of your own to adapt the process to different life situations. Here, then, are the seven basic steps in a typical decision-making process:

1. Define your needs or wants.
2. Analyze your resources.
3. Identify your choices.
4. Gather information.
5. Evaluate your choices.
6. Make a decision.
7. Plan how to reach your goal.

Now take a look at *Figure 2-1* on the next page to see how these seven steps can be applied to buying a car.

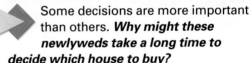

YOU'RE THE BOSS!

Solving Workplace Problems

As the owner of a fast-food franchise, you have trouble keeping reliable employees. This is the first job for most of the young people you hire, and they need weeks of training. You often feel that, once your employees are well trained and productive, they move on to other jobs. What will you do about this situation?

Would You Buy This Car?
How to Use a Seven-Step Decision-Making Process

Step 1	**Define Your Needs or Wants**	Chances are, you want a car that is not too expensive and is in reasonably good condition.
Step 2	**Analyze Your Resources**	Your main resource in this case is money. How much do you have? How much do you need to buy the car?
Step 3	**Identify Your Choices**	Now it's time to think about where you will get the car. You might make a list of sources, including new-car dealers, used-car dealers, owner-advertised cars in the classified ads, and your second cousin Ellen, who offered to sell you her 1985 station wagon for "next to nothing."
Step 4	**Gather Information**	Next, you must take time to evaluate each source on your list. Call each person or place, and make an appointment. Look at each available car, and ask questions. Take notes on such factors as cost, condition, insurance, warranty, and appearance. Take test drives. Draw sketches. At this point, you may eliminate some choices. For example, a new car may be too expensive.
Step 5	**Evaluate Your Choices**	Now is the time to review your notes. You might make a chart rating each car on the basis of four or five factors. In evaluating your choices, you will need to consider which factors are most important to you.
Step 6	**Make a Decision**	Working from your notes or chart, decide which car you want to buy.
Step 7	**Plan How to Reach Your Goal**	Focusing now on the car you have chosen, list the steps you need to take before you can actually drive the car home. These may include informing the dealer that you want the car, making a down payment, arranging a loan, and buying insurance.

▲ Figure 2-1   A seven-step decision-making process can help you make informed choices. Why is it important to make conscious decisions?

 What you enjoy doing is an important personal resource that needs to be considered as you plan your career. *What do you think these carpenters enjoy about their work?*

Choosing a Career

You can also use the seven-step process in choosing a career. However, since the stakes are much higher than they are in buying a car, the process will be more complex. You will work through each of the following steps in detail as you proceed through this and the next three chapters.

EXCELLENT BUSINESS PRACTICES

Personal Empowerment

Rhino Foods Inc. of Burlington, Vermont, a small frozen-dessert company, has a "wants" program designed to help employees achieve their life goals. All employees are encouraged to work with "wants coordinators" who coach employees in identifying what they want and setting steps to achieve goals or to cultivate skills. These wants may range from buying a house to writing a book or seeking a promotion. The program helps workers develop strong connections between their work and personal lives.

The company also takes a personal interest in employees. When Rhino Foods faced a temporary overload of 25 percent of its workforce, the company helped employees find temporary work at local companies. If the other companies paid them lower wages, Rhino paid the difference. Employees kept their seniority, benefits, and accrued vacation, and came back to Rhino when jobs opened up again.

Thinking Critically

How can a job be an essential component to attaining specific "wants"?

Step 1. Define Your Needs by Using Your Hopes and Dreams

The path to a career starts with considering your hopes and dreams for the future. Where will you want to live? Do you want a job that will allow you to travel or to stay at home? How much money will you need to earn? How much of your time and energy will you be willing to devote to your job? Later in this chapter, you will explore such questions and generate information about your personal goals.

Step 2. Analyze Your Personal Resources

In choosing a career, your resources relate to who you are and what you have to offer. Such resources include your values, interests, aptitudes and abilities, and personality traits and styles of learning. By being aware of all that you are, you will be more likely to make a realistic career choice. In the next sections of this chapter, you will examine these various aspects of yourself.

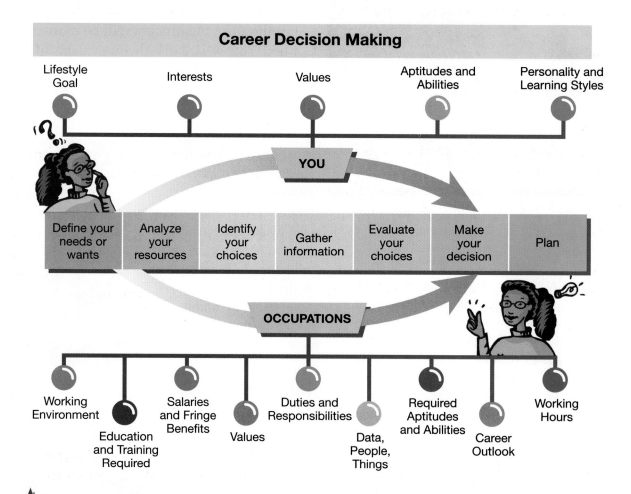

Figure 2-2 Over the next few chapters, you will be proceeding through the seven-step decision-making process, trying to choose a career for yourself. This diagram previews your course. What two general areas will you be exploring before you actually make a career decision and begin to plan for it?

Step 3. Identify Your Career Choices

This step involves selecting several possible careers that you think may match your personal goals and resources. If you are like many teenagers, you may not be able to think of a career you would enjoy. You can jump-start your thinking by increasing your awareness of life's possibilities. Keep your eyes and ears open to discover "what's out there." Even if you decide not to follow certain paths, at least you will know your options. Chapters 3 and 4 will help you uncover many career possibilities.

Step 4. Research Your Career Choices

Have you ever heard the phrase "research and development"? The two terms go together because successful people know that there is no development without research. Chapter 3 will show you how to go about researching the careers you've identified as possible choices for yourself. In Chapter 4, you will see if being in business for yourself is the right path for you.

Step 5. Evaluate Your Career Choices

By the time you reach this fifth step, you will have gathered much information both about yourself and about various career possibilities. Evaluating your career choices involves systematically looking at them to see whether they match your personal goals and resources. *Figure 2-2* shows how the decision-making process is central to career evaluation. If the process looks complicated, don't worry. Chapter 5 will suggest a helpful strategy for making this evaluation process manageable.

Steps 6 and 7. Make Your Decision and Plan How to Reach Your Goal

Though you may change your career goal several times, it is still important to make a decision and a plan. You may also discover at some point that your career goal is unrealistic or undesirable. You can then repeat the decision-making process to arrive at a new goal. Chapter 5 will help you focus on these last two steps.

SECTION 2-1 *Review*

Understanding Key Concepts

Using complete sentences, answer the following questions on a separate sheet of paper.

1. Imagine that you've won a $1,000 gift certificate for buying audio/video equipment at a local store. Explain how you would use the seven steps in the decision-making process to decide what to buy.

2. Explain the importance of having a strategy for choosing a career.

Setting Lifestyle Goals

OBJECTIVES

After studying this section, you will be able to:

- **Identify your values and describe how they affect your career choices.**
- **Identify your interests and describe how they affect your career choices.**
- **Determine whether you prefer working with data, people, or things.**

KEY TERMS

lifestyle goals
values
data

"Know thyself!" This inscription was carved at the Ancient Greek temple in Delphi, where people once traveled seeking advice about their futures. This bit of ancient wisdom is no less valid today. By getting to know yourself, you can plot your future better and choose a career you'll be interested in pursuing. A good place to begin this inward exploration is by considering lifestyle goals.

Lifestyle goals are the way you want to spend your time, energy, and resources in the future. Brainstorm about the lifestyle you'd like to have someday. Ask yourself a few questions.

- What do you want to accomplish in life?
- Do you want to raise a family?
- Where would you like to live—in a house or in an apartment? In a city or in the country?
- How would you like to spend your free time?
- Do you want a high income or just enough money to be comfortable?

Now imagine your life 5 or 10 years from today. Write down or sketch the way you'd like to be living. What career would make this lifestyle possible? To begin to see whether this career would be a realistic choice for you, you'll need to take a closer look at yourself.

Many people prefer a career that allows them to live near their family and friends. *What kind of career might give you a chance to work in your community?*

What Are Your Values?

Becoming aware of your values is an important way of getting to know yourself. Your **values** are the principles that you want to live by and the beliefs that are important to you. For example, if you spend a good deal of time playing your guitar and

This woman works as an aide in a veterinary clinic. *What other career would be appropriate for a person who cares about animals?*

listening to music, you probably would say that one of your values is artistic expression.

Besides principles and beliefs, your values may also include concrete things, such as money and fine clothing. As you think about a future career, you should consider how well it suits your values.

Six General Values

Your values may change as you go through life. However, you will probably keep a core set of basic values that you learned early on from the people who were most important to you. To help determine your current values, think about the following list of six general values. Which ones are very important to you, and which ones concern you less? Can you think of any careers especially suited to each of these values?

1. *Responsibility.* Being responsible means fulfilling obligations in a dependable and trustworthy way. You may decide to take on responsibilities, such as caring for a sick friend. Other responsibilities may be automatically expected of you as part of your position in life, say, as a parent or team leader.

2. *Relationships.* If you value relationships, your family and friends are important to you. You may then make career decisions that will allow you to work with people you like or to live near your family.

3. *Compassion.* Having compassion means you care deeply about people and their well-being. You may also feel compassion for other creatures, such as threatened animals. A compassionate person may choose a career that would help people lead better lives.

4. *Courage.* Courage is the ability to conquer fear or despair. You use courage, for example, when you speak up for an unpopular cause. It may take courage to follow your values!

5. *Achievement.* Valuing achievement means you want to succeed in whatever you do, whether you are an artist, an auto mechanic, a wilderness guide, or a computer programmer.

6. *Recognition.* If you value recognition, you want other people to appreciate and respect your accomplishments. You want to be rewarded for your work in some noticeable way—with a good salary, through job promotions, or with approval and praise.

Now make your own list, ranking your values in order of importance. You may include some or all of the six general values, and you may add as many others as you wish. (Keep this list for later use.) Can you imagine a career that would satisfy your particular mix of values?

Putting Your Values into Practice

While many people may share the same value—such as believing it is important to help others—each person may put that value into practice in a different way. For example, Chris Watson is a paraprofessional at an elementary school in suburban Chicago. He helps disabled children get around by assisting them

Chris works at a school for children with special needs. He makes friends with all the children at the school. This behavior helps students with disabilities become more a part of things. *How else could Chris help the children he works with?*

with their wheelchairs and walkers. Through his work, Chris helps one person at a time. Janet Gregory, in contrast, helps others indirectly by working as an administrator for a charity organization that shelters the homeless in the Bronx, New York. In trying to match a career to your own set of values, you will probably find that you have a range of choices. Narrowing your choices will mean looking even deeper into yourself.

What Are Your Interests?

In addition to recognizing your values, you need to pay attention to your interests when considering a career. Your interests are the things you enjoy doing. You may, for example, like singing in a choir or doing dissections in biology class. If you aren't sure what your interests are, one way to find out is to try activities you haven't done before. You might try, for example, taking karate classes or volunteering at a hospital.

Favorite Activities

You probably already enjoy a variety of activities, so make a list of your 10 favorite ones and try to rank them. Think of activities you like to do with friends or quietly by yourself—at school, at home, at work, or outdoors. (Keep this list for later use.)

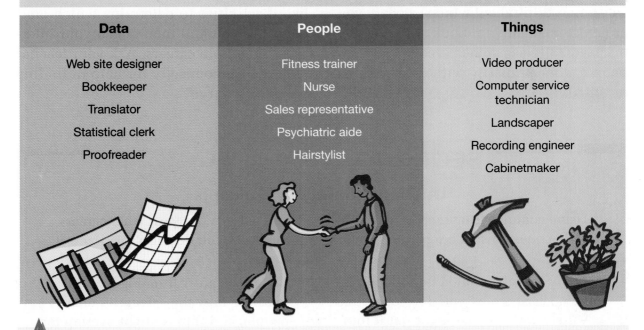

Careers Related to Data, People, and Things

Data	People	Things
Web site designer	Fitness trainer	Video producer
Bookkeeper	Nurse	Computer service technician
Translator	Sales representative	Landscaper
Statistical clerk	Psychiatric aide	Recording engineer
Proofreader	Hairstylist	Cabinetmaker

▲ Figure 2-3   This chart shows some careers in each of three categories. Which career interests you the most? Why? You can find other listings at your library in the U.S. Department of Labor's <u>Dictionary of Occupational Titles.</u>

Data, People, or Things?

Identifying your interests can help you recognize whether you would prefer to work with data, people, or things. These three categories described below can form the basis for describing different kinds of careers.

- The **data** category involves working with information, ideas, facts, symbols, figures, or statistics.
- The people category includes working with people *and* animals.
- The things category involves working with physical objects of any size, such as instruments, tools, machinery, equipment, raw materials, and vehicles.

Since any career you choose would probably involve an overlapping of these categories, think about which category you are *most* interested in. Look at *Figure 2-3* on page 33 to see some careers in which people work primarily with data, people, or things.

You're a newly hired sales clerk in an office supply store. A group of students comes into the store regularly. You've seen these students steal several small items. When you mention this to a more experienced employee, she just shrugs. Will you discuss your observations with anyone else? Why or why not?

Interest Surveys

Another helpful way to identify and assess your interests is to take an interest survey, which is like a test that has no right or wrong answers. You choose from a long list of activities to determine which ones appeal to you and then match your interests to possible careers. Ask your teacher or guidance counselor for help in finding an interest survey.

SECTION 2-2 *Review*

Understanding Key Concepts

Using complete sentences, answer the following questions on a separate sheet of paper.

1. Choose a value that is important to you. Discuss how you developed this value and how you might put it into practice in a career.

2. Choose one of your interests, and write down reasons why you enjoy this activity. Suggest what career might let you develop this interest further.

3. Choose a career from Figure 2-3. Describe how the categories data, people, and things might overlap for a person working in that career.

Exploring Careers: Communications and Media

Carolina Narváez
Public Relations Specialist

Q: What *is* public relations?

A: My company deals with corporate public relations. We try to build a positive public image of each client's company or corporation. We do that by writing press releases about things going on in the company—new products, staff changes, policy changes, events that promote the company's image. We contact the media; such as television, radio, newspapers, or magazines.

Q: What skills are most useful in your job?

A: The most useful skills are people skills. I work with the client and with others at the company who are on the client's team. I have to be able to communicate clearly. I also have to be detail-oriented, organized, and patient. Writing, editing, and proofreading skills are also necessary.

Q: What background did you have before going into public relations?

A: I majored in communications in college and had some experience in the communications field. I thought it would be interesting and a good learning experience to handle multiple tasks and accounts at once.

Thinking Critically

What types of companies need public relations specialists? Explain.

CAREER FACTS

Nature of the Work:
Develop and maintain a favorable public image for a client through media contacts, public events, and publications.

Training or Education Needed:
English, journalism, or communications degree preferred; experience working in a related field.

Aptitudes, Abilities, and Skills:
Math, listening, speaking, and interpersonal skills; problem-solving skills; decision-making and reading and writing skills; ability to allocate time, material, and human resources; ability to work under pressure; skills in persuasion; creativity; self-reliance; attention to detail.

Salary Range:
Start $15,000 to $20,000; up to $50,000 or more.

Career Path:
Start at a newspaper or as a secretary or research assistant at a public relations firm, gradually taking on a wider range of responsibilities; advance within the firm or by moving to other firms.

Are Your Goals Realistic?

OBJECTIVES

After studying this section, you will be able to:

- **Identify your aptitudes and abilities and describe how they affect your career choice.**
- **Identify and match your personality and learning style to career choices.**

KEY TERMS

aptitude
ability
personality
self-concept
learning styles

Now that you have identified some of your values and interests, what's next? You'll want to consider your skills and personality.

Aptitudes and Abilities

Aptitude and ability are the "before and after" of a skill. An **aptitude** is your potential for learning a certain skill. An **ability** is a skill you have already developed. Suppose you discover that you have the knack for training your new pet dog. If you continue to study and work with other dogs to become a professional trainer, then your aptitude will become your ability.

How do you discover your own aptitudes and abilities? First, you need to realize that there are many kinds of skills. Look at these general examples from the list of SCANS Skills:

creative thinking	decision making
knowing how to learn	seeing things in the mind's eye
responsibility	self-esteem
friendliness	adaptability
honesty	self-control

What other skills can you think of?

What Are *Your* Aptitudes and Abilities?

To get a clear picture of your aptitudes and abilities, make a list of all your skills that you can think of. Need help? Try these techniques:

- Make a chart with the headings Mental, Physical, and Social. List your aptitudes and abilities in each category.

- Meet with a friend, family member, neighbor, or anyone else you trust. Talk about what you think your aptitudes and abilities are, and ask the other person to write them down. After you finish, discuss the list. Does this person agree with your evaluation? What ideas does he or she have about your aptitudes and abilities?

Matching Your Aptitudes and Abilities to Careers

Now review your list of aptitudes and abilities, and try to think of at least one career that requires each of your skills. For example, if one of your aptitudes is caring for children, a good match might be a career as a day care provider or teacher. Finding a realistic career match for your aptitudes and abilities will make your working life more enjoyable.

Once you have identified some of your aptitudes and abilities, you will probably feel that you are really getting to know yourself. Next, look at how your personality influences your career choice.

Your Personality and Learning Styles

All the special qualities that make you an individual form your personality. **Personality** is the combination of your attitudes, behaviors, and characteristics. To explore your personality, you need to examine your self-concept and styles of learning.

Self-Concept

The way you see yourself is your **self-concept**. When you look in the mirror, do you see someone who is confident, curious, dependable, funny, observant, sympathetic? You may have some or all of these traits, and more. Some of your personality traits may even seem to contradict one another. You may, for example, feel shy in new situations but outgoing in familiar surroundings. On some days you may think you're a fairly interesting person, and on other days, you may think you're not that interesting. Everyone has highs and lows. However, you probably do have a fairly consistent self-concept— a feeling that you know the kind of person you are.

Personality Types and Learning Styles

The way you interact with the world around you to gather information and turn it into knowledge is a key component of your personality. The different ways that people naturally think and learn are called **learning styles** (see *Figure 2-4*). When you are aware of your own learning styles, you are able to determine the best approach for you to learn something new. You also can judge what kind of field would be good for your particular personality type, because you'd probably do well in a career that used your strongest learning style.

Read the list of the seven styles of learning given in *Figure 2-4.* Which ones apply to you? Which one do you think is your main style of learning?

Being aware of all the aspects of yourself that make you who you are will give you a great advantage as you explore career choices. Look at *Figure 2-5* on page 39 to see how one person developed her special qualities on the path to a career. Then write a description of yourself in your journal, adding drawings if you wish. Include at least some of your values, interests, aptitudes and abilities, and personality traits and learning styles.

In Chapter 3, you will find out how to research careers—and you will come closer to knowing what you want to do.

Seven Styles of Learning

Type of Learner	Likes	Best Ways to Learn
Linguistic	Likes to read, write, and tell stories; good at memorizing names and dates.	Learns best by saying, hearing, and seeing words.
Logical/Mathematical	Likes to do experiments, work with numbers, explore patterns and relationships; good at math, logic, and problem solving.	Learns best by making categories, classifying, and working with patterns.
Spatial	Likes to draw, build, design, and create things; good at imagining, doing puzzles and mazes, and reading maps and charts.	Learns best by using the mind's eye and working with colors and pictures.
Musical	Likes to sing, hum, play an instrument, and listen to music; good at remembering melodies, noticing pitches and rhythms, and keeping time.	Learns best through rhythm and melody.
Bodily/Kinesthetic	Likes to touch and move around; good at hands-on activities and crafts.	Learns best by interacting with people and objects in a real space.
Interpersonal	Likes having lots of friends, talking to people, and joining groups; good at understanding people, leading, organizing, communicating, and mediating conflicts.	Learns best by sharing, comparing, and cooperating.
Intrapersonal	Likes to work alone and pursue interests at own pace; good at self-awareness, focusing on personal feelings, and following instincts to learn what needs to be known.	Learns best through independent study.

Figure 2-4 Although most people may have a preferred style of learning, they can usually shift between styles to acquire new skills and knowledge. Can you think of a career that would be especially suited to each type of learner?

Figure 2-5

The Path to a Career

Sasha's awareness of her values, interests, aptitudes and abilities, and personality and learning styles helped her develop a career as an event planner.

A **Values and Interests.** Sasha always valued her friends. She was a "people" person. She also loved to play sports.

B **Aptitudes and Abilities.** In school, Sasha developed her talent for creative thinking and problem solving. She also had a knack for seeing things in her mind's eye.

C **Personality and Learning Styles.** Sasha was outgoing and liked to be in groups of people. She is an interpersonal learner and enjoys working with people.

D Sasha now has her own business, planning banquets, corporate events, and fund-raisers.

Chapter 2 • Getting to Know Yourself **39**

Brainstorming about your aptitudes and abilities with a person you trust can help you learn more about yourself. *Why is it useful to get suggestions or advice about careers from an older person?*

Career Do's & Don'ts

To Find Out More About Yourself...

Do:
- spend quiet moments to identify what is important to you.
- keep an open mind to all ideas, people, and opportunities.
- make a list of personal strengths and weaknesses.
- start something you always wanted to do.

Don't:
- place more importance on personal appearance than on who you are inside.
- reject criticism unless it is totally unfounded.
- believe that your way is the only right way.
- make excuses for your behavior.

SECTION 2-3 *Review*

Understanding Key Concepts

Using complete sentences, answer the following questions on a separate sheet of paper.

1. Name something you feel you have an aptitude for. Design a plan for developing it into an ability.

2. Choose a learning style and name a career that you think would match it. Explain why that career would be appropriate for the learner.

SECTION 2-1 Summary

- Careful planning for your future career will allow you to be in control of one of the biggest decisions in your life.

- The longer a decision will affect your life, the more time you need to think about the consequences beforehand.

Key Terms

decision-making process *(p. 24)*

SECTION 2-2 Summary

- When beginning to think about a career, consider your lifestyle goals. Imagine how you would like to spend your time, energy, and resources in the future.

- Consider your values, or the principles that you want to live by, when you are planning for a career. General values include responsibility, relationships, compassion, courage, achievement, and recognition.

- Your interests are your favorite activities. You probably want to plan for a career that would involve your interests. You need to determine whether you prefer working with data, people, or things.

Key Terms

lifestyle goals *(p. 30)*
values *(p. 31)*
data *(p. 34)*

SECTION 2-3 Summary

- An aptitude is your potential for learning a certain skill. An ability is a skill you have already developed. You want to discover your aptitudes and abilities because you will want to use them in the career of your choice.

- Your personality and main learning style can influence the kind of career that would be right for you. Personality includes your attitudes, behaviors, and characteristics. There are seven learning styles, which relate to how you think and learn.

Key Terms

aptitude *(p. 36)*
ability *(p. 36)*
personality *(p. 37)*
self-concept *(p. 37)*
learning styles *(p.37)*

Reviewing Key Terms

On separate paper, write a yearbook profile of yourself using the following terms as headings.

lifestyle goals   aptitudes
values   abilities
data   self-concept
learning styles   personality

Recalling Key Concepts

On a separate sheet of paper, tell whether each statement is true or false. Rewrite any false statements to make them true.

1. The first step in the seven-step decision-making process is to gather information.

2. In choosing a career, your resources pertain to who you are and what you have to offer.

3. People who share the same values always practice them in the same way.

4. Your interests are the things you like to do.

5. Working with data means you are working with things.

6. Aptitudes are skills you have already developed.

7. Learning styles are the different ways that people think and learn.

Thinking Critically

Using complete sentences, answer each of the questions below on a separate sheet of paper.

1. What role do you think your instincts should play in the decision-making process when considering possible careers?

2. What consequences might result from settling on a career that conflicts with your personal values?

3. Classify the following skills according to data, people, or things and explain your reasoning: supervising, repairing, communicating, designing, organizing, operating.

4. Volunteer to help a friend discover his or her aptitudes and abilities. What questions would you ask to encourage your friend to become better aware of his or her personal skills?

5. Think of three people you know well, and decide which learning styles fit them. Explain your choices.

SCANS Foundation Skills and Workplace Competencies

Basic Skills: *Speaking*

1. Decide on three values that you feel are important. Give a brief talk to the class explaining why you care about these values. Give examples to illustrate each value. You may want to write out your whole speech and practice at home before speaking to the class.

Information: *Organizing and Maintaining Information*

2. Create a chart to help you keep track of what you have learned about yourself. Use these column headings: Lifestyle Goals, Values, Interests, Aptitudes, Abilities, and Learning Styles. Write or brainstorm to fill in the chart. You can add to it as the year goes on.

Connecting Academics to the Workplace

Social Studies

1. Research the system of values in another culture. Look in library books, an encyclopedia, or CD-ROM, or interview someone who grew up in a different culture. Name and describe three values. How do these values affect the world of work in that culture? Share your findings in a report to the class.

Math

2. Conduct a study on the learning styles in your class. Follow these steps:

- Take a survey. Ask each student to identify his or her main learning style. Record the total number of students for each style.

- Make a bar graph showing the number of students for each learning style.

- Write up a brief report of your class's learning styles. Is there one main style? Are all the learning styles represented?

Art

3. Draw a picture that reflects one (or some) of your values or interests. Use a pencil, markers, watercolors, or collage techniques. Make the picture abstract or realistic, but be prepared to explain your artwork.

Developing Teamwork and Leadership Skills

Work with a small group and decide on a value that you can put into practice that will benefit your community. Brainstorm about different values and various possible projects you could do as a group. Then choose one project, plan how to go about doing it, and get to work—as a team.

Real-World Workshop

With a partner, role-play abilities as they might be used in the workplace. Each of you can choose an ability, such as adaptability or decision making. Improvise situations until you feel comfortable that you are expressing the ability, then show your role-play to the class. Can the others guess what ability you are acting out?

School-to-Work Connection

Interview the director of human resources at a local business to find out what methods the company uses to match applicants to particular jobs. Does the company use interest surveys or other means of assessing aptitudes and abilities? Prepare questions in advance, and take a pen and notebook to write down the responses. Write what you learned in an interview format, showing your questions and the director's answers.

Individual Career Plan

Look at Figure 2-5. Then make a chart for yourself similar to this one showing Sasha's steps. Does this give you an insight into a career choice? If not, show your chart to a family member, friend, or teacher. Ask the person to suggest an appropriate career.

ASPECTS OF INDUSTRY:
Technical and Production Skills

Overview

In Unit One, you read about why people work, and focused on evaluating your skills and aptitudes. In this Unit Lab, you will use what you have learned while exploring one of the aspects of industry: **Technical and Production Skills.**

The Technical and Production Skills aspect of industry covers the actual techniques and abilities you'll need on the job. It also covers how you'll work—whether you'll time-share, telecommute, or rotate jobs with someone else.

Tools

1. *Occupational Outlook Handbook*
2. Trade and business magazines
3. Consumer magazines
4. Information on apprenticeship programs
5. College/Specialty school catalogs

Procedures

STEP A

Choose one of the following 15 job clusters that interests you: Agribusiness and Natural Resources; Business and Office; Communications and Media; Construction; Family and Consumer Services; Environment; Fine Arts and Humanities; Health; Hospitality and Recreation; Manufacturing; Marine Science; Marketing and Distribution; Personal Service; Public Service; Transportation.

Choose three jobs in the job cluster that you would seriously think about pursuing. Research each of the three, listing the skills you would need to perform the job (reading, computer use, carpentry, math, etc.). Use the *Occupational Outlook Handbook (OOH)* and other career references, trade and business magazines, and consumer magazines to get your information. Some of these sources are on the Internet.

In your research, look for comments that indicate how the work is performed by computer, individually, in groups, and so on. Mention if the way the work is done is changing.

STEP B

If you have not already done so, make lists of your skills, interests, aptitudes, and values. You may want to brainstorm with two or three classmates.

Compare the list of your skills, aptitudes, interests, and values to the lists of skills you made for the three jobs.

Choose the job that most closely matches your skills, interests, aptitudes, and values.

STEP C

Have your teacher, counselor, or parent help you arrange a short (20- to 30-minute) interview with a person in that job. If someone in your first choice job is not available, go on to your second choice.

During the interview, ask the following:

1. Which skills are most important in performing the job?

2. How did the person get the skills to perform the job? (Formal training? Experience?)

3. How have the job skill requirements changed in the past five to ten years? Are they expected to change in the next five to ten years?

4. How does the person perform his or her job? (Telecommuting? In groups? Alone?)

During the interview, take careful notes. Do not record the interview without permission. Be punctual and be courteous.

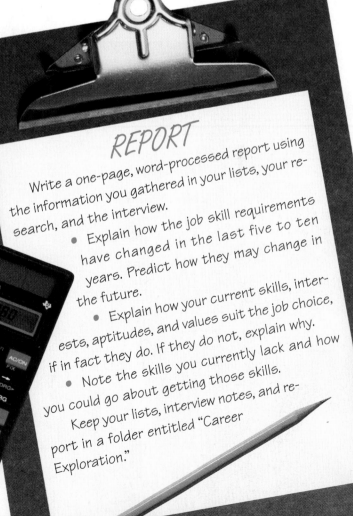

REPORT

Write a one-page, word-processed report using the information you gathered in your lists, your research, and the interview.

- Explain how the job skill requirements have changed in the last five to ten years. Predict how they may change in the future.
- Explain how your current skills, interests, aptitudes, and values suit the job choice, if in fact they do. If they do not, explain why.
- Note the skills you currently lack and how you could go about getting those skills.

Keep your lists, interview notes, and report in a folder entitled "Career Exploration."

UNIT 2
Exploring Careers

UNIT 2 QUIZ:

What Do You Know About Exploring Careers?

- What is the difference between job shadowing and an internship?

- What kind of job benefits are important to you?

- Would you want to start your own business or work for someone else?

- What career interests you?

47

Chapter 3

Researching Careers

Section 3-1
Exploring Careers

Section 3-2
What to Research

In this video segment, learn how your friends can help you research careers.

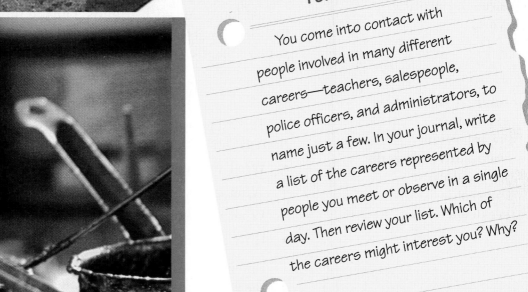

Journal
Personal Career Plan

You come into contact with people involved in many different careers—teachers, salespeople, police officers, and administrators, to name just a few. In your journal, write a list of the careers represented by people you meet or observe in a single day. Then review your list. Which of the careers might interest you? Why?

Exploring Careers

Now that you've thought about your own interests and abilities, it's time to learn more about the real world of work. The U.S. Office of Education lends a hand by dividing careers into 15 clusters. Look at *Figure 3-1.* Which cluster—or clusters—seems to fit the kind of person you are? Narrow your search by choosing a cluster. Then start exploring related careers that might be right for you.

Research—It's Right Before Your Very Eyes

You can discover what the world of work has to offer by simply keeping your eyes and ears open. Look around as you travel to school, as you play, eat, shop, or just hang out with friends. During the next week, list all the careers that you notice. You'll be amazed at how effective this kind of informal research can be.

Been There, Done That

Talk to people you know about their career experiences. Just ask a few basic questions.

- What was your favorite job?
- What was your least favorite job?
- What was your most unusual job?
- How do you like your current job?

Put your SCANS listening skills to work as you gather firsthand information.

The U.S. Office of Education Job Clusters

Career Clusters	Job Examples
Agribusiness and natural resources	Small-animal breeder, horse groomer, poultry farmer, forestry technician
Business and office	Receptionist, bookkeeper, computer servicer, claim examiner
Communications and media	Cable television technician, book editor, computer artist, technical writer
Construction	Air-conditioning, heating, and refrigeration mechanic; roofer; building inspector; surveyor
Family and consumer services	Child-care worker, pet-care worker, jeweler, floral designer
Environment	Environmental technician, hazardous waste management technician, pollution-control technician, sanitary engineer
Fine arts and humanities	Actor, cartoonist, dancer, musician
Health	Operating-room technician, dental hygienist, nurse's aide, home health aide
Hospitality and recreation	Cruise director, fitness instructor, park ranger, pastry chef, baker
Manufacturing	Industrial laser machine operator, toolmaker, stationary engineer, production supervisor
Marine science	Ocean technician, diver, fish culture technician, marine engineer
Marketing and distribution	Insurance agent, real estate agent, auto sales worker, retail buyer
Personal service	Barber and hairstylist, cosmetologist, massage therapist, bridal consultant
Public service	Teacher, member of the armed services, firefighter, paralegal aide
Transportation	Airline reservations agent, airline pilot, railroad conductor, automotive mechanic

Figure 3-1 The U.S. Office of Education has grouped careers into 15 clusters based on similar job characteristics. Which areas appeal to you? Why?

What's Happening?

Have you ever seen a situation in a movie and thought, "Wow, that's the job I want"? Think about movies and TV shows that you've seen and magazines and newspapers that you've read. Are people doing things you'd like to do? If so, learn more about them. That's how Jen Kizer found her career. She never missed her favorite TV program—real-life rescues of people in danger. When she stopped to think about it, she realized that emergency rescue work was exactly what she wanted to do with her life.

Formal Research

Consider yourself a detective, hot on the trail of a satisfying career. While informal research gives you some clues, formal approaches yield even more.

Libraries—Check Them Out

Your first stop might be your school or public library. Many libraries have job information or career centers. The information is well organized, and it's free. You'll find reference books, magazines, videotapes, and other sources of career information. You can also search the card catalog or electronic catalog.

Books. Look for three useful books published by the U.S. Department of Labor.

- The *Dictionary of Occupational Titles* describes more than 20,000 jobs.

- The *Occupational Outlook Handbook*, updated every two years, describes the type of work, the training and education required, and the future outlook for hundreds of careers.

- The *Guide for Occupational Exploration* groups careers into categories, such as mechanical careers and careers protecting people,

Libraries have a broad range of career materials, including videotapes and audiotapes. *Why do you think a videotape that shows someone at work might be more engaging than reading about someone at work?*

and describes many careers within each category.

Additional Print Resources. Libraries also contain other print resources, including magazines, government reports, and newspapers.

- With the *Reader's Guide to Periodical Literature*, locate magazine articles on specific industries and career trends. Business magazines, such as *Forbes, Business Week, Entrepreneur,* and *Wired*, cover the hot topics and inside news of many industries.
- The *Occupational Outlook Quarterly*, published by the Department of Labor, provides up-to-date information on employment trends.
- Job listings in your local newspaper show what is available in your local job market.

VCR Resources. Many labor organizations and industry service groups produce audiotapes and videotapes of workers in action. The library collects them for you, so take advantage of them.

Computerized Guidance. Some libraries also offer special computer programs that can speed up your career search. These programs let you call up detailed information on particular occupations. You can also do some career browsing: Tell the program what you like doing, and it suggests possible careers. In the process, you'll grow more skilled at using computers, a SCANS competency.

Internet Job Services

Computer users can find huge amounts of career information on the Internet, particularly on the World Wide Web. The Web offers such **Internet job services** as Web sites, newsgroups, and bulletin boards created by trade organizations, companies, and individuals—all designed for job recruitment and career research. You can surf the Net to find everything from global statistics (How many plumbers are there in India?) to occupational chat rooms ("Let me tell you about the design problem I solved today!").

Exploratory Interviews

Ask your family, friends, neighbors, teachers, and counselors to help you build a list of people who work in careers that

An exploratory interview is a perfect opportunity to let your personal qualities shine. *Name at least three social skills that will help make an interview go smoothly.*

you find interesting. After doing some initial research into a career, call the appropriate person and arrange an **exploratory interview**. That's simply a short, informal talk with someone who works in a career that appeals to you.

Ask questions such as these:

- How did you start your career?
- What education and training did it require?
- What do you like about your job?
- What do you do on a typical day at your job?

Don't be afraid to ask people for interviews. They may have started out by receiving someone else's help and may be more than happy to pass the favor along.

The story of John Liu is a great example. When he was a teenager, John thought he wanted a career in retailing. He asked everyone he knew until he found the perfect contact—a friend's aunt who worked as a department store buyer. "I learned more about buying and selling in an hour with her than I could have imagined. She was smart, savvy, and she loved her work." The interview paid off. John went on to become a well-known marketing consultant. "I'm really grateful for her advice, and I help students today whenever I'm asked."

Part-Time Work

The most direct way to learn about a career is to work. If your schedule allows it, working part-time will enable you to observe a career from the inside. You'll gain experience, make personal contacts, and put some money in your pocket at the same time. Paula Terrano started doing part-time work after school setting up displays at a convention center. Her carefulness and enthusiasm, she says, were noticed, and she moved up the ladder of responsibility. She eventually accepted full-time work at the center as assistant event coordinator.

Work Experience Programs

You may find a part-time job through a vocational education program. Such programs are designed to give you a chance to learn job skills while you are still in high school. As a bonus, the work also earns you class credit and a grade.

Some local corporations team up with schools, hiring students to perform jobs that are taught in their high school classes. This is called a **cooperative program**. A high school in California, for example, used math and science classes to prepare students for work at a local chemical company.

Some schools create school-based businesses. One enterprising high school in Minnesota bought a grocery store that was going out of business. Students learned

You can learn about careers through part-time work. *What job skills might be needed for the job pictured here?*

marketing and retailing in classes and then applied their knowledge working at the school store.

Job Shadowing

You don't need to be a spy to "shadow" someone. **Job shadowing,** which involves following a worker for a few days on the job, means learning the ropes by watching and listening.

Today Elena Kazinski is a television camera operator for a major production company, but when she was a student she didn't know anyone in the industry. As she tells it, "I was always hanging around our local TV studio, and one day I just asked the camera operator if I could talk to her about her job. She offered to let me shadow her. I got the OK from the station, and I stuck to her like glue for a week. I even helped with some equipment. After that, I was hooked. TV production has been my life ever since."

Volunteering and Internships

You may think that volunteers don't get paid. True, they don't usually draw a salary, but they are paid in valuable experience. Don't underestimate the value of volunteering as another way to explore

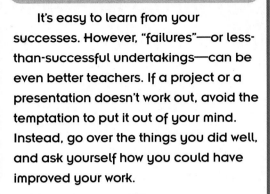

Attitude Counts ✔

It's easy to learn from your successes. However, "failures"—or less-than-successful undertakings—can be even better teachers. If a project or a presentation doesn't work out, avoid the temptation to put it out of your mind. Instead, go over the things you did well, and ask yourself how you could have improved your work.

careers. What you learn can help you make major decisions later. Hospitals, senior citizen centers, and museums are just a few places that use volunteers.

An **internship** is a more formal position and usually requires a longer-term commitment than volunteering. Like volunteers, interns are usually unpaid, but they learn vital job skills. An intern is on the spot, working where the action is. With one foot in the door, interns who work hard can sometimes step into full-time paying positions.

In addition, many communities and schools offer **service learning**. In such programs, community service—for example, cleaning up a neighborhood—becomes part of your schoolwork.

SECTION 3-1 *Review*

Understanding Key Concepts

Using complete sentences, answer the following questions on a separate sheet of paper.

1. Why are talking to people and using media resources called informal methods of researching jobs?

2. What kinds of career information can you find in libraries and on the Internet?

3. What are some benefits of doing unpaid part-time work?

Exploring Careers: Marine Science

Dawn Murray
Biologist/Senior Interpreter,
Monterey Bay Aquarium

Q: **What is your work like?**

A: I work with the interpretive programs in the aquarium's education department. We interpret—or explain—marine science to aquarium visitors. I train 750 volunteers in shifts, three times a day, seven days a week, working with a different group of volunteers each shift. I tell them what's new at the aquarium, or give them information on anything from how birds fly to how a mollusk makes its shell.

Q: **How did you get into this field?**

A: When I was eight, I went with my family to the Great Barrier Reef in Australia. I'll never forget the manta rays and the turtles. I remember thinking, "This is what I want to do—study marine life." So I studied biology in college and started working as an intern at the aquarium after graduation. The aquarium kept rehiring me, first part-time, then full-time.

Q: **What makes your work important to you?**

A: The fact that I can have such an impact. People don't know much about marine biology. We're just now beginning to figure out what it's like out in the ocean. I can take a class at the university, write a lecture about what I've learned, and teach it to the volunteers, who teach it to the public. If I can get my spark into the volunteers, they can get that spark into the public.

Thinking Critically

What are some other kinds of jobs that might use educational interpreters?

CAREER FACTS

Nature of the Work:
Enrich visitors' experiences through tours, lectures, classes. Design training and public programs; teach.

Training or Education Needed:
Bachelor's or master's degree in education or in science; experience working in aquariums, museums, zoos.

Aptitudes, Abilities, and Skills:
Math, listening, speaking, and interpersonal skills; self-management skills; problem-solving and decision-making skills; reading and writing skills.

Salary Range:
Start at $28,000; up to $65,000; depends on the institution.

Career Path:
Start as a volunteer or an intern; take on more responsibility as an instructor, a resource coordinator, or an education director.

What to Research

After studying this section, you will be able to:
- **Target key questions that you can ask in researching careers.**
- **Examine some of the characteristics that make up a career profile.**

work environment
flextime
fringe benefits

Once you know *where* to get career information, the next question is *what* information should you get? You'll want to know what the career is like and whether it is right for you. You can find that out by examining careers in terms of these 10 characteristics:

1. values,
2. tasks and responsibilities,
3. working with data-people-things,
4. work environment,
5. working hours,
6. aptitudes and abilities,
7. education and training,
8. salary and fringe benefits,
9. career outlook, and
10. international career outlook.

Try to gather information on each of these factors for each career you investigate. This will enable you to compare careers directly and make a wise career decision.

Values

When you look into a career, ask yourself if your values match the values that will help you in that career. What do you really care about? What do people in that career really care about? Justice? Art? Money? Health? Fame?

Tasks and Responsibilities

When you go to work each day, what will you actually be doing? Find out by asking basic questions, such as these:

- What specific tasks do workers in this career perform?
- Are the workdays repetitive or full of new experiences?
- Is the pace easy, or is the career a high-pressure one?
- Is the work primarily physical or mental?

Working with Data-People-Things

Careers involve working with data, people, and things. Many careers entail working with all three categories, as *Figure 3-2* shows. For any given career, though, one area tends to predominate. Statisticians, for example, work mainly with data, home health aides work primarily with people, and technicians usually work with things.

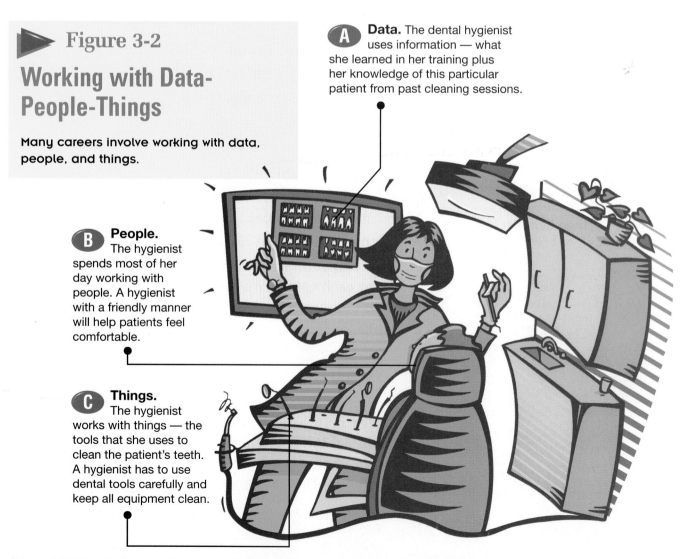

▶ Figure 3-2

Working with Data-People-Things

Many careers involve working with data, people, and things.

A **Data.** The dental hygienist uses information — what she learned in her training plus her knowledge of this particular patient from past cleaning sessions.

B **People.** The hygienist spends most of her day working with people. A hygienist with a friendly manner will help patients feel comfortable.

C **Things.** The hygienist works with things — the tools that she uses to clean the patient's teeth. A hygienist has to use dental tools carefully and keep all equipment clean.

Work Environment

Because you'll be spending about 40 hours a week at work, do yourself a favor: Consider your **work environment**. Your physical and social surroundings can affect your well-being. Do you want to work indoors or outdoors? Would you rather work alone or with other people?

Take a few minutes to visualize your ideal work environment. Then draw a picture or write a paragraph describing what you envisioned. As you research careers, try to find those that match that image.

Working Hours

When you think about work, do you assume you'll be starting at 9:00 A.M. and quitting at 5:00 P.M.? Of course, many people do work those hours—but in the world of work, variety rules. Andrew Barros, a restaurant host, starts work at 3:00 P.M. and leaves after the last guest does at about 11:00 P.M. Andrew's restaurant buys produce from Janet Cho, who works from 4:00 A.M. to noon. Many careers are simply not 9-to-5 careers. When are you at your best? Are you a night owl or a morning person?

Some careers allow flexible scheduling. With **flextime**, workers construct their work schedules to suit their lives. Some people work four 10-hour days and enjoy three-day weekends. Some work from 7:00 A.M. to 3:00 P.M. so that they can be home when their children return from school. Some people telecommute: They work at home and communicate with clients and colleagues by phone, fax, and computer.

Flextime scheduling allows some workers to more easily match their work schedules with the demands of family life. Many employers that offer flextime require workers to be on-site during certain core hours, typically from 10:00 A.M. to 4:00 P.M. *Why do you think this is the case?*

Aptitudes and Abilities

As you know, skills for any kind of work are more easily learned if you have an aptitude for learning them. In Chapter 2 you analyzed your own aptitudes and abilities. As you do your research, find out

Career Do's & Don'ts

To Identify a Career Path ...

Do:
- visualize yourself doing every job you come across.
- acknowledge that developing a career is a process.
- seek personal satisfaction.

Don't:
- underestimate the skills and discipline required to do any job well.
- be discouraged by the long educational process or years of experience required for some careers.
- consider a field you would not like even if it's known for high pay.
- choose a career path only because family members have that career.

which aptitudes and abilities are needed for each career. You can then match your natural talents with careers that require those same abilities. Anthony McCabe was a high school student who loved to talk. He talked about anything to anybody, and he had the knack of getting people to relax and open up to him. When it dawned on him that talking was what he was really good at, his career started to take shape, and today he hosts his own radio talk show.

Education and Training

Careers demand different kinds and levels of education and training. You may need a two-year associate's degree, a four-year bachelor's degree, or a technical or business school license or certificate. As you research, note how much time, money, and effort it will take to get the necessary education and training for various careers.

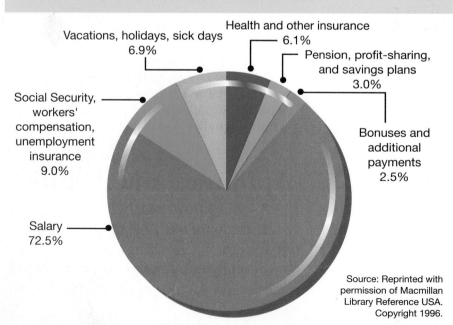

Salary and Fringe Benefits

Vacations, holidays, sick days 6.9%

Social Security, workers' compensation, unemployment insurance 9.0%

Salary 72.5%

Health and other insurance 6.1%

Pension, profit-sharing, and savings plans 3.0%

Bonuses and additional payments 2.5%

Source: Reprinted with permission of Macmillan Library Reference USA. Copyright 1996.

 Figure 3-3

This chart shows salary and fringe benefits in relation to overall employee compenstion. What is the difference between a salary and a fringe benefit?

Salary and Fringe Benefits

Occupational directories often include general information on what careers pay. They list an hourly rate or a weekly or annual salary, as well as ranges based on national averages.

Of course, many company employees receive more than their paychecks. **Fringe benefits** may include health insurance, paid vacation and holiday time, and a retirement plan. As *Figure 3-3* shows, fringe benefits can add substantially to what you earn.

Career Outlook

What will your career area be like in 10 years? Many of the research materials described in Section 3-1 can tell you about industry prospects and help you make big decisions.

Kathy Silno's research helped her. Kathy was mechanically inclined, and she considered a career in manufacturing. Her research, however, pointed to an upcoming increase in service jobs. Kathy decided on automotive repair and found a service job with a good future.

EXCELLENT BUSINESS PRACTICES

Looking at a Career in Tourism

Century Plaza Hotel and Tower in Los Angeles, California, has made a commitment to help high school students learn about the tourism industry. The 1,072-room hotel gives teenagers from two inner-city high schools an opportunity to experience the behind-the-scenes workings of a luxury hotel.

During the two-day program, managers provide information about opportunities in the hotel industry, including educational requirements, professional careers, and rates of pay. They also discuss the hotel's standards.

Students choose the department they want to "work" in and are fitted with uniforms they wear while shadowing an employee through his or her shift.

The program has helped students understand more about the working world and visualize themselves making tourism their career.

Thinking Critically

How does following someone through a day's work give you a more complete understanding of that person's job than just talking about it?

International Career Outlook

With growth in the global economy, more and more careers involve working internationally. Brainstorm with your friends and family. Do they know someone who has worked in a foreign country? Pool your resources with other students and make a list of international career possibilities, such as English teacher, civil engineer, or health-care worker.

You can find plenty of international jobs by using library resources. Browse the Web as well.

▶ In today's global economy, many jobs are opening up in foreign countries. *In what foreign country do you think you might like to work? Why?*

SECTION 3-2 *Review*

Understanding Key Concepts

Using complete sentences, answer the following questions on a separate sheet of paper.

1. What aspects of the work environment are important when evaluating a career?

2. Why should you consider a career's outlook?

Key Terms

Internet job services *(p. 53)*
exploratory interview
    (p. 54)
cooperative program *(p. 54)*
job shadowing *(p. 55)*
internship *(p. 55)*
service learning *(p. 55)*

SECTION 3-1 Summary

- The U.S. Office of Education divides careers into 15 clusters.
- You can research careers informally from the world around you, friends and family, and media resources.
- You can research careers formally in books, magazines, and other printed matter; videotapes and audiotapes; and in computerized job resources.
- You can obtain a wealth of up-to-date information on the Internet, especially the World Wide Web.
- You can research a career and then interview someone who works in that field.
- You can obtain part-time work in many different ways: through educational programs, job shadowing, volunteering, internships, and service learning.

Key Terms

work environment *(p. 59)*
flextime *(p. 59)*
fringe benefits *(p. 61)*

SECTION 3-2 Summary

- Consider whether the values that a career reinforces match your values.
- Investigate exactly what tasks and responsibilities a career entails.
- Look for a career that balances working with data, people, and things in a way that suits you.
- Evaluate the work environment a career offers.
- Find out what scheduling flexibility is possible within a career.
- Determine what aptitudes and abilities you have that a career requires.
- Investigate what education and training you need for a career.
- Many career resources describe the salary ranges of different careers.
- Consider whether the number of people working in a career is expected to increase or decrease in the future.
- Consider international careers in the growing global economy.

Reviewing Key Terms

Work with a partner to practice your vocabulary. On a separate sheet of paper, write an example of each term, and see if you and your partner can match each other's examples with the correct terms.

Internet job services
service learning
exploratory interview
work environment
flextime
cooperative program
fringe benefits
job shadowing
internship

Recalling Key Concepts

Choose the correct answer for each item below. Write your answers on a separate sheet of paper.

1. The *Dictionary of Occupational Titles* is a guide to ____.

   (a) employers (b) job titles

   (c) career magazines

2. The *Reader's Guide to Periodical Literature* helps in finding ____.

   (a) magazine articles (b) career videos

   (c) Internet listings

3. Working in a homeless shelter as part of course work is called ____.

   (a) an internship (b) fringe benefits

   (c) service learning

4. Driving a tow-truck and repairing engines are examples of ____.

   (a) a career outlook (b) values

   (c) tasks and responsibilities

5. One characteristic that makes up a career profile is ____.

   (a) salary (b) internships (c) data

Thinking Critically

Using complete sentences, answer each of the questions below on a separate sheet of paper.

1. What are some advantages of doing formal career research?

2. Why is it a good idea to research a career before having an exploratory interview?

3. What might motivate a career professional to allow a student to shadow him or her on the job?

4. What personal values would match someone to a career in the military?

5. How might a compatible work environment contribute to job satisfaction?

 ## SCANS Foundation Skills and Workplace Competencies

Personal Qualities: *Self-Esteem*

1. List qualities that make you a good candidate for a part-time job.

Resources: *Allocating Time*

2. Imagine that you have volunteered for after-school service learning. Estimate how many hours per week and on which days you could work. What factors influenced your estimate?

Technology: *Selecting Technology*

3. Compare searching for career information using the *Reader's Guide to Periodical Literature* with searching on the Internet.

Connecting Academics to the Workplace

Art

1. Henry volunteers at the Mayfield Senior Citizen Center. He is in charge of publicity for a yard sale intended to raise funds for a group trip. Design a flyer, by hand or with a computer, advertising the event.

Social Studies

2. Eriko is an intern at the local radio station, which is doing market research for a station profile. Its listening audience is mostly 30- to 40-year-olds. Eriko must research the major historical and cultural events that occurred when these listeners were teenagers. What five events would you suggest?

Math

3. A listing in the *Occupational Outlook Handbook* puts the average weekly salary range for a career at $250 to $300. What would the yearly salary range be? If a worker earning the minimum of this range received a 5 percent raise, what would the new weekly salary be?

Developing Teamwork and Leadership Skills

Join forces with three other students to form a career recruitment team. Choose one of the U.S. Office of Education career clusters shown in Figure 3-1. Each team member should research one career within that cluster. Then pool information and work together to create posters, brochures, and other materials that explain the characteristics of each career. Present the materials to the class.

Real-World Workshop

Using one of the resources mentioned in the chapter or another resource that you locate, identify five employers in your area who hire part-time workers. (Do not use fast-food restaurants, service stations, or supermarkets for any of the examples.)

School-to-Work Connection

Find someone who will agree to allow you to job shadow over a weekend or a holiday. Make notes on the career in terms of the 10 characteristics described in this chapter. Report to your class about the career.

Individual Career Plan

Write a letter introducing yourself to someone working in a career that interests you. In your letter, describe your interest in the career and request an exploratory interview. Supplement your letter with a list of questions for your interview subject.

Entrepreneurship

In this video segment, find out how your interests may lead to entrepreneurial opportunities.

Journal
Personal Career Plan

Entrepreneurs create and develop their own businesses. It's an exciting undertaking—but it's not for everyone. How does the prospect of entrepreneurship fit your own values, interests, and abilities? In your journal, list the advantages entrepreneurship might offer you as an individual. Then write a list of the disadvantages.

What Is Entrepreneurship?

Are you a fan of the *Star Trek* movies and TV programs? In this sci-fi adventure, the crew of a starship travels across the universe, exploring places where no one has gone before. The starship is called the *Enterprise*—and for good reason. The word comes from an Old French word, meaning "to take action, take risks, take responsibility."

You might be surprised to learn that the word *entrepreneur* comes from the same root as *enterprise*. An **entrepreneur** is someone who organizes and then runs a business. An entrepreneur's life is challenging. The risks can be high, but the rewards can also be great. Entrepreneurs must make wise decisions and search out inventive solutions.

Does this adventure appeal to you? Are you willing to set off into the unknown and find your way? Maybe your career path leads to entrepreneurship.

Advantages of Entrepreneurship

If you think entrepreneurship would demand a great deal from you, you're right. What, then, are the advantages?

- *You're in charge.* Entrepreneurs decide when and how hard to work and how their businesses will operate.

- *There is great job satisfaction.*

- *Entrepreneurship can lead to a good income.*

 Entrepreneurs can't go home at 5:00 P.M. if there's still work to be done. **What rewards does the entrepreneur reap for all the long hours put in?**

Disadvantages of Entrepreneurship

Entrepreneurship can be exciting and rewarding, but there are also drawbacks.

- *There is financial risk.* You can lose your investment and sometimes more.

- *Entrepreneurs often work long hours.*

- *Competition can be stiff.*

- *There are no guarantees of success.* Almost two of every three new businesses fail within their first four years.

ETHICS in Action

For years, you've worked in your town's only copy shop. The owner has trained you well and given you unusual opportunities and responsibilities. Now a financial backer offers to help you open your own copy shop—in direct competition with your current employer. Will you take advantage of this opportunity? Why or why not?

Traits of Entrepreneurs

Most entrepreneurs share certain behaviors and attitudes. If the ones described below don't quite match traits you see in yourself, you can develop them.

Motivation

Successful entrepreneurs are very self-motivated. They know what they want to achieve, and they believe in their ability. They keep themselves motivated by setting short- and long-term goals. Then they make and follow a plan for achieving those goals.

Sight and Foresight

Entrepreneurs recognize opportunities (see **Figure 4-1**). They see problems and find a way to build success on them. That's how Daryl Bernstein got his start when he was 17 years old.

► Figure 4-1

Viewing Problems as Opportunities

For the entrepreneur, every problem is an opportunity.

A Entrepreneurs are alert to situations around them. The difference between the advertisements produced by major corporations and those produced by small businesses is apparent. The entrepreneur might ask, "What is the difference between these ads? How can I help make small businesses more competitive?"

FRANK'S FRESH FRUIT

Ford New

1. Logos for small businesses.
2. Start ad agency specializing in small businesses.

B The entrepreneur looks for solutions to the problem. Ideas may come from brainstorming, reviewing similar situations to see how problems were solved or avoided, talking to people who are involved in the problem or have experience in the same conditions, or doing library research. Every idea is saved because there is no telling which idea might contribute to a solution.

Pros and Cons of Logo Business	
Pros	**Cons**
Do it myself.	Selling to small businesspeople will be hard.
I have computer and software.	
Low overhead.	No one to advise me on logo design.

C Each idea is evaluated to see whether it represents the best solution. The evaluation may include research into the costs of implementing the idea, surveys to learn customer preferences, and interviews with experts. When the facts are gathered, the entrepreneur compares the pros and cons of each idea to find the best solution.

D If the solution ideas have been fully researched, nothing remains but to put the idea into action. Implementation may reveal more problems. The entrepreneur uses the problems as a springboard for making adjustments to the solution.

Daryl noticed that large companies used logos to promote their services and products. He thought logos would also benefit small companies. As a result, he started a business creating logos for small companies. It took a while, but his business became a success. In the process, he helped his clients increase their profits by giving them a greater identity and ultimately more recognition.

Viewing problems as opportunities can be seen as a process. *Figure 4-1* on pages 70–71 shows how Bernstein might have used this skill to develop the idea for his business.

Decision Making

Entrepreneurs make business decisions every day, and the decisions must be good ones. Refer back to Section 2-1 of Chapter 2 for more information on how to make decisions.

Career Do's & Don'ts

When Starting Your Own Business...

Do:
- talk to several people who started their own businesses.
- make a plan for starting a business.
- be open to even the craziest ideas.
- make having your own business an ongoing lifetime goal if you know it's right for you.

Don't:
- limit yourself by thinking all the "good ideas are already taken."
- hold yourself back from working hard.
- get involved with "partners" who can't contribute their share.
- let others crush your dreams.

SECTION 4-1 *Review*

Understanding Key Concepts

Using complete sentences, answer the following questions on a separate sheet of paper.

1. Give an example of a successful business in your community. How might the traits of an entrepreneur have helped this business succeed?

2. Are the advantages or the disadvantages of entrepreneurship more important to you? Why?

Ways of Becoming a Business Owner

OBJECTIVES

After studying this section, you will be able to:
- **Identify the four main ways of becoming a business owner.**
- **Explain the advantages and disadvantages of each major route to business ownership.**

KEY TERMS

start-up costs
lease
goodwill
market outlook
franchise

If you decide entrepreneurship is for you, you'll have to decide how you're going to get your own business. Here are the four main ways of doing so:

1. starting a new business,
2. buying an existing business,
3. buying a franchise, and
4. taking over the family business.

Starting a New Business

Starting a new business is a dream many people share. What an exciting adventure! If you start a new business, look for challenges as well as rewards.

The Challenges

No matter how you get into business, you will face challenges. If you're starting a new business, you'll face a few additional ones.

- A new business requires more time and effort than an established business.
- Start-up costs are often high. **Start-up costs** are the expenses involved in going into business. Examples include renting or buying space and buying equipment, office supplies, and insurance.
- If you borrow money, you'll have to convince lenders that your business idea will work.
- It's risky. No matter how well you plan, you won't know if the business will succeed until you've tried it.

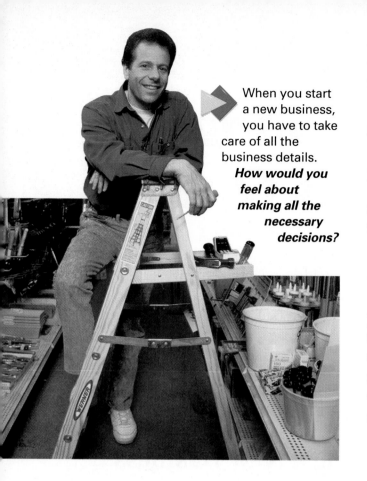

When you start a new business, you have to take care of all the business details. *How would you feel about making all the necessary decisions?*

are many reasons why a business might be for sale. A successful one may be for sale because the owners are retiring or entering a new business. Perhaps business is so good, they can't handle it all anymore.

There may also be many reasons why an unsuccessful business is for sale. The bottom line, however, is that it is losing money. Perhaps it's still a good investment, if it can be turned around.

A Fast Start

Buying an existing business can put you several steps ahead. First, you can save on start-up costs by taking advantage of the previous owner's business agreements, such as a lease signed when rents were lower. A **lease** is a contract to use something for a specified period of time.

The Rewards

Tough challenges await those who build a business. What are the rewards? Besides those enjoyed by all entrepreneurs, consider these benefits:

- You don't inherit a previous owner's mistakes.
- You can try fresh ideas and build your business your way.
- You get personal satisfaction from knowing you built the business yourself.

Buying an Existing Business

If you don't want to start a new business, you might buy an existing one. There

 When buying an existing business, check out customer goodwill. *Why should you think twice about buying a business that lacks goodwill?*

There are more than 500,000 franchised businesses in the United States. *Why do you think such businesses are so popular with entrepreneurs?*

If the business has been successful, you can build on that success. The **goodwill**, or loyalty, of customers is one of a business's most valuable assets. You may also benefit from an established reputation and a trained staff.

Drawbacks

Every business has its problems, but if it's struggling, look for the reasons.

- The location may be poor.
- The competition may be taking business away.
- The **market outlook**, or potential for future sales, may have changed.
- The building or equipment may need expensive repairs or replacement.
- The business may have a reputation for poor products.

Buying a Franchise

A type of existing business that offers specific advantages is the franchise. A **franchise** is the legal right to sell a company's goods and services. Many fast-food restaurants and real estate offices are franchises.

When you buy a franchise, you are actually buying the right to sell another company's products. In addition to paying for the franchise, you will continue to pay a percentage of your profits to the parent company.

Like any business owner, you are in charge. However, you must follow the parent company's guidelines. These may dictate how to make or distribute the goods or services.

Less Risk

A franchise may be a wise choice for people with limited business experience. Here are some other benefits you'll gain:

- a recognized product name,
- established management systems,
- a business reputation and customer goodwill,
- training and support services,
- advertising, and
- financing.

Less Gain

A franchise is not the right choice for everyone. A franchise may be less profitable because you pay a portion of your profits to the parent company. Since you didn't build the company from scratch, there may be less satisfaction.

Taking Over the Family Business

Does your father, mother, or another relative own a business? If so, it might be a shortcut into entrepreneurship.

Smoothing the Way

Taking over a family business can have the advantages of the franchise without the fees.

- Your relatives might help you finance the business.
- Family members tend to be loyal and to trust each other.
- Family members working as a team can achieve more than individuals.
- Relatives can teach you the business.

Bumps in the Road

In addition to the usual hazards of business ownership, a family business presents special ones. To begin with, it's sometimes hard to have normal business relationships with relatives. Moreover, when the family is part of the business, you can't always go home and leave the business behind.

Joining a family business can be an easy entry into business. Relatives provide emotional as well as professional support. *What do you think would be the hardest part of joining a family business?*

SECTION 4-2 *Review*

Understanding Key Concepts

Using complete sentences, answer the following questions on a separate sheet of paper.

1. Describe four ways to enter the fast-food business. Which one do you think would offer you the best chance for success? Why?

2. State the advantages and disadvantages of buying an existing business rather than starting a new business.

Exploring Careers: Hospitality and Recreation

Ben Abebe
Travel Agent

Q: Why did you become a travel agent?

A: First of all, I love to travel. Travel is always exciting. As a travel agent, I send people to places they've been waiting to visit for a long time. It always makes me happy to see my customers happy.

Q: What training did you have?

A: I had a year of training as a ticket reservationist at Ethiopian Airlines, where I worked before coming to this country. That helped me in this business because the basic principles are the same.

Q: What skills are important for a travel agent?

A: I think you need to know the specific areas your clients are going to. For example, I book people who want to go to Africa, especially Ethiopia. I know the area and what airlines are going there. Knowing your own product really helps you promote yourself.

Q: What is the future like for travel agents?

A: Many airlines have cut the commissions they pay travel agents. Most people book their own travel with their personal computers. Electronic ticketing is crippling for travel agents. However, the business will probably continue to be good for experienced agents.

Thinking Critically

People are traveling more than ever before. Can you name ways that a travel agent might go into the business despite the restrictions mentioned above?

CAREER FACTS

Nature of the Work:
Help clients plan trips; make reservations; write tickets.

Training or Education Needed:
Training in a travel school or experience in a related travel field.

Aptitudes, Abilities, and Skills:
Math, listening, speaking, and interpersonal skills; problem-solving skills; reading and writing skills; interest in travel, world cultures, and geography; sales ability; detail-oriented; decision-making skills; office skills; foreign language skills.

Salary Range:
Salary, commission, or a combination. Start at $13,000; average $20,000 with 5 years of experience; up to $65,000 or more with 10 years of experience.

Career Path:
Start in a related travel field or a travel agency office. Because of shrinking demand, work may be scarce.

Getting Started in Your Own Business

OBJECTIVES

After studying this section, you will be able to:

- Describe the different legal forms of business ownership.
- Identify key factors in selecting a business location.
- Describe the documents needed when financing a new business.

KEY TERMS

sole proprietorship
partnership
corporation
operating expenses
income statement
revenue
gross profit
net profit

Let's say that you've decided to become an entrepreneur. Will you own the business by yourself, or do you want someone to share the work and the risks? Where will you locate your business—in your home or in a building elsewhere? Think about the business you'd like to start. How would you answer these questions?

Forms of Legal Ownership

Suppose you decide that you want to own a business. You must now decide what form the ownership will take. This is a legal issue, so think carefully about it. You have three choices: sole proprietorship, partnership, or corporation. *Figure 4-2* compares the advantages and disadvantages of each form of ownership.

Sole Proprietorship

Most businesses begin as a **sole proprietorship**. This means the business is completely owned by one person. About 75 percent of all U.S. businesses are sole proprietorships.

Partnership

A **partnership** is a legal arrangement in which two or more people share ownership. Control and profits are divided between or among partners, according to

Form of Legal Ownership	Advantages	Disadvantages
Sole Proprietorship	• Owner makes all decisions • Easiest form of business to set up • Least regulated of the three forms of business	• Limited by the skills, abilities, and financial resources of one person • Difficult to raise funds to finance business • Owner has sole financial responsibility for company; personal assets sometimes at risk
Partnership	• Can draw on the skills, abilities, and financial resources of more than one person • Easier to raise funds than in sole proprietorship	• More complicated than sole proprietorship • Tensions and conflicts may develop among partners • Owners liable for all business losses; personal property sometimes in jeopardy
Corporation	• Easier to finance than other forms of business • Financial liability of shareholders limited (usually, can lose only what they've invested)	• Expensive to set up • Record keeping often time-consuming and costly • Often pays more taxes than other forms of business

Figure 4-2 Every form of business ownership has its advantages and disadvantages. What business do you know of that is owned as a sole proprietorship? A partnership? A corporation?

a partnership agreement. A partnership is the least common of the three forms of business ownership.

Corporation

A **corporation** is a business chartered by a state that legally operates apart from the owner(s). The owners buy shares, or parts, of the company. They are called *shareholders* and earn a profit based on the number of shares they own.

Location, Location, Location

Suppose you want to open a fast-food restaurant. Is location important? Of course! You've got to be near your customers. What about a mail-order business? As long as a good postal service is available, you can ship goods from anywhere. In this case, location may not be so important.

 Good locations are usually expensive, yet business owners usually choose the best location they can afford. *What advantages does this site offer the business owner?*

YOU'RE THE BOSS!

✓ *Solving Workplace Problems*

You've developed a successful business designing and selling T-shirts. One of your regular customers places an unusually large order for special T-shirts. However, the customer has requested a slogan that goes against your most basic values; making and selling these shirts would be difficult for you. How will you respond?

When location is important, consider these factors:

- the type of businesses in the area,
- the condition of streets and buildings,
- the cost of property,
- the location of the competition, and
- the location of your customers.

Working at Home

What about working out of your home? It's cheaper than leasing a location and more convenient. You'll also enjoy more flexibility and a relaxed atmosphere.

What about the problems? First, some communities restrict the kinds of businesses that can operate in residential areas. In addition, the isolation of working at home troubles many business owners. Jean Ainsworth left a large office to start a home-based business. "I hadn't realized how much I enjoyed saying 'Good morning' to people, sharing the weekend, hearing about the football games," says Ainsworth. "I had a grandchild last August and I didn't have a set of people to show the pictures to."

Financing

Whatever type of business you launch, you'll need money to get it going. You might draw on your savings or get a loan from friends. More likely, you'll need to borrow money from a commercial lender. To apply for a loan, you'll need a business description and a financial plan.

A *business description* gives specific information about your business. It describes your product and states where your business will be located. It specifies how many employees you will hire and what their salaries will be. It describes your competitors and points out their strengths and weaknesses. It also describes your timetable for starting the business.

A *financial plan* spells out your start-up costs, operating expenses, and other costs for the first few months. **Operating expenses** are the costs of doing business, such as the costs of manufacturing and selling the product.

Producing these reports will require you to apply the SCANS skills of math and writing. If you're planning on entrepreneurship, now is the time to master these skills.

Operating Your Own Business

Whatever business you choose, you will use many of the SCANS skills and competencies. These include reading, writing, math, listening, and speaking skills.

Africa Brown started a business called Africa's Clothing when she was a 16-year-old high school student in Washington, D.C. She got the idea after participating in an entrepreneurship program offered by the Business Kids Institute and the city of Washington, D.C. Brown makes clothing to order, mainly for her classmates. She must listen effectively to take orders accurately and to get the job done right. She must speak well so that she can explain her service. Think about the business you'd like to start. How will you use listening, speaking, reading, writing, and math skills?

EXCELLENT BUSINESS PRACTICES

Responsibility to the Planet

Ben & Jerry's Homemade, Inc. of Burlington, Vermont, manufactures and markets ice cream and franchises shops. Part of the company's mission is to initiate innovative ways to improve the quality of life on local, national, and international levels.

The company created a foundation that sets aside 7.5 percent of pretax profits to support progressive social change by funding small grassroots organizations.

In manufacturing its product, Ben & Jerry's also supports small businesses. During a period of volatile prices in the dairy industry, Ben & Jerry's paid a dairy premium totaling a half million dollars to the Vermont family farmers who supply the milk for their products. Brownies used in one product come from a bakery which employs disadvantaged people from the local community. Nuts used in another product are imported directly from South American rain forests, supporting the local industry.

Ben & Jerry's opened shops in Petrozavodsk and Kondopaga, Russia. Profits from the shops are designed to fund cross-cultural exchanges.

Thinking Critically

If you operated your own successful company, what values would you support and which activities would you fund?

Entrepreneurs whose businesses are based on technical or mechanical skills need good communication skills. *What are some situations in which listening is important in business?*

Mountain Air Bikes Income Statement

Year Ended December 31

Revenue:		
Sales	$212,015	
Cost of goods sold	109,614	
Gross profit		$102,401
Operating expenses:		
Salaries	$24,019	
Rent	11,211	
Utilities	4,514	
Advertising	2,422	
Total operating expenses		$42,166
Net profit (before taxes)		$60,235

You'll need math skills for almost every aspect of business, from setting prices and calculating payroll to balancing your business checking account.

One essential record for business owners is the **income statement**. This document shows how much the business has earned or lost. *Figure 4-3* shows such a statement. The first item in the income statement is **revenue**, or income from sales. Another item is **gross profit**, or the difference between the cost of goods and their selling price. **Net profit** is the amount left after operating expenses are subtracted from the gross profit.

Figure 4-3 An income statement shows whether a company has made a profit or suffered a loss. If this business had lost money, how would the entries on the income statement be different?

SECTION 4-3 *Review*

Understanding Key Concepts

Using complete sentences, answer the following questions on a separate sheet of paper.

1. Imagine that you are starting a trucking company. What form of ownership will you choose? Why?

2. What should you consider in choosing a location for this business?

3. You have decided to organize your trucking company as a corporation. How will you go about financing it?

Highlights

Key Term

entrepreneur *(p. 68)*

SECTION 4-1 Summary

- Entrepreneurship offers you the chance to run your own business, to enjoy job satisfaction, and to earn a high income. The downside is financial risk, long hours, and no *guarantee* of success.

- Entrepreneurs are self-motivated and recognize opportunities around them.

Key Terms

start-up costs *(p. 73)*
lease *(p. 74)*
goodwill *(p. 75)*
market outlook *(p. 75)*
franchise *(p. 75)*

SECTION 4-2 Summary

- If you start a new business, you don't inherit problems. However, it's risky, takes time, effort, and money.

- If you buy an existing business, you may have low start-up costs, an operating business, and goodwill. However, you may inherit a poor location, stiff competition, a dwindling market, bad equipment, or a poor reputation.

- When you buy a franchise, you get a proven product, established systems, and company support. However, a franchise can be expensive, and you must pay part of your profits to the parent company.

- If you enter a family business, relatives may help you finance it and may teach you the business. However, having normal business relationships with relatives is often difficult.

Key Terms

sole proprietorship *(p. 78)*
partnership *(p. 78)*
corporation *(p. 79)*
operating expenses *(p. 81)*
income statement *(p. 82)*
revenue *(p. 82)*
gross profit *(p. 82)*
net profit *(p. 82)*

SECTION 4-3 Summary

- There are three legal forms of business ownership: sole proprietorships, partnerships, and corporations.

- Location is extremely important for many businesses.

- A home-based business has low costs and flexible working conditions. However, you may feel isolated.

- A business loan application requires a business description and a financial plan.

Reviewing Key Terms

On separate paper, describe a business you would like to own. Use the following key terms in your description.

entrepreneur	partnership
start-up costs	corporation
lease	operating expenses
goodwill	income statement
market outlook	revenue
franchise	gross profit
sole proprietorship	net profit

Recalling Key Concepts

On a separate sheet of paper, tell whether each of the following statements is true or false. Rewrite any false statements to make them true.

1. Entrepreneurs often work long hours, but they enjoy great job satisfaction.

2. Once a franchise is paid for, all profits go to the entrepreneur.

3. Entrepreneurs who plan to work out of their homes should consider whether they can take the isolation.

4. In a partnership, the owners can never lose their personal property if the business fails.

5. A financial plan shows how much a business has earned or lost.

Thinking Critically

Using complete sentences, answer each of the questions below on a separate sheet of paper.

1. Is a family business more like a franchise or more like a business you might start from scratch? Explain your answer.

2. Why would someone wish to enter into a partnership instead of operating as a sole proprietor?

3. After six months of operation, an entrepreneur prepares an income statement. It shows that while he has had strong sales and high revenue, instead of a gross profit, he has a gross loss. What should he understand about the cost of the goods he is selling?

SCANS Foundation Skills and Workplace Competencies

Basic Skills: *Listening Skills*

1. Work with a group of four or five other students. Individually, prepare a detailed message. Give the message orally to a group member, who should pass it on to the next group member, who should also pass it on. When you receive a message, write it down before passing it on. When all messages have returned to their authors, discuss with your group the accuracy of the messages given and received. Write a one-paragraph summary of your conclusion.

Interpersonal Skills: *Serving Clients/Customers*

2. Alicia owns a bakery. During busy hours, she and her one employee cannot serve customers quickly enough. The customers become upset when she waits on them out of order. Sometimes they leave if the line is too long. Without hiring more employees, what might Alicia do to keep her customers happy?

Connecting Academics to the Workplace

Math

1. Brad sells ice cream and soft drinks at outdoor festivals. He buys soft drinks for 50 cents per can and ice-cream bars for $75 per hundred. He marks up all items by 100 percent, selling the drinks for $1.00 and ice-cream bars for $1.50. One day, he sold 100 cans of soft drinks and 90 ice-cream bars. Expenses totaled $31.50. What was his net profit?

Social Studies

2. Carlos wants to operate a landscaping business out of the garage behind his house. In your neighborhood, would it be legal to run such a business at home? Research your community's guidelines for home businesses.

Human Relations

3. Because of a downturn in business, Christy must lay off three employees. What local or state agencies can help them find new jobs or provide training for new careers? Research services provided in your area.

Developing Teamwork and Leadership Skills

With a team of four people, create a plan for a T-shirt shop. Decide what products to sell, what prices to charge, and where to locate the shop. What other decisions must be made? Select one team member as a facilitator to keep the team on target. Give a formal presentation of your plan to the rest of the class. Include visuals.

Real-World Workshop

Write a business description of a small business you would like to start. Include the goods or services to be provided, your business location, number of employees and their salaries, and your competitors' strengths and weaknesses. Choose a business that fits your interests, skills, and work experience. Research if necessary.

School-to-Work Connection

Identify one small business in your community that interests you. Interview the owner about the business. Ask questions about how and why the owner got into the business. What does he or she like about it? What are some problems? What special skills are needed? What advice would the owner give someone who wanted to get into the business? Prepare a brief report to share with the class.

Individual Career Plan

Choose a business that interests you. Research the skills and experience you would need to get into the business and be successful. Finally, develop short-term and long-term goals for learning those skills and getting the necessary experience.

Developing an Individual Career Plan

Section 5-1
Evaluating Career Choices

Section 5-2
Your Plan of Action

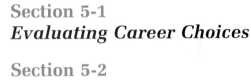

In this video segment, learn how to develop your own individual career plan.

Journal
Personal Career Plan

Think of a goal you've set for yourself. Once you set that goal, what steps did you take toward achieving it? What progress have you made? Why? Record your experiences and ideas in your journal.

Evaluating Career Choices

OBJECTIVE

After studying this section, you will be able to:

- **Evaluate various career possibilities.**

KEY TERMS

evaluation
personal career
profile form

Throughout Chapters 2, 3, and 4, you have been completing the first four steps in the decision-making process to explore career possibilities. This process began in Chapter 2 with your taking a close look at your own personal needs and resources. You then identified your choices and began gathering information as part of your career research.

If you've done your research well, you've turned up many career choices. Narrowing these choices to a few "winners" involves comparing your personal data with the career information you've gathered. This step needs to be done with special care.

Evaluate Your Choices

Evaluation can take several forms. Usually it involves comparing and contrasting sets of data to rank them and determine winners. You will do this to find the best possible match between yourself and a career. Why is choice A better than choice B? Why is choice C less realistic than choice D?

Evaluation can also involve weighing possible outcomes. If I take this course of action, what will happen?

Finally, evaluation can involve thinking about your choices in light of your values. If I make this choice, will I be living up to what I truly believe in?

Personal Career Profile Form

Name Gloria Perry   **Date** December 14   **Career** Fashion Industry Publicist

Personal Information	Career Information	Match (1–10)
Your Values I believe in equal opportunities for all people, especially women! I like to do creative things too.	**Career Values** All kinds of people work in fashion. As a publicist, I would be able to use my creativity, as well as work with other creative people.	9
Your Interests My hobbies include reading Victorian novels. I love fashion and keep very up-to-date on the new styles, but I hate sewing! I also enjoy parties.	**Career Duties and Responsibilities** As a fashion publicist, I would make contacts with stores and buyers, arrange fashion shows and launch parties, and send out press releases.	8
Your Personality I'm very outgoing and enjoy having lots of friends. I get bored just sitting in class, unless there are open discussions. I have a good imagination.	**Personality Type Needed** A publicist must be outgoing and friendly. She must also be responsible and keep on top of things. Communication skills are important.	6
Data-People-Things Preferences I like being with people best of all. I find people fascinating. Sometimes facts interest me, too, but I prefer spending time with people!	**Data-People-Things Relationships** Publicists work mostly with people. In the fashion industry, you must be on top of trends, which are constantly changing. You don't work much with things—except for clothes and accessories!	9
Skills and Aptitudes My best subject is history. I have a natural sense of design and color, but I'm about average at actually drawing. My teacher says I'm "excellent" at reading comprehension, but I hate grammar.	**Skills and Aptitudes Required** Good verbal and writing skills are essential for a publicist. You also must be a good "people person." History doesn't matter so much, but you never know—it could help.	7
Education/Training Acceptable I would love to go to fashion school in New York City. I suppose I need some business training as well.	**Education/Training Required** I guess a four-year fashion school would be best—one that has a good business department.	9

▲ **Figure 5-1** Gloria Perry completed a personal career profile form for each career possibility that she researched. Do you think Gloria would be successful as a fashion industry publicist?

A good tool to use in evaluating your choices is the **personal career profile form** shown in *Figure 5-1.* This is a chart in which you can arrange side by side what you have learned about yourself and what you have learned about a career possibility. In the third column, you are asked to use a 1-to-10 rating system to express how

Attitude Counts ✓

Your current project—whatever it is—will never be completely perfect. For that matter, neither will you! Of course, that's no reason to stop trying. Keep striving to improve your work—and yourself. However, don't expect yourself or the people around you to be perfect. If only perfection can satisfy you, you'll always be disappointed.

closely your personal and career information match. A perfect 10 (or as close as possible) in all six categories wins the gold.

Use the following questions to help you assign a score for each category:

- *Values.* Does this career match up well with my values?

- *Interests Versus Responsibilities.* Will the day-to-day responsibilities interest me? Will I be good at them?

- *Personality.* Will I be happy with the work environment and hours?

▶ Choosing the right career path can seem bewildering. *Why is it important to keep your career plans flexible at this stage in your life?*

- *Data-People-Things.* Do the data-people-things requirements of this career match up well with my own preferences?
- *Skills and Aptitudes.* Do I have the skills I need for this career—or the aptitudes to develop them?
- *Education/Training.* Am I willing to get the education and training necessary for this career?

You should complete a personal career profile form for each career choice you have identified for yourself. Then you should tally the scores on all the forms and see which career choice ranks the highest. You are now ready for the next step.

Make Your Decision

Now's the time to make a choice. Which career will you pursue? You may be afraid to commit yourself, but try to have confidence in your research and evaluations. Remember: Unless you define a goal, you are unlikely to reach it. Also,

remember that your choice is flexible—one that you will probably change as your life develops.

In the next section, you will work on the final step in the decision-making process: drawing up your plan of action.

YOU'RE THE BOSS!

✓ *Solving Workplace Problems*

As a vet, you run your own small animal clinic. Recently, a customer's sick cat was so frightened by another customer's dog that the cat ran out the door and was lost. The owner of the missing cat is very angry. How will you respond to the cat owner? What changes should you make to prevent this kind of problem from recurring?

SECTION 5-1 *Review*

Understanding Key Concepts

Using complete sentences, answer the following question on a separate sheet of paper.

1. Your uncle has been urging you to pursue a career as a real estate broker. However, you feel you'd prefer working as a sales representative for a sporting goods manufacturer. How would you go about evaluating these two career possibilities to see which one might be better for you?

Exploring Careers: Agribusiness

Jean Lesley
Farrier

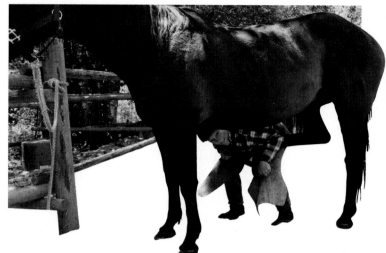

Q: Have you always worked with horses?

A: I had horses until I was 22. Then I sold them and went to college. Though I worked in stables in my 20s and loved it, I thought I should do something traditional, more white-collar. I worked as a graphic designer for 15 years before realizing the position didn't suit my personality. I wanted to be outside with horses.

Q: What drew you to horseshoeing?

A: When you train horses or teach riding, you deal more with the person, not the horse. As a farrier, I work directly with the horse.

Horseshoeing requires craftsmanship. I have a lot of ability with my hands, and I enjoy working with my hands. I like creating shapes—as I did as a graphic designer. Now, however, I work in three dimensions with metal instead of two-dimensional shapes.

Farrier work is also very independent. You work for yourself. You're not in a team situation. In an office, you work with other people.

Q: How do you train to be a farrier?

A: I went to the farrier school at Oregon State University. It's a three-month program in which students work every day, eight hours a day, with horses. It gives you a lot of hands-on experience. Others become farriers by apprenticing with other farriers.

Thinking Critically

Where is a farrier likely to work and under what kinds of conditions?

CAREER FACTS

Nature of the Work:
Fit shoes to horses with tools; keep careful notes on each horse.

Training or Education Needed:
Experience working with other farriers; training in a specialty trade school.

Aptitudes, Abilities, and Skills:
Ability to work with tools; decision-making and problem-solving skills; ability to work intuitively; self-management skills; responsibility; ability to work with large animals; patience; riding skills.

Salary Range:
$20,000 first five years; after five years: average $50,000 to $60,000; up to $100,000.

Career Path:
Start in a training or apprenticeship program; work for stables; work for self.

Your Plan of Action

OBJECTIVES

After studying this section, you will be able to:

- Establish a plan of action and intermediate career goals.
- Identify the education and training you will need.
- Develop an individual career plan.

KEY TERMS

individual career
 plan
on-the-job training
apprentice
vocational-technical
 center
trade school
continuing education

Making your career goals a reality means planning a course of action, called an **individual career plan.** This is the seventh and final step in the decision-making process leading to a career. There is no substitute for planning if you want to be successful and happy. Having a plan doesn't guarantee success, but it greatly improves your chances. You may get help from many sources, but the most workable plan will probably be the one you design yourself. Consider, for example, how Ronald Jones of Chelsea, Massachusetts, is planning for his future.

Since graduating from high school, Ron has been working five nights a week as a waiter at a French restaurant in Boston. During the day, he attends a culinary arts institute, where he is learning to become a gourmet chef. He describes his job as follows:

"It's a little hectic most of the time, but when things slow down, I can watch how the kitchen is run and how various dishes are prepared. I'm making good tips, which is helping me pay for school. I wouldn't want to have this waitering job forever, but the restaurant experience I'm getting—not to mention the cash—is helping me prepare for the career I really want."

Like Ron, it's time for you to start making plans. How will you begin?

Plan How to Reach Your Goal

To reach your ultimate career goal, you will first need to establish some intermediate planning goals. These are the steps you will take to get from where you are now to where you want to be. For example, if your career goal is to be a real estate broker, one intermediate goal is to find out what training you will need to qualify for a real estate license in your particular state.

*Ron dreams of becoming a great chef. **How do you get from where you are now to your ultimate goal?***

Taking Aim

The more specific your intermediate career targets, the more likely you are to hit the bull's-eye. If your ultimate career goal is to become a medical technician, it is not enough to say your intermediate goal is "to get a job working in a hospital." That's like throwing a dart in the general direction of the board. Instead, "to enroll in a program that will train me to be an emergency room technician" is much closer to the mark.

In your journal, write down a few intermediate goals for your particular career choice. Then see if you can make each one more specific.

With Your Feet on the Ground

Besides being specific, your planning goals should be realistic. To plan realistic goals for the future, you must think about who and where you are today.

It would be almost impossible to hit that bull's-eye if you didn't know where you were standing in relation to the dartboard. It would be just as difficult to reach your career goals if you were not honest with yourself about where you are starting from on your career path.

For example, if you dislike math, you may not be happy as an engineer. On the other hand, even if your math skills are weak right now, you may still strongly believe that you would enjoy being an engineer. Therefore, a realistic—and necessary—intermediate goal would be to strengthen your math skills in the near future.

An important note: Be careful not to confuse the words *realistic* and *traditional*. For example, women were traditionally more limited in their job options than men. Today, however, it is realistic for women to consider all available jobs. Also, since you will be developing your career in the years to come, do not limit yourself by the current reality of the world. Be creative in your thinking. You may end up starting a trendsetting business, as Meredith Hunter has done. (See **Figure 5-2** on page 96).

EXCELLENT BUSINESS PRACTICES

Providing a Second Chance

The DELSTAR Group of Phoenix, Arizona, believes in giving people a chance to rebuild their lives after having experienced personal problems. DELSTAR owns and operates retail specialty shops in airports and resorts. The company lists openings at nonprofit agencies and recruits job candidates from various community groups.

DELSTAR's special program provides meaningful work and creates an environment for growth and achievement. Participants receive training, evaluation, and support on a one-to-one basis. They learn about certain personal issues, such as how to manage finances or use a checking account.

A special training program teaches employees how to become small-business entrepreneurs. Employees take the course on their own time. More than a dozen have used the training to open their own businesses.

Thinking Critically

How can organizing your personal life help you do well at work? How can a steady job help you in your personal life?

Stepping-Stone Goals

Think of your ultimate goal as a green meadow on the far side of a river. If you simply plunge into the river, chances are you will be carried way off course. Now imagine a series of stepping-stones. By using each one in turn, you will be able to cross the river safely—and relatively quickly. Think of the stepping-stones as your short-, medium-, and long-term planning goals.

Ronald Jones, whom you read about earlier, has established several stepping-stone goals. While his ultimate career goal is to be head chef at a fine restaurant, he is currently working on a short-term goal: to get practical restaurant experience while serving as a waiter. He is also working on a medium-term goal: to earn a certificate within a few years from the culinary institute he attends. One long-term goal he has is to study with a master chef in France.

Figure 5-2

Setting Planning Goals

Stepping-stone goals are short-, medium-, and long-term goals that can help you reach your ultimate career goal in realistic stages.

A Several years ago, Meredith Hunter made a career decision. She wanted to start a company that would create computer games based on well-known, high-quality children's books. Since she had little experience with business or computers, she knew that she had a long way to go before she could achieve her goal. However, she also knew that listing specific planning goals was a good place to start.

B Meredith's first short-term goal was to attend business school to acquire the knowledge and skills she would need to start her own business. She planned to take courses in business incorporation, management, and law, as well as in computer programming.

Having stepping-stone goals will also allow you to make a "course correction" if you decide your ultimate goal is not right for you. At any point along the way, you can change your mind and head off in a different direction. On the basis of his waitering experience, for example, Ron might decide he would prefer to own and operate a restaurant. He could then revise his medium-term goals to include taking business courses.

C One of Meredith's medium-term goals was to get a job with a successful computer game company—preferably one in which she would have some creative input. She accomplished that goal. At this job, she learned as much as she could about how games are researched, developed, manufactured, and distributed.

D Another medium-term goal of Meredith's was to find out which children's books were the most popular. During her time off from work, she did research at libraries and bookstores.

E Meredith has reached her long-term goal. Having found businesspeople willing to invest in her idea, she hired a creative team of artists. Today she runs a company that creates computer games.

This person is working part-time to learn more about the restaurant business. In the future, she would like to own a restaurant. *Why is it helpful to have stepping-stone goals in planning for a career?*

Deciding on Education and Training

One of your first stepping-stone goals should be receiving the education and training you will need to achieve your ultimate career goal. Almost every job requires some special training, and having advanced education and training means more career opportunities to choose from. *Figure 5-3* shows that workers who have more than a high-school diploma are generally better prepared to succeed at their jobs than those who do not.

Many options are available for getting the education and training you will need.

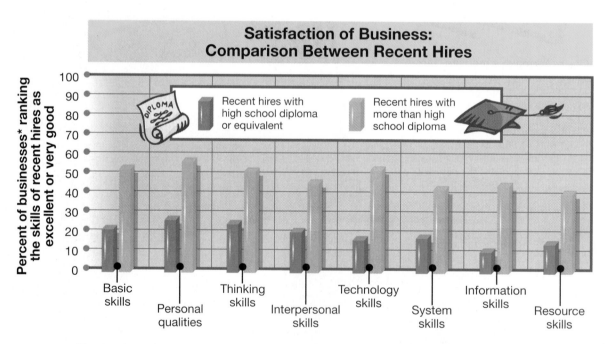

Satisfaction of Business: Comparison Between Recent Hires

*Racine Area Manufacturing and Commerce (RAMAC) Members, Racine County, Wisconsin
Source: RAMAC Education Committee Workforce Survey

Figure 5-3 A survey by the Racine Area Manufacturers and Commerce Education Committee found that employers tend to be more satisfied with workers who have received some post–high school training. How do you suppose such extra training affects an employee's wages over the course of a career?

On-the-Job Training: Learning by Doing

Offered by many companies, **on-the-job training** is on-site instruction in how to perform a particular job. It may consist of a few days of orientation for new employees or more formal long-term instruction. Workers at nuclear power plants, for example, undergo continual training in technical and safety procedures.

The need to be on the cutting edge of new trends makes many large companies stress ongoing training for their employees. For instance, companies that use computer networks generally offer courses to keep their workers up-to-date with the latest software and computer technology.

Apprenticeship

The practice of training young people through apprenticeship to master a craft goes back many hundreds of years. Today an **apprentice** is someone who learns how to do a job through hands-on experience under the guidance of a skilled worker.

Kattai Wendall of Pittsburgh, Pennsylvania, for example, found her apprenticeship as a sheet-metal worker through her state apprenticeship agency. Although she does not make very much money now working at a manufacturing plant, she feels lucky because she is getting paid to learn a trade that will eventually earn her a better position and salary.

Vocational-Technical Centers

You can prepare for many careers by attending a **vocational-technical center.** This is a school that offers a variety of

The practice of serving as an apprentice to learn a craft from a master is centuries old. *What advantages does this form of training have?*

Career Do's & Don'ts

When Finding the Right Career ...

Do:
- talk to people about their career choices.
- work at a job in the field you are interested in to see if it feels right.
- recognize that you may choose several careers in your lifetime.
- map out the steps to achieving the level you want to attain in each career path you identify.

Don't:
- overlook internships or volunteer work.
- limit your options because some of the academic requirements are not your strongest subjects.
- be discouraged by job outlooks in a particular career; there's room for you if you want to do it.
- get sidetracked by a job that won't help you reach your goals.

skills-oriented programs, such as courses in automotive or computer technology. Most vocational-technical centers have evening classes and are relatively inexpensive.

Trade Schools

The culinary arts institute that Ronald Jones attends in Massachusetts is an example of a trade school. A **trade school** is a privately run institution that trains students for a particular profession. Trade schools are usually more expensive than vocational-technical centers. However, they sometimes offer programs that vocational-technical centers do not.

Community and Technical Colleges

Community colleges and technical colleges offer two-year and certificate programs in many occupational areas, such as accounting, tourism management, paralegal work, retailing, and desktop publishing. These colleges usually offer night and weekend classes and are less expensive than trade schools or four-year colleges. One who graduates from a community or technical college with a two-year associate's degree can usually transfer his or her credits to a four-year college or university.

Four-Year Colleges and Universities

Some careers—such as teacher and physical therapist—require a minimum of a bachelor's degree from a four-year college or university. Other careers—such as those in law, architecture, and medicine—require even more advanced degrees. In choosing a college, you will want to consider such factors as location, size, cost, the quality of your particular program, entrance requirements, and the availability of financial aid.

Continuing Education

Many adults return to school at some point in their lives to complete their education, brush up on old skills, or pursue you think you might be cut out for the military, you may be able to receive training in one of more than 200 different occupations, including health technician and air-traffic controller. Depending on the career you choose, you must enlist for up to six years of active duty.

Sometimes you can attend school before or during your service. At other times, the military will pay for your education after you serve.

Committing Yourself on Paper

Are you feeling overwhelmed? That's only natural when faced with so many career options, but don't waste your energy worrying. Instead, take out a large notebook and begin formulating your individual career plan on paper.

Questions and Answers

Start by creating a list of questions to answer about your career goals, education, and training. You might begin with these questions and add others that you feel apply to your particular situation:

- What is my ultimate career goal?
- What is my first "stepping-stone" or short-term goal?
- Which educational programs offer the training I need to prepare for my career?
- How much money will I need to pay for my education and training? Where will this money come from?

The military is one place you can get post–high school training. *Why might the armed forces be a good career choice for some and not for others?*

new paths. Many high schools, colleges, and universities offer **continuing education**—programs geared toward adult students. Some even offer correspondence courses. Some of these programs lead to academic degrees.

Military Service

Did you know that the military is the largest employer in the United States? If

Where Do You Go from Here?

Now write up your individual career plan, such as Ronald Jones's shown in **Figure 5-4** below. In chronological order, write your short-, medium-, and long-term goals. Make sure to include your projected starting and ending dates. You can modify the goals and dates as you get closer to your ultimate goal.

Also, remember that your decisions and plans are flexible. They are not set in stone. Expect to change them. The advantage to having a plan, though, is that you will continue to move ahead until you find the career that is right for you.

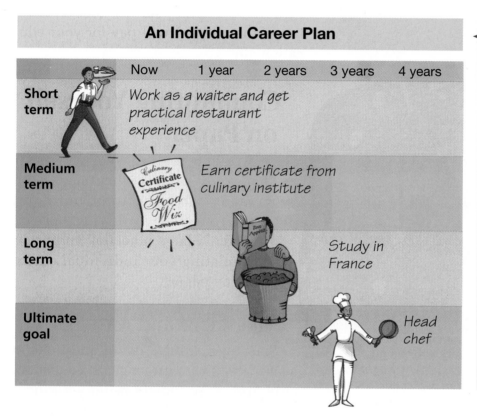

An Individual Career Plan

	Now	1 year	2 years	3 years	4 years
Short term	Work as a waiter and get practical restaurant experience				
Medium term	Earn certificate from culinary institute				
Long term	Study in France				
Ultimate goal	Head chef				

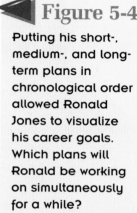

Figure 5-4

Putting his short-, medium-, and long-term plans in chronological order allowed Ronald Jones to visualize his career goals. Which plans will Ronald be working on simultaneously for a while?

SECTION 5-2 *Review*

Understanding Key Concepts

Using complete sentences, answer the following questions on a separate sheet of paper.

1. Explain why having "stepping-stone" planning goals is important for reaching your ultimate career goal.

2. Suppose that you have a friend who wants to be a fashion designer. What education or training options would you advise your friend to explore?

3. What is the advantage of committing your career plans to writing?

Highlights

Key Terms

evaluation *(p. 88)*
personal career profile
   form *(p. 89)*

SECTION 5-1 **Summary**

- In evaluating possible careers, you should match the career information you've gathered to your personal interests and resources.

- Using a personal career profile form allows you to analyze career possibilities in a systematic way.

SECTION 5-2 **Summary**

- The most workable career plan will probably be the one you design for yourself.

- Establishing intermediate career goals will make your ultimate goal easier to reach.

- For your planning goals to be realistic, you must be honest with yourself about your personal strengths.

- Setting short-, medium-, and long-term goals will enable you to evaluate your career path as you go along.

- Acquiring more education and training means having more career opportunities to choose from. Your options include on-the-job training, apprenticeship, vocational-technical programs, trade schools, community and technical colleges, four-year colleges and universities, continuing education programs, and military service.

- Committing your plan of action to paper will help you develop specific career plans. It will also allow you to revise your plans while you continue to move ahead toward a career that will be right for you.

Key Terms

individual career
   plan *(p. 93)*
on-the-job training *(p. 99)*
apprentice *(p. 99)*
vocational-technical
   center *(p. 99)*
trade school *(p. 100)*
continuing education
   (p. 101)

Reviewing Key Terms

Write a one- or two-page article for your school newspaper about how a typical high school senior might go about making a career decision. Use the following terms in your article:

evaluation
personal
  career
  profile form
individual
  career plan
apprentice

on-the-job training
vocational-technical
  center
trade school
continuing
  education

Recalling Key Concepts

On a separate sheet of paper, tell whether each statement is true or false. Rewrite false statements to make them true.

1. You can use a personal career profile form to match what you know about yourself with what you know about different careers.

2. Once you establish an individual career plan, you should not change it.

3. Vocational-technical centers are more expensive than trade schools.

4. An individual career plan should include short-, medium-, and long-term goals.

Thinking Critically

Using complete sentences, answer each of the questions below on a separate sheet of paper.

1. What consequences might result from settling on a career that conflicts with your personal values?

2. When evaluating your hopes and dreams, it helps to visualize your future. How might good visualization skills help you in your job or career?

 ## SCANS Foundation Skills and Workplace Competencies

Basic Skills: *Writing*

1. Determine your top three career choices. Research the education and training needed for each career. Summarize your findings in a 150-word report.

Thinking Skills: *Decision Making*

2. Andrew just graduated from high school. His interests are radio and television, and he plans to build a career in the communications industry. He has just been offered an excellent job as publicity coordinator for a local radio station. The problem is that it is a full-time job with irregular hours and Andrew has been planning to attend college full-time. How should Andrew reach a decision? What do you think a good decision might be?

Interpersonal Skills: *Participating as a Team Member*

3. As a class make a list of the names and addresses of vocational-technical centers, trade schools, community and technical colleges, and four-year colleges and universities. Then, break the class down into teams of three students. Each team should select a

different institution. As a team write a letter requesting information from the institution you have selected. Send your letter to the institution. When you receive the material, use it to create a class display.

Connecting Academics to the Workplace

Vocational Education

1. Lynn recently graduated from high school. Her career goal is to become a computer programmer. She is interested in learning computer programming. However, she must stick to a very strict budget. Using the library, the Internet, or the telephone, research the costs of computer-training programs in your area. Determine which program offers the best training for the lowest cost.

Art

2. You have been told you have excellent art skills and should pursue a career in the art field. Using resources in your school library, develop a list of five careers that require artistic skills. Explain the job task involved in each career that would require your art skills.

Science

3. You are interested in becoming a physical therapist. Research the career to find out more about it. Then develop a list of short-, medium-, and long-term goals that would help you reach this ultimate career goal.

Developing Teamwork and Leadership Skills

Working with a classmate, select several careers you are each interested in. Then help each other establish a list of intermediate planning goals to reach your ultimate career goals.

Real-World Workshop

Use copies of the personal career profile form shown in Figure 5-1 to compare four or more possible careers within your general area of interest. For example, if your interests lie in the area of fine arts, you might use the forms to evaluate and then compare such careers as individual artist, art gallery owner, museum tour guide, and state art council program administrator. After you complete your evaluations, write a summary in which you identify the most promising career choice for you.

School-to-Work Connection

Arrange to spend a day at an apprentice program, vocational-technical center, trade school, or one of the other kinds of education or training sites discussed in this chapter. If possible, arrange to sit in on a typical class, and take notes on what you observe. Give an oral presentation on your findings to the class.

Individual Career Plan

Using Figure 5-4 as a guide, create your own individual career plan. Include your short-, medium-, and long-term goals.

Aspects of Industry:
Planning

Overview

In Unit Two, you began thinking about what kind of work is right for you and developing your career plan. In this Unit Lab, you will use what you have learned about careers while exploring another aspect of industry: **Planning.**

The Planning aspect of industry covers the various types of business ownership—sole ownership (proprietorship), partnership, cooperative, corporation—and how businesses of all types affect and are affected by the economy, politics, and society.

Tools

1. Internet
2. Trade and business magazines
3. Business newspapers
4. Personal interviews

Procedures

STEP A

Choose one of the 15 job clusters from Figure 3-1 in Chapter 3. You may choose the same cluster you explored in the previous Lab, or a different one.

Choose two jobs in the job cluster that you would seriously think about pursuing. Using trade and business magazines, newspapers, and the Internet, research how the industry represented by the jobs you have chosen is affected by economic, political, or social changes.

STEP B

Identify a local corporation that employs people in one of the jobs you have chosen. Ask friends, family, teachers, and counselors for leads. You may also check with your local Chamber of Commerce, which may have a directory of member businesses.

If possible, research that particular corporation. The Chamber of Commerce may have profiled the business in its newsletter, or the local newspaper may have run stories about the business.

Contact a manager at the corporation and ask permission to do a short (20- to 30-minute) interview. You want to find out why the business is organized as a corporation and what the advantages and disadvantages are of that form of business.

Some of the questions you might ask at the interview are:

1. How does the corporate form of business allow the company to expand, change, and meet challenges?

2. How are important decisions made in the corporation?

3. What are the advantages and disadvantages of working for a corporation?

Write out your questions beforehand. If you are doing the interview in person, be prompt and courteous, and dress appropriately.

STEP C

You will now repeat instructions for Step B, but for a sole proprietorship. Identify a sole proprietorship that employs people in the other job you have chosen.

Contact the business owner, and ask permission to do a short (20- to 30-minute) interview. Find out why the owner

chose sole proprietorship. What are the advantages and disadvantages of that form of business? Some of the questions you might ask are:

1. How does being a sole proprietorship allow the company to expand, change, and meet challenges?

2. What are the advantages and disadvantages of being a sole proprietorship?

3. How are important decisions made in a sole proprietorship?

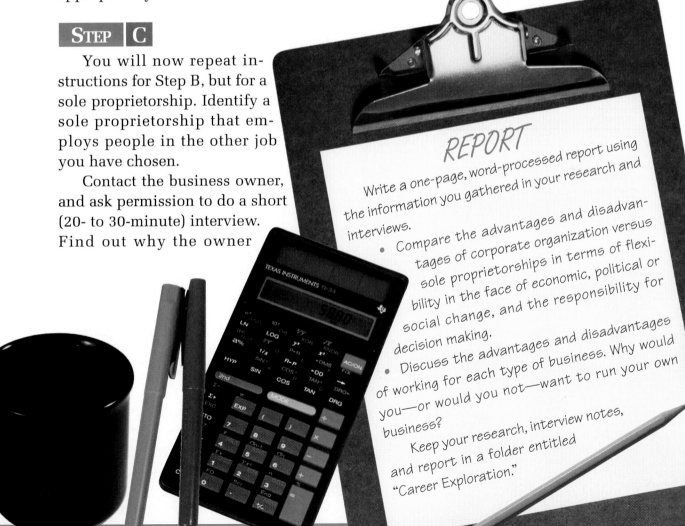

REPORT

Write a one-page, word-processed report using the information you gathered in your research and interviews.

• Compare the advantages and disadvantages of corporate organization versus sole proprietorships in terms of flexibility in the face of economic, political or social change, and the responsibility for decision making.

• Discuss the advantages and disadvantages of working for each type of business. Why would you—or would you not—want to run your own business?

Keep your research, interview notes, and report in a folder entitled "Career Exploration."

Finding a Job

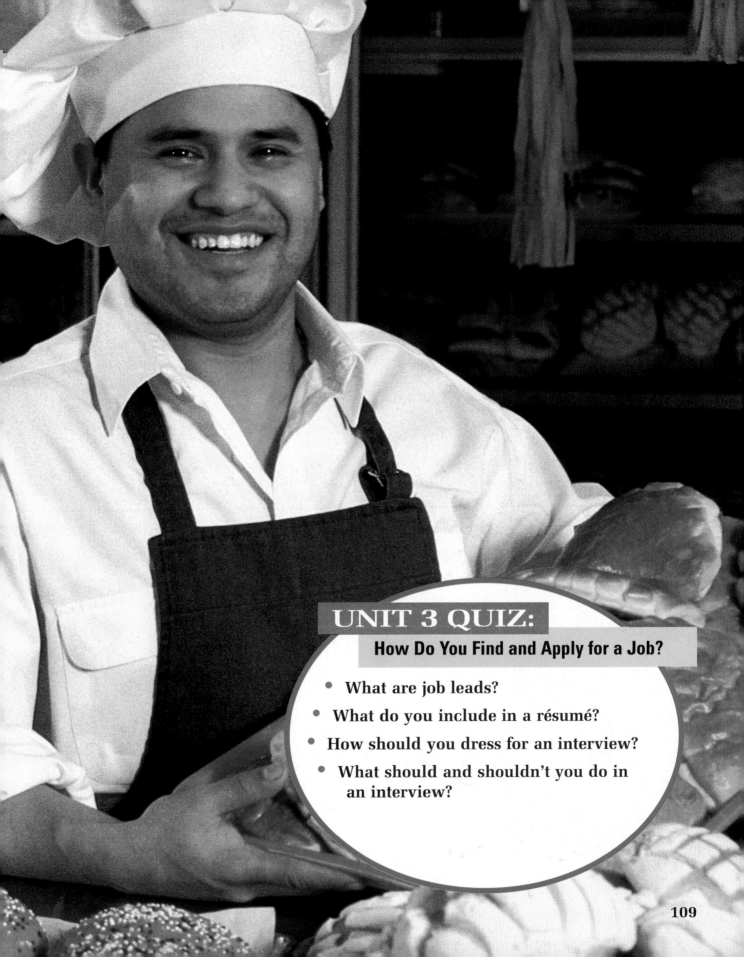

UNIT 3 QUIZ:

How Do You Find and Apply for a Job?

- What are job leads?
- What do you include in a résumé?
- How should you dress for an interview?
- What should and shouldn't you do in an interview?

Finding and Applying for a Job

Section 6-1
Exploring Sources of Job Leads

Section 6-2
Applying for a Job

In this video segment, discover how practicing with friends can help you improve your interview techniques.

Journal
Personal Career Plan

During the next week, explore as many sources of job leads as possible. Record your explorations in your journal, noting details about each job opening and how you learned about it. At the end of the week, write a paragraph summarizing what you have learned from this exploration.

Exploring Sources of Job Leads

OBJECTIVES

After studying this section, you will be able to:

- Explain why networking is effective for developing job leads.
- Create and maintain a career network and contact list.
- Identify sources for job leads.
- Apply knowledge of the Internet in a job search.

KEY TERMS

job lead
networking
contact list
referral
school-to-work
    programs
Internet

Getting a job is the beginning of a new lifestyle. There will be new friends, new surroundings, new challenges, and your own income. Think of the possibilities! To get started on this adventure, you need a job. Not just any job will do, though. You need the right job. This is the one that you will enjoy and do well at.

Finding the right job begins with a job lead. A **job lead** is information about a job opening. It can be a tip from a friend, a classified (help-wanted) ad in the newspaper, or information from a teacher or school guidance counselor.

Networking

How do you go about developing job leads? One of the best ways is by networking. **Networking** is communicating with people you know or can get to know to share information and advice.

How well does networking work? Compare it to other ways of getting a job shown in *Figure 6-1.*

What makes networking so useful is that your contacts may be "insiders." Often, they work at the company that is hiring. They can tell you what the company is looking for and give you a recommendation that really counts.

Creating Your Own Network

Networking is not as difficult as you might think. You know people, don't you? Those people will form the basis for your network.

School counselors can provide advice about sources of job information. *What advantages can you see in beginning your job search now, while you are still in school?*

To get started, make a **contact list**. This is simply a list of people you know. Include everyone—family friends, neighbors, classmates, friends of friends, and even casual acquaintances.

Now begin networking by contacting the people on your list. Ask for any information that will lead to a job. You may think your aunt doesn't know anything about job openings. Maybe she doesn't, but her neighbor might, so don't give up on your aunt. Ask whether she knows anyone who works in the business you're interested in or for a company you'd like to work for.

Build your contact list by getting a referral from everyone you talk to. A **referral** is someone such as your aunt's neighbor to whom you've been directed, or referred. By contacting referrals, you

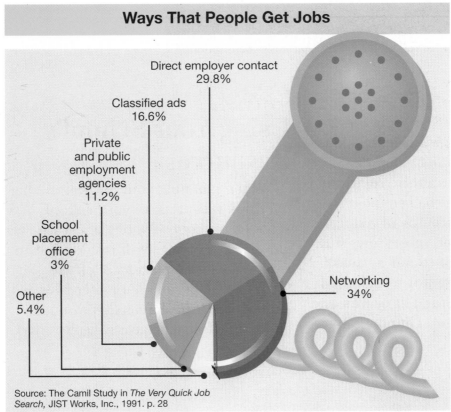

Ways That People Get Jobs

Direct employer contact
29.8%

Classified ads
16.6%

Private and public employment agencies
11.2%

School placement office
3%

Other
5.4%

Networking
34%

Source: The Camil Study in *The Very Quick Job Search*, JIST Works, Inc., 1991. p. 28

Figure 6-1

The graph shows the proportion of jobs people get from different sources. Why do you think most people get jobs by networking and contacting employers directly?

Associations in Successful Networks

Associations	Description	Examples
Personal	All the people you know personally; according to a recent MTV poll, 85 percent of young workers found jobs through personal associations	Brothers, aunts, classmates, neighbors, family friends
Professional	The people you work with or know because of the business you're in or professional organizations you belong to	Coworkers, supervisors, customers, colleagues in other companies
Organizational	People you know because of non-job-related organizations or clubs you belong to	Members of your Sierra Club chapter, computer club, softball team, church or synagogue
Opportunistic	People you bump into by chance	The clerk at the music store, the woman sitting next to you on the train, the contractor who's repairing a neighbor's house

Figure 6-2

Successful networks include four types of associations: personal, professional, organizational, and opportunistic. Why should you try to include all four in your network?

build your network. (See *Figure 6-2*.) Eventually, networking will lead to a job.

Take Carrie Lannon, for example. She found her job in hotel public relations through networking. She had an interview with a promotions director of a hotel. Nothing came of that interview, but she added the director to her network. A month later, the director telephoned Lannon with a job lead. There was an opening at another hotel. Lannon got an interview and the job.

Using Your School's Resources

When planning your job search, don't overlook resources at your school. Your school has a counselor or teacher who can guide you in your job hunt. Your school may even have a placement office.

A counselor can set up interviews with employers. He or she can help you identify and follow leads in specific career areas.

Your school counselor may also be able to help you get into **school-to-work programs**. These programs bring schools and local businesses together. Students gain work experience and training. When they graduate, they usually get preference for jobs at the businesses.

Job Advertisements

The classified ads can be one part of your job search, but it should not be the only one. Only a small percentage of job seekers find their jobs through ads.

In pursuing this method of job hunting, don't limit yourself to newspaper classifieds. There are many other sources. Check these out:

- *National Business Employment Weekly*;

- *Black Enterprise*, *Hispanic Business*, and similar publications that are geared to specific ethnic groups; and

- magazines that specialize in particular industries, such as *Advertising Age* and *Computerworld*.

Using the Telephone

The telephone is one of your most useful job-hunting tools. Use it to make hot calls. A *hot call* is a call to a referral or a call to follow up a lead. It's *hot* because you know whom you're

 You can begin networking with your friends. ***How can they help you find a job?***

Career Do's & Don'ts

When Looking for a Job...

Do:
- make it a top priority.
- create a professional résumé.
- tell everyone you know that you're looking for a job.
- be prepared to sell yourself on the phone to get an interview.

Don't:
- accept a job until you clearly understand the position.
- forget to ask questions about the company, the opportunities, and the benefits.
- put yourself down.
- ignore the importance of making a good first impression.

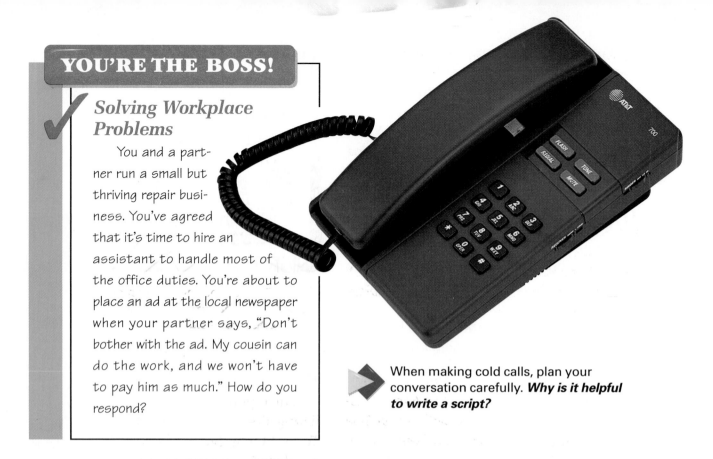

YOU'RE THE BOSS!

✓ *Solving Workplace Problems*

You and a partner run a small but thriving repair business. You've agreed that it's time to hire an assistant to handle most of the office duties. You're about to place an ad at the local newspaper when your partner says, "Don't bother with the ad. My cousin can do the work, and we won't have to pay him as much." How do you respond?

When making cold calls, plan your conversation carefully. **Why is it helpful to write a script?**

calling and you know there's a job or information at the other end of it.

You may also make *cold calls*. These are blind calls. You're not calling to follow up on a specific job lead or a referral but just to get information. Does the company have any openings? Whom can you talk to there? If you make cold calls, plan them carefully.

- Scan the Yellow Pages for companies you might want to work for, and call them. Ask for the personnel director or the supervisor of a department.

- Write an introductory script to use when calling. Tell who you are, why you're calling, and what you want.

- Write questions that will get you information about job openings. Be sure to request referrals.

A telephone call may be your first personal contact with an employer. Make it effective. Practice the SCANS skills of speaking and listening.

Employment Agencies

An employment agency is a matchmaker between job seekers and companies with job openings. Job seekers fill out applications at the agency. Businesses call the agency when they have openings. The agency brings the two together.

There are two kinds of employment agencies—public and private. Public agencies provide free placement services. Private agencies charge a fee, which may be paid by either the job seeker or the employer. Private agencies may give more personal service and list jobs not on file with the public agency.

Using the Internet

Using the job-hunting tactics discussed so far, you can contact hundreds of potential employers. That's not bad, but there's a way to reach thousands. It's the **Internet**, a worldwide electronic community that links millions of computers and computer users. You can view on-line job ads, post your résumé, and find advice and information at career centers.

Getting on the Internet

What do you need to get hooked up to the Internet? A computer, a modem, a telephone line, and an account with an on-line server, such as America Online, CompuServe, or Prodigy.

Even if you don't have a computer, access to the Internet is available. Check with your school and public libraries. Many are already connected to the Internet. You might also check with community colleges, universities, copy shops, and your state employment office.

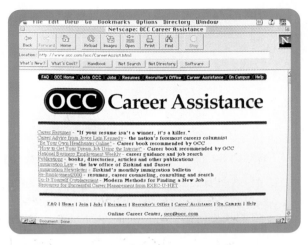

The Internet is the newest tool for finding jobs. *What keywords might lead you to jobs in the field you're interested in?*

Navigating the Internet

Once you're on-line, hundreds of job-listing sites are just a few keystrokes away. To find them, type in keywords. *Keywords* are descriptive words that tell your computer what to search for. Examples are *employment opportunities*, *job listings*, and *careers*.

Keywords will lead you to some of the many job-related sites on the Internet, such as America's Job Bank, Online Career Center, or Federal Job Openings.

SECTION 6-1 *Review*

Understanding Key Concepts

Using complete sentences, answer the following questions on a separate sheet of paper.

1. Explain why networking is one of the most effective means of finding a job.

2. Whom should you include on your contact list? Why?

3. Which source for job leads will you use first in job hunting? Why?

4. What are six keywords you might use in a job search on the Internet?

Exploring Careers: Construction

Bill Jagger
Building Contractor

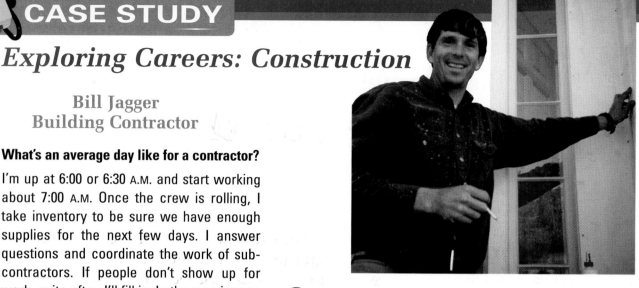

Q: What's an average day like for a contractor?

A: I'm up at 6:00 or 6:30 A.M. and start working about 7:00 A.M. Once the crew is rolling, I take inventory to be sure we have enough supplies for the next few days. I answer questions and coordinate the work of sub-contractors. If people don't show up for work, quite often I'll fill in. In the evenings or on weekends, I do the paperwork: pay bills, send bills, type contracts. Ten-hour days are not uncommon.

Q: How did you acquire your skills?

A: I worked for a friend's father in high school—pounding nails, cleaning up job sites. I ended up going to technical college and earning an associate degree in building construction. I've worked for many contractors over the years. Being a contractor is an acquired trade. The more you do, the better you are. I've worked at it about 20 years.

Q: What are some of the difficulties?

A: We sometimes have problems with labor. Sometimes lumber doesn't show up, or the order is wrong. There's a lot of risk. You're dealing with large sums of money. People don't forget if something goes wrong. But it's gratifying to stand back and look at a house you've built and say you've had a part in it.

Thinking Critically

What are the many ways that contractors use math skills on a daily basis?

CAREER FACTS

Nature of the Work:
Order supplies for construction jobs; coordinate work crews and subcontractors; work on the job; bill clients; pay invoices. work with tools and equipment; ability to work intuitively; reading and writing skills; ability to allocate resources.

Training or Education Needed:
Experience on construction sites; work with other contractors; business skills.

Aptitudes, Abilities, and Skills:
Math and interpersonal skills; problem-solving and decision-making skills; ability to read blueprints and diagrams; ability to

Salary Range:
Average starting salary—$30,000; average top salary—$60,000.

Career Path:
Start on the job; develop skills in one or more trades; learn business of contracting; act as sub-contractor; start own business or work for a large contracting firm.

Applying for a Job

OBJECTIVE

After studying this section, you will be able to:

- **Outline procedures for applying for a job: filling out applications, preparing a résumé and cover letter, and taking tests**

KEY TERMS

Social Security number
work permit
standard English
references
résumé
cover letter

Think of a personnel director with three piles of applications before him. One pile is labeled "Yes." One is labeled "Maybe." One is labeled "No." Your job is to get your application into the "Yes" pile. How will you do that?

It comes down to how well you present yourself in your phone calls, job application, résumé, and cover letter. Your knowledge of the SCANS skills of writing, problem solving, creative thinking, and reasoning will show.

Employers are looking for the best person to fill the job. They want to know whether or not you have the ability to do the work. They will be influenced by the way you dress and whether or not you are well-groomed. They will also notice if you use slang or any other language that is not standard English. In fact, they will want to know everything about you that relates to the job.

Be Confident and Be Prepared

You may feel anxious and insecure when applying for a job. That's natural, but don't show it. Project confidence and a positive, businesslike image. Display this image every time you communicate with an employer by phone, in writing, or in person.

Be Prepared

An employer will require you to have certain documents. If you don't have them when you apply for a job, it shows you aren't prepared. Get them before you go job hunting.

First, you'll need a **Social Security number**. You probably already have one. If not, you can get one at the post office. This number is issued by the federal government.

If you are under 16, you will also need a work permit. Some states require work permits for workers under 18. A **work permit** shows that you have been advised of laws restricting the hours young people can work and the kinds of jobs they can hold. You should be able to get a work permit at your school's guidance office.

Communicating Effectively

The way you talk and write is one of the first and strongest impressions you'll make, so use **standard English**. This is the form of writing and speaking you've learned in school. It is the form used in newspapers and on television news programs. If you have trouble with grammar and usage, now is the time to polish these SCANS skills.

Filling Out the Job Application

A *job application* is one way an employer screens applicants. This form asks questions about your skills, work experience, education,

A job application is a type of interview. *What could an employer learn about you from your handwriting?*

and interests. Always fill out a job application completely and accurately. Keep these additional suggestions in mind:

- Read and follow directions exactly.
- Keep the application neat and clean.
- Make your statements positive. If you believe that answering a question might disqualify you, write "Will explain in interview."
- Keep your options open. Do not state the salary you want. Write "Negotiable." If you are asked whether you will work nights, write "Will consider."
- Prepare any lists of information in advance. Many applications, for example, ask for a list of schools

attended. If you've attended a number of schools, you might prepare this information in advance for your own reference. Then you can enter the information quickly and accurately.

Applications often request **references.** These are people who will recommend you to an employer. Choose references carefully and be prepared to list them on the application. Employers trust teachers or former employers the most. Make sure you ask permission to use people as references.

Employers don't have a right to ask about your race, religion, sex, children, or marital status. You don't have to tell if

EXCELLENT BUSINESS PRACTICES

Interactive Technology That Lists Your Résumé

Texas Instruments of Dallas, Texas, manufactures electronic components, defense electronics, and digital products. Texas Instruments designed a method of helping students list their qualifications on the company's employment database. During visits to college campuses or by mail, the company distributes a brochure and interactive floppy disks with a program called "Engineer Your Future." The interactive program was designed to streamline the recruitment process and teach job-searching skills.

Using the disks, students identify work styles and preferences with a career-mapping feature. They can then create résumés that will be submitted to the company.

Students return completed profiles on disk. When the company receives the information, it is entered into the employment database and reviewed, as appropriate, when job positions need to be filled. Each student receives a copy of the career profile generated by the program.

Thinking Critically

How would a recruitment tool designed specifically for one company help you in a job search at other companies?

you've been arrested, although you are required to tell if you've been convicted of a felony. If you are asked for this information on an application form, you might indicate that you'll explain in the interview.

Preparing a Résumé

A **résumé** is a brief summary of your personal information, education, skills, work experience, activities, and interests. You will send it to an employer when applying for a job by mail or via the Internet. An employer may also request that a copy be attached to your job application or brought to an interview. A résumé can get you an interview or kill your chance for a job. Don't be shy. Make yourself look good!

You do this by carefully choosing what you'll include, what you'll emphasize, and how you'll describe your experience. Do not include any negative information. If you don't have work experience, don't mention it. Focus on the skills, education, and training you do have. Don't hesitate to include awards, hobbies, or activities. References can be included, or you can indicate you'll provide them on request.

The best résumés are brief. Keep yours to one or two pages. It must be typed or computer generated. Of course, it must be neat, and there should be no errors in spelling, grammar, or usage. There are two basic forms of résumés.

A *chronological résumé* gives your experience in time order. You list your most recent job first, then your previous job, and so on. You organize your education and other information in the same reverse time order. *Figure 6-3* shows an example of a chronological résumé.

The advantage of a chronological résumé is that it shows your growth in experience. It works best for a person with continuous work experience.

A *skills résumé* highlights your skills and accomplishments. It is organized around skills or strengths, such as attention to detail or interpersonal skills. After each heading is a description. The advantage

The information you include on a résumé must be accurate and true. What you include and how you state it is up to you. *What can you do to make yourself look good on a résumé?*

Figure 6-3

Chronological Résumé

Résumés may be organized in different formats. However, most will include the following kinds of information. Keep your résumé brief. An outline form is best because it is easy to read. Use titles and spacing to identify major categories of information.

1 **Name and Address.** Give your name, full address, and telephone number (with area code) at the top of your résumé.

2 **Job Objective.** State the job you are applying for. Be sure to change this item if you are using the same résumé when applying for different jobs.

3 **Work Experience.** List your work experience, beginning with your most recent job. Include volunteer work if it relates to the job you are applying for.

4 **Education.** List the schools you have attended and diplomas or degrees you have received. You may also include any subjects or programs you specialized in.

5 **Honors and Activities.** Include any honors or awards you have received or activities you have participated in that relate to the job you want.

6 **Special Skills and Abilities.** Identify any business or other skills and abilities that you have gained in school, on a job, or in other situations.

7 **References.** If your résumé is short, you may include references. If not, say "Available upon request."

The résumé reads:

Laura Calero
621 Bradley Street
Kirkwood, MO 63122
314-555-8210

JOB OBJECTIVE

Seeking a position as a junior production editor. Desire position with opportunity for career growth.

WORK EXPERIENCE

July 1995–present: Production Assistant, Benjamin Publishing Company, Chesterfield, Missouri. Responsible for a variety of tasks involved in textbook production, including photo acquisition, proofreading, and inputting of corrections on computer.

August 1993–June 1995: Sales Associate (part-time), J. H. Covington Company, St. Louis, Missouri. Responsible for customer service, some record keeping, and the taking of inventory.

Summers, 1992 and 1993: Swimming instructor, Kennedy High School, Webster Groves, Missouri. Taught diving and life-saving techniques to intermediate level students.

EDUCATION

High School Diploma (College Preparatory Program), Kennedy High School, Webster Groves, Missouri

HONORS AND ACTIVITIES

Dean's Honor List, Student Council Member, Yearbook Sports Editor, Swimming Team Member

SPECIAL SKILLS AND ABILITIES

Skilled on both Macintosh and IBM-compatible computers, Windows, Microsoft Word, and Quark. General familiarity with textbook publishing production. Strong math skills. Excellent attendance record.

REFERENCES

Available upon request.

of this résumé is that you can emphasize your strengths. *Figure 6-4* shows one way to organize a skills résumé.

Electronic Résumés

Increasingly, companies *scan* résumés into their computers. That is, they copy and store them in their computers. When companies need to hire someone, they do an electronic search of the résumés. They look for keywords that describe skills or job experiences they're seeking, such as *food service*, *mathematics*, and *French*.

Try to create a résumé that works in today's electronic age. Here are some tips for making your résumé "scannable":

- Keep the résumé clean.
- Use crisp, dark type.

Skills Résumé

Laura Calero
621 Bradley Street
Kirkwood, MO 63122

Home: 314-555-8210
Fax: 314-555-8200

JOB OBJECTIVE:	Seeking a position as a junior production editor. Desire position with opportunity for career growth.
SKILLS AND ABILITIES:	**Computer Skills** Skilled on both Macintosh and IBM-compatible computers. Classes using IBM-compatible computers in middle and high school. On-job training on Macintosh with Benjamin Publishing Company. Familiar with Windows, Microsoft Word, and Quark.
	Communications Excellent writing and speaking skills. Good with grammar and usage. Have had short stories published in high school journal, *The Athenaeum.*
	Hardworking Have worked outside of school since I was sixteen as a swimming instructor during summer vacation and as a part-time sales associate for J. H. Covington Company. Worked 20 hours per week while going to school.
	Customer Relations As a sales associate with J. H. Covington, had direct customer contact. Successfully handled both sales and returns. Won "Sales Associate of the Month" award.
	Attention to Detail I am precise and careful in my work. As a production assistant for Benjamin Publishing Company, I did proofreading and also input corrections on the computer.
EDUCATION:	High School Diploma, Kennedy High School, Webster Groves, Missouri. Followed College Preparatory Program.
ACTIVITIES AND AWARDS:	High School activities included member of Student Council, yearbook sports editor, member of swimming team. Awards included Dean's Honor List in high school.

Figure 6-4

A skills résumé lets you highlight skills, aptitudes, and experience that you have. What categories would you list under Skills and Abilities?

- Avoid italics, underscores, and other fancy type.
- Use white paper.
- Use keywords in describing your experience.

Writing Cover Letters

Do not send your résumé by itself. Always include a **cover letter**. This is a one-page letter telling the employer who you are and why you're sending the résumé. It is sometimes called an *application letter*. Keep it concise and to the point. A cover letter has three parts. (See *Figure 6-5* below.)

- The opening explains why you are writing. Drop names! Say where, or from whom, you learned about the job.

Cover Letter

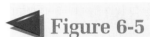

621 Bradley Street
Kirkwood, MO 63122
November 16, 1997

Mr. David Schweizer
Managing Editor
Premiere Publishing Company, Inc.
St. Louis, MO 63108

Dear Mr. Schweizer:

Ann Leiter, the editorial director for Sunshine Publishing, suggested I contact you about the position of junior production editor that is open with your company. Please consider me an applicant for this position.

I have been working since July 1995 as a production assistant for Benjamin Publishing Company in Chesterfield, Missouri. I've had an opportunity to develop skills in desktop publishing and to learn about many aspects of textbook publishing. Please review my résumé, which is enclosed. It provides more details about my experience and the skills I can bring to your company.

I am especially interested in pursuing a career with Premiere Publishing because of your reputation for creative use of graphics and page design. I believe employment with your company would offer me a wonderful opportunity to use my skills and advance in my career.

May I have an interview? I shall be glad to call at your convenience. My home telephone number is (314) 555-8210.

Sincerely,

Laura Calero

Laura Calero

Figure 6-5

Make the purpose of your cover letter clear. Let your personality come through. How has this writer included the key elements of the three parts of the cover letter?

- The body is your sales pitch. It tells why you are right for the job.
- The closing tells how you will follow up. Include your phone number so the employer can contact you.

Try to personalize your letter. One woman applied for a job with Playskool. As a child, she had loved the company's toys. She mentioned this fact in her cover letter. It helped her get the job.

Taking Tests

When you apply for a job, you may have to take one or more tests.

- A performance test evaluates how well you can do a particular task. An example is a typing test.
- A drug test is a blood or urine test for illegal drugs. Most companies in the nuclear power and transportation industries use drug tests.
- A polygraph test is a lie detector test. It may be required if you are applying for a job in law enforcement or government.

When taking a test for a job, relax, stay calm, and keep focused. *What techniques do you have that help you relax during tests?*

ETHICS in Action

You've been looking for a part-time job, but you haven't had much luck. A classmate mentions a job you hadn't known about. "They said they'd call back tomorrow, and I really think I'll be hired. It's just the job I've been looking for." It's just what you've been looking for, too. Will you go and apply for the job this afternoon? Why or why not?

SECTION 6-2 *Review*

Understanding Key Concepts

Using complete sentences, answer the following question on a separate sheet of paper.

1. Why should you use standard English throughout the job application process?

Highlights

SECTION 6-1 Summary

- There are numerous sources for job leads. They include networking, employment agencies, school placement centers, classified ads, and the Internet.

- Networking means talking with people who can help you in your job search. Contact lists provide the foundation of networks.

- You build a network by getting referrals from people you know.

- School counselors and placement centers can help you identify and apply for jobs.

- You can find classified ads in newspapers and a variety of other publications. They should not be the only method for finding job leads.

- Employment agencies match job seekers with businesses seeking new employees. There are public and private employment agencies.

- The Internet has job lists, on-line career centers, and sites where you can post your résumé.

Key Terms

job lead *(p. 112)*
networking *(p. 112)*
contact list *(p. 113)*
referral *(p. 113)*
school-to-work
    programs *(p. 115)*
Internet *(p. 117)*

SECTION 6-2 Summary

- Before you apply for a job, you should get a Social Security number, and you may need a work permit.

- When you apply for a job, use standard English, the form of speaking and writing that you learned in school.

- Employers screen applicants through job applications, résumés, and cover letters. You want to project a positive image of yourself in these documents.

- Some employers require tests—such as performance tests, drug tests, or polygraph tests—as part of the application process.

Key Terms

Social Security
    number *(p. 120)*
work permit *(p. 120)*
standard English *(p. 120)*
references *(p. 121)*
résumé *(p. 122)*
cover letter *(p. 125)*

Reviewing Key Terms

On a separate sheet of paper, write one or two paragraphs describing how you would conduct a job search. Use the terms below in your description.

job lead

networking

contact list

referral

school-to-work

    programs

Internet

Social Security

    number

work permit

standard English

references

résumé

cover letter

Recalling Key Concepts

Choose the correct answer for each item below. Write your answers on a separate sheet of paper.

1. Getting a job lead is the first step in ____.
   (a) building a network (b) finding a job
   (c) locating a school-to-work program

2. You build your network by asking for ____.
   (a) contact lists (b) job leads
   (c) referrals

3. A fee may be charged by a ____.
   (a) private employment agency
   (b) public employment agency
   (c) school placement center

4. When completing a job application, you should ____.
   (a) make it scannable
   (b) make your statements positive
   (c) ask for referrals

5. A résumé that lists your last job first is a ____.
   (a) skills résumé
   (b) chronological résumé
   (c) electronic résumé

Thinking Critically

Using complete sentences, answer each of the questions below on a separate sheet of paper.

1. Many employers like to hire people referred to them through a network. Why do you think this is so?

2. If you were an employer, what would you think of an applicant who did not use standard English?

3. List information you would include on your résumé, and explain why.

4. Why would an employer give applicants a skill test before hiring them?

5. If you were an employer, what would you look for in an applicant's cover letter?

 SCANS Foundation Skills and Workplace Competencies

Thinking Skills: *Knowing How to Learn*

1. In a paragraph, describe how your school placement office can help you find job leads.

Personal Qualities: *Integrity/Honesty*

2. Jennifer is filling out a job application. She was fired from her last job. She wants to answer no to the question "Have you ever been fired?" What should she do and why?

Resources: *Allocating Time*

3. Imagine you are looking for a job. Prepare a daily schedule for your job search.

Connecting Academics to the Workplace

Mathematics

1. Bill has 20 people on his first contact list. If each person on his list refers him to two more people, and each of those people refers him to one more person, how many people will be on his new list?

Social Studies/Language Arts

2. Laura is interested in sending a résumé to a corporation. Choose a corporation she might be applying to and do research to learn about it. Then write a cover letter she might send to the corporation. Use your research in your letter.

Computer Science

3. Sheila wants to find out about opportunities in nursing in Texas. Use the Internet to find some on-line job bulletin boards. Find some jobs for Sheila. Contact an on-line career service to get some advice for her.

Developing Teamwork and Leadership Skills

Pair up with another student in a job-search team. As a team, choose a particular job and research openings through methods described in the chapter. Then present your findings to the class.

Real-World Workshop

Collaborate with a classmate to research ways to write résumés. You might read career books or find information on the Internet. Then write your résumé. Exchange résumés with your partner for review and proofreading. Check each other's résumé for standard English.

School-to-Work Connection

Call an employment agency or a business and ask to speak to the personnel director. Interview this person about common mistakes that people make on their job applications, cover letters, and résumés. What advice would this person give for preparing these documents? Present your findings to the class.

Individual Career Plan

Select a field that interests you. Do research to learn about companies that employ people in this field. Interview a person who knows about work in the field. This might be an employer or an employee in the field. Present your findings to the class in an illustrated oral report.

Interviewing

Section 7-1
Before an Interview: Getting Ready

Section 7-2
During an Interview: It's Show Time

Section 7-3
After an Interview: Following Up

In this video segment, learn the right way to interview for a job.

Journal
Personal Career Plan

In your journal, write three or four questions you would want to ask a job applicant. Think of questions that would help you understand the applicant as an individual and as a possible employee, regardless of particular job skills. Now switch roles from interviewer to applicant; record your ideas for answering the questions.

131

Before an Interview: Getting Ready

Your heart's pounding and your palms are sweaty. You're feeling that mix of confidence and excitement that is part of your first job interview. You prepared well, and you're ready to shine!

The **interview**—a formal meeting between an employer and a job applicant—is the employer's chance to meet you as a person, not just as a name on a résumé. Here's where research and rehearsal pay off.

Know Before You Go

How can you stand out in a job market packed with qualified people? Cheryl Nickerson of Nike says, "Please do your research. Be able to ask intelligent questions about the company and what's going on in the industry." Employers, Nickerson adds, want people with a "willingness to learn and grow."

Here are some smart ways to research a company before an interview:

- Use the library for books, magazines, and newspaper articles about the company and current industry events.

- Ask the public relations department for the annual report or press kit to check out the company's history.

- Visit the company's Internet site for up-to-the-minute information.

- Talk to people who work for the company.

Do your homework before you go to an interview. *What is the advantage of reading articles in current magazines?*

Do these techniques work? Absolutely. The more you know about a company, the better you can showcase your ideas.

Rehearsal Time

Think of a television comedy. The program lasts less than half an hour, but it takes days of rehearsal to get it right. In an interview, you're the cast, and practice will improve your performance.

- **Practice your telephone skills.** When you request an interview, speak clearly and repeat the appointment time and location. Remember: You make your first impression on the telephone.

- **Interview with a friend.** Have a friend ask you typical questions and comment on your interview style.

- **Use a mirror.** Are you sitting straight? Are you fidgeting? Is your facial expression alert and pleasant?

- **Use a tape recorder.** Are your words clear? Do you sound confident?

- **Prepare answers to typical questions.** For example, "What can you tell me about yourself?" One clever strategy is to prepare a 30-second "commercial" that highlights your unique talents and skills.

Rehearsing before an interview will make the interview less stressful. **What should you practice?**

Dress for Success

What does an employer see first when you walk through the door? Not your great personality or your long list of accomplishments. It's your clothes.

Carefully plan what you will wear to your interview. Dress as you would for an actual day on the job, but a little bit better. Match your clothes to the job and, if you can, visit the workplace to see what other workers are wearing.

When in doubt, think conservative. Let your skills stand out, not your tie or dress. Be sure you're neat, clean, and well-groomed, with shined shoes and no fancy jewelry. What would an employer think of the Don'ts in *Figure 7-1?*

Career Do's & Don'ts

When at the Interview...
Do:
- arrive on time and alone.
- have a positive attitude.
- act enthusiastically.
- make sure you are up on current events.

Don't:
- make yourself at home in someone's office until you have been invited.
- chew gum.
- give one-word, yes-or-no answers.
- appear desperate.

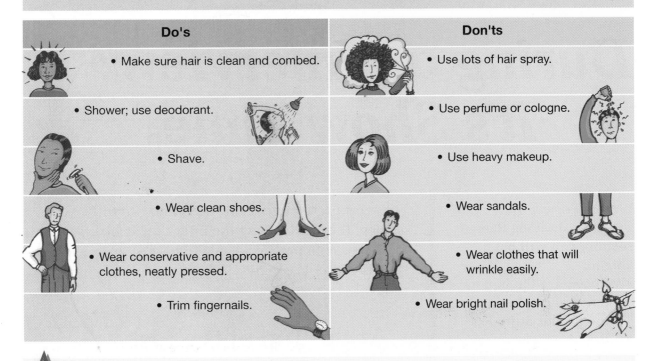

Dressing for Success

Do's	Don'ts
• Make sure hair is clean and combed.	• Use lots of hair spray.
• Shower; use deodorant.	• Use perfume or cologne.
• Shave.	• Use heavy makeup.
• Wear clean shoes.	• Wear sandals.
• Wear conservative and appropriate clothes, neatly pressed.	• Wear clothes that will wrinkle easily.
• Trim fingernails.	• Wear bright nail polish.

▲ **Figure 7-1** Dressing for success means following a certain dress code. What is the most important message you can send with this code?

From Door to Door

Here's a simple but vital tip: Arrive at the interview alone and on time (maybe even make a trial run the day before). It's the mark of a responsible individual.

Bring a pen, a notepad, and two copies of your résumé—even if you've already sent one. Be prepared to fill out an application too, with Social Security number and references ready.

SECTION 7-1 *Review*

Understanding Key Concepts

Using complete sentences, answer the following questions on a separate sheet of paper.

1. How can you research an employer?

2. What methods can you use to rehearse an interview?

3. Why is it important to dress for success at a job interview?

During an Interview: It's Show Time

OBJECTIVES

After studying this section, you will be able to:

- Recognize the importance of displaying the proper attitude.
- Practice clear and accurate communication.
- Answer typical and tough questions.
- Identify strategies for dealing with interview stress.

KEY TERMS

body language
role-playing
problem solving
stress

By preparing for an interview carefully, you can meet the challenge of the interview itself with confidence. With practice, you will be able to project a positive attitude, communicate effectively, and lessen the level of stress.

At the Top of the List: Attitude

When James Coblin of Nucor Steel interviews applicants for a mill in South Carolina, he doesn't focus on job skills. Coblin knows that he can teach workers how to make steel. What he looks for is the right *attitude*. He wants people who can speak honestly to each other, understand other people's feelings, and pitch in to solve problems together.

Let your smile and enthusiasm project your positive attitude. As Brian Johnson of the Dogwater Cafe, a Florida restaurant chain, puts it, "When I'm interviewing, I'm looking for someone with a lot of energy who wants this job more than anything." What do you think *Figure 7-2* says about attitude?

Body Talk

When you interact with people, you communicate through **body language**—the gestures, posture, and eye contact you use to send messages.

Eye contact, for example, shows that you're paying attention. A firm handshake signals self-confidence. Nodding your head shows that you are thinking, while

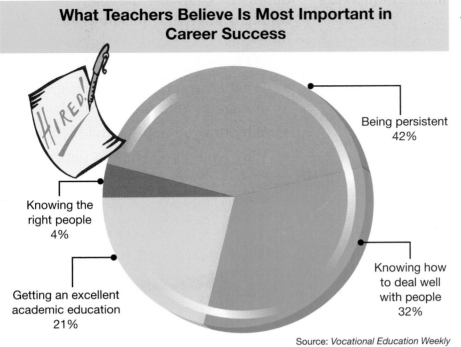

What Teachers Believe Is Most Important in Career Success

- Being persistent 42%
- Knowing how to deal well with people 32%
- Getting an excellent academic education 21%
- Knowing the right people 4%

Source: *Vocational Education Weekly*

Figure 7-2

Persistence is one part of a good attitude. How can you demonstrate to an interviewer that you're persistent?

biting your nails may suggest that you're too nervous to handle the job. What message is body language sending in *Figure 7-3* on pages 138–139?

Good manners count too. Don't chew gum or eat during the interview. Don't throw your coat or papers on the interviewer's desk, and wait until the interviewer asks you to be seated.

meet you" in a clear, confident voice immediately creates a positive, adult impression. Listen attentively too. Listening can calm you and keep you focused.

When you speak, use standard English, as you did on your résumé. Don't speak too quickly; enunciate so that the interviewer doesn't have to strain to understand you.

Speaking for Success

Interview success depends not only on what you say but also on how you say it. Saying "Hello, it's nice to

A good attitude is crucial in the workplace. *What are some essential components of a good attitude?*

Show the SCANS communication skills that employers look for.

Typical Questions

At an interview, an employer tries to find out who you are and what you can do for the company. Be ready to answer standard interview questions such as the following:

- What goals have you set for yourself?
- What do you think are your greatest strengths? Your greatest weaknesses?
- Why did you apply to our company?
- Why would you be right for this job?

Figure 7-3

Body Language

At a job interview, make sure your body language says that you're a positive, confident person.

A Establish eye contact. If the interviewer holds out a hand, give it a firm handshake, and be sure to smile. Practice your handshake beforehand, making sure it's firm but not crushing.

B Lean forward slightly in your chair. Look at the interviewer, and listen to questions. Nod your head, when appropriate, as you listen to the interviewer.

Honesty is the best policy. If you don't understand a question, ask the interviewer to clarify it. Interviewers also prefer specific answers that show you think clearly. Compare these answers:

Question: "Do you enjoy working with others or on your own?"

Answer 1: "I enjoy working with others."

Answer 2: "Well, that depends. Some tasks demand teamwork. Our soccer team, for example, won the city tournament because we worked together to put our strategy into action."

Which answer do you prefer? Why?

C Think about your hands as you speak. Don't clench your fists or bite your nails. Use your hands in a relaxed, confident way.

D Be friendly as the interview closes. Shake the interviewer's hand. Even if you don't get this job, the interviewer may be able to refer you to someone else.

Tough Questions

Sometimes an interviewer may toss a tough question your way. Don't be surprised. The interviewer might want to see how you respond, how you act when you're rattled, or how you think under pressure. You might hear eyebrow raisers such as these:

- How can the company be assured that you'll give us your best effort?

- What qualities do you have that offset your lack of experience?

- Are you going to move to a better job as soon as you gain experience here?

You may want to storm out of the office, but stay calm and don't get defensive. Turn the question around to focus on your skills. For example: "You're right. I'm not experienced, but my work on the Smith project proves that I'm a great organizer!"

If a panel of several people interview you simultaneously, stay calm and address

Don't panic under tough questioning. *How can you prepare for tough questions?*

one question at a time. You may also face think-on-your-feet questions designed to stump you. Remember: There's often no right answer. It's how you react that counts.

Be prepared to ask your own questions too. Asking nuts-and-bolts questions can demonstrate genuine interest.

- What are the employee benefits?

- What does the health plan cover?

- Does the company pay for training?

Standing in the Spotlight

Some interviews include **role-playing**, in which you are asked to play a role in an invented situation and are evaluated on the skills

Role-playing means acting out a role assigned to you during your interview. *What can an interviewer learn about you through this technique?*

you display. Microtraining Plus in Connecticut, for example, trains people to use computers. Job candidates, however, play the role of teachers and make a presentation on a topic other than computers. David Knise, the company's CEO, says, "We're hiring people for their ability to get up in front of six people they don't know and present material."

You also may face a question that requires **problem solving**. For example, "If you faced a deadline you couldn't meet, what would you do?" Remember that the interviewer is evaluating your thinking skills and your attitude (SCANS skills), not looking for one right answer.

 Interviewing can be stressful. The key is handling it well. **Can you think of some techniques for relaxing?**

EXCELLENT BUSINESS PRACTICES

Exploring Opportunities

Patagonia, Inc. designs and distributes clothing for the outdoors. The company has an internship program that allows employees to take paid leaves-of-absence from their jobs for one week to one month and work for a nonprofit organization of their choice.

Employees identify and secure the internships on their own. They also design plans to cover their own job while they are absent.

Employees have volunteered for such diverse tasks as tagging and tracking salmon, monitoring growth of trees in a rain forest, and working at a family planning agency.

All parties involved benefit from this program. The company can support nonprofit groups with labor. Employees get time away from their regular jobs and can add to their personal growth and knowledge of issues important to them and the company.

Thinking Critically

What are the benefits—both to you and to the nonprofit organization—of volunteering your time?

Can They Ask You That?

An interviewer does not have the right to ask you about certain matters. For example, you don't have to answer questions about children or child care, age, disabilities, citizenship, lawsuits, or AIDS or HIV status.

If an interviewer asks you a question that isn't job-related, you might say, "I assure you that this area is not a problem. Let me tell you about the skills I have that fit this job."

The Stress Factor

During an interview, you may experience **stress**—mental or physical tension that is the body's natural response to conflict. You may feel stress before you perform in a concert or play in a big game. What should you do?

First of all, tell yourself you're doing well. (You probably are.) Don't worry about saying "the right thing." That can make you more tense. Stop trying so hard—relax and be yourself.

Most important, keep the experience in perspective. The worst thing that can happen is that you don't get the job. There are

other jobs. Besides, if the interviewer does not think you're right for the company, the company may not be right for you.

Wrapping It Up

At the end of the interview, you may be offered the job on the spot. If not, thank the interviewer and come up with a reason to check back soon. You might say, "What is a convenient time to call you if I have other questions?"

YOU'RE THE BOSS!

Solving Workplace Problems

You are a computer consultant, looking for a part-time employee to help with office chores; you are definitely not looking for an assistant or a trainee. During the interview, the most promising applicant tells you, "I'm so glad to find an opportunity to train as a computer consultant. It's what I've always wanted to do!" How do you respond?

SECTION 7-2 *Review*

Understanding Key Concepts

Using complete sentences, answer the following questions on a separate sheet of paper.

1. Why is a positive attitude essential to succeeding in the workplace?

2. Where in the job market do you see yourself in five years?

3. Why do you think employers ask tough questions?

4. How do you control interview stress?

Exploring Careers: Personal Service

Helen Choi
Hairstylist

Q: How did you get interested in hairstyling?

A: My profession in Korea was painting. It was hard to use my painting skills here, in the United States. I had a friend who was in beauty school. I used to take her to school and pick her up. As I waited for her, I thought, "I could do this. I could go to beauty school."

Q: Was beauty school your only training?

A: Most of my classmates got out of beauty school, got their licenses, and went to work, but I wanted to learn more. I decided to be a hairstylist's assistant and to learn from more experienced people. I was lucky. I had the best teachers. I spent about a year as an assistant. I started out sweeping the floor. It was hard work but good experience. Eventually, the boss said I could begin cutting customers' hair. When I didn't have customers, I watched the other hairstylists. I came in early and stayed late. The customers appreciated that. You build a business relationship and clientele that way.

Q: What do you like about your work?

A: It's exciting, challenging, and stimulating. It's creative. It's nonstop studying. Hairstyles change when the fashion changes.

Thinking Critically

What kinds of personal services do you think might grow in demand in the future?

CAREER FACTS

Nature of the Work:
Counsel clients about hairstyles; keep up on styles; cut hair; schedule appointments; maintain customer relations.

Training or Education Needed:
Approximately one year of beauty school; licensing may be required.

Aptitudes, Abilities, and Skills:
Listening, speaking, and interpersonal skills; problem-solving and decision-making skills; self-management skills; ability to work with your hands; an interest in trends and fashion; an enjoyment working with people; detail-oriented; ability to stand for hours.

Salary Range:
Average starting salary—$15,000; average salary after 5 to 10 years—$30,000-$50,000.

Career Path:
Work as an assistant to a hairdresser; rent space in a salon; start own salon.

After an Interview: Following Up

OBJECTIVES

After studying this section, you will be able to:

- **Apply procedures for following up on an interview, including self-evaluation.**
- **Recognize proper methods of accepting and rejecting employment.**

The interview process doesn't end when you walk out the door of an employer's office. It's important to consider how you did at the interview. What went well? What skills do you need to sharpen? Another major consideration is how you will follow up on the interview. For example, how will you thank the interviewer? How will you get the interviewer to remember you? Most important, of course, is what you'll do if you're offered a job—or rejected.

Tying Up the Loose Ends

You've gotten through the interview! Now's the time to evaluate your own performance.

- Jot down some notes. Did you speak clearly? Did you use standard English? Show enthusiasm? Forget something important? Can you think of any additional information about yourself that you should have provided? Use the notes to improve your next interview.

- Send a follow-up letter soon—even the same day as the interview—in which you thank the interviewer, reinforce how your skills can benefit the company, and restate your continued interest in the job.

- Don't forget to call back.

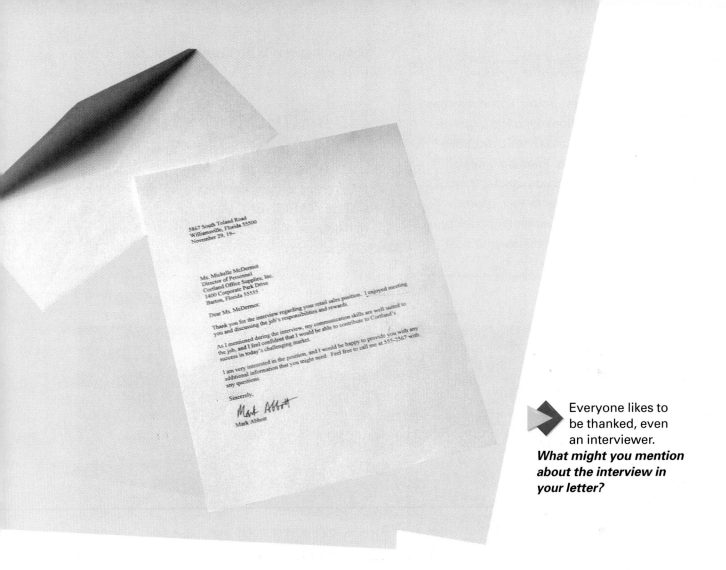

5867 South Toland Road
Williamsville, Florida 55500
November 29, 19—

Ms. Michelle McDermot
Director of Personnel
Cortland Office Supplies, Inc.
1400 Corporate Park Drive
Barton, Florida 55555

Dear Ms. McDermot:

Thank you for the interview regarding your retail sales position. I enjoyed meeting you and discussing the job's responsibilities and rewards.

As I mentioned during the interview, my communication skills are well suited to the job, and I feel confident that I would be able to contribute to Cortland's success in today's challenging market.

I am very interested in the position, and I would be happy to provide you with any additional information that you might need. Feel free to call me at 555-2567 with any questions.

Sincerely,

Mark Abbott

Mark Abbott

Everyone likes to be thanked, even an interviewer. *What might you mention about the interview in your letter?*

Accepting: See You Monday Morning

You hear those magic words: "The job's yours." Now what do you do? Believe it or not, you don't have to say yes immediately. If you want time to think about it, ask the employer if you can take a day to decide. List the job's pros and cons before calling back to accept the job. Ask for a formal offer letter for your files. Send an acceptance letter, and keep a copy.

Rejecting: Thanks, But No Thanks

Suppose an employer wants to hire you, but the salary is low or the job isn't exactly what you were looking for. Don't say no at the interview. Take a day to think about it, and talk it over with other people. You might change your mind, or you might be able to negotiate the salary. When you call back, thank the interviewer, give a reason for your answer, and keep your options open. Who knows what the future may bring?

Handling Rejection

If an employer turns you down, consider it a learning experience. Ask why you weren't hired. Do you need more training? How did you come across in your interview? Feedback will help you in future interviews.

Sometimes it helps to make a pro/con list before deciding whether to take a job. *What might be on such a list?*

SECTION 7-3 *Review*

Understanding Key Concepts

Using complete sentences, answer the following questions on a separate sheet of paper.

1. What questions could you ask yourself to evaluate an interview?

2. What are some disadvantages to instantly accepting or rejecting a job?

CHAPTER 7 · *Highlights*

Key Term
interview *(p. 132)*

SECTION 7-1 Summary

- Prepare carefully for an interview. Research the company and current events in the industry.
- Rehearse before an interview. Practice with a mirror and a tape recorder, and ask a friend for comments.
- Plan what you will wear at an interview. Dress conservatively and avoid flashy items. Appear neat and well-groomed.
- Arrive on time.

Key Terms
body language *(p. 136)*
role-playing *(p. 140)*
problem solving *(p. 141)*
stress *(p. 142)*

SECTION 7-2 Summary

- Employers will be evaluating your attitude and your communication skills. Be positive and enthusiastic.
- You will probably be asked some typical questions at an interview. Be prepared to answer them.
- You may be asked some tough questions designed to rattle you. Be prepared to respond to them with a calm and positive attitude.
- Some questions may involve role-playing or problem solving to evaluate your ability to think on your feet.
- Some questions are illegal for an employer to ask during an interview. You are not required to answer them.

SECTION 7-3 Summary

- Evaluate your performance after an interview. Send a follow-up letter.
- Follow standard procedures for accepting or rejecting employment. Don't say no during an interview. Always leave the door open for the future.

Reviewing Key Terms

On a separate sheet of paper, write a paragraph describing how you would prepare for an interview. Use the terms below in your paragraph.

interview
body language
role-playing

stress
problem solving

Recalling Key Concepts

Choose the correct answer for each item below. Write your answers on a separate sheet of paper.

1. Researching a company before an interview enables you to ____.

   (a) ask intelligent questions

   (b) impress your friends

   (c) dress for success

2. Preparing a 30-second "commercial" about yourself is a good way to ____.

   (a) research a company

   (b) negotiate a salary

   (c) rehearse for an interview

3. Which of the following topics is illegal for an employer to ask about? ____

   (a) your skills (b) your goals

   (c) your citizenship

4. Interviewers look for applicants ____.

   (a) wearing fashionable clothes

   (b) demonstrating a positive attitude

   (c) with a sense of humor

5. In a follow-up letter, you should ____.

   (a) restate your continued interest

   (b) invent additional references

   (c) apologize for being nervous

Thinking Critically

Using complete sentences, answer each of the questions below on a separate sheet of paper.

1. In what ways can you stand out positively at an interview?

2. Summarize the importance of body language at a job interview.

3. Compare rehearsing for an interview alone and rehearsing with a friend. Identify the advantages of each method.

4. What would you infer about a job applicant who asks questions about a job's responsibilities and chances for advancement in the company?

5. Imagine that you are an employer. List the five most important qualities of a great job applicant in order of priority. Give reasons for the order.

SCANS Foundation Skills and Workplace Competencies

Basic Skills: *Speaking*

1. Compose a 30-second "commercial" to summarize your abilities. In it, act as if you were being interviewed.

Thinking Skills: *Reasoning*

2. An interviewer asks Wendy: "Do you plan to have children anytime soon?" How should she answer this question?

Personal Skills: *Self-Esteem*

3. Michael is in the middle of a job interview. Suddenly, he feels very stressed. Write a paragraph telling what he can do to calm down and finish the interview successfully.

Interpersonal Skills: *Exercising Leadership*

4. An interviewer says to you: "You have no experience in this field. Why should I hire you?" In a few sentences, describe how you could answer this tough question in a way that shows maturity and ability to take charge of a situation.

Connecting Academics to the Workplace

Social Studies

1. Ella wants to research trends in the computer industry before her job interview at a software company. Using the library, current magazines, newspapers, or the Internet, find relevant information. Then describe some ways she might use this information in an interview.

Human Relations

2. Kyle has an interview scheduled with a company that is based in a foreign country. He wants to make sure he understands the body language in this country. Choose a country (such as Japan, Saudi Arabia, Kenya, Norway), and research its "rules" about body language. What movements and gestures should Kyle be aware of?

Math

3. It is a 20-minute ride to Laura's job interview. However, due to construction, she will have to take a detour that will add 15 minutes. If she wants to arrive 15 minutes early, how much time should she allow for the trip?

Developing Teamwork and Leadership Skills

You are part of a hiring team for a chain of department stores. You need to hire a person for an entry-level position in sales. Describe the job and identify the skills it requires. Then create a four-person role-playing exercise that will enable candidates to display those skills. As a team, decide which person you would hire, and explain the reasons for your decision.

Real-World Workshop

In groups of three, identify a job that interests you. Then research skills involved in the job. Separately, develop interview questions. Have two members act as interviewer and applicant, while the third member evaluates the applicant. After each member of the team has served in each role, comment on each other's interview style.

School-to-Work Connection

Talk to an employer or a manager who has interviewed job applicants. Ask this person about common mistakes that people make during job interviews. What advice would this person give every applicant? Report your findings to the class.

Individual Career Plan

Using standard business style, write a thank-you letter to an employer. Mention your unique skills, and express your enthusiasm for the job. Proofread for standard English, spelling, and punctuation.

ASPECTS OF INDUSTRY:
Management

Overview

In Unit Three, you learned about the process of finding, applying for, and interviewing for a job. In this Unit Lab, you will use what you have learned while exploring another aspect of industry: **Management.**

The Management aspect of industry covers the decisions managers make about their products and services, company growth, and profitability. It also includes managing employees—not only assigning and overseeing their work, but also planning how to keep employees interested in and enthusiastic about their work. Continuing education, involvement in company decisions, and flexible working schedules are a few ways to achieve that goal.

Tools

1. Internet
2. Trade and business magazines
3. Business newspapers

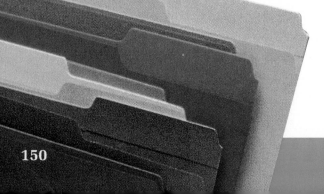

4. Personal interviews

Procedures

STEP A

Choose one of the 15 job clusters from Figure 3-1 in Chapter 3 that interests you. You may choose the same cluster you explored in the previous Lab, or a different one. Choose two jobs in the job cluster that you would seriously think about pursuing.

Using trade and business magazines, newspapers, and the Internet, research how the industry represented by the jobs you have chosen is affected by new management practices.

STEP B

Identify a local corporation that employs people in one of the jobs you have chosen. Ask friends, family, teachers, and counselors for leads. You may also check with your local Chamber of Commerce, which may have a directory of member businesses.

If possible, research that particular corporation. The Chamber of Commerce may have profiled the business in its newsletter, or the local newspaper may have run stories about the business.

Contact the personnel manager at each company. This should not be the same manager that you interviewed in previous assignments. Ask permission to do a 20- to 30-minute interview. Make it clear that you are not interviewing for a job, but that you are seeking information for a class presentation.

Some of the questions you might ask are:

1. What qualities are most important in an employee?

2. What does the employer look for during an interview?

3. What might convince a manager to hire a student with little experience?

4. What kind of training/ education program does the company offer, if any?

5. Do employees participate in company decision or policy making?

6. What kinds of benefits do employees receive?

Remember, you are building your contact list through these exercises. Present yourself in as positive a light as possible.

STEP C

Working in groups of three or four, compare notes on your interviews. On what topics did the managers agree? On what did they disagree? What suggestions did the managers make? What kinds of attitudes did they display?

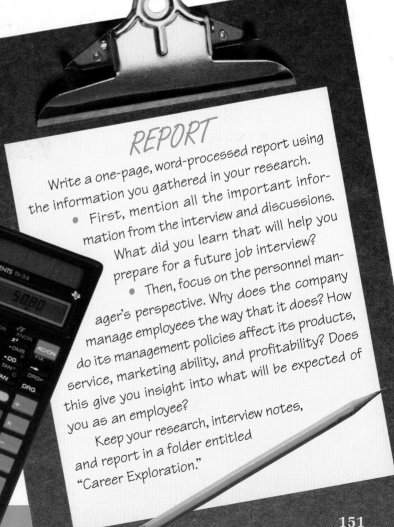

REPORT

Write a one-page, word-processed report using the information you gathered in your research.
- First, mention all the important information from the interview and discussions. What did you learn that will help you prepare for a future job interview?
- Then, focus on the personnel manager's perspective. Why does the company manage employees the way that it does? How do its management policies affect its products, service, marketing ability, and profitability? Does this give you insight into what will be expected of you as an employee?

Keep your research, interview notes, and report in a folder entitled "Career Exploration."

Joining the Workforce

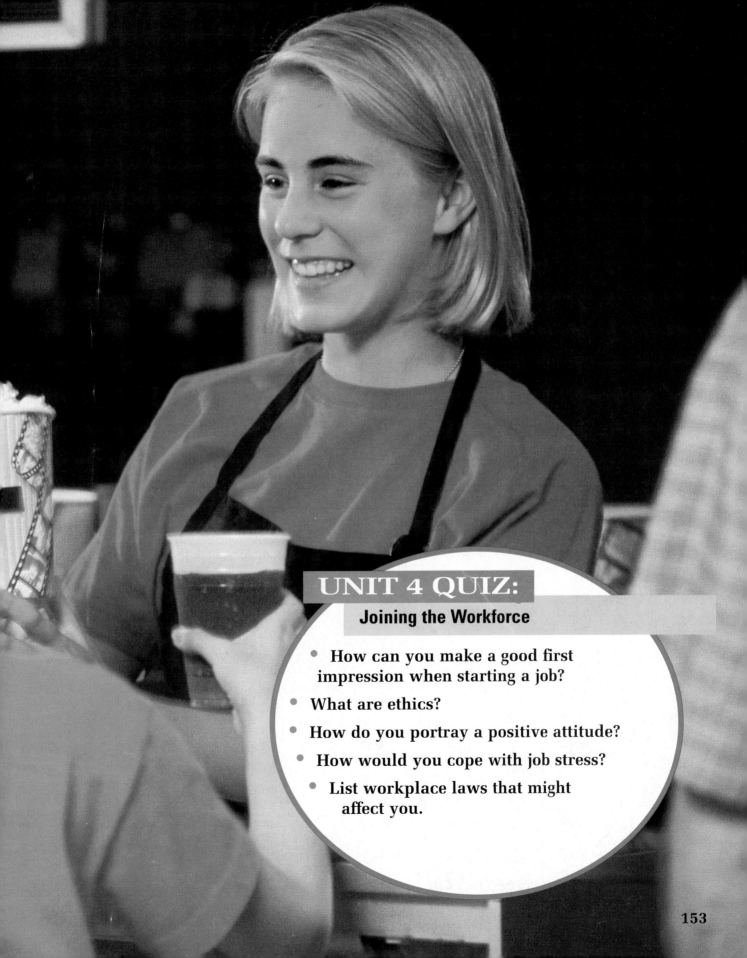

UNIT 4 QUIZ:

Joining the Workforce

- How can you make a good first impression when starting a job?

- What are ethics?

- How do you portray a positive attitude?

- How would you cope with job stress?

- List workplace laws that might affect you.

Beginning a New Job

Section 8-1
Preparing for Your First Day on the Job

Section 8-2
What You Can Expect from Your Employer

In this video segment, find out what to expect on the first days of your new job.

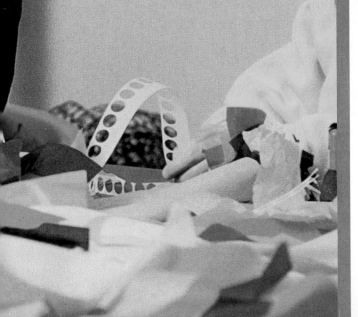

Journal
Personal Career Plan

The first day on a new job is a time of excitement and anxiety. In your journal, write a list of questions and concerns you might have on your first day of work. Then think about the facts and ideas that might give you confidence on your first day. Write another list of your confidence-inspiring ideas.

Preparing for Your First Day on the Job

OBJECTIVES

After studying this section, you will be able to:

- **Anticipate and manage the anxieties and challenges of a first day at work.**
- **Discuss the proper ways to dress for work.**
- **Understand company policies.**

KEY TERMS

company culture
orientation
mentors

Getting a new job is like moving to a different country. Who knows what's waiting for you there? Many unexpected things can happen. What can you do to prepare? What do employers expect from you? How can you deal with first-day anxieties?

Having a Good First Day

Your first day on the job can be exciting. Enjoy it. It will almost certainly be stressful as well. You can't avoid the stress, but you can prepare yourself for it.

Figure out how long it will take you to get ready and to get to work. Then get up even earlier. Don't make yourself more nervous by running late and then hurrying to get to your job on time.

At work, you'll be introduced to your new coworkers. You'll probably forget their names. Don't worry. You can't be expected to remember everyone's name at first. Just ask again. A simple trick that may help you remember is to repeat each person's name out loud as you're introduced. Then use the name again while talking to the person.

Company Culture

As soon as you walk in to work as an employee, you'll become immersed in the **company culture**. This is the behavior, attitudes, values, and habits of the employees and owners that are unique to a particular company.

Plan to get to your new job early. **What would your new supervisor think if you were late?**

Learning the company culture will take you a while. Until you understand it, take your time trying to fit in. You don't have to do a lot of talking your first few days. Concentrate on listening and observing. Watch your coworkers to learn how they work and interact. The SCANS skills of listening, knowing how to learn, and sociability will help you.

Dressing for the Job

One anxiety about your first day of work may concern how to dress. What's appropriate? How dressed up should you get? What makes this matter even more confusing is that dress codes keep changing. Unless your job calls for a uniform, it's hard to know what to wear.

Office workers once wore suits and ties, skirts and high heels. That rule no longer applies in most places. The majority of companies are now moving toward more casual dress. Unfortunately, there's no "norm." What's correct in one office is inappropriate in another. Jeans and a rugby shirt might be fine at one place but too casual at another.

To complicate matters further, many companies now have "casual Fridays" and "jeans days." These allow even more casual dress. Even on these days, though, not everything goes.

If you work in a manufacturing plant, in a garage, or on a construction site, your choices may be more predictable. Even dress codes for these jobs have changed in recent years, however.

How do you know what to wear? When you show up for your interview, observe what other people are wearing. Make a point of asking about the dress code. It's

Office casual means casual "business" clothing, not casual wear. You may need a separate wardrobe of work clothing. **What's wrong with the clothing these people are wearing? What's right?**

YOU'RE THE BOSS!

Solving Workplace Problems

Your growing mail-order business has two new employees who take orders over the phone and process orders received by phone, fax, or mail. One is charming and efficient on the phone, but not very organized in processing orders; the other is very organized, but too shy to be very effective on the phone. What will you do?

also a good idea to ask for examples because "office casual" means different things in different companies.

Still uncertain? Consider these pointers:

- Err on the side of conservative dress.

- Avoid bright or garish colors and clothes that are faddish.

- Keep jewelry simple and not too large.

- Wear clean clothes, and never wear clothes that are frayed or worn out.

- If you're meeting the public, wear more traditional business clothing. A business suit might be right if you're in sales, for example.

Learning the Ropes

You'll have a lot to prepare for and to think about on your first day. Your employer will also be preparing for you.

Orientation

To help new employees get started, companies provide **orientation**. This is a program that will introduce you to the company's policies, procedures, values, and benefits. You may get a tour of the company, meet coworkers, and be shown where the lunchroom and restrooms are.

At a small company, orientation may be informal. You may simply meet with the office manager to talk about benefits, have lunch with your supervisor, and tour the workplace. Most large companies have more elaborate orientations. You may receive a company manual and hear formal presentations. Orientation may last a few hours, all day, or much longer.

At some companies, the new employee may be paired with a senior coworker who acts as a mentor. **Mentors** are informal teachers. They introduce new employees to their coworkers and coach

Even if a company does not assign a mentor to young workers, it is a good idea to look to experienced workers for advice. *How could this arrangement benefit the new and the experienced worker?*

EXCELLENT BUSINESS PRACTICES

Employing the Older Worker

The McDonald's Corporation, of Oak Brook, Illinois, is known for its success in employing workers who are 55 years of age and older. The fast-food company developed specific recruiting materials to sell McDonald's as a career opportunity for older workers. The materials emphasized flexibility in scheduling and working within government regulations so that older workers wouldn't jeopardize their Social Security benefits.

These new hires receive the same training as other workers. But special programs were established, for example, to teach computer skills to people who had never worked with computers before. McDonald's also sets up a buddy system so that each older worker has someone to help him or her learn the way things are done at McDonald's.

More than 40,000 older employees serve McDonald's customers worldwide. Older workers are known for better attendance, lower turnover rates, and lower accident rates. They also tend to excel in hospitality skills and customer service.

Thinking Critically

Which jobs are more suitable for younger workers and which might need workers with more experience? Why is attitude more important than age?

them in the skills and procedures needed for their jobs. Mentors help new employees learn the company culture and company policies.

After three months, new employees often meet with their supervisors to talk about their new jobs, the company, and their future. *Figure 8-1* gives you an idea of the scope of some orientation programs.

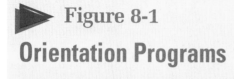

Figure 8-1

Orientation Programs

About 85 percent of businesses with more than 100 employees have an orientation program for new workers. Such programs differ in length and in type, but they all have a dual purpose: to make newly hired workers feel at home and to sharpen their job skills to fit their new employer's needs.

A In the past, orientation often consisted of filling out insurance forms and reading lengthy company policy manuals. At some companies today, this is what you will still find.

B Many companies now offer interactive training programs. The programs enable new workers to ask questions and to meet each other as they learn about their employer.

However your company handles orientation, use it to get a clear idea of your responsibilities and the company goals. Get answers to the following questions:

- What is the company's mission, or purpose? How do your job and your department fit into the mission?
- What are your exact job responsibilities? What should you do first? Next?
- How will your performance be evaluated? When?

C Some employers even use games such as scavenger hunts to help introduce their new employees to the workplace.

D Employers may also include team-building activities to help new employees develop their abilities to work together.

E Orientation does not necessarily stop with new employees. Employers often "reorient" their entire staff to boost morale and to help employees keep up with changes within the company.

Company Policies

Every company has specific policies that spell out what the company expects of you and what you can expect of the company. You will probably be given a company manual or other written statement of official policies. You should learn about these policies right away. Following are questions about just a few company policies.

- When will you be paid?

- What happens if you're late for work?

- How many sick days will you be paid for each year? What happens if you need more days than you're allowed?

- How much vacation time will you get, and when can you take it?

- What paid holidays does the company grant?

- When will you receive a raise? What will be the basis for it?

Career Do's & Don'ts

When Starting a New Job...

Do:
- learn the organization's corporate culture or rules.
- understand what your boss expects from you.
- be tactful.
- express interest in all aspects of the company and coworkers' jobs.

Don't:
- act like a know-it-all.
- constantly explain how things were done at your other job.
- complain or demand.
- sit there with nothing to do unless you've been instructed to.

SECTION 8-1 *Review*

Understanding Key Concepts

Using complete sentences, answer the following questions on a separate sheet of paper.

1. What worries you about starting a new job? How can you prepare for your first day at work?

2. How will knowing about your new employer's dress code help make your first day on the job successful?

3. Why should you learn about company policies as soon as possible?

Exploring Careers: Health

Marcelitte Failla, D.C.
Chiropractor

Q: **Why did you choose chiropractic over conventional medicine?**

A: My parents and grandparents in Louisiana used natural plant substances to cure illnesses. I realized that responding to illness with natural foods was better than trying to cover up symptoms with medicines. As a health-care professional, I wanted to go back to the way my parents had cared for our health. Chiropractic makes that possible.

Q: **What kind of training have you had?**

A: I have a bachelor's degree in pre-med. Then I went through a four-year chiropractic college program.

Q: **What's involved in chiropractic treatment?**

A: I interview a patient to get a medical history. Then I give an exam, looking for signs of injury to the spine. If the patient is in a lot of pain, I usually don't adjust him or her then. I give other treatments instead. I keep asking questions to help me rule out other things that could be causing the pain.

Q: **In addition to having diagnostic skills, do you have to be strong?**

A: You do need a certain amount of upper-body strength. I'm only 5 feet 3 inches tall, so I work out. I also use some of the tools and techniques that chiropractors have available to them to make things easier.

Thinking Critically

Why would chiropractors take pre-med programs in college if they are not going to be doctors?

CAREER FACTS

Nature of the Work:
Diagnose illness and injury; treat patients with adjustment and exercise.

Training or Education Needed:
A minimum of two years of college, or a bachelor's degree; training at an accredited chiropractic college.

Aptitudes, Abilities, and Skills:
Math, listening, speaking, and interpersonal skills; physical strength; an aptitude for the sciences; a strong desire to help people; ability to work well with hands.

Salary Range:
Average starting salary—$20,000 to $30,000; average top salary—$90,000.

Career Path:
Start as vacation relief for other chiropractors; work in a chiropractic clinic; go into partnership with other chiropractors, or start a practice.

What You Can Expect from Your Employer

OBJECTIVES

After studying this section, you will be able to:

- Describe typical ways that employers pay workers.
- Explain benefits that employers offer workers.
- Discuss the significance of employee performance reviews.

KEY TERMS

hourly wages
overtime
nonexempt
   employees
exempt employees
salary
commission
profit-sharing plan
performance bonuses
pension plan
probation
layoff

Every employee works for a reason. What's yours? A salary? Health insurance? A pension? The challenge of interesting work? Job security? You may want and expect these and other things from your employer.

The answers keep changing as business moves closer to the global market. Companies must be more efficient and more competitive. The result is a changing relationship between workers and their employers. *Figure 8-2* shows how the relationship has changed in recent years.

Payment

Of course, you expect to get paid for the work you do. This is one aspect of the employer-employee relationship that has not changed. However, your pay may be calculated in any number of ways.

Basic Payment Methods

Most entry-level employees receive **hourly wages**. In other words, the employer pays a fixed amount of money, such as $7, for each hour worked. At the end of each week, pay is calculated by multiplying the number of hours worked times the hourly rate.

Hourly wages may be affected by whether or not workers are paid **overtime** for working more than 40 hours in a week. Usually workers on overtime are paid one and one-half times their normal pay for each hour in excess of 40 hours. For example, if workers are normally paid $10 per hour, they will get $15 when working overtime.

Figure 8-2

Changing Worker Expectations

	In the Past	Today
Job Security	• Lifetime job security • Length of time with a company or experience in a career field guarantees job security • Company responsible for worker's security	• Limited job security • Continuing training provides job security • Current job skills allow mobility among companies and careers • Freedom from company ties
Salary	• Based on experience • Based on number of years with company	• Based on current value of the work

Source: "The New Deal" by Brian O'Reilly, *Current*, October 1994

The competitive global and technology-based economy has changed the expectations of the American worker. What are the advantages for today's worker? What are the disadvantages?

Not everyone gets paid overtime. Who does? A federal law requires that certain types of workers must be paid overtime. Workers who are covered by this law are called **nonexempt employees**. These workers are normally paid an hourly wage. Workers who are not covered by the law are **exempt employees**. Most exempt employees earn a **salary**. That is, they are paid a fixed amount for a certain period of time, usually a month or a year. Exempt employees do not have to be paid overtime.

Workers in some kinds of jobs—such as sales or telemarketing—may be paid a **commission**. These workers' earnings are based on how much they sell. They might, for example, earn 2 percent of the value of the merchandise they sell. By basing pay directly on their performance, this system aims to motivate salespeople to work harder.

Many workers who are paid an hourly wage must "clock in" at a time clock.

This worker normally works seven hours per day, five days per week. This week she has worked eight hours per day for five days. *How many hours of overtime is she entitled to?*

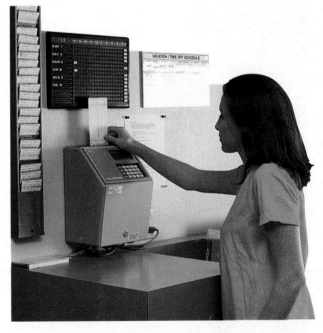

These four members of a magazine advertising sales team have been offered a sales incentive. If the team can sell $200,000 worth of advertisements, each member will receive $1,000. *What are the benefits of a sales incentive such as this one?*

Incentive Plans

One change in how workers are paid is in incentive plans. These plans reward workers for achievement.

In a **profit-sharing plan**, workers receive a share of the company's profits. The better the company performs, the more the workers receive.

Performance bonuses reward workers for high levels of performance. Some companies pay bonuses to workers who increase the quantity or quality of their work. These bonuses vary greatly in amounts and how they are awarded. At Dow Brands, for example, employees may receive cash awards of several hundred dollars for doing good work. At Steelcase, factory workers are paid relatively low salaries, but their bonuses can almost double their incomes.

Fringe Benefits

The rewards for working are not limited to a paycheck. Various fringe benefits may come with a job. Fringe benefits are the "extras" that a company provides in addition to pay. Usually there is a waiting period for many of these benefits.

The kinds and value of fringe benefits vary dramatically from employer to employer. However, they can be substantial. A recent study showed that benefits average about 40 percent of employers' payrolls.

Health Benefits

Health insurance is probably the most sought after benefit. It's also the most costly one for employers. Health-care costs have risen sharply over the past 20 years, and the trend is likely to continue. *Figure 8-3* shows the expected increase in these costs for the nation's 500 largest companies. Employers sometimes change their health insurance plans to find lower-cost alternatives.

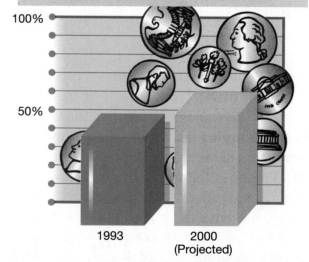

Employer Health-Care Costs*

100%

50%

1993   2000 (Projected)

* As a percentage of annual profits

Source: Joseph Pizzorno, M.D., *Total Wellness.* Prima Publishing, Rocklin, CA, 1996, p. 7

Figure 8-3 These graphs show the projected growth in health-care costs for the nation's 500 largest companies. How might this rising expense affect workers in a negative way?

Retirement Plans

Many companies offer a **pension plan** that builds a retirement fund for each worker. Some employers make contributions for each worker. Some plans allow workers to contribute a portion of each paycheck to the fund. Many companies match the amount of each worker's contribution up to a certain percentage of his or her salary.

Convenience Benefits

Some employers also provide *convenience benefits*—services that make workers' lives easier. There is great variety in the types of convenience benefits. They range from flexible work hours and legal counseling services to on-site oil changes for employees' cars. Quad/Graphics, Inc., provides an accredited kindergarten for employees' children, a fitness center, and popcorn carts, where employees can get a

snack for a quarter. Hallmark Cards provides twice-monthly seminars to help employees handle family issues, such as elder care and parenting. Such benefits are designed to reduce employee stress, improve workers' health, and make workers more productive, loyal, and satisfied.

Cafeteria Plan

A *cafeteria plan* is not a benefit but a policy that lets employees choose the benefits they want. Employers realize that not all employees want or need the same benefits, so they let employees choose those they do want. For example, rather than vacation time, an employee may prefer disability insurance.

Honest and Fair Treatment

You have a right to expect your employer to be honest with you. You should be paid the amount you agreed to. You should receive all the benefits promised when you were hired. If your work situation changes, you should be told as soon as possible.

You also have a right to be treated fairly by your employer, supervisor, and coworkers. If you feel you have been treated unfairly, discuss it with the person involved or with your supervisor. Try to resolve the problem before it gets out of hand. Chapter 12 discusses additional options you have if your rights are violated.

Evaluations

How well are you succeeding at your work? Many companies have formal, scheduled *performance reviews*. These are

Some workers receive health-club memberships as an employee benefit. *How does this service benefit these employees? How does it benefit their employer?*

When businesses are forced to lay off workers, they often lay off more recently hired workers before those who have worked for the company longer. **Why do you think this is so?**

During your probation period, your employer will decide whether you are suited to the job. When you are hired, ask if your company has a probation period policy. If it does, ask what guidelines will be used for the evaluation.

Standard Separation Procedures

Most people, at some time during their careers, will lose their jobs. There are several reasons why a company will *terminate*, or end, a worker's employment.

Employees may be terminated, or fired, for poor job performance. Your employer should have a clear policy for handling these situations.

Sometimes companies have to terminate employees because business is slow. This kind of job loss, which often affects many workers at once, is a **layoff**. Workers who are laid off may be rehired once a company's business improves.

Because you can't always avoid job loss, you should prepare for it. Keep your job-hunting network active and your skills up-to-date. Put aside money to help you through a time of unemployment.

meetings between you and your supervisor to evaluate how well you're doing your job.

Reviews are important to you and to your supervisor. Promotions, pay increases, new responsibilities, and your future with the company may be based on these evaluations. If your company does not have regular evaluations, ask for one. You need feedback to improve your performance and build your career.

In some companies, new employees are put on **probation**. This is the period after you are first hired when you are "on trial."

SECTION 8-2 *Review*

Understanding Key Concepts

Using complete sentences, answer the following questions on a separate sheet of paper.

1. Why does working for a commission offer less financial security than working for a salary?

2. How do fringe benefits improve employee morale?

3. Why are performance reviews as important to workers as to their employers?

Highlights

Key Terms

company culture *(p. 156)*
orientation *(p. 158)*
mentors *(p. 159)*

SECTION 8-1 **Summary**

- Reduce anxiety on the first day of work by giving yourself ample time to get ready and to get to work.

- Learn the company culture by listening and observing how your coworkers work and interact.

- Dress codes for work are changing, and different companies have different standards. Ask about the dress code at your interview. Observe what other workers are wearing.

- Companies help new employees learn policies, procedures, values, and benefits through orientation programs.

- Company policies spell out what the company expects of new employees and what employees can expect from the company. Learn these policies as soon as possible.

Key Terms

hourly wages *(p. 164)*
overtime *(p. 164)*
nonexempt
  employees *(p. 165)*
exempt employees *(p. 165)*
salary *(p. 165)*
commission *(p. 165)*
profit-sharing plan *(p. 166)*
performance
  bonuses *(p. 166)*
pension plan *(p. 167)*
probation *(p. 168)*
layoff *(p. 168)*

SECTION 8-2 **Summary**

- The basic methods of payment include hourly wages, salary, and commission.

- Incentive programs such as profit-sharing plans and performance bonuses offer workers a chance to share in their company's success.

- Workers usually receive fringe benefits, such as health insurance and a retirement plan. They may also receive convenience benefits.

- Employees have a right to honest and fair treatment from their employer.

- Employers and employees both benefit from performance evaluations.

- Some employers have probation periods for new employees.

- Employers sometimes terminate a worker's employment. This may be because of poor worker performance or bad business. Companies should have a clear termination policy.

- You can prepare for possible job loss by maintaining your network of contacts, keeping your skills up-to-date, and having some money saved.

Reviewing Key Terms

On a separate sheet of paper, write a one- to two-page employee manual. Use the terms listed below to explain the policies of an imaginary employer.

company culture
mentors
overtime
exempt employees
commission
performance bonuses
pension plan
orientation
hourly wages
nonexempt employees
salary
profit-sharing plan
probation
layoff

Recalling Key Concepts

On a separate sheet of paper, tell whether each statement is true or false. Rewrite any false statements to make them true.

1. Companies are beginning to insist on more formal business clothing.

2. During orientation, new employees are introduced to the company's policies, procedures, values, and benefits.

3. Typically, workers are paid an hourly wage, a salary, or a commission.

4. A cafeteria plan is a convenience benefit that allows workers to eat free meals while at work.

5. If you are on probation, it means that you are being considered for a pay raise.

Thinking Critically

Using complete sentences, answer each of the questions below on a separate sheet of paper.

1. How can watching other employees help a worker succeed on the job?

2. Why do some companies devote so much time to new-employee orientation?

3. If fringe benefits are so expensive, why do companies provide so many for employees?

4. How does fair and honest treatment contribute to a good workplace?

5. Why do some companies place new employees on probation?

 ## SCANS Foundation Skills and Workplace Competencies

Thinking Skills: *Knowing How to Learn*

1. Working with a partner, role-play your first conversation with your new employer, who has called to congratulate you and answer any questions you may have about your first day at work. What questions will you ask?

Personal Qualities: *Sociability*

2. Brainstorm a list of suggestions for ways to get to know coworkers.

Technology: *Selecting Technology*

3. Your employer plans to link the personal computers in the accounting department. What issues should the employer address in making this change?

Connecting Academics to the Workplace

Math

1. Kumar earns $7.00 per hour. If he works an average of 40 hours a week, what does he earn a week? How much does he earn a year if he works 50 weeks? One week he worked 10 hours of overtime, for which he earned time-and-a-half pay. What were his total earnings that week?

Health and Physical Education

2. Your employer has decided to create a company wellness program to improve employee health and fitness. Write a one-page questionnaire for workers to complete that will inform your employer about the habits that affect their health and general well-being.

Foreign Language

3. You work in a company's shipping room. You have been assigned to be a mentor for a new employee whose native language is not English. Her duties include copying order forms, filling out address labels, and wrapping packages. How would you explain these tasks to her?

Developing Teamwork and Leadership Skills

Working with a group, prepare an orientation program for a company. You can make up the company or choose an existing one. Design an informative presentation using any combination of skits, talks, and written or audiovisual materials to welcome new employees (your classmates) to their new jobs.

Real-World Workshop

Your school is your present workplace and has a "company culture." Students and teachers have specific ways of behaving, interacting, talking, and doing work. If a new student entered this workplace and you were appointed his or her mentor, what would you tell the student about the company culture? Write a description of your school's culture.

School-to-Work Connection

Choose a local company and research its fringe benefits. You might call the human resources department or interview someone who works there. Write a report that outlines the benefits that the employer offers.

Individual Career Plan

What job would you like to have? For what company? Look through your wardrobe. Which outfits would you consider appropriate for the job? What additional clothing would you need to get to have a good work wardrobe? Create a list indicating your current work-appropriate clothing and what you would need to add.

Chapter 9

Workplace Ethics

Section 9-1
Desirable Employee Qualities

Section 9-2
Ethical Behavior

In this video segment, explore the importance of workplace ethics.

Journal
Personal Career Plan

What basic ethics should guide the behavior of a well-known business leader? In what ways—if any—should that leader's ethics differ from those of a part-time worker in that leader's company? How do the leader and the part-time worker affect each other's work ethics? Write a journal entry discussing your ideas.

Desirable Employee Qualities

OBJECTIVES

After studying this section, you will be able to:

- **Identify the qualities that employers look for in employees.**
- **Describe ways that employees can become self-managing.**

KEY TERMS

cooperativeness
initiative
responsibility
self-management

In the past, employers looked for workers with specific skills. They wanted people who excelled at computer keyboarding, bookkeeping, or graphic art, for example. Skills such as these may still get you a job, but the workplace is changing. According to Raymond Brixley, director of human resources for the Quaker Oats Company, employers are beginning to ask for more. " ... we look for someone capable of doing lots of things well," he says, "and more importantly, someone who 'fits' into the organization's structure."

How do you prepare for doing lots of things well and fitting in? Master the SCANS skills. Solid thinking skills, skills in math and communications, and strong personal qualities will help you adapt to the changing needs of today's workplace.

Cooperativeness

One of an employee's most valued qualities is cooperativeness. **Cooperativeness** is a willingness to work well with everyone else on the job to reach a common goal. Cooperativeness is part of several of the SCANS skills, including listening skills, responsibility, self-esteem, and self-management.

Be forewarned. Your first job will put your cooperativeness to the test. You may get the worst tasks and little responsibility. If this happens, all you can do is smile, do the job well, and demonstrate a spirit of cooperativeness.

How can you be cooperative?

- Do tasks you don't like without complaining or trying to avoid them.
- Do your fair share of a job when working with others.
- Pitch in to help a coworker who has a tough job or has fallen behind.
- Volunteer to help coworkers meet a deadline or reach a goal.

Willingness to Follow Directions

On the job, you will be asked to complete many tasks. To complete a task, you must first follow directions. This is a vital skill on any job.

Following directions requires many SCANS skills. Listening is one of the most important ones. These suggestions may help you follow directions:

- Stop whatever you are doing, and listen to the directions being given.
- Listen carefully, even if you think you already know the procedure. Some details might surprise you.
- Take notes, if possible. Even simple directions can become murky if you or your supervisor is hurried.
- Identify the goal or purpose of the task. Then try to visualize the steps leading to the goal.
- If you do not understand the directions, don't guess at what is needed. Ask questions!

Workers can show cooperation by willingly doing whatever tasks they are assigned. *Why is it important to demonstrate cooperation?*

Asking questions is the best way to learn a new job. It's also a good way to avoid making embarrassing mistakes. *What should you do if you ask a question and, after receiving an answer, still don't understand what to do?*

Willingness to Learn

Think ahead a few months or years. You've completed your education and walked into your first full-time job. You may think you're done with learning. You're not. You'll have lots to learn about your new job, even if the job is one you've been trained for. Every company has its own ways of doing things. You'll have to learn the system and how to work with your coworkers.

Because you're a new employee, your employer will not expect you to know everything. So don't pretend to know something you don't. Ask questions.

Be willing to learn any job, no matter how small. When the copier gets jammed, watch how to fix it. Next time, you can take care of it yourself.

Learn all you can about your job and about the company. This information will help you do your job better and will prepare you for a promotion.

Look for opportunities to get more training. Many companies will pay for their employees to attend workshops, training programs, or college. Take advantage of any chance to learn more.

Initiative

You may get by, just by doing what you're told. Employers expect more from you, however. They want employees to show **initiative**. Taking initiative means doing what needs to be done without being told to do it.

Disney World deliberately seeks out employees who have initiative. Robert Sias, a trainer for Disney, gives an example of what it wants. A mother had just bought her son a box of popcorn, he explains. The child, about four years old, stumbled and dropped the popcorn, spilling it all over. The little boy burst into tears, and the mother became upset. Just at that moment, a costumed employee who was on his way to another attraction walked by. Without a pause, he scooped up the empty popcorn box, got it refilled by the vendor, handed it to the little boy, and went on his way.

The employee showed initiative. He saw a problem and fixed it. It was no big deal, but it made a customer happy. That's what employers want.

Willingness to Take on More Responsibility

Business today is more competitive than ever. Companies must do more to satisfy customers. Employers know the key is empowered employees. They want employees to take more responsibility. **Responsibility** is the willingness to accept an obligation and to be accountable for an action or situation.

YOU'RE THE BOSS!

✓ *Solving Workplace Problems*

A review of the records of your CD/tape store shows unusual losses of inventory. You have six employees, all of whom seem loyal and reliable. The losses seem to have begun around the time your newest employee started work, but you have no evidence that she has been dishonest. What will you do?

Marriott Hotels has this attitude. One of its employees is Tony Prsyszlak (Prush-lak). If he worked for another hotel, he might be called a doorman. At Marriott, he's called a "guest service associate." The difference is more than the title. Prsyszlak picks up a guest's luggage at the curb and carries it up to the room. He can also check the guest in, obtain theater tickets for a play, reserve a table at a restaurant, or provide other services for the guest.

"I'm a bellman, a doorman, a front-desk clerk, and a concierge all rolled into one," Prsyszlak says. "I have more responsibilities. I feel better about my job, and the guest gets better service."

Human resource managers look for employees who help customers without being told to do so. *How can workers prepare themselves for showing initiative on their jobs?*

What do you get out of taking on more responsibility? Your job becomes more interesting. You gain experience and a chance at better jobs. You increase your value to the company and earn job security.

Prove to your employer that you can accept greater responsibility. Show that you're not afraid of change. Volunteer for new jobs. Look for opportunities to do more than you were hired to do. Practice looking ahead. Don't think about extra work as just unpaid overtime. Think about where the added responsibility will get you in a year.

Self-Management

Who do you think is going to get you a job, a promotion, a raise? Only you. You've got to take responsibility for the work you do and the career you want. This is called **self-management**. It means doing the things necessary to build a better career. Here are some tips:

- Set career goals, and develop a plan for reaching them. As you achieve goals, or as your situation changes, set new goals.

- Monitor your work habits and performance. For example, you might keep

EXCELLENT BUSINESS PRACTICES

Reaching the Global Marketplace

Eli Lilly and Company of Indianapolis, Indiana, is an international pharmaceutical firm with 27,700 employees. About 12,700 work overseas in 90 countries.

Lilly has made an effort to communicate the corporate strategy and company values to all employees worldwide. Employees learn to be sensitive to local differences and creative about finding ways to do business.

In some instances, however, Lilly does not want employees to follow the local culture. In some countries, "payoffs" are common, where a drug company representative pays doctors a fee every time they prescribe the company's product. Lilly does not allow this practice.

To help families of workers from other countries assimilate to American culture, Lilly has provided funds to the International School of Indiana. There, children of international workers can attend a special school that offers a cross-cultural curriculum.

Thinking Critically

In what ways does an international company have more challenges to maintain a firm position on ethics?

a diary to track how you spend your time. Then you can identify ways to be more time-efficient.

- Ask for feedback on how you're doing your job. Ask coworkers and supervisors. Act on what you learn to improve your work habits and skills.

Loyalty

You know what it means to be loyal to your country and your school. It's also important to be loyal to your company. After all, you, your coworkers, your supervisors, and the owners are all in the business together. You're a team working toward a common goal.

How do you show loyalty at work? Don't run down the company or a supervisor in conversation. Be positive. Look for solutions. Don't point fingers.

When there's a crisis, pitch in and help the company get through it. This may involve self-sacrifice, some overtime, maybe even unpaid overtime. Remember you're doing it for yourself, too.

Business owners today know they must do more to earn customer loyalty. *How does empowering employees with greater responsibility improve customer service?*

SECTION 9-1 *Review*

Understanding Key Concepts

Using complete sentences, answer the following questions on a separate sheet of paper.

1. Consider the qualities employers are seeking in employees. How will employees with these qualities allow companies to do less "managing"?

2. How is self-management good for you and good for your employer?

Exploring Careers: Fine Arts and Humanities

Erica Eysenbach
Graphic Designer

Q: How did you get your job as an art director?

A: I sort of slipped in the back door. I had an art history education and took a lot of art design and studio classes. I wanted to work at L. L. Bean, so I started as a customer service representative. Because of my background in art and my experience in working with the customers, I was eventually given the opportunity to work with the catalog. I started as an editor, then worked as an artist and editor, and finally became an art director.

Q: What skills are most important in your work?

A: You have to be a logical thinker. It's important to be able to juggle a lot of tasks. You have to be flexible and accept change because so many people have input into what you do. You should be able to work with many different people—from copywriters to corporate vice presidents to models.

Q: What are some of the changes you've seen in eight years?

A: The biggest change is the use of computers. We no longer draw everything by hand. We don't paste up the design. Typesetting is done directly on the computer. I think the use of computers will grow as computers develop.

Thinking Critically

What are some of the many ways graphic design is used today?

CAREER FACTS

Nature of the Work:
Use a variety of media and methods to communicate the client's ideas.

Training or Education Needed:
Bachelor's degree in art, specializing in graphic design; computer-design experience or training.

Aptitudes, Abilities, and Skills:
Math, listening, speaking, and interpersonal skills; problem-solving and decision-making skills; self-management skills; a good design sense, including an eye for color, form, and layout; the ability to work under deadline pressure; the ability to work alone and as part of a team; computer skills.

Salary Range:
Average starting salary—$18,000; average top salary—$50,000.

Career Path:
Start in a graphic design firm, publishing house, or advertising firm; take on more complex work and responsibility as an assistant art director and then as an art director; possibly open own business.

Ethical Behavior

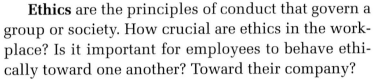

OBJECTIVES

After studying this section, you will be able to:

- **Explain why ethics are important in the workplace.**
- **Describe ways to behave ethically in the workplace.**

KEY TERMS

ethics
confidentiality
prejudice

Ethics are the principles of conduct that govern a group or society. How crucial are ethics in the workplace? Is it important for employees to behave ethically toward one another? Toward their company?

Many businesspeople think ethical behavior is critically important to success. Why? *Figure 9-1* on pages 182–183 shows how unethical behavior can have repercussions throughout a company.

Some companies have created programs to promote ethics. Do you think this is a good idea? Write down your answer to this question in your journal. List reasons for your opinion. As you read this section, add other reasons you discover.

Honesty

Employers expect their employees to be honest. Often, they're disappointed. Dishonesty is at the root of most ethics problems in the workplace.

What's the penalty for dishonesty? On a personal level, it can be devastating. One lie can destroy your reputation. How much does your reputation matter? If you were an employer, would you hire someone with a reputation for dishonesty? Be honest with your employer and your company. As an honest worker you will have a much better chance of being successful in your work.

Honesty About Time

One of the most common ways in which employees can demonstrate honesty concerns their work hours. This is especially true for employees whose work takes them away from the company, who work at home, or who work on flextime, or flexible schedules. In each case, employees are trusted to work the hours they say they will. What might be the consequence if employees are dishonest about the time they work?

 ## Figure 9-1

The Effects of Unethical Behavior

Unethical behavior in the workplace has a spiraling effect. A single act can affect many people.

A There are many forms of unethical behavior. These workers have a responsibility to ship quality products. By deliberately shipping damaged goods, they're cheating their employer and the customer.

B Unethical behavior rarely goes unnoticed.

Honesty About Money

Taking money out of the cash drawer is clearly dishonest. In many instances, the issue is more subtle. Consider the following case.

Juanita Benes is a salesperson. On a business trip, she spent more for meals than her expense account allowed. She thought she'd have to pay the difference out of her own pocket. On the other hand,

C The owners of Quality Televisions, Inc., will replace the damaged television sets, but they can't repair their reputation. Word of the problem spreads among customers. Customers will purchase television sets from another supplier.

D A company's reputation is its most important asset. Once the reputation is lost, business will be lost. Eventually, everyone who depended upon the company for a living will be affected.

A recent study by the Ethics Resource Center revealed that one-third of all employees interviewed observed some kind of unethical behavior during a one-year period. This graph shows the most common observations. Does the information on this chart surprise you? Why or why not?

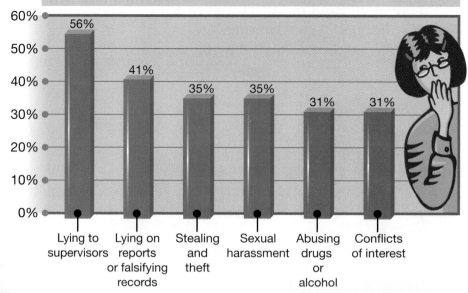

Observed Unethical Behavior

- Lying to supervisors — 56%
- Lying on reports or falsifying records — 41%
- Stealing and theft — 35%
- Sexual harassment — 35%
- Abusing drugs or alcohol — 31%
- Conflicts of interest — 31%

Source: Ethics Resource Center survey in Flynn, Gillian. "Make Employee Ethics Your Business," *Personnel Journal*, June 1995, v74 n6 p. 30.

she thought she could make up the difference by adding the amount to two blank taxi receipts. Would this be dishonest?

Benes at first reasoned that it was only a technicality. Other employees probably did it. She wouldn't feel guilty telling her husband. Then she thought about telling her children. She realized that in their eyes, it would be dishonest.

Often you may think there is a thin line between honesty and dishonesty. As you reason through such cases in your career, think how your action might appear to others. *Figure 9-2* shows the types of unethical behavior observed during a one-year period.

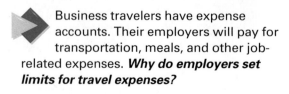

► Business travelers have expense accounts. Their employers will pay for transportation, meals, and other job-related expenses. *Why do employers set limits for travel expenses?*

Respecting Employers' Property

Another way to risk your reputation and job is to be careless with company property. Don't illegally copy company software for your personal use. Don't take office supplies home for your own use. These items may seem petty, but the small costs do add up. Also, think about it from your supervisor's point of view. If he or she knows you're stealing stamps, will he or she put you in charge of more costly items?

Interacting with Others

Whatever business you enter, you'll be talking and working with others. Occasionally, your interactions may involve ethical issues.

Confidentiality

As an employee, you may have information that would harm the company if others learned about it. This information might have to do with new products, expansion plans, promotions, and so on. Your company will expect you to observe **confidentiality**. In other words, don't tell secrets to people who are not supposed to know them.

Confidentiality is behavior your friends, family, and coworkers also expect from you. They don't want their secrets told either.

Any business may face a crisis from time to time. When it happens, everyone needs to pull together. *Why is it important to have a good attitude, even if you don't like the extra work?*

Career Do's & Don'ts

On the surface, confidentiality seems easy. Sometimes, though, there are conflicting interests. Take the situation involving Sheila Williams.

Williams ran into a former coworker and friend at a seminar. They had dinner together. While talking, Williams learned about a new product her friend's company was developing. It was a product similar to one Williams's own company was working on. Not only that, but her friend's company had solved a problem that Williams's company was stuck on. Her friend didn't know Williams's company was a rival. Should Williams use the information to help her company beat out the rival?

The Ethics Quiz in *Figure 9-3* may help you with such decisions. Use it to resolve Williams's dilemma.

Coworkers often become good friends. *Why is confidentiality especially important when one of the friends moves to a new job?*

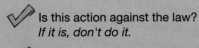

Ethics Quiz

✓ Is this action against the law?
If it is, don't do it.

✓ Do you know the action is wrong?
If so, don't do it.

✓ Is the action contrary to company values?
Every company has a set of values. Sometimes they are written policy. Sometimes they are not written but are part of an unwritten code of behavior.

✓ Will you feel bad if you perform this action?
If so, don't do it.

✓ Are you unsure if the action is wrong?
Ask someone. Check with coworkers, your supervisor, friends or associates outside of work.

✓ If this action were reported on the five o'clock news, what would viewers think about it?

✓ If you asked an eight-year-old about the action, what would he or she tell you to do?

Source: Flynn, Gillian. "Make Employee Ethics Your Business," *Personnel Journal,* June 1995, v74 n6 p. 30 ff.

▲ **Figure 9-3** Questions about ethical issues often do not have definite or clear-cut answers. You must simply use your best judgment. Why does it help to try to see the situation through a child's eyes?

Fairness

Virtually every business includes men and women of different races and religions. You'll interact with them as customers, owners, and coworkers. Treat everyone fairly, openly, and honestly.

Prejudice—an unjustifiable negative attitude toward a person or group—is an ethical issue. Prejudice comes in many forms, including racist or sexist comments, stereotyping, name calling, and generalizations. Prejudice in any form, however, is hurtful, offensive, and unacceptable; it cannot be tolerated in today's workplace. Not only can employees be fired for prejudicial comments, but they and their companies can be sued.

Handling Unethical Practices

What if you're the victim of unethical practices? What if you experience prejudice in the workplace? What if you observe unethical business practices?

Consider whether it was an isolated incident or an ongoing practice. Maybe it can be cleared up by a calm, open discussion.

If the offense is deliberate, don't ignore it. Don't act rashly either. First, consider your options. If you're dealing with a customer, you might simply walk away. You don't have to sell a product to an abusive or dishonest customer. Report the incident to your supervisor.

If you're dealing with a coworker, you might tell him or her you will not tolerate his or her prejudiced behavior. If that does not work, talk to your supervisor. Look for solutions, not revenge.

What if your employer is unethical? You can choose to live with the situation. You can keep quiet and find another job. You can report it to the appropriate authority. The choice may not be easy. If you decide to take action, these pointers may help:

- Keep a written record as shown in *Figure 9-4*. Describe each incident. Record the date and time.

- Check your observations with others. Maybe they can explain matters. Maybe they will help.

- Get advice from people you trust.

- Check your motives. Are you acting for the right reasons?

- Collect any evidence you can, such as receipts, invoices, or contracts.

- Decide whether you want to remain anonymous or to speak up openly.

- Report only facts or observations. Don't exaggerate or speculate.

July 23, 10:45 A.M.
I saw Mr. Jones meeting with Andrew Mathes, a sales representative for XYZ Company. They met in his office for 25 minutes. When they left, Mr. Jones said, "I'll take care of it. When I get your company's bid, I'll see it's given preferential treatment."

July 27, 3:30 P.M.
A courier arrived with an envelope for Mr. Jones. I signed for the envelope. It was from Mr. Mathes. Mr. Jones opened the envelope in front of me. It contained two play-off tickets.

Figure 9-4 Accurate, complete records of unethical behavior can serve as partial proof of the events. Why would it be a good idea to have a coworker keep additional records?

SECTION 9-2 *Review*

Understanding Key Concepts

Using complete sentences, answer the following questions on a separate sheet of paper.

1. Imagine that you've observed a coworker lying to a customer. How might this unethical behavior affect you?

2. Of the different kinds of ethical behavior, which do you think will be your biggest challenge? Why?

Key Terms

cooperativeness *(p. 174)*
initiative *(p. 176)*
responsibility *(p. 177)*
self-management *(p. 178)*

SECTION 9-1 Summary

- Today's employers want employees who can do many things and who will fit into the company's structure. A key is cooperativeness. This means working well with coworkers and managers.

- Employees must be skilled at listening to and following directions.

- You should be prepared to continue learning throughout your working career.

- Businesses are looking for employees who show initiative. These are people who will step forward and do what needs to be done without having to be told.

- Most employers want workers to take on more responsibility. Taking on additional responsibility will make your work more interesting and make you more valuable to your employer.

- To succeed in the world of work, you must manage your own career.

Key Terms

ethics *(p. 181)*
confidentiality *(p. 185)*
prejudice *(p. 187)*

SECTION 9-2 Summary

- Ethics are the moral rules of society. Ethics are very important because unethical behavior can have negative repercussions throughout a company.

- As an employee, you should strive to be honest, especially as this relates to time, money, and your employer's property.

- Every career involves interactions with other people. Respecting the confidentiality of your employer and coworkers and acting fairly with everyone are critical to your success.

- You must maintain your own values. When you are the victim or observer of unethical behavior, there are several ways to respond. Choosing the correct response can be a difficult decision.

Reviewing Key Terms

On a separate sheet of paper, write a paragraph about the qualities employers seek in employees. Use each of the key terms.

cooperativeness   initiative
responsibility   self-management
ethics   confidentiality
prejudice

Recalling Key Concepts

Choose the correct answer for each item below. Write your answers on a separate sheet of paper.

1. A willingness to work with others is ____.

   (a) initiative (b) cooperativeness

   (c) ethics

2. When you are given directions, you should ____.

   (a) listen (b) show initiative

   (c) experiment

3. When you take on unassigned tasks, you are demonstrating ____.

   (a) honesty (b) initiative (c) caution

4. The ethics of your coworkers ____.

   (a) cannot affect a business's success

   (b) should not concern you

   (c) can affect your job security

5. If you observe confidentiality, you ____.

   (a) report a coworker's dishonesty

   (b) work the hours you are expected to work

   (c) don't tell company secrets

Thinking Critically

Using complete sentences, answer each of the questions below on a separate sheet of paper.

1. Why might you need a strong sense of self-esteem to be cooperative in the workplace?

2. How might learning tasks that are not part of your regular job make you a more valuable employee?

3. What are some positive and some negative consequences that might result from reporting a coworker's unethical behavior?

 SCANS Foundation Skills and Workplace Competencies

Information: *Acquiring and Evaluating Information*

1. Employees in retail stores spend time at a variety of tasks, such as helping customers, checking them out at the cash register, stocking shelves, taking inventory, and ordering products. To operate efficiently, store managers must know how much time employees spend at each task. Create a chart that might be used to collect and record this information.

Basic Skills: *Math*

2. Because retail stores are busier at certain times of the day, more employees are needed to run the cash registers at different hours. Construct a line graph that presents the following information: one employee at 8:00 A.M.,

two at 9:00, two at 10:00, three at 11:00, four at 12:00, five at 1:00 P.M., two at 2:00, one at 3:00, one at 4:00, two at 5:00, five at 6:00, six at 7:00, six at 8:00, four at 9:00, two at 10:00.

Connecting Academics to the Workplace

Science

1. Li works for a small manufacturing company in your area. The owner has 50 cans of latex paint stored in the back of his warehouse. The paint is no longer good, and the owner wants to dispose of it. He has asked Li to investigate options for safely disposing of the paint. Find out how old paint can be legally disposed of in your area, and provide two practical options.

Social Studies

2. Andrew works in the human resources department of a small publishing company. The owners have asked Andrew to investigate the pros and cons of flextime. They also want to know if flextime is suitable for their kind of business. Do research to learn the answers. You might use library resources or the Internet or talk with human resource managers whose companies have flextime.

Developing Teamwork and Leadership Skills

Work with four or five other students. Assume that your group works in the human resources department of a company that is participating in a job fair at your high school. As a group, select a business. Then develop and give a presentation in which you describe three openings in your company and the skills and personal behavior required.

Real-World Workshop

Imagine that you work for a company that is no longer profitable. Layoffs are possible, and morale is low. Work with four classmates, who will be your coworkers. Choose a business and create a list of problems you have witnessed. Examples include lack of training, bad morale, and poor customer service. Then brainstorm solutions to this question: What can we, as employees, do to improve morale and protect our job security?

School-to-Work Connection

Interview the owner or human resource manager of a local business. Find out what skills and personal behavior the company is looking for in a person just entering the workforce. Does the company provide training for new employees? Report your findings to your class.

Individual Career Plan

What job would you like to have when you finish school? What skills and personal qualities will this job require? How do you measure up right now? Do you have the skills needed? Write an assessment of your skills and personal qualities.

Developing a Positive Attitude

Section 10-1
Attitudes for Success

Section 10-2
Acting Like a Professional

In this video segment, discover how a positive attitude can lead to job success.

Journal
Personal Career Plan

It happens to everyone—you wake up in a bad mood. How could this mood affect your relationships with other people? Your school activities? Your work? In your journal, make a list of at least six possible effects of your bad mood. Then think about how you might overcome your bad mood. List at least four specific things you could do.

Attitudes for Success

OBJECTIVES

After studying this section, you will be able to:

- **Discuss how a positive attitude and high self-esteem lead to success on the job.**
- **Explain the value of enthusiasm at work.**
- **Describe how to assert yourself at work.**

KEY TERMS

**attitude
self-esteem
enthusiasm
assertiveness
arrogance**

School-to-work students Roy Marcus and Gary Sikes have just received some surprising news. Amy Ngo, their coworker at the administrative offices of LaSalle Industries, is moving to another city. She will be leaving in two weeks and will not be replaced. After celebrating with Amy over lunch, Roy and Gary discuss their reactions in private.

Roy thinks the news is great—not only for Amy but also for himself and Gary. Without Amy, they will have the opportunity to learn more about running the business. They will be able to prove themselves to the company. They may even earn permanent positions at LaSalle.

Gary, on the other hand, considers the situation a problem. "What's so great?" he scowls. "All this means is we'll be doing more work for the same pay."

Does this scene sound familiar? If not, be prepared. You may face a similar one at work. While you can't control everything that happens on the job, you can control how you react.

If you are more a "Gary" than a "Roy," pay special attention to this section. Your **attitude,** or basic outlook on life, matters. It determines how you react to certain situations and, often, how you are perceived by others. It is your way of looking at the world and the people in it. How well you get along with your employer and your coworkers will depend on your attitude. If you have a positive attitude, you are already on your way to success on the job.

Building a positive attitude is like climbing a spiral staircase. *How can positive thinking help you get ahead?*

I'm Positive!

The first step in building a positive attitude is to think positively. When you think positively, you reap many rewards.

What Positive Thinking Can Do for You

Have you ever heard people attribute their success to "the power of positive thinking"? Well, they may be right. Evidence shows that thinking positively can bring you power—in your life and on the job. Think back to Roy and Gary. Whom do you think is more likely to succeed at work? Why?

Here are some ways that positive thinking can lead you to positive results:

- *Positive thinkers get along better with others.* When you think positively, you are more receptive, or open, to the people around you.

- *Others feel more comfortable with positive thinkers.* Whom would you rather be around: someone who is optimistic or someone who is negative?

- *Positive thinkers handle problems more effectively.* Consider this "upward spiral": When you think positively, you elevate your mood. When you elevate your mood, you make better decisions. When you make better decisions, you feel even better, and so forth.

- *Positive thinking can help you reach your goals by motivating you to act.* As Les Brown, author of *Live Your Dreams*, explains: "People who expect to achieve their goals don't

▶ Figure 10-1

Building a Positive Attitude

If you want to build a positive attitude, it helps to practice the four steps shown here.

B Surround yourself with positive thinkers. Positive energy is contagious. Unfortunately, negative energy can be as well. You should not make a practice of deserting friends in need. However, if most of your friends are in a negative place, and particularly if they are bringing you down, it may be a good idea to seek out new friends.

A Promote positive thoughts by taking positive actions. Instead of sitting around complaining about problems, mobilize and act. Join or form a group or club for a one-time or ongoing action.

D Present your ideas positively, without apologizing. Attending a school-, job-, or community-related meeting offers an excellent opportunity to work on this step. Remember to speak slowly and clearly and to watch your body language.

C Turn a negative into a positive by listing good aspects of something that appears to be bad. Even the worst situations may have some benefits. For example, having to work overtime to catch up with a project may let you feel more in control. It may also mean a larger paycheck or extra vacation time.

stand around talking about them. They're engaged in action."

- *Positive thinkers are healthier.* In fact, a study has shown that pessimistic students get sick twice as often as optimistic ones.

How to Build a Positive Attitude

OK, you may be thinking, a positive attitude is good. Now how do I go about getting one? The answer is you must build one, step-by-step. *Figure 10-1* shows some of the steps in the process.

Developing Self-Esteem

As *Figure 10-1* shows, when you present your ideas without apologizing, you show **self-esteem**, or a recognition and regard for yourself and your abilities. Self-esteem is essential for a positive attitude.

Here's another "upward spiral": Self-esteem breeds confidence. Confidence generates success. Success boosts self-esteem.

Overcoming Doubt

Do you have a little voice inside your head? Does it sometimes whisper negative messages, such as "You don't deserve to get that new job" or "You're not smart enough to pass that test"? Most people suffer twinges of inner doubt. Would you like to get rid of that voice? One technique that works for many people is called positive self-talk.

Positive self-talk means you "outtalk" your negative inner voice. When the voice says, "You can't," you answer, "I can—and

✓ **Solving Workplace Problems**

You've had your own law practice for nearly 10 years. Originally, you planned to defend the interests of children in family and criminal court. Recently, however, you've felt dissatisfied; you realize that you're making a lot of money, but you aren't working for or with children at all. What changes will you make?

The Importance of Enthusiasm

What do employers look for in their employees? Experience? Skills? Many employers value an upbeat attitude most. They look for enthusiastic people who take pride in their work and show initiative.

It's easy to have **enthusiasm,** or eager interest, when you love your work. However, even your dream job will have its down moments. What then?

You may have to push yourself to act with enthusiasm. While this may not feel natural, it's worth the effort. An upbeat attitude will help you develop a reputation as a hard and willing worker. When you act with enthusiasm, you are more likely to end up really feeling enthusiastic.

I will!" Making a list of positive statements also can help. Statements might include "I am in charge of my life" and "I can achieve whatever I want." Try repeating these statements to yourself throughout the day.

How to Build Self-Esteem

Once that negative voice is on its way out, self-esteem is on its way in. Here are some ways you can speed its arrival:

- Make lists of your abilities and successes. Look at them often.

- Set reachable goals, and work to achieve them.

- Think about how you have made a difference in someone else's life.

Dealing with Mistakes

No one is perfect. Everyone makes mistakes. The difference between highly successful people and those who are less successful is not that the successful people make fewer mistakes. It's that

▶ Your negative inner voice is like a bully who is always putting you down. *How can positive self-talk help you get rid of that "bully"?*

While this woman had less experience than some of the other applicants, she got the job because of her outgoing manner. **Why do employers value enthusiasm?**

they don't give up. Instead of letting mistakes bring them down, they use them as opportunities to learn and grow.

Remember: Whenever you make a mistake, be patient with yourself. You will probably have the opportunity to correct the mistake. Also, you will have other opportunities to succeed.

Once you have accepted that you will make mistakes from time to time, you can prepare yourself to act effectively when you do. When you think you have made a mistake, try following these steps:

1. Make sure it's really a mistake. Because a project didn't turn out the way you planned doesn't mean it's wrong.

2. It's easier to handle a mistake you acknowledge than one you try to hide. Tell your supervisor immediately, and accept responsibility.

3. Offer a way to solve the problem.

4. Find a lesson you can learn from your mistake.

5. Forgive yourself. Don't dwell on your mistake. Learn from it, and move on.

Asserting Yourself

Most people who work hard to do a good job want to be recognized for their efforts. How do you get the credit you deserve from those around you? You do it by practicing **assertiveness**. When you confidently present yourself and your abilities to those around you, you are showing assertiveness.

Representing Yourself

In some cultures, asserting individuality is frowned upon. In the United States, however, especially in the business world, presenting yourself confidently is usually admired. How should you go about it?

The first step in practicing assertiveness is to be friendly and outgoing. When you notice a coworker you haven't met, find a good moment and introduce yourself. Use positive body language and speak with confidence.

Make an effort to get to know your supervisor better too. If he or she has an "open door" policy, take advantage of it. Offer your opinions or suggestions from time to time. Asking for advice is also an excellent way to let your supervisor know that you care about your job.

Here are some other ways to make yourself better known:

- Volunteer for committees and projects.
- Keep informed. Become an expert on your job or company.
- Keep a journal of your accomplishments. Include the date, what you did, and how it helped your employer. Bring your journal to performance reviews.

This person has made a mistake pricing merchandise. He is informing his supervisor. *Why is it important to admit mistakes you make at work?*

This woman keeps a record of her accomplishments on the job. *How can keeping a journal help your reputation as a good worker?*

Assertiveness—Not Arrogance

Here's an important distinction to remember: Most employers will accept, and even admire, employees who confidently indicate their real accomplishments and abilities. That is assertiveness. However, no one likes employees who are overbearing and full of self-importance. That is **arrogance**, which you want to avoid. The difference has to do with respecting other people and *their* abilities. It's a question of using the proper attitude and tone.

SECTION 10-1 *Review*

Understanding Key Concepts

Using complete sentences, answer the following questions on a separate sheet of paper.

1. How might having a positive attitude help an employee get a raise or a promotion?

2. On Sheila's second day on her new job at an accounting firm, her supervisor asks her to reorganize the storage closet. Sheila knows this will involve many hours of tedious work. How should she respond to the request? Why?

3. Marco's supervisor is about to prepare her quarterly evaluation of him. He is fairly sure she doesn't realize that he worked much harder than his coworkers on a recent team project. How can Marco get the credit he deserves?

Exploring Careers: Marketing and Distribution

John Gabaldon
Internet Specialist in Marketing

Q: What kind of background do you have as an Internet specialist?

A: In college I worked with computers a lot, doing everything—word processing, programming, desktop publishing. Much of the time I felt isolated. So I focused on a career in marketing because of the interaction with people. I taught myself about the Internet—reading all the good books on it, learning about the programs.

Q: What do you do for your clients?

A: I help them market their products on-line through promotions and Web pages. I can help them link with other Web sites that get lots of hits so that they get more exposure.

When people give us information on the Internet, we can keep track of the statistics. We can then target markets for them when there are future products. It can be a real cost-cutter for the client.

With the new programs it's so much easier for people to find things out about a product. For example, you can get a video that can show you a car, interior and exterior, from all angles.

Q: What's the future for someone who wants to do Internet marketing?

A: All the big companies are getting a Web site presence. In the future, small- to medium-size companies will be getting into this kind of marketing.

Thinking Critically

What are the advantages of marketing through the Internet?

CAREER FACTS

Nature of the Work:
Develop and maintain Web sites; devise marketing plans for clients.

Training or Education Needed:
Training in computer programming; experience using various programs.

Aptitudes, Abilities, and Skills:
Very strong computer skills; listening, speaking, and interpersonal skills; problem-solving and decision-making skills.

Salary Range:
Average starting salary—$30,000; average top salary—$65,000.

Career Path:
Work as a programmer or in traditional marketing fields; freelance; start own business.

Acting Like a Professional

OBJECTIVES

After studying this section, you will be able to:

- **Describe how to accept criticism at work.**
- **Give examples of how to professionally handle workplace pressure and gossip.**
- **Explain how to control anger on the job.**

KEY TERMS

professionalism
constructive
    criticism
defensiveness
gossip

Think back to a difficult time at school or work. Maybe you had a classmate who challenged you every time you spoke up. Perhaps you were so overworked you felt you would explode if someone told you to do just one more thing.

Now divide a sheet of paper into three columns. In the first column, briefly describe the *situation* you recalled. In the second, list the *feelings* you experienced. In the third, describe the *action* you took. Turn the paper over. Then answer these questions: Was your reaction a mature response to your problem? Was your answer constructive? What could you have done differently?

When you experience difficulties, these will be important questions to ask yourself. Particularly in the workplace, you should question yourself before you react to a problem. At work, you will need to show **professionalism**. That is, you will need to handle problems and criticism gracefully and maturely. Instead of reacting prematurely, think things through before you take any action.

Accepting Criticism

You already know that properly handling criticism can be difficult. However, it is vital to your survival in any job.

Have you ever had a day like this? **Why should you learn to handle pressure gracefully?**

What Makes Criticism Constructive?

Criticism that is presented in a way that can help you learn and grow is **constructive criticism**. When you see criticism as potentially helpful, it becomes easier to handle. Believe it or not, some employees welcome criticism. They have found that it teaches them better ways to succeed at their jobs.

EXCELLENT BUSINESS PRACTICES

Stress Reduction in the Workplace

Cigna Corporation, a Philadelphia-based health-care, insurance, and financial services organization, has a stress-reduction program for employees. Called "Fast Break," the program is designed to help employees manage tension and focus their energies, whether they are stressed from personal issues or work pressures.

Employees decide if they need to relax or energize and can choose a break of 5, 10, or 15 minutes. Employees can relax with New Age music, meditation, and stretching, or they can increase their energy levels by listening to tapes of empowering thoughts or by moving to upbeat music.

Some of the breaks are conducted by instructors from Cigna's Employee Wellness Center, an on-site health and fitness center which offers free confidential counseling (for employees and their families) and classes on stress reduction, tai chi, and yoga.

Thinking Critically

How does stress affect a person's job performance?

Of course, not all criticism is equally productive. *Figure 10-2* compares constructive criticism to less helpful criticism. You can use the standards in this figure to evaluate criticism you receive. You can also use them if your job requires you to evaluate employees.

Responding to Criticism

What does the term *defensiveness* bring to mind? Consider this situation:

Janet's coworker Paolo has been late many times. Recently, Janet overheard her supervisor tell a colleague that if Paolo continued to be late, he would lose his job. After work, Janet told Paolo what she had heard and suggested he try to get to work on time. Paolo snapped back, "But it's not my fault! My car is always breaking down. Besides, who are you to judge me?" Janet understood why Paolo was upset. However, she wished that he had really listened to what she had to say. After all, she felt the criticism had been for his own good.

Defensiveness means putting up an emotional guard against negative opinions. Remember the upward spirals from Section 1? Here's a downward spiral: When Paolo reacts defensively, he becomes closed. When he is closed, he cannot listen. When he cannot listen, he cannot grow. The only way he could have benefited from Janet's criticism was to be receptive and not defensive.

What Makes Criticism Constructive?	
Constructive Criticism	**Less Helpful Criticism**
Addresses behavior	Addresses attitude
Is specific	Is general
Is offered immediately	Is not offered immediately
Makes some mention of positive points	Focuses exclusively on negative points
Offers specific actions to solve the problem(s)	Offers no solution to the problem(s)
Is given in private	Is announced in public

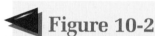

Figure 10-2

You can learn to give and accept constructive criticism. Why is it easier to accept <u>constructive</u> criticism?

Here are four steps that can help you respond effectively to criticism:

1. Listen to the criticism.

2. Make sure you understand the criticism. If the speaker does not specify the problem, ask him or her to do so.

3. Identify a solution to the problem.

4. Take action to remedy the problem. If the problem is complex, break it down into smaller bits. Then you can take action one step at a time.

If you are closed to criticism, you may be following a downward spiral. *How can defensiveness prevent growth?*

On-the-Job Pressures and How to Handle Them

◄ **Figure 10-3**

Every job has pressure. Why is it important to have a plan for handling the different kinds of on-the-job pressure?

Meeting Deadlines 	Learn to break large tasks into smaller steps. Carefully schedule when you will complete each step. If the deadline seems unrealistic, ask for help *as early as possible*.
Juggling Tasks 	A daily "to do" list, where you define and prioritize your duties, can be a lifesaver. As you complete each task, cross it off the list. For example: A. ~~Call MF and LS about the meeting Wednesday.~~ B. ~~Prepare minutes from last month's meeting.~~ C. Copy fund-raising report for GG. D. Make calls to caterers about May event.
Having More Than One Supervisor 	If two supervisors give you assignments due at the same time or if they give you conflicting instructions, speak up! Request a meeting with both supervisors so that they can sort out their priorities together.

A final word on responding to criticism: In the end, you must use your own judgment. Even if the rest of the world thinks you've made a poor decision, you may know inside that you did the right thing. This is especially true when you need to stand up for your values.

Handling Pressure

Pressure is everywhere! Supervisors set deadlines. Coworkers make demands. Difficult customers need polite attention. You wonder if you are making the right decisions. You wonder if you will ever be able to get all your work done. You wonder if you are succeeding at your job. You wonder if you are in the right job at all. …

Sound familiar? *Figure 10-3* offers some tips that can help you handle on-the-job pressure.

Handling Gossip

Idle talk that usually consists mostly of rumors is called **gossip.** The problem with such talk is that the information it spreads is often untrue—and hurtful. According to Adele Scheele, a writer for *Working Woman* magazine, people gossip so that they can feel important. "Gossip is a bribe," she says, "a way of enhancing your status at someone else's expense."

In the end, gossip usually hurts the gossiper most. The more an employee gossips, the less coworkers will confide in that person. Eventually, the gossiper develops a reputation as someone who cannot be trusted. Before you join in gossip, ask yourself these questions:

- What is my motivation for gossiping?
- Could my comments damage someone else's reputation unfairly?

This woman has some gossip about a coworker. *Should she share it with her other coworkers? Why or why not?*

Controlling Anger

Some frustration is inevitable in any job. As you work to develop new skills and advance in your career, things will not always go well. However, you must avoid letting frustration turn to anger and your anger boil over on the job. If you do get angry, here are some tips for "damage control:"

- Count to 10. It gives you a chance to calm down and not say something you will regret later.

- Consider what you are really angry about. Are you angry about a situation at work or with friends?

- Channel your energy into problem solving. Here's a five-step model: (1) define the problem, (2) decide on possible solutions, (3) evaluate those solutions, (4) make a decision, (5) take action.

Career Do's & Don'ts

When Learning to be Positive...

Do:
- accept challenges.
- be considerate and responsive to everyone, even if it's not reciprocated.
- compliment others.
- be at peace with yourself.

Don't:
- say "It's not my job."
- allow other people to whine or complain to you unless they recommend solutions.
- put people on the defensive.
- gossip.

SECTION 10-2 *Review*

Understanding Key Concepts

Using complete sentences, answer the following questions on a separate sheet of paper.

1. Sean's supervisor wants to speak to him about some problems with the project he just completed. Sean feels that he worked hard on the project and did an excellent job. What should he do when he meets with his supervisor?

2. Jake is overwhelmed by the amount of work he must complete every day. What is one step Jake can take to reduce the pressure he feels?

3. What is the difference between sharing helpful information with your coworkers and gossiping?

4. List three tips for controlling anger on the job.

CHAPTER 10 *Highlights*

Key Terms
attitude *(p. 194)*
self-esteem *(p. 197)*
enthusiasm *(p. 198)*
assertiveness *(p. 200)*
arrogance *(p. 201)*

SECTION 10-1 Summary

• While employees cannot control everything that happens on the job, they can control how they react. A positive attitude can help workers succeed.

• A positive attitude is based on self-esteem. Self-esteem and confidence in your abilities are closely related.

• To build self-esteem, you can train your positive inner voice to "outtalk" your negative inner voice.

• Employers value an upbeat attitude. You can learn to act with enthusiasm even during your job's down moments.

• Be patient with yourself. It's OK to make mistakes as long as you try to learn from them.

• Being assertive, but not arrogant, can help you get the recognition you deserve on the job.

Key Terms
professionalism *(p. 203)*
constructive criticism *(p. 204)*
defensiveness *(p. 205)*
gossip *(p. 207)*

SECTION 10-2 Summary

• Employees need to handle criticism gracefully and to react maturely. These are important aspects of professionalism.

• It is best to avoid being defensive when receiving constructive criticism.

• Learning to handle pressure effectively will help you succeed at your work.

• People usually gossip to enhance their status. However, gossipers often end up damaging their own reputations.

• Things at work don't always go the way you want them to. Employees must learn to prevent frustration from becoming anger and anger from boiling over.

Reviewing Key Terms

On separate paper, write a short story about a high school graduate's first week of work. Use the terms below in your story.

attitude
self-esteem
enthusiasm
assertiveness
arrogance

professionalism
constructive
criticism
defensiveness
gossip

Recalling Key Concepts

On a separate sheet of paper, tell whether each statement is true or false. Rewrite any false statements to make them true.

1. Optimists get sick less often than pessimists.

2. When you act with enthusiasm, you are more likely to start feeling enthusiastic.

3. Failure is who you are, not something you did.

4. Assertiveness is assuming you know everything and bragging about your accomplishments.

5. People usually gossip so that they will feel more important.

Thinking Critically

Using complete sentences, answer each of the questions below on a separate sheet of paper.

1. Why do you think positive "self-talk" can help you build self-esteem and confidence?

2. Do you think it's OK to "push" enthusiasm when you're feeling down on the job? Is this dishonest? Why or why not?

3. When you are angry, counting to 10 can help you calm down and think clearly. What other techniques might accomplish the same goal?

 ## SCANS Foundation Skills and Workplace Competencies

Thinking Skills: *Knowing How to Learn*

1. Explain how each of the following SCANS skills can help you develop a better attitude on the job: writing, thinking, listening.

Interpersonal Skills: *Participating as a Team Member*

2. Abigail, Dara, and Thomas work as a team as cashiers and baggers at a supermarket. All of them are being considered for one new managerial position. Though the three are good friends, Thomas and Dara tell Abigail that they think she is "playing up" too much to their supervisor by always complimenting him on his supervision. How should Abigail respond to this criticism? Should she change her behavior? Why or why not?

Connecting Academics to the Workplace

Human Relations

1. Arrange to interview the human resource administrator or a manager at a company that employs many workers. What human relations problems are of particular concern at that company? Find out how the administrator works

to solve those problems and improve the working environment. Report your findings to the class.

Health and Physical Education

2. Do research in the library or on the Internet to find out what long-term effects a negative job attitude and work-related stress and anger can have on a person's health. What do doctors recommend to prevent these health risks?

Music/Science

3. Many companies pipe music into certain areas of the workplace in an attempt to improve the working environment and boost worker performance. What kinds of music do employers in your area use and why? Contact such employers as supermarkets, mall stores, and doctors' offices to find out.

Developing Teamwork and Leadership Skills

In a team of five or six students, develop a one-act play about an employee struggling with a supervisor who is critical of his or her work. Two students might work as writers, one as a director, and two or three as actors. Alternatively, the team can write the play collectively. Present the play to the class. Have the class discuss the "employee's" behavior.

Real-World Workshop

As a class, simulate an office environment. Each student may choose a role to play. Roles should include executives, department directors, administrative assistants, outside clients, a receptionist, and so forth. Students should take turns playing a new employee on his or her first day at work. "New employees" should introduce themselves to people in the office, applying the skills they learned in the chapter. After each student takes a turn at role-playing, the class should discuss and evaluate his or her performance.

School-to-Work Connection

Using the Yellow Pages or the Internet, identify a local business of career interest. Arrange an informational interview to discuss what qualities that business looks for when hiring new employees.

Individual Career Plan

Write a brief report on the personal qualities you believe are most important for the career you have chosen. Base your report on the chapter you have just read and the information you collected at your informational interview in the School-to-Work Connection activity. For each quality you name, consider to what extent you already have that quality and how you might develop it further.

Chapter 11

Workplace Health and Safety

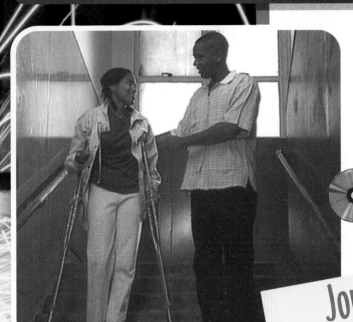

Section 11-1
Becoming a Healthy Worker

Section 11-2
Safety on the Job

In this video segment, learn how to create a safe and healthy work environment.

Journal
Personal Career Plan

How healthy are you? Write a brief journal entry, describing your own health. Then, after you have studied this chapter, reread your journal entry. Has your understanding of your own health changed? Write a second journal entry explaining your new ideas.

Becoming a Healthy Worker

OBJECTIVES

After studying this section, you will be able to:

- **Recognize the relationship between good health and career success.**
- **Explain the health benefits of exercise, a balanced diet, and rest.**
- **Describe causes and effects of stress.**
- **Develop effective strategies for coping with stress.**

KEY TERMS

nutrients
Food Guide Pyramid
sedentary
addiction

Athletes know that good health makes success possible. Without it, there are no touchdown passes, no 20-foot jump shots. To score the kinds of goals you want in whatever career you choose, you, too, need to pay attention to your health.

What It Takes to Be Healthy

Good health means more than being free of pain and illness. It means having the mental and physical energy to do what you need and want to do. You can't have total control over your health, but you can influence these major health factors:

- diet,
- exercise, and
- rest.

You can also do one more thing—stay on guard against disease and addiction. Following this advice will help you build a solid foundation for career success.

Eating Wisely

Maria Cisneros, a telemarketer, assumed she was healthy. Yet after a busy day at work, all she wanted to do was pick up a pizza, collapse on the couch, and watch television. "I was really tired, and I blamed my job," she recalls. "I gave it all I had." Then her doctor explained that she was tired because she wasn't getting enough **nutrients**—the substances in food that the body needs to produce energy and stay healthy.

Check for the nutrients you need in *Figure 11-1* on page 216, which shows the **Food Guide Pyramid**. This is a guideline created by the U.S. Department of Health and Human Services to help you get the nutrients you need each day.

Exercising for Fitness

Exercise takes energy, but it also gives *back* energy. Exercise helps you do the following:

▶ Eating wisely does not necessarily mean eating less. It means eating foods that nourish you. *What foods would make up another nutritious breakfast?*

YOU'RE THE BOSS!

✓ *Solving Workplace Problems*

Last week a customer suffered a heart attack in your pharmacy. You were able to administer CPR while your clerk phoned for an ambulance, and the customer is recovering well. However, you have discovered that all your employees consider phoning 9-1-1 the only response to accidents and emergencies. What will you do?

- build strength and endurance,
- feel mentally alert, and
  - reduce tension and anxiety.

Employees who exercise are productive and don't get ill as often as employees who don't exercise. Exercise is particularly important if you have a **sedentary**

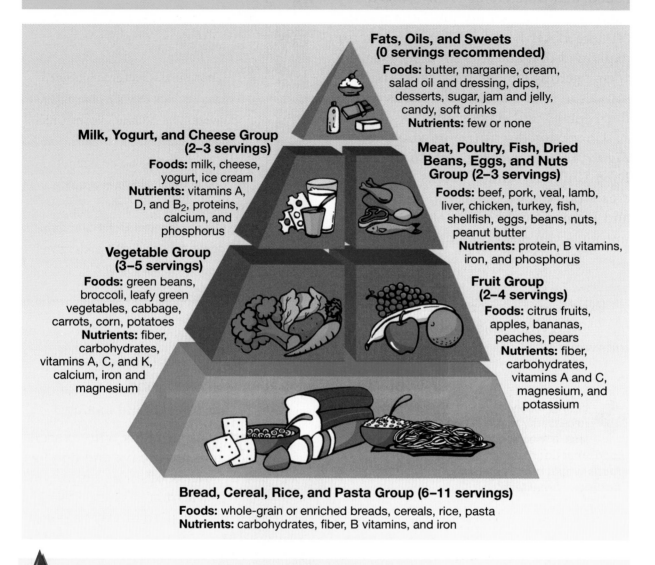

The Food Guide Pyramid

Fats, Oils, and Sweets (0 servings recommended)
Foods: butter, margarine, cream, salad oil and dressing, dips, desserts, sugar, jam and jelly, candy, soft drinks
Nutrients: few or none

Milk, Yogurt, and Cheese Group (2–3 servings)
Foods: milk, cheese, yogurt, ice cream
Nutrients: vitamins A, D, and B_2, proteins, calcium, and phosphorus

Meat, Poultry, Fish, Dried Beans, Eggs, and Nuts Group (2–3 servings)
Foods: beef, pork, veal, lamb, liver, chicken, turkey, fish, shellfish, eggs, beans, nuts, peanut butter
Nutrients: protein, B vitamins, iron, and phosphorus

Vegetable Group (3–5 servings)
Foods: green beans, broccoli, leafy green vegetables, cabbage, carrots, corn, potatoes
Nutrients: fiber, carbohydrates, vitamins A, C, and K, calcium, iron and magnesium

Fruit Group (2–4 servings)
Foods: citrus fruits, apples, bananas, peaches, pears
Nutrients: fiber, carbohydrates, vitamins A and C, magnesium, and potassium

Bread, Cereal, Rice, and Pasta Group (6–11 servings)
Foods: whole-grain or enriched breads, cereals, rice, pasta
Nutrients: carbohydrates, fiber, B vitamins, and iron

Figure 11-1 Foods are usually grouped according to the nutrients they provide. This pyramid shows you how many daily servings from each food group you need. Why doesn't the Food Guide Pyramid recommend any servings of fats, oils, and sweets?

job—one in which you spend much of your time sitting. Think you're too busy to exercise? Think again. Health professionals say you need only 20 minutes of exercise three times a week to reap the benefits. So what do you like? Aerobics? Dancing? Basketball? Go for it!

Recharging Yourself—Sleep

There's a lot happening in Laurie McBride's life. Three nights a week, she has a class at the community college. At other times, she goes out with friends. Most nights, after taking care of household

The secret of a successful exercise program is doing something you enjoy. *If you exercise regularly, what are some of the health benefits you experience?*

Staying on Guard

Beyond maintaining a balanced diet and getting the right amounts of exercise and rest, you need to stay on guard to stay healthy. That means following rules of hygiene, getting regular check-ups, and guarding against drug and alcohol addiction.

Addiction is a physical or psychological need for a substance. Addictive substances can include alcohol and prescription drugs, as well as illegal substances such as marijuana and cocaine. Addiction can lead to devastating physical and mental effects, including depression, heart attack, liver disease, and even death.

Addiction can have a drastic impact on business, causing injuries, absenteeism, and poor productivity. That is why many

chores and winding down in front of the television set, she usually gets about six hours of sleep. What's the result? Laurie struggles to stay alert at work.

Almost everyone needs about eight hours of sleep a night. Too little sleep can cause difficulty concentrating and make a person more prone to accidents.

Sleep restores the body and recharges the brain. To get a good night's sleep, try to go to bed about the same time every night. Avoid caffeine-rich foods and drinks, such as chocolate and caffeinated sodas, before bed.

Eating or drinking certain foods, such as milk, before bedtime helps some people sleep well. *What other nighttime routines might help this person get a good night's rest?*

companies have established *drug-testing programs*, programs designed to detect illegal drug use. Some companies might test you when you apply for a job; others have a policy of testing employees periodically. Companies are not likely to hire job applicants who test positive for drugs. Employees with positive drug tests face possible job termination or may be referred to counseling and treatment.

Managing Stress

Another vital factor in staying healthy is learning to manage stress. Sam Burnett, a real estate agent, faced a hectic daily schedule. An economic downturn in his region made selling homes a difficult task. Although some amount of stress is natural, Sam found that the pressure gave him severe headaches. The stress—which is one's physical and emotional reaction to change or conflict—was getting to him.

In a recent survey by *U.S. News and World Report* and the advertising agency Bozell Worldwide, Inc., 7 out of 10 people said that they feel stress at least once a workweek, and 43 percent reported physical and emotional symptoms. The survey estimated that stress costs the United States $7,500 per worker per year.

Stress—Positive and Negative

Stress is a natural reaction to conflict. When you are challenged, your heart rate and breathing accelerate, your muscles tighten, and your blood pressure climbs. In the short term, these effects can be positive because they help you focus more clearly and act more decisively. When the challenge is over, your body returns to normal.

Stress becomes negative, however, when your body doesn't return to normal but stays in an unnecessary state of alertness. This state can wear you out and produce such effects as headaches, chest pain, irritability, and depression.

Coping with Stress

Health experts say that one of the most effective ways of dealing with stress is to identify the cause of the stress and then to

The major sources of stress are change, conflict, the environment, and overwork. *What could this man do to cope with the stress of his job?*

Coping with Stress

Figure 11-2

You can use your SCANS problem-solving skills to manage stress on the job. What positive aspects of a workplace might relieve stress?

Recognizing the Problem	Finding Solutions
Major changes, such as marriage, a new job, or the death of a family member	Try to limit changes in other areas of your life. If you've just started a new job, for example, you might want to delay other changes (such as getting married).
Conflict or uncertainty caused by disagreements with coworkers or unclear instructions about what is expected of you	Talk the problem out with a trusted coworker, human relations worker, or company counselor. If the problem persists, consider getting someone to mediate—to listen to what you both have to say—and negotiate.
Prolonged overwork or pressure when you have to pick up the work of employees who have been laid off or when you have to work additional hours during seasonal deadlines	Review your responsibilities with a coworker or mentor. Can one person do them all? Are there ways to do them more efficiently? If the workload is not doable, discuss getting help from your supervisor. Until help comes, set priorities, and take one step at a time.
Environmental stresses, such as noise, uncomfortable temperatures, crowding	Brainstorm with coworkers. Bring comforts from home, such as headphones, a small fan or heater, or a desk lamp. Use visualization to move to a calmer, quieter place.

address the problem directly. ***Figure 11-2*** identifies some problems and their possible solutions. In addition, you can develop your own relaxation techniques. Here are three widely used methods:

- *Deep breathing.* Slowly fill your lungs with air. Hold it. Release.

- *Visualization.* Close your eyes and picture yourself in a calm place—for example, resting on a beach or under a tree.

- *Taking a time-out.* Get away from a pressure-packed situation for a few minutes—for example, take a walk outside. When you return, you may see solutions you didn't see before.

The benefits of reducing stress can be increased productivity, greater job satisfaction, and better self-management (a SCANS skill). Handling stress is also a leadership skill: Only people who can manage themselves can lead others effectively.

Attitude Counts

Exercise is terrific for your physical health, but its benefits go beyond fitness. Regular exercise can improve your attitude and your outlook on life. So, when the stresses of work make you feel pessimistic and exhausted, set aside a half hour in the day to exercise. Not only will this do wonders for you physically, but it will help you mentally too.

 Cathy, the character in this cartoon, is overwhelmed by her work. *What advice would you give Cathy?*

cathy®

by Cathy Guisewite

SECTION 11-1 *Review*

Understanding Key Concepts

Using complete sentences, answer the following questions on a separate sheet of paper.

1. In what ways can being healthy help your career?

2. Name three obstacles that keep people from regularly managing their diet, exercise schedule, and rest schedule?

3. What negative effects could stress have on your work?

4. Why is it important to prepare yourself to cope effectively with stress on the job?

Exploring Careers: Communications and Media

Suzanne Wade
Trade Magazine Editor

Q: What training did you have to become an editor?

A: I received my bachelor's degree through a university co-op program. After my freshman year, I alternated spending six months in school and six months working as a reporter for a local newspaper. My co-op experience was critical in getting the job experience I needed to move into the field.

Q: What is a typical day like for a magazine editor?

A: What I love about being an editor is that there's no such thing as a typical day. I may talk to writers, edit material, or work with the production department. I have to be able to set my priorities—there are always 20 different projects clamoring for attention. I have to determine what can wait. It's stressful working with deadlines.

Q: Did you always know you wanted to work for a magazine?

A: I decided very young to be a writer. When I was deciding what I wanted to do for a living, I stumbled onto journalism. I'm a better writer than journalist—I like regular hours as opposed to the hours you keep as a reporter. I never intended to be the editor of a trade magazine. I don't know where I'm going from here.

Thinking Critically

Writing skills are critical for an editor. How might you depend on writing skills in your chosen career?

CAREER FACTS

Nature of the Work:
   Plan content of magazine; assign work to writers; edit, organize, rewrite articles; work with sales and design staff.

Training or Education Needed:
   English, journalism, or communications background preferred.

Aptitudes, Abilities, and Skills:
   Listening, speaking, and interpersonal skills; problem-solving skills; reading and writing skills; ability to allocate time, material, and human resources.

Salary Range:
   Depends on the size of the magazine's circulation; average starting salary—$25,000; average top salary—$45,000.

Career Path:
   Start as a writer, or an editorial assistant; advance to managing editor; move to other magazines or other types of publishing.

Safety on the Job

OBJECTIVES

After studying this section, you will be able to:

- Identify rules and procedures for maintaining a healthy and safe work environment.
- Identify workplace conservation and environmental practices and policies.
- Describe American Red Cross procedures.
- Explain how to respond to fire and weather emergencies.

KEY TERMS

Occupational Safety and Health Administration (OSHA)
workers' compensation
repetitive stress injuries
ergonomics
first aid

Accidents happen—but they don't have to happen regularly or to have such serious consequences. More than 6.5 million people are injured on the job every year. Part of your job is to make sure you're not one of them. Accidents cost businesses billions of dollars annually in lost wages, medical expenses, and insurance claims.

Rules and Regulations

Government, employers, and workers all have a stake in preventing accidents. Therefore, they cooperate to make workplaces safer.

The Government's Role

The federal government protects American workers by setting workplace safety standards and by making sure that accident victims receive care. The **Occupational Safety and Health Administration (OSHA)** is the branch of the U.S. Department of Labor that sets job safety standards and inspects job sites. If a company fails to meet OSHA's standards, it can face fines and other penalties. OSHA keeps pace with the world of work by revising standards when work conditions change or new technology, such as the use of lasers, is developed.

The government also makes sure that workers are compensated, or paid, if they have an accident and can't work. **Workers' compensation** laws guarantee that if you are hurt on the job, you will receive financial help to cover lost wages and medical expenses.

Employers' Roles

Safety regulations for employers can be very complex. In a nutshell, employers must do the following:

- provide a workplace free from recognized health and accident hazards,

- provide equipment and materials needed to do the work safely and teach employees how to use them,

- inform employees when materials or conditions are hazardous, and

- keep records of job-related illnesses and injuries.

In addition, employers establish policies and procedures for conservation and environmental protection. These procedures—such as those for recycling glass and safely disposing of hazardous waste—may vary from company to company. It is everyone's responsibility, however, to see that they are carried out in line with government regulations. If you work in an office, for example, you may be asked to sort wastepaper into separate bins for recycling. If you work with chemicals, you'll have to follow strict guidelines to prevent injury to coworkers and damage to the environment.

Employers are also concerned with new risks fostered by emerging technologies. For example, each year several hundred thousand workers, from computer users to meatpacking plant workers, suffer from **repetitive stress injuries**, ailments that develop after the same motions are performed over and over. To address this problem and other similar injuries, industrial engineers are engaged in a new field of applied science called **ergonomics**, in which they redesign workstations to make them safer, more comfortable, and more efficient.

Workers' Responsibilities

Workplace safety is also the responsibility of individual employees. In addition to following regulations for environmental

Employers and employees are responsible for protecting the environment. **What is one step you can take to do this?**

protection, workers must learn and follow safety regulations set down by OSHA. These include the following:

- learning to perform a job safely,
- knowing how to operate, maintain, and troubleshoot tools and equipment safely, and
- reporting unsafe conditions or practices immediately.

Responding to Emergencies

Your own safety and the safety of other employees can depend upon your awareness of what to do in an emergency. Knowing **first aid**—what to do *first*, before help arrives—may mean the difference between life and death.

Juwon Taylor, a student driving home in a heavy windstorm, watched helplessly as a giant tree limb came crashing down on the car in front of him. Stopping his own car, Juwon started toward the damaged vehicle to see if anyone was injured. Quickly taking in the scene as he approached, Juwon spotted an exposed power line draped across the car's hood. By looking around before touching the car, Juwon saved his own life and allowed himself to get help for the injured motorist.

Always survey an accident scene before you do anything. Don't make any assumptions. Quickly figure out what has already happened, and try to determine what may happen next. If someone is injured and you are nearby, follow the easy-to-remember American Red Cross guidelines in the following sections.

Provide A-I-D

The letters of the word *AID* help you remember what to do.

- **A**sk for help. If someone is seriously injured, call the Emergency Medical Service immediately.
- **I**ntervene, but ask the victim first.
- **D**o no further harm. Do not move a victim whose back or neck may be broken.

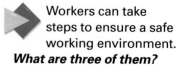
Workers can take steps to ensure a safe working environment. *What are three of them?*

Know Your ABCs

The ABCs are another easy way to remember priorities in an emergency.

- **Airway.** If necessary, clear the victim's airway (the passage that allows the person to breathe). Do this by placing one hand on the person's forehead and two fingers of the other hand under the person's chin. Tilt the head back by pushing on the forehead and lifting the chin.

- **Breathing.** Check to see if the victim is breathing.

- **Circulation.** Check to see if the victim has a pulse and whether he or she is bleeding severely. If so, press a clean cloth on the wound, and hold firmly with your palm.

Always follow the ABCs. If necessary, administer rescue breathing, shown in *Figure 11-3* on pages 226–227.

When the Elements Strike

Nature's fury can cause emergencies too. You need to know what to do to protect yourself and those you live and work with in case of fire or weather emergencies.

EXCELLENT BUSINESS PRACTICES

The Effect of Fitness Screenings

The Victorville, California, Fire Department recognizes the value of keeping firefighters physically fit, especially since their work makes them particularly prone to injury and heart attacks.

Victorville hires a firm to perform fitness screenings twice a year. These screenings include measuring cholesterol levels and blood pressure, blood profiles to screen for irregularities, treadmill tests, and nutrition profiles. Participants also are measured for such physical performance as abdominal endurance, push-ups, and vertical jump and grip strength. Individuals receive confidential consultations with a professional who makes recommendations for improving their health and fitness status.

Since the fire company initiated the program, the firefighters have shown improvements even as they get older. The average cholesterol level has dropped, and strength performance has increased. The firefighters are motivated to lower their risks for injury and illness. As a result, the department has had fewer injuries and those who have been injured have healed quickly.

Thinking Critically

In what ways does even moderate physical fitness enhance performance?

Fire

Your best protection against fire is to be prepared. Learn the location of fire exits at your workplace, and know your escape routes. If a fire breaks out, take these precautions:

- Leave the building immediately. Take the stairs or go out a window; do not use an elevator.

- If you cannot leave, stay close to the floor to avoid smoke.

- Before opening a door, put your hand on it. If the door is hot, don't open it. Find another way out or wait for help.

▶ **Figure 11-3**

Rescue Breathing

Rescue breathing is an important first-aid method.

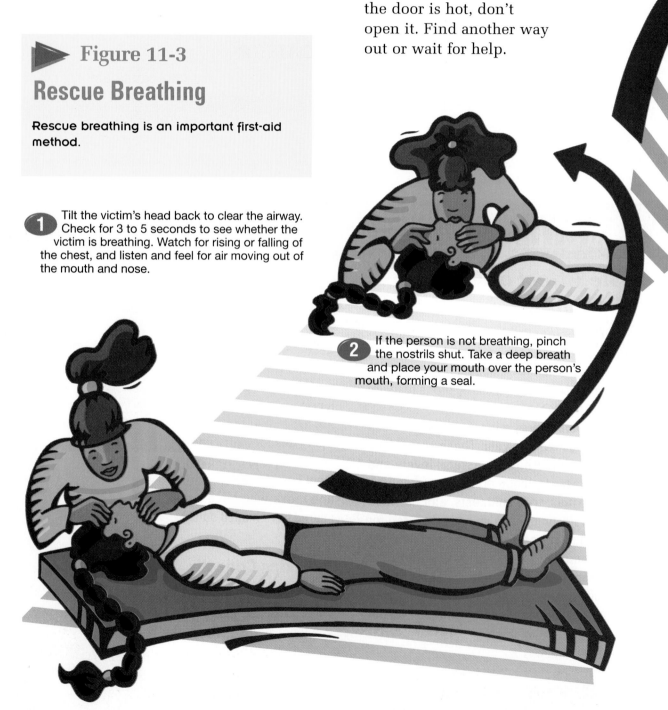

1 Tilt the victim's head back to clear the airway. Check for 3 to 5 seconds to see whether the victim is breathing. Watch for rising or falling of the chest, and listen and feel for air moving out of the mouth and nose.

2 If the person is not breathing, pinch the nostrils shut. Take a deep breath and place your mouth over the person's mouth, forming a seal.

3 Give the person two full breaths that last 1 to 1½ seconds each. After two breaths, remove your mouth and allow the victim to exhale (the chest should fall).

- If your clothes catch fire, stop, drop to the floor, and roll to put the fire out.
- Leave fire fighting to the experts. Don't try to put out the flames yourself.

4 Repeat steps 2 and 3, giving about one breath every 5 seconds, until the person is breathing on his or her own.

Source: American Red Cross.

Earthquakes

The most common danger in an earthquake comes from collapsing structures, falling objects, and glass. When an earthquake strikes, follow these precautions:

- If you are inside, stay inside. Move to a doorway or under a table or desk.
- If you are outdoors, stand in the open, away from tumbling trees, utility poles, and buildings.

Hurricanes

These powerful storms can pack raging winds and driving rains. When a hurricane threatens, take these precautions:

- Listen to bulletins from the National Weather Service. Be prepared with candles and matches, a flashlight, and a battery-operated radio.

Be prepared to handle emergency situations. *What should you do if a fire breaks out at work?*

When Ensuring Your Health and Safety...

Do:

- make your health and safety your highest priority.
- clean your own workplace and move any obstructions you see elsewhere.
- follow all safety regulations you are taught at work.
- offer suggestions for making a work area or work process more safe.

Don't:

- ignore potential health or safety hazards.
- fail to report an accident.
- do physical work that is too strenuous in general or if you are particularly tired.
- be pressured by coworkers into doing something that is not safe.

- At home, board up windows and doors. Tie down or remove loose objects or furniture.
- If evacuation is ordered, follow police instructions.

Tornadoes

These unpredictable funnel-shaped windstorms have enough power to pick up entire buildings and smash them down miles away. If a tornado threatens, take these precautions:

- Go indoors and stay away from windows. (Hallways and basements are

safest.) Cover yourself with a mattress or blanket.

- If you cannot get inside, dive into a ditch or another low ground area, and stay down.

SECTION 11-2 *Review*

Understanding Key Concepts

Using complete sentences, answer the following questions on a separate sheet of paper.

1. What does the acronym OSHA stand for, and how does OSHA help workers?

2. How might you protect the environment at work?

3. How can clear thinking skills help you in an emergency situation?

Key Terms

nutrients *(p. 215)*
Food Guide Pyramid
   (p. 215)
sedentary *(p. 215)*
addiction *(p. 217)*

SECTION 11-1 Summary

- Being healthy means having the mental and physical energy to pursue your goals.

- Nutrients are the substances in food that your body needs to produce energy and stay healthy. The Food Guide Pyramid shows how you can achieve a balanced diet.

- Everyone needs to exercise regularly and get enough rest.

- Addiction is a physical or emotional dependence on alcohol, illegal substances, or prescription drugs. It can cause devastating effects.

- Stress—a natural reaction to change or conflict—needs to be managed. People can cope with stress by identifying the causes of stress and by taking action to minimize its harmful effects.

Key Terms

Occupational Safety and
   Health Administration
   (OSHA) *(p. 222)*
workers' compensation
   (p. 222)
repetitive stress injuries
   (p. 223)
ergonomics *(p. 223)*
first aid *(p. 224)*

SECTION 11-2 Summary

- Government, employers, and employees share responsibility for creating and maintaining safe workplaces.

- The government sets and enforces safety standards.

- Employers must provide hazard-free workplaces, safe equipment, and health and safety information.

- Employees should know and follow safety rules.

- When an emergency occurs, you should follow American Red Cross guidelines: first survey the scene, then follow AID and ABC guidelines.

- To respond safely to fire and weather emergencies, be prepared and know what to do in each emergency.

Reviewing Key Terms

On separate paper, write a company newsletter describing proper health and safety practices to be used on the job. Use the terms below in your newsletter.

nutrients

Food Guide
  Pyramid

sedentary

addiction

first aid

OSHA

workers'
  compensation

ergonomics

repetitive stress
  injuries

Recalling Key Concepts

Choose the correct answer for each item below. Write your answers on a separate sheet of paper.

1. The main purpose of following the Food Guide Pyramid is to ____.
   (a) lose weight (b) save money
   (c) get the nutrients your body needs

2. In order to cope with stress, ____.
   (a) take a deep breath
   (b) take a brief break
   (c) do both a and b

3. Workers' compensation is ____.
   (a) pay for working overtime
   (b) medical coverage and partial pay for an injury
   (c) time off without pay

4. In order to help protect the environment, businesses often ask employees to ____.
   (a) wash their hands
   (b) avoid repetitive stress
   (c) recycle paper

5. The first thing you should do in an emergency is ____.
   (a) survey the scene
   (b) check the victim's breathing
   (c) call for help

Thinking Critically

Using complete sentences, answer each of the questions below on a separate sheet of paper.

1. Why would a prospective employer be interested in your health?

2. Compare the effects of positive and negative stress.

3. Describe how government, employers, and employees—working together—create a comprehensive system to ensure workplace safety.

4. Explain how the ABCs of first aid help you deal with emergencies effectively.

5. What are the advantages and disadvantages of workplace fire drills? What would you do to make them more useful?

 ## SCANS Foundation Skills and Workplace Competencies

Thinking Skills: *Problem Solving*

1. Mark and Keisha work on an assembly line in a toy factory. Lately, they are both feeling negative stress because their workload has increased and their boss is pressuring them to perform more efficiently. Describe in writing a strategy for solving their problem and reducing their symptoms of stress.

Explain the benefits of learning to handle stress effectively.

Technology Skills: *Maintaining and Troubleshooting Technology*

2. Research employee manuals or interview a supervisor in a company to find out how one company ensures safe operation and maintenance of its equipment. Prepare a report that identifies three pieces of equipment and the training and maintenance procedures that lead to a safe workplace.

Connecting Academics to the Workplace

Art

Tom, a teacher's aide at your school, says he doesn't have time to do the shopping and cooking it takes to eat wisely. Design a Food Guide Pyramid poster for people such as Tom, including foods that are easy to buy and prepare. Use paints or a collage to make the poster as appealing as possible.

Developing Teamwork and Leadership Skills

Working in a small group, create a weather emergency plan for a new office building in your town or city. Choose a specific weather emergency that could occur in your area: hurricane, flood, tornado, earthquake, blizzard, or other severe condition. Identify the specific procedures for workers to follow in an emergency. Include as many details as you can, and present your plan to the class.

Real-World Workshop

With a partner, create and role-play a situation in which an employee reports an unsafe or unhealthy condition to an employer. Identify the type of workplace and have the employee describe the health or safety hazard in detail. The employer should describe what he or she is going to do to solve the problem.

School-to-Work Connection

Interview someone in an industry you are interested in to learn about conservation and environmental practices followed in his or her workplace. Find out how the company works with local government to conserve resources and how the company attempts to protect the environment. Prepare a report that describes the findings from your interview, as well as any additional recommendations you might have for the company.

Individual Career Plan

Write a profile of how one particular career area of interest to you matches your personal outlook on health and fitness. What aspects of the career seem to fit well with your health and fitness habits? What aspects of this career area might be challenging for you? What changes might you make in your health habits if you decide to pursue a career in this particular field?

Chapter 12

Workplace Legal Matters

Section 12-1
Laws About the Workplace

Section 12-2
You and the Legal System

In this video segment, find out about legal issues that affect the workplace.

Journal
Personal Career Plan

In your journal, list five words or phrases that each of these terms brings to mind:

- police officer
- lawyer
- judge

What do you think your responses say about your understanding of—and attitude toward—our legal system?

Laws About the Workplace

OBJECTIVES

After studying this section, you will be able to:

- Identify laws that affect the workplace.
- Describe discrimination in the workplace and identify some of the laws that fight it.
- Recognize sexual harassment and identify actions to take against it.

KEY TERMS

minimum wage
compensatory time
collective bargaining
discrimination
affirmative action
sexual harassment

You're standing at a major intersection, and cars are whizzing by as you wait to cross. Then the light facing you turns green. Sure, you take a quick glance to either side before you step into the street. Still, you assume that drivers will obey the law and stop so that you can cross. This everyday event reminds us that the life of our society—from crossing the street to electing a leader—depends on laws.

Labor Laws

Just like traffic laws, labor laws set some ground rules. The difference is these laws are designed to protect you from unfair treatment on the job. They strive to ensure that all Americans have an equal opportunity to get and to keep a job, to be paid a just wage, to be considered fairly for promotion, and to be protected in times of personal and economic change. It is important that you understand your rights and responsibilities concerning labor laws.

Laws About Work and Pay

In 1938, the federal government passed the Fair Labor Standards Act (FLSA). This important law requires employers to pay a **minimum wage**—the lowest hourly wage that an employer can legally pay for

 This photo, taken in the early 1900s, shows the inside of a cotton mill factory. *How would you describe this work environment? Does it strike you as unfair?*

a worker's services. Believe it or not, the first minimum wage was set at 40¢ per hour, although it has risen to more than $5 over the years. The FLSA also set the 40-hour workweek and created the practice of *overtime* for hourly workers who work more than 40 hours a week. You read about this practice in Chapter 8. In addition, employees may receive **compensatory time,** paid time off from work rather than cash in exchange for working overtime. Employees, however, must agree in advance to this arrangement.

Child labor laws are another product of the FLSA. Imagine a 10-year-old working 60 hours a week in a factory! Sad to say, children worked under terrible conditions in this country less than 100 years ago. To put an end to a practice that robbed children of their childhood—and often of their good health as well—the FLSA set the minimum age for factory jobs at 16.

The Organization of Labor Unions

In another effort to protect people who work, the Wagner Act of 1935 (also called the National Labor Relations Act) made it legal to organize labor unions and engage in union activities. Labor unions represent workers in their dealings with employers. The workers elect union leaders, who establish and extend employee rights through **collective bargaining.** In other words, unions use the power of their numbers (the workers in the union) to bargain for better wages, increased benefits, better safety rules, and other job improvements. Today, about 15 percent of all American workers belong to a union.

Providing a Safety Net

State laws provide for unemployment insurance to help workers cope with the loss of a job. For example, Ben Dyal worked for five years selling athletic gear to department stores. The competition was fierce, and when his company suddenly went out of business, Ben had trouble landing a new job right away. "I had to eat," he said. "I had to pay the rent. So I went down to the local government office and filed for unemployment." Soon he received an unemployment check each week. "It allowed me to pay my basic living expenses until I found a new job. The temporary funds gave me a chance to get back on my feet."

Many workplaces include individuals from a variety of racial and ethnic backgrounds. *What advantages could this bring to business?*

Sometimes accidents and illness throw lives out of balance as well. Workers need to know that if they get sick, their jobs won't be given away to other workers. Some people need to take time off from work to care for relatives. To meet these needs, Congress passed the Family and Medical Leave Act in 1993. This law guarantees employees (at companies with more than 50 employees) up to 12 weeks' leave for family or personal medical care or for the birth or adoption of a child.

Drawing the Line

Law goes a long way toward protecting workers, but it draws the line at people who are working illegally. The Immigration Reform and Control Act of 1990 makes it very difficult for illegal immigrants (noncitizens living in our country without authorization from our government) to find work. Employers should make sure that *all* new employees have proper working papers and identification. Businesses can face huge fines if they break this law.

Discrimination

Under laws passed by Congress, it is illegal for employers to engage in **discrimination**—unequal treatment based on such factors as race, religion, nationality, *gender* (being male or female), age, or physical appearance.

EXCELLENT BUSINESS PRACTICES

Resolving Conflicts

Brown & Root Inc., a Houston-based engineering, construction, and maintenance company of 35,000 employees, has a dispute-resolution program. The program allows workers to voice their complaints. Through the company's employee hot line and legal consultation program, employees may receive free and confidential advice from professional advisers.

Employees may take complaints to any level of management in the organization, individually or in conference, through the company's open-door policy.

More than 500 employees have used the program since it was implemented, and about 80 percent of disputes have been resolved in fewer than four weeks.

Thinking Critically

How can a legal counselor save you time and help you avoid worrying about what to do? Why would the advice have to be confidential?

People with Disabilities in the Workforce

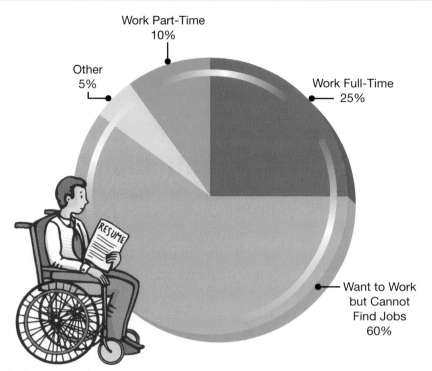

Work Part-Time
10%

Other
5%

Work Full-Time
25%

Want to Work
but Cannot
Find Jobs
60%

Estimated number of people with disabilities in America aged 16–64: 27 million

Source: Carol Kleiman, *The 100 Best Jobs for the 1990s and Beyond,*
Berkley Books, New York, 1992, p.10.

Figure 12-1

Entering the world of work can be a challenge for Americans with disabilities. Use your basic math skills to figure out the total number of people with disabilities who would like to work but are unable to find jobs.

Major Antidiscrimination Laws

Every employee has a legal right to fair treatment under one of a number of state and federal laws.

- The **Civil Rights Act of 1964** bans discrimination in employment based on race, color, religion, or gender.

- The **Age Discrimination Act of 1967** makes it illegal to discriminate against people over 40 in hiring, promoting, or discharging employees.

- The **Rehabilitation Act of 1973** and the **Americans with Disabilities Act of 1990** protect the rights of individuals with *disabilities*—conditions that include blindness, visual or hearing impairment, mental illness,

or paralysis. For example, the law requires businesses to provide aids such as wheelchair ramps and other special equipment for disabled workers. *Figure 12-1* shows statistics on people with disabilities in the workforce.

Courts have recognized some exceptions to the fundamental discrimination laws. Some employers are allowed to hire only people with certain qualifications if those qualifications are necessary to do a particular job. Models and actors, for example, may need to be a particular age or gender to do a particular job.

The government also created **affirmative action** plans that aim to provide access to jobs for those who suffered discrimination in the past and to give everyone a fair chance to compete in the working world. These plans, which continue to be the subject of intense debate, sometimes set numerical goals for the hiring of groups such as ethnic minorities, females, or people with disabilities.

Equal Rights on the Job

Look at *Figure 12-2,* which shows how the percentage of women in the workforce has grown. Before 1960, few women worked full-time, and those who did worked in positions not usually held by men. Now men and women often compete for the same jobs and aim for the same raises and promotions. Have you ever wondered how being a male or a female might affect your career?

Hilary Frye worked as a laborer with a landscaping company. One day she had lunch with a male coworker who casually mentioned his salary. Hilary was surprised to find that he was getting paid $3 an hour more than she was—for doing the same job with the same amount of experience for the same amount of time. Hilary was a victim of discrimination. **The Equal Pay Act of 1963** requires equal pay for equal work.

Sexual Harassment

Another gender-related problem in the workplace is **sexual harassment**—any unwelcome behavior of a sexual nature. Such behavior may include jokes, gestures,

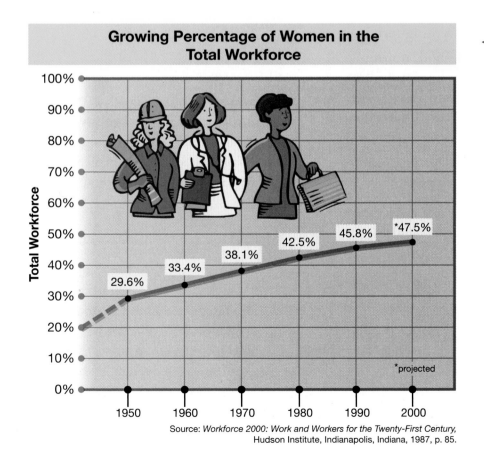

Growing Percentage of Women in the Total Workforce

29.6% 33.4% 38.1% 42.5% 45.8% *47.5%

*projected

Source: *Workforce 2000: Work and Workers for the Twenty-First Century,* Hudson Institute, Indianapolis, Indiana, 1987, p. 85.

 Figure 12-2

Women have steadily taken their places in the world of work since World War II. What do you predict will happen in terms of the percentage of women in the total workforce in the 21st century? Base your prediction on the pattern shown in this graph.

repeated or threatening requests for dates, and unwanted touching. Although most reported victims are female, males have also been the victims of sexual harassment.

Would you consider the following two examples cases of sexual harassment? Courts have declared that they are.

- A male worker's female boss told him that he could keep his job only if he started to date her.

- Female employees were "rated" by male employees, who also made comments about their physical appearance, as the women walked past the male employees' desks.

What if you feel you are the victim of sexual harassment? Here are some practical suggestions:

- Immediately tell the person to stop. Be clear and direct; don't assume the harassment will stop if you ignore it.

- Write down what happened, noting the date, time, and place. Include the names of any witnesses and your own comments about how the harassment directly affected your work.

- Inform a trusted supervisor or human resource officer of the incident.

Career Do's & Don'ts

When Protecting Your Legal Interests...

Do:
- be honest.
- voice any legal concerns as soon as possible.
- use company channels.
- deliver your company's part of any contract if it's part of your job.

Don't:
- be afraid of confrontation.
- take on someone else's battle.
- deny or cover up a potential legal problem.
- threaten legal action without first investigating all other options.

- If the issue is not resolved within your company, you can get help from your local human rights office or the office of the U.S. Equal Employment Opportunity Commission.

SECTION 12-1 *Review*

Understanding Key Concepts

Using complete sentences, answer the following questions on a separate sheet of paper.

1. Describe one law that is designed to establish and maintain fairness in the workplace.

2. How do employers benefit from hiring people over 40?

3. How does sexual harassment create problems in the workplace?

Exploring Careers: Construction

Dave Hiebert
Plumber

Q: **Why did you choose plumbing as a career?**

A: I actually got into it by accident. I answered an ad for a delivery person. That's how most people start out in the trade—driving a truck or working as a helper. They eventually work into the apprenticeship program.

Q: **Why did you stay in the field?**

A: It was the opportunity to do something mechanically minded. The second reason is that, as a plumber, I could go anywhere in the world and have a job.

Q: **What do you like about plumbing?**

A: Actually, there isn't a whole lot I don't like about it. I'm one of the few who absolutely love plumbing. I like the mechanical side of it. I love the problem solving. Additionally, by being a service plumber, I get to meet people.

Q: **What advice would you give someone who wanted to become a plumber?**

A: Be very attentive and be aggressive. By that, I mean always find something to do. Do not ever stand around. There are work ethics to our trade, which have been handed down from the older generation. If an experienced plumber happens to see you standing around, you won't go very far.

Thinking Critically

Why is problem-solving ability so critical to a plumber?

CAREER FACTS

Nature of the Work:
Solve plumbing problems; make repairs, often in small, cramped areas.

Training or Education Needed:
A four- to five-year apprenticeship; state licensing to become an experienced plumber; continuing education to maintain your license.

Aptitudes, Abilities, and Skills:
Math and listening skills; problem-solving skills; self-management skills; ability to work with your hands; physical stamina; mechanical aptitude; patience; ability to concentrate; communication skills.

Salary Range:
Experienced plumbers earn approximately $20 to $35 an hour, depending on the location.

Career Path:
Work as an apprentice; work for a plumbing firm; possibly start own business.

You and the Legal System

Most of us have recited the Pledge of Allegiance, which ends: "with liberty and justice for all." You have seen how labor laws strive to make these noble words a reality in the workplace, protecting workers and serving as a ballast in times of personal and social change. Many job-related situations, however, are not clear-cut or easily resolved. Therefore, one responsibility of the legal system is to provide a set of procedures for resolving conflicts. In court, lawyers, judges, and sometimes jurors make decisions about *disputes,* or disagreements, between employers and employees. It is important that you learn some basic facts about the law and how it affects you. As you become more responsible for your own actions, you will have more dealings with the law.

The Legal Battlefield

Many court cases involve **civil law,** which applies to conflicts between private parties, concerning rights and obligations. Divorce, custody battles, and personal injury cases all fall into this category. Companies may also become involved in civil law disputes. Here are a few examples of civil law cases:

- Tracy worked as a bank teller, and her employment contract stated that the company provided paid maternity leave. When she became pregnant, the bank fired her, claiming that it couldn't

 When a high court makes a decision about a labor law, it sets the standard for future cases. *How do you think this process helps laws keep up with changes in society?*

afford to pay for her benefits. According to civil law, the bank broke the contract and was *liable,* or responsible, for doing what it had originally promised.

- John, an accountant, sued his employer because he developed chronic bronchitis as a result of being placed in an office with several heavy smokers. The employer was found guilty of *negligence,* or disregard, of John's right to a smoke-free environment.

- Michael, an autoworker, was physically searched by his company's security guards, who suspected him of stealing. The guards found no stolen goods, and Michael's shoulder was bruised during the search, when he was shoved against a wall. A court found the company guilty of *deliberate* (purposeful) injury.

How do cases such as these move from the workplace to the courtroom? The process starts when a person files an official complaint with the court. The court clerk delivers a **summons,** or an order to appear in court, to the accused party. This person (or company) then files an answer.

For some business problems, small-claims court is an effective low-cost solution. *Small-claims court* is designed to handle minor disputes and small claims on debts. It does not require lawyers. Rules vary from state to state, but in general, small-claims court procedures and paperwork are less complicated than those in other courts.

Most people resolve their civil cases before they get to court. Opponents often come to a mutual agreement, or *settlement,* that does not state that either party is right or wrong. A settlement often takes

▶ **Figure 12-3**

Avoiding a Trial

The court system is overcrowded with cases. Taking advantage of other methods of settling disputes can save you time and money.

A Many states require workers to file a formal complaint with the Equal Employment Opportunity Commission or a similar agency. Sometimes these labor agencies can settle labor-management disputes.

B You may be able to settle a dispute by discussing it with your employer. Some companies have complaint procedures in place to handle legal problems between workers.

the form of a cash award or a correction of the situation that caused the complaint. Many states require that both sides in a civil case first try to settle out of court, thus avoiding trial. *Figure 12-3* explains still other ways to resolve civil disputes and avoid trials.

D *Mediation* is a process in which you and your opponent present the case to a neutral third person, who helps you both talk to each other and reach a compromise, or a settlement.

E Union disputes are often resolved through *arbitration*. Both sides present evidence and witnesses to an arbitrator, who issues a written decision, just as a judge or a jury would do.

C If your dispute involves less than $5,000, you may be able to go to small-claims court and argue your own case for a fee as low as $25. The judge's decision carries just as much weight as a state or federal court decision.

The employer and employee shown here with the employee's lawyer have just settled a dispute out of court. **Why might a company agree to pay an employee for damages rather than take the dispute before a judge and jury?**

Civil laws cover most workplace disputes, but sometimes incidents will occur on the job site that fall under criminal law. Under **criminal law,** the government brings an *indictment,* or list of charges, against a person or a business. The charges state that a crime, such as assault or fraud, has been committed. A serious crime punishable by imprisonment or death, such as murder or rape, is called a **felony.** A less serious crime is called a **misdemeanor** and could be anything from shoplifting to striking another worker during a dispute.

Using Legal Services

If you have tried to solve a problem too big for small-claims court and feel that other legal action is the only answer, then your best bet is to contact a lawyer. Laws are very complex, and legal procedures are often confusing. It usually takes an expert to argue a case in court.

Finding a Lawyer

If you had a cavity, you wouldn't dream of going to an eye doctor to get it taken care of. One doctor isn't the same as another. Similarly, you'll want to take your legal problem to a lawyer with just the right specialty. To start your search, try the following:

- Use your phone book to find legal referral services. The local bar association and your state's chapter of the Association of Trial Lawyers of America are possible sources of help.

- Ask friends and family members if they know any lawyers. These contacts may lead you to others.

Many lawyers will have an initial meeting with you before charging you a

ETHICS in Action

Although you are a minor, you and a neighbor have entered into an oral work contract. You have agreed to do certain repair work, and the neighbor has agreed to pay you a set amount. However, after you've done the work, your neighbor refuses to pay you. What steps are you willing to take toward your neighbor?

The media often cover exciting criminal court cases. *Why do you think people are often so interested in criminal cases?*

fee. Use this opportunity to interview a lawyer carefully. Is the lawyer efficient and organized? Does he or she have the kind of experience you need? Do you feel you can trust this person?

Lawyers' Fees

Lawyers generally charge an hourly rate or set a flat fee based on how much work they expect to do for you. Some lawyers work for a **contingency fee.** This means that they take as payment a percentage of any money that you win in the lawsuit. Make sure you understand the fee system and projected costs before you agree to anything. Legal advice can be expensive.

Low-cost legal assistance in civil cases may be available from the Legal Aid Society. In criminal cases, the office of the public defender can provide free legal representation.

No matter where you go for legal advice, be prepared for the meeting:

bring documents, records, and names of witnesses. Remember, too, that legal proceedings can take a very long time—months or even years.

YOU'RE THE BOSS!

Solving Workplace Problems

You are the owner of a busy convenience store. When you witness one of your part-time employees, a high school student, taking money from the cash register, you fire him but agree not to file criminal charges. Then the student's father calls. He's irate that his son has been fired, and threatens to sue you. What will you do?

SECTION 12-2 *Review*

Understanding Key Concepts

Using complete sentences, answer the following questions on a separate sheet of paper.

1. Why might you want to resolve a civil case out of court rather than through a trial?

2. Describe a workplace situation that could lead to a civil case and one that could lead to a criminal case.

3. Do you think it is a good idea to defend your own case in court? Why or why not?

Key Terms

minimum wage *(p. 234)*
compensatory time *(p. 235)*
collective bargaining
    (p. 236)
discrimination *(p. 237)*
affirmative action *(p. 238)*
sexual harassment *(p. 239)*

SECTION 12-1 Summary

- Labor laws set basic rules for fair treatment in the workplace.

- Labor unions organize workers and bargain with employers to protect workers' rights.

- Labor and employment laws help employees deal with medical and financial emergencies.

- Antidiscrimination laws protect workers from job discrimination based on factors such as race, religion, age, gender, and disability.

- The government creates programs to help employers put antidiscrimination laws into action.

- Sexual harassment is unwelcome behavior of a sexual nature. If you experience harassment, you should take immediate steps to deal with it.

Key Terms

civil law *(p. 242)*
summons *(p. 244)*
criminal law *(p. 246)*
felony *(p. 246)*
misdemeanor *(p. 246)*
contingency fee *(p. 248)*

SECTION 12-2 Summary

- The legal system—with its courts, judges, and lawyers—provides a set of procedures for resolving conflicts.

- Civil law applies to conflicts between private parties, such as an employee and a company, concerning rights and obligations.

- There are several ways to resolve a civil dispute without going to trial, including mediation and arbitration.

- Criminal law involves cases in which the government charges a person or a business with committing a crime. More serious offenses are called felonies, and less serious offenses are called misdemeanors.

- If you need to take legal action, consider going to small-claims court or hire a lawyer. Before you hire a lawyer, search carefully for the best person, make sure you understand what the fees will be, and provide all pertinent information to the lawyer you choose.

Reviewing Key Terms

You are interviewing a lawyer who specializes in labor and employment law. On a separate sheet of paper, write out a list of questions, using each of the following terms.

minimum wage
compensatory
   time
collective
   bargaining
discrimination
affirmative
   action

sexual
   harassment
civil law
criminal law
summons
felony
misdemeanor
contingency fee

Recalling Key Concepts

On a separate sheet of paper, tell whether each statement is true or false. Rewrite any false statements to make them true.

1. The minimum wage has remained the same since it was first created.

2. Antidiscrimination laws protect certain groups of citizens from unfair employment practices.

3. Sexual harassment is any unwelcome behavior of a sexual nature.

4. Civil law refers to charges the government brings against a person.

5. You do not need to hire a lawyer if you are taking a case to a court other than small-claims court.

Thinking Critically

Using complete sentences, answer each of the following questions on a separate sheet of paper.

1. Why are antidiscrimination laws important?

2. How could effective communication skills help you defend yourself against an unfair situation at work?

3. How might sexual harassment interfere with a person's career advancement?

4. Explain the difference between criminal law and civil law.

5. Give an example of a case that you might take to small-claims court.

SCANS Foundation Skills and Workplace Competencies

Basic Skills: *Reading and Writing*

1. Working in a team of three, locate and read several articles on sexual harassment in the workplace. Together, create a list of do's and don'ts for a fair and comfortable business environment.

Thinking Skills: *Problem Solving*

2. Working in a group of three, come up with an imaginary dispute that requires arbitration. Decide who will be the arbitrator, and have the other two group members defend their side of the dispute. After listening to both arguments, the arbitrator should make a judgment in favor of one side, explaining his or her reasons. Then switch roles until all group members have had a chance to play arbitrator.

Connecting Academics to the Workplace

Language Arts

1. Tamika is applying for a job. On the application form, she is asked the following questions:
   - Where were you born?
   - How much do you weigh?
   - Do you plan to have children?

   Explain why it would be a violation of antidiscrimination laws for the employer to base an employment decision on Tamika's answers to these questions.

Social Studies

2. Labor laws have played a major role in American history and culture. Choose one aspect of the world of work—such as hours, wages, child labor, minorities, unions, safety, benefits, or pollution—and research one federal or state law that has affected that aspect. Report to the class on what conditions were like before the law existed and how conditions changed after the law was passed.

Developing Teamwork and Leadership Skills

Working with a small group, develop a short handbook for employers that will show their legal responsibilities in terms of hiring and promotion practices as well as labor issues. Conduct research as needed to find additional facts about an employer's legal responsibilities. Present the handbook in an easy-to-use format.

Real-World Workshop

Using the phone book or the Internet, locate the local branch of a state or federal labor organization such as the Department of Labor or the Equal Employment Opportunity Commission. Research the procedures for filing a claim by either visiting the appropriate office or requesting information over the telephone. Report your findings to the class.

School-to-Work Connection

Arrange a visit to a state or federal courthouse, and sit in on a trial. You can do this by writing a letter to the court clerk or by calling the courthouse. (Check the telephone book's government pages under "Courts.") Take notes on the court process, indicating at least four career opportunities in the court system.

Individual Career Plan

The law states that all new employees must fill out an I-9 form to prove their eligibility to work. When you fill out this form, you will be asked for three forms of identification. Conduct research to find out what identification is required, and gather the various cards and papers you could present. The Immigration and Naturalization Service, part of the Justice Department, can provide information.

ASPECTS OF INDUSTRY:
Health, Safety, and Environmental Issues

Overview

In Unit Four, you read about starting a new job and the ethics and proper attitude that will sustain you throughout your working career. You also began to look into some of the health, safety, and legal issues that arise in the workplace. In this Unit Lab, you will use what you have learned while exploring another aspect of industry: **Health, Safety, and Environmental Issues.**

The Health, Safety, and Environmental Issues aspect of industry covers an employee's health, safety, and environment while at work. It also covers how businesses affect the health, safety, and environment of the community at large.

Tools

1. Internet
2. Trade, health, environmental, and business magazines
3. Newspapers

Procedures

STEP A

Choose one of the 15 job clusters shown in Figure 3-1 in Chapter 3. You may choose the same cluster you explored in the previous Lab, or a different one.

Choose one job in the job cluster that you would seriously think about pursuing. Use trade, health and environmental magazines, newspapers, and the Internet to pinpoint a health, safety, or environmental issue that affects workers in that industry. Examples of some issues might be the use of chemicals, working high above the ground, or working with computers.

Next, pinpoint a health, safety, or environmental issue in the industry you have chosen that affects the community at large. Some issues might be hazardous waste disposal policies, building standards, or air pollution.

Keep copies of the articles you find. You may want to refer to them later when you write your Report.

STEP B

Find and research two local companies that employ people in the job you've chosen. Choose companies that have a positive record in dealing with health, safety, and environmental issues.

Contact the person at each company who is in charge of worker safety or community relations, probably someone in the personnel department for employee issues. Ask permission to do a 20- to 30-minute interview for a class project.

Some of the questions you might ask about employee working conditions are:

1. What situations on the job might affect a worker's health or safety?

2. What steps does the company take to ensure employees' health and safety? (Thorough training? Safety equipment?)

Some questions you might ask about the affect of the industry on the community are:

1. How might the work of the industry affect the health, safety, and environment of the community?

2. What steps does the company take to minimize risk to the community?

Use the same interview etiquette in this Lab as in the previous Labs. Be prompt, courteous, and send a thank-you letter.

REPORT

Write a one-page, word-processed report using the information you gathered in your research, interview, and team discussion.

● Does the attitude of the industry you've chosen toward worker health and safety correspond to the conditions under which you want to work? Is this an industry-wide attitude? How would you feel about working for the company you interviewed, or the industry in general?

● Does the industry's attitude toward public safety correspond to your values? Explain.

Keep your research, interview notes, and report in a folder entitled "Career Exploration."

UNIT 5

Professional Development

UNIT 5 QUIZ:

What Do You Know About Professional Development?

- What does it take to get along with coworkers?
- How do you create an effective team?
- What makes a great leader?
- How are communication skills used in the workplace?
- How would you handle decisions and problems people face every day in the workplace?
- How is technology used in the workplace?
- What is the secret to managing your time and information?

255

Chapter 13

Interpersonal Relationships at Work

Section 13-1
Your Personal Traits at Work

Section 13-2
Applying Interpersonal Skills

In this video segment, learn how to get along with others in the workplace.

Journal
Personal Career Plan

Imagine yourself working full-time in the career of your choice, and consider the people with whom you'll come in contact. In your journal, write a list of the traits you hope to find in those people. Then respond to these questions: Which of those listed traits do you have? Which should you try to develop?

Your Personal Traits at Work

What do you think is the most important workplace skill? According to a recent survey, many employees believe it is "getting along with others at work." Whether you're working already or beginning to plan your career, you need to think about your relationships with coworkers.

If you develop good interpersonal relationships with your coworkers, you'll enjoy your time at work more. After all, think of all the hours you'll be spending together. In addition, you'll be able to do your job more successfully. By showing a willingness to cooperate with your coworkers, you'll probably receive their cooperation in return.

What can you do to develop good relationships with your coworkers? Begin by assessing your own traits. (Look back at the work you did in Chapter 2 on getting to know yourself.) What traits do you already have that help you work well with other people? What traits do you need to develop?

Important Personal Traits

The personal traits that help you get along with others at your job are the same ones that help you at school or in social situations. As you learned in Chapters 9 and 10, the following SCANS skills are important personal qualities for the workplace:

- *Responsibility*, including dependability and positive motivation;
- *Self-esteem*, including confidence;

By cooperating with one another, these employees get their job done efficiently. *How can working well with others help you in your career?*

- *Sociability*, including friendliness, enthusiasm, adaptability, and respect for other workers;
- *Self-management*, including self-control and **tact**, the ability to say and do things in a way that will not offend other people; and
- *Integrity/Honesty*, including loyalty and trustworthiness.

Self-Awareness on the Job

Understanding your own unique blend of qualities can help you adjust to new work situations. If you are self-aware, you know not only your strengths but also the traits you need to improve.

Tracy Kagan of Miami, Florida, learned a great deal about her personal traits when she changed jobs at the same restaurant. After working for two years as a server, Tracy was promoted to assistant manager. While she had been well liked as a server, Tracy was not popular when she first became an assistant manager.

"I wasn't confident that I could handle my responsibilities," she explains. In her nervousness, she yelled at the cooks and criticized servers in front of customers. Fortunately, Tracy's supervisor recognized the problem. She spoke with Tracy about her need to control her emotions and to be tactful. Still, changing was not easy.

"Whenever I felt pressured, I had to remind myself to be polite," Tracy says.

Tracy needed help from her supervisor to improve her personal traits at work. *Why is it important to be able to listen to constructive criticism?*

"I made it a habit to take a deep breath when I felt myself getting upset. Then I'd smile."

In time, Tracy developed her self-management skills. Now she enjoys her job and has won back the respect of her coworkers.

Figure 13-1

Four Steps to Self-Improvement

Self-improvement takes time and effort. The process involves a series of clearly defined steps.

Improving Your Personal Traits

Can you improve yourself? Of course you can. One of the most successful people in American history—Benjamin Franklin—used a notebook to keep track of how effectively he practiced the personal qualities he wanted to improve. Each day he'd write notes for himself about such traits as justice, diligence, and sincerity.

Step 2 **Draw up a plan and stick to it.** Kylor makes a list of several things he can do on a regular basis to help out around the house. He makes sure he takes responsibility for at least one chore each day.

Step 1 **Zero in on one trait at a time.** Kylor is confident that he is sociable and honest. He's decided that he needs to focus on becoming more responsible, however.

Look back at the list of important personal traits on pages 258–259. In your journal, write down which traits you think are your strong points and which you would like to improve. **Figure 13-1** shows four steps to self-improvement and how one person put them into action.

Becoming an Effective Coworker

Remember the "upward spirals" you read about in Chapter 10? Here's another one: By developing your positive traits, you will be better able to get along with your coworkers. By getting along with your coworkers, you will be more effective at your job. By being more effective at your job, you will be more likely to advance in your career.

Being effective—that is, getting a job done quickly and well—seldom happens in isolation. Within the workplace, you'll find that effectiveness comes about when workers cooperate with one another. Four interpersonal behaviors are essential for being an effective coworker: respect, understanding, communication, and good humor.

Step 3 **Keep track of your progress.** Kylor checks his progress each night by keeping a record of every responsibility he's fulfilled that day. He also writes notes to himself about areas in which he might do better. Once a week he asks his family, "How am I doing?"

Step 4 **Move on.** Once Kylor feels that he has made progress in becoming more responsible, he starts to work on improving another trait. He has decided to work on boosting his self-esteem by reading to students in a local elementary school.

Respecting Others

Without mutual respect, there can be little cooperation in the workplace. Which two negative traits do you think do the most to prevent respect? One is an "I'm-better-than-you" attitude. The other negative trait is jealousy.

An "I'm-better-than-you" attitude is simply the idea that you are superior to someone else. Remember that each worker—no matter what his or her job may be—has something important to contribute. Any job well done grants dignity to the worker who performs it.

Jealousy can act like a poison in the workplace. Workers who become jealous of their coworkers view them as rivals. They withhold respect, and cooperation becomes more difficult—a downward spiral. A jealous worker refuses to admit that coworkers may have worked more effectively and deserve raises or promotions.

Remember that respect is a two-way street. In most cases, the more you give, the more you'll gain in return.

Understanding Others

You don't have to have a deep understanding of your coworkers in order to work well together. Instead, you can develop understanding by being an interested observer.

Career Do's & Don'ts

To Delegate Effectively...

Do:
- assign tasks you've already mastered.
- pick associates with the skills for the job.
- make sure delegated assignments benefit the organization.
- specify what you want done, in writing if necessary.

Don't:
- give others work just to keep them busy.
- hover over their shoulders, watching every move.
- wait until the deadline to follow up.
- dwell on mistakes without offering positive guidance for the future.

People show their feelings through body language, whether they mean to or not. *What kind of message is the woman on the right conveying? What leads you to this conclusion?*

- Notice the personal traits of your coworkers.

- Ask your coworkers about their short-term and long-term career goals.

- Try to **empathize** with your coworkers—that is, try to see things from their point of view and to gain an understanding of their situation.

- Pay attention to your coworkers' body language—how their physical actions express emotions. Be alert to facial expressions, which very often give clues to a person's inner feelings.

EXCELLENT BUSINESS PRACTICES

Networking

American Express Financial Advisors, of Minneapolis, Minnesota, sees so much value in networking that it has developed official employee networks. The groups represent the diversity of the company of 650 employees.

To receive official status, the networks present a formal mission statement to the company. The company provides each network with $5,000 to create relationships with nonprofit organizations that represent the network's mission. These may include a partnership with a museum, a special health-care interest, or other community services.

The program enhances awareness of different cultures and promotes diversity. It supports the special interests of employees and is an opportunity for the company to serve the community directly. Networking also is a means of making contacts, learning about an industry, and cultivating relationships with other people in the community who have similar interests and values.

Thinking Critically

How can participating in the same special-interest group help develop a relationship with a coworker?

convey information promptly and clearly can disrupt a project. It can make everyone on the team look bad.

Don't be reluctant to speak up and ask a coworker or supervisor for help if you need it. Remember that being effective means producing results. A coworker can often provide the guidance you'll need to overcome problems and get the job done.

Communicating, however, does not mean talking about your private life. You can be warm and friendly without revealing personal secrets. In the workplace, it's better to spend time discussing work-related matters.

Communicating with Others

Communication, like respect, is a two-way street. How you listen is as important as what you say. Both listening and speaking well are especially important when you are working as part of a team. If you don't listen well, you won't benefit from being part of the team. Failure to

Keep Smiling!

Your sense of humor can carry you—and your coworkers—through times of stress. It can also help unite a team and make people feel better about themselves. You don't have to be a comedian. Just try to find ways to see the light side of a situation.

SECTION 13-1 *Review*

Understanding Key Concepts

Using complete sentences, answer the following questions on a separate sheet of paper.

1. Describe a situation in which you effectively applied one of the SCANS skills listed on page 258–259. What did you learn from this experience?

2. Which of the four interpersonal behaviors discussed in this section do you think is the most important? Why?

Exploring Careers: Family and Consumer Services

Rose Johnson
Automotive Customer Service Adviser

Q: How did you become a service adviser?

A: I had a broken-down car and no money to fix it. I'm good with my hands, so I figured out how to fix my car myself. When I went to the community college, I trained to be an automotive technician. However, I realized I would be physically unable to do that kind of work for a long time.

Q: So you switched to service advising?

A: Dealerships are reluctant to give that kind of position to someone just out of college. So I started out washing cars and moving them around the lot. As a cashier, I learned computer skills. Later, as a dispatcher, I scheduled up to 100 cars a day, making sure they were done on time. From there, I moved to the position of service adviser.

Q: What skills are most important in your work?

A: It's necessary to know about cars. That's the most helpful skill in giving advice to customers. If customers hear doubt in your voice, they are doubtful about your advice. Computer skills, math skills, and good phone etiquette are also important. You have to be able to work long hours—up to 11 hours a day, 5 days a week. You have to be very detail-oriented. There's no room for mistakes. You have to be able to deal with people. It's a big race every day to get everything done.

Thinking Critically

What would make an automotive service adviser's work stressful?

CAREER FACTS

Nature of the Work:
Write up estimates for car repairs; handle customer complaints and problems.

Training or Education Needed:
Training on the job or through a community college.

Aptitudes, Abilities, and Skills:
Math, listening, speaking, and interpersonal skills; reading and writing skills; problem-solving skills; self-management skills; ability to manage people.

Salary Range:
Combination of base pay and commission; average starting earnings—$18,000; with experience, average top earnings—$50,000.

Career Path:
Work your way up through the industry from car washing to advising about auto service; move up to service manager.

Applying Interpersonal Skills

OBJECTIVES

After studying this section, you will be able to:

- Understand and practice proper workplace etiquette.
- Understand and practice effective methods of conflict resolution.
- Appreciate and increase sensitivity to diversity in the workplace.

KEY TERMS

etiquette
conflict resolution
diversity
stereotype

Etiquette may sound more like something you need to have at a wedding than at the workplace. However, **etiquette** really just means having good manners in your dealings with people.

How do you identify the right behavior for your workplace? First, use common sense. Treat people as you would want them to treat you. When in doubt, observe experienced and well-liked workers who are successful in their jobs. How do they conduct themselves at work? What do they do to get along with other people? What kinds of actions or responses do they avoid?

Workplace Etiquette

Here are a few basic do's and don'ts of etiquette that apply to all workplaces:

- *Be courteous.* Greet your coworkers when you come to work, and address people by name whenever you can. Don't interrupt private conversations, and don't talk so loudly that you disturb other people, especially those working near you. Avoid tying up equipment that other people may need to use.

- *Dress appropriately.* Whether your job has a dress code or not, you should wear neat, clean clothes. As a new employee, don't use your wardrobe or hairstyle to attract attention. Let your on-the-job performance speak for itself.

- *Be punctual.* Be at work on time, arrive at meetings promptly, and meet your deadlines. If you promise someone that you'll call at a certain time, be sure to keep your word.

- *Avoid workplace gossip.* Gossiping wastes valuable work time and can result in the spread of false or hurtful rumors. Gossiping is just plain unprofessional.

Respecting Privacy

Workplace etiquette also involves respecting your coworkers' privacy. This concerns more than not listening in on telephone calls and private conversations.

- *Faxes, E-mail, and voice mail.* Treat these means of electronic communication as you would treat private mail. Don't read or listen to them unless they are addressed to you.

- *Computers.* Sharing a computer with a coworker does not give you the right to examine or alter files that

you have not created—unless you have permission.

- *Shared office space.* Respect your coworkers' private spaces. Never look in a locker, file cabinet, or desk that is not your own.

Working with Your Supervisor

If you treat your supervisor with the same proper respect and courtesy that you do your coworkers, you should get along well. Naturally, however, you face the added element of wanting—and needing—your supervisor's approval. Here are some things you can do to develop and maintain a good working relationship with your supervisor:

- Deal with any criticism from your supervisor in an objective and professional manner. Do not get defensive.

- Practice initiative instead of bothering your supervisor with details that do not need his or her approval.

- Whenever you can, offer to help your supervisor.

- If you have a work-related complaint, discuss it with your supervisor. Be prepared, however, to suggest your own solution.

Conflict Resolution

Even when coworkers practice mutual courtesy and respect, it is a rare workplace that does not experience tension from time to time. When conflicts arise in the workplace, you will have to decide how to deal with them.

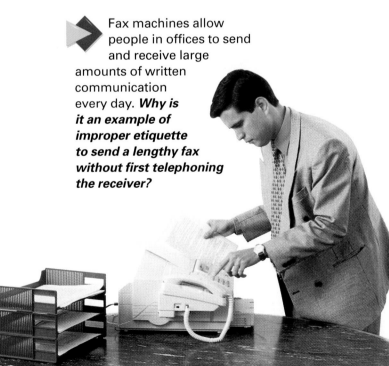

Fax machines allow people in offices to send and receive large amounts of written communication every day. **Why is it an example of improper etiquette to send a lengthy fax without first telephoning the receiver?**

Steps in Conflict Resolution

Define the problem

Each party takes a turn describing the problem from his or her point of view. Participants should show respect for each other.

Suggest a solution

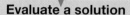
Each party suggests a solution to the problem.

Evaluate a solution

The solutions are discussed. Each party explains the part of a suggestion that (1) they agree with and (2) they cannot accept.

Compromise

If the parties are fairly close to agreeing, they may *compromise,* or settle the dispute by each agreeing to give something up.

Think creatively

If the parties cannot compromise, they brainstorm different ways to approach the problem and try again to reach a compromise.

Seek mediation

If no solution is reached, the parties invite a third party to listen and make suggestions.

Seek arbitration

The method of arbitration is used when the parties agree that a solution must be found but cannot agree on what the solution should be. The parties submit the conflict to a third party who will make the final decision. The parties agree beforehand to abide by the arbitrator's decision.

▲ **Figure 13-2** Conflict resolution is a way for the people involved in a dispute to work out a solution to their problem. They try to work together to bring the conflict to an end. Why do you think this diagram shows a choice of steps for finding a resolution?

As a worker, you may find yourself involved in a process called **conflict resolution.** This is a problem-solving strategy for settling disputes. Its aim is to find a solution that will allow each side to "save face" and leave the least amount of ill-feeling. *Figure 13-2* shows the steps in this strategy.

Remember that conflict resolution focuses on the issues, not on the personalities of the people involved. How can you best prepare yourself for conflict resolution in the workplace? You can do so by practicing your communication and problem-solving skills in school and in the minor disputes you may have with friends.

Diversity in the Workplace

The United States has always been a nation of **diversity**, or variety, where each group contributes something special. In most workplaces in this country, many different kinds of people come together for a common purpose—to get a job done and to earn a living. ***Figure 13-3*** shows how the U.S. population is expected to continue to become more diverse.

Embracing this diversity is one way to discourage conflict at work. How can you accomplish this? Begin by showing respect for cultural differences as well as for differences in religion, age, gender, and viewpoint. Embracing diversity in the workplace is a way of acknowledging that you are part of a community of workers with common needs and goals. It's also a way to broaden your understanding—and perhaps make some exciting discoveries as well.

Overcoming Stereotypes

To succeed in a diverse workplace, workers need to look beyond stereotypes of groups of people. A **stereotype** is an oversimplified and distorted belief about a person or group. The danger of thinking in stereotypes is that it does not allow for individuality. In addition, it encourages an "us versus them" mentality.

How can you get along with a diverse group of people? As in any group situation, respect, understanding, and communication are important. In addition, you'll need to develop a sensitivity to your coworkers' different situations. Many businesses

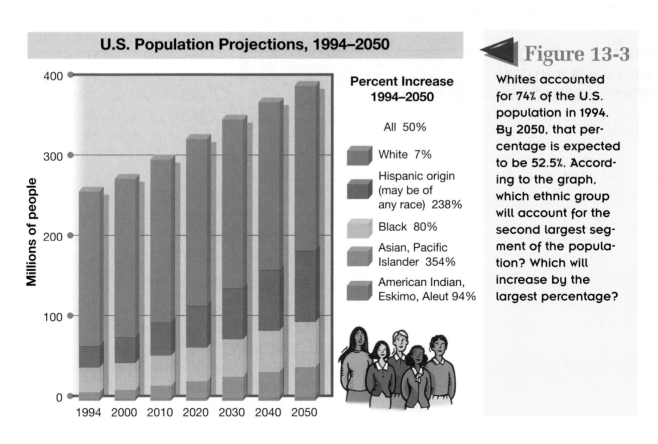

U.S. Population Projections, 1994–2050

Millions of people

400
300
200
100
0

1994 2000 2010 2020 2030 2040 2050

Percent Increase 1994–2050

All 50%

White 7%

Hispanic origin (may be of any race) 238%

Black 80%

Asian, Pacific Islander 354%

American Indian, Eskimo, Aleut 94%

Figure 13-3

Whites accounted for 74% of the U.S. population in 1994. By 2050, that percentage is expected to be 52.5%. According to the graph, which ethnic group will account for the second largest segment of the population? Which will increase by the largest percentage?

today sponsor diversity training programs to help employees overcome stereotyping in the following areas.

- *Cultural distinctions.* People from different ethnic backgrounds have different customs. What's polite in one society may be rude in another, such as certain gestures or forms of address. It's important

to remember, however, that cultural blunders happen even among the best-intentioned people. Learn by reading and observing, and apologize if you are unintentionally impolite.

- *Gender distinctions.* Effective coworkers have mutual respect for members of the other sex. It is not sexist to acknowledge that women and men may have different styles of working and interacting. It is wrong—and illegal—however, to harass anyone because of his or her gender.

- *Generational distinctions.* People of one age group sometimes feel they have little in common with other age groups. As a young person, you may have a different point of view from someone several years older than you. You can bridge the difference by listening carefully to the other person's point of view and finding ideas on which you can agree.

Overcoming stereotypes can lead to good working relationships. *How can getting along with different people at work affect other aspects of your life?*

SECTION 13-2 *Review*

Understanding Key Concepts

Using complete sentences, answer the following questions on a separate sheet of paper.

1. How does technology affect etiquette in the workplace? Give an example.

2. Why is creative thinking an important part of conflict resolution?

3. Why are respect, understanding, and communication especially important in a diverse workplace?

Key Terms

tact *(p. 259)*
empathize *(p. 263)*

SECTION 13-1 Summary

- Getting along with your coworkers means you will have greater job satisfaction and enjoy your time at work more.

- Personal traits you need to develop to get along with your coworkers include responsibility, self-esteem, sociability, self-management, and integrity/honesty.

- To improve your personal qualities, work on one trait at a time, devise a plan for working on the trait, check your progress, and then proceed to work on other traits.

- To be an effective coworker, you need to respect others, try to understand them, communicate well, and maintain a sense of humor.

Key Terms

etiquette *(p. 266)*
conflict resolution *(p. 268)*
diversity *(p. 269)*
stereotype *(p. 269)*

SECTION 13-2 Summary

- Basic etiquette in the workplace includes being courteous, dressing appropriately, being punctual, and avoiding gossip. Etiquette also includes respecting your coworkers' privacy.

- You can develop and maintain a good working relationship with your supervisor by dealing with criticism objectively, practicing initiative, offering your help, and suggesting solutions to problems.

- When trying to resolve a conflict, discuss issues, not people. When compromise is not possible, creative thinking may lead to a solution. Mediation and arbitration are other possible ways to arrive at solutions.

- The U.S. workplace is diverse, and workers need to be sensitive to cultural, gender, and generational differences.

Reviewing Key Terms

On a separate sheet of paper, write one or two paragraphs on getting along with coworkers. Use the terms below in your paragraph(s).

tact · conflict resolution
empathize · diversity
etiquette · stereotype

Recalling Key Concepts

On a separate sheet of paper, tell whether each statement is true or false. Rewrite any false statements to make them true.

1. The personal traits that help you get along with others at your job are different from the ones that help you in school or in social situations.

2. Effective coworkers display respect, understanding, and good communication skills.

3. It is acceptable to read a fax that arrives for a coworker because the fax machine is there for everyone to use.

4. When you compromise to resolve a conflict, you let the other person have his or her way.

5. Being sensitive to diversity helps overcome stereotyping.

Thinking Critically

Using complete sentences, answer each of the questions below on a separate sheet of paper.

1. How are the personal traits of responsibility and self-management related to each other?

2. Identify two sources of praise you might receive in the workplace and two sources of criticism. Tell how you would respond to each.

3. When trying to improve yourself, why should you work on one trait at a time?

4. Why does conflict resolution focus on the problem rather than the personality of the opposing person?

5. Describe how you might broaden your perspectives by communicating with others in a diverse workplace.

SCANS Foundation Skills and Workplace Competencies

Personal Qualities: *Self-Management*

1. Write a one-page paper on why it is important to control emotions in the workplace. Discuss ways that emotions can be channeled properly to allow people to work together effectively. Within the paper, note possible consequences of lack of emotional control.

Interpersonal Skills: *Working with Diversity*

2. Research some of the cultural differences between your culture and that of another country. Focus on differences that affect the workplace. Summarize your findings for the class.

Connecting Academics to the Workplace

Computer Science

1. Imagine that you are an employee in an office that has just acquired new

word-processing software. Luckily for you, it's a program you are familiar with. Describe steps you would take to teach a coworker to use it. Keep in mind that this coworker is much older than you and has limited knowledge of computers.

Human Relations

2. Brittany is an administrative assistant in a human resources department. Her supervisor wants to develop a checklist of positive attitudes for the workplace. He has asked Brittany to submit a list of her own. Draw up a list that Brittany could submit to her supervisor. In addition, make a list of attitudes to avoid.

Math

3. Stephen works in a busy music store at a mall. Part of his job is to check the addition on purchase orders before they are sent to the distributor. Stephen's coworker, Max, suggests that he make a rough estimate before adding the prices on a calculator. Stephen thinks estimating is a waste of time. Imagine that you are Max, and explain to Stephen why estimating helps accuracy.

Developing Teamwork and Leadership Skills

To gain insight into interpersonal relationships, observe how you work with your fellow students. With a small group of students, plan and make a pamphlet or other visual presentation that describes personal qualities people need to be part of a successful team. Examine your own teamwork

on this project, and include that information in your presentation.

Real-World Workshop

Working in a group of three, find and read one article or book chapter on conflict resolution. Then, with other group members, create a realistic workplace conflict situation. Role-play how this conflict might be resolved successfully, using information from your textbook and the outside resource that you found. Present your role-play to the class.

School-to-Work Connection

Set up an informational interview with a manager working in a career field that interests you. Choose a workplace that employs 25 or more people. Ask the manager to explain the diversity of his or her workplace and provide details about how that diversity benefits workers and the business. Question the supervisor about ways this particular workplace has encouraged diversity and what procedures are in place for handling problems that may arise. Present a report on your interview to the class.

Individual Career Plan

Write a thank-you letter to the manager you interviewed for the School-to-Work Connection activity. Describe the positive things you learned during the interview, and express your appreciation of the way the workplace is working to encourage diversity.

Chapter 14

Teamwork and Leadership

Section 14-1
Teamwork

Section 14-2
Leadership

In this video segment, discover how teamwork benefits everyone in the workplace.

Journal
Personal Career Plan

Think about your recent group activities in school or at work. In most situations, are you more comfortable as a group leader or as a cooperative group member? Why? Record your ideas in your journal.

Teamwork

OBJECTIVES

After studying this section, you will be able to:

- **Explain how teamwork benefits both team members and businesses.**
- **Describe the steps involved in team planning.**
- **Identify common obstacles to team success.**
- **Define** *total quality management* **and discuss its effect on workers.**

KEY TERMS

self-directed
functional team
cross-functional
  team
team planning
facilitator
total quality
  management
  (TQM)

Have you ever worked in a cooperative learning group at school? A learning group is one type of team. This is a group of people who work together to reach a common goal. Working as a team member in school will prepare you for today's business world.

Teamwork in Business

Today, businesses rely more and more on teams of workers to get jobs done. Once, such teamwork was rare. For example, in the past, automobile assembly-line workers did just one task. They might attach a radiator or put on a door. They would perform the same job over and over again. Today, workers are more likely to be part of a team. Teams work together to complete an entire phase of production. Members of such teams share the responsibilities and the rewards of their efforts.

Some teams are supervised by managers. Others are **self-directed,** or responsible for choosing their own methods for reaching their goals. Self-directed teams work without supervision. If you were a member of such a team, you might work without a manager from the start to the finish of a lengthy project.

Why Businesses Encourage Teamwork

Companies have found that teamwork pays off. It's good for team members and for businesses. Why? Teams tend to be more productive than the same number of employees working separately. Greater productivity means greater profits. Other business benefits include:

- improved quality and customer service,
- increased employee morale, and
- fewer layers of management.

Individual workers also benefit from being part of a team. Workers report the following rewards:

- *Greater job satisfaction.* Teams often rotate tasks among members. This variety reduces boredom and allows each team member to develop an array of skills.

- *Improved self-esteem.* As a rule, each team member is given the authority to help make and carry out decisions. Many team members report that the most satisfying part of their jobs is feeling in charge of their own work. Of course, team members must be *self-starters.* They have to work without always being told what to do.

- *Better communication.* Here's an extra bonus. When people work in a team, they've got to talk. As a result, they get to know each other better.

Career Do's & Don'ts

To Become a Leader...

Do:

- get involved.
- expand your boundaries beyond your job description.
- cultivate your intuition.
- earn the respect of your peers first; respect from higher-ups will follow.

Don't:

- be controlling.
- be afraid of taking risks.
- be a perfectionist.
- discard established practices—work within the system.

ter. Workers learn about each other's behavior, attitudes, and ways of thinking. They get along better and are not so quick to judge one another. Tension and conflict among workers are reduced.

These students are working on a science project. *Why do you think their teacher requires them to work in teams?*

The members of this team are from a variety of national and ethnic backgrounds. *How might their working on a team benefit their company?*

Types of Teams

On a business team, you may work with as many as 9 or 10 other people. As *Figure 14-1* shows, your team will be either a **cross-functional team** or a **functional team.**

Team Planning

Imagine that you and your friends have decided to throw a surprise birthday party. If each of you goes ahead and does what you think should be done, the result may be chaos. If, however, you plan who will send invitations, set up decorations, be in charge of music, and buy the food, the result will probably be a great party.

The same goes for running a successful team project at work. Before you start, make a plan. Since you will be working as a team, plan as a team. **Team planning** involves setting goals, assigning roles, and communicating regularly.

Setting Goals

Do you remember the personal career goals you set in Chapter 5? When you work in a team, think about group goals. Your company's overall goal, or *mission,* is a place to start.

Figure 14-1

Two Types of Business Teams

	Definition	Examples
Functional Team	A group of people from one company department or area of expertise, working together to reach a common business goal	• Six architects designing a building complex for an architectural firm • Seven chemists developing a cold medicine for a medical laboratory
Cross-Functional Team	A group of people from two or more departments or areas of expertise, working together to reach a common business goal	• A building maintenance supervisor, two bricklayers, a landscaper, and a financial officer planning the gardens around a company's new headquarters

Cross-functional teams are becoming more and more common in the business world. What is an advantage of a cross-functional team?

A company's mission includes its purpose and values. It can often be stated in one sentence. For example, Volkswagen's mission statement is "to provide an economical means of private transportation."

Keep your company's mission in mind. Then set short-, medium-, and long-term project goals. Imagine that you are working on a team for a sportswear company. Your goals might include the following:

- **Short-term goal:** Analyze the team's procedure for assembling jackets.

- **Medium-term goal:** Figure out more efficient procedures.

- **Long-term goal:** Produce more jackets in less time.

As you know from reading Chapter 5, the best way to approach a large project is to use "stepping-stone goals." First, break

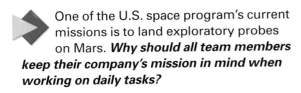

One of the U.S. space program's current missions is to land exploratory probes on Mars. *Why should all team members keep their company's mission in mind when working on daily tasks?*

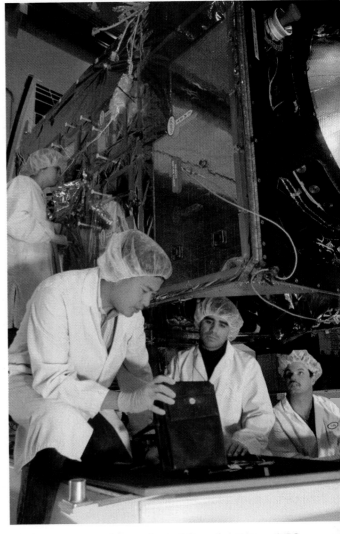

the project into smaller tasks. Then assign a start date and an end date for each task. A useful tool for teams is a *tracking schedule.* Such a schedule identifies the people who will be working on each part of a project. It tells when they will start and when they will finish.

Assigning Roles and Duties

Remember the party you planned? You could have chosen one friend to oversee the process. Then the tasks might have been done even more efficiently. Likewise, team projects often work more smoothly if the team appoints a **facilitator,** or leader. This is especially true for self-directed teams. The facilitator coordinates the tasks so that the team works efficiently.

When assigning roles in the workplace, it is important to match tasks to abilities. For example, Jason Sedrick works on the landscaping crew at a community zoo. Recently, he was assigned to a self-directed functional team to work on a new zoo entrance. The team chose a facilitator who had experience in landscape design. Jason knew about stonework. He agreed to handle this part of the job. Other members were assigned roles based on their skills.

Jason explains: "I felt uncomfortable at first. I wasn't used to working without a supervisor to report to. I thought, 'What if we do something wrong? What if no one finds out until it's too late?' I got used to taking responsibility, though. Now it feels good to be trusted. I like relying on the team and making our own decisions."

 When you are part of a team, you need to take time-outs occasionally to communicate about strategy. *How can asking and answering questions help a team succeed?*

Regular Assessment

If a project doesn't get assessed regularly, small problems can become major obstacles. Communication is the key to assessment. Jason's team, for example, meets daily for quick updates. They meet weekly to evaluate overall progress. Sometimes the team has to rethink its goals.

Potential Obstacles

Can there be trouble in "team paradise"? Of course. These are some common team problems:

- unclear goals,
- misunderstandings about how much authority the team has and how much authority individuals have.
- confusion about how to assess the performance of individuals,
- competitiveness among various team members,
- resentment at lack of individual recognition, and
- reduced effort by individuals on the team, especially as the size of the team increases.

EXCELLENT BUSINESS PRACTICES

Building Teamwork Through Experiential Training

To improve teamwork skills, Evart Glass Plant, a division of Chrysler Corporation, sent all 257 plant employees on a high-adventure training program at Eagle Village. Eagle Village is an experiential-based adventure center near the automobile plant. All employees were well-briefed about the program beforehand and the training took place during regular shift work hours.

Employees participated in a number of activities, such as juggling as a team, going through a maze, solving puzzles blindfolded, or lifting someone through an "electric fence." During the process they learned that all members affect the outcome and each individual has strengths. They also learned that a team can achieve something an individual can't, and some people are natural leaders. The activities helped them support and trust each other, go past their personal comfort zones, and value emotional and verbal support in pushing boundaries.

Employee attitudes became more positive as a result of the training. Employees were more likely to help others and to include everyone's opinion in discussions. Employees experienced higher overall motivation, increased abilities to work within a team, and more personal confidence.

Thinking Critically

Why is trusting each other important when individuals work as a team?

Most obstacles can be overcome if teams define goals clearly, take action promptly, and—above all—keep communicating. Poor communication can create serious obstacles to success—from a single missed deadline to repeated personality clashes. Talking with the team leader or calling a team meeting is a good way to start to solve problems.

Being a Valuable Team Member

What makes a person a good team player? The following list describes valuable attitudes and actions. How can these help you overcome the obstacles you just read about?

- Make the team's goals your top priority.
- In meetings, listen actively and offer suggestions. Continue to communicate with team members outside meetings.
- Follow up on what you've been assigned to do.
- Work to resolve conflicts among team members. Respect the other members of your team.
- Try to inspire other employees to get involved.

Total Quality Management

Total quality management (TQM) is a theory of management that seeks to continually improve product quality and *customer satisfaction*. TQM is sometimes referred to as the "quality movement."

According to TQM, quality comes first at every stage of the business process. It begins with planning and design and carries through to production and distribution. Every worker at every stage is challenged to find ways to improve the quality of the product. The goal? To maximize customer satisfaction.

Here's a twist, however: TQM defines a *customer* as anyone who receives the results of your work. That can mean either a coworker within the company or an outside consumer. This way of defining customers means that the responsibility for providing quality isn't limited to the salespeople. It involves each employee all the way down the line. Each person, in fact, is encouraged to determine how his or her own job might be done better. *Figure 14-2* shows the upward spiral that can result when TQM is put to work.

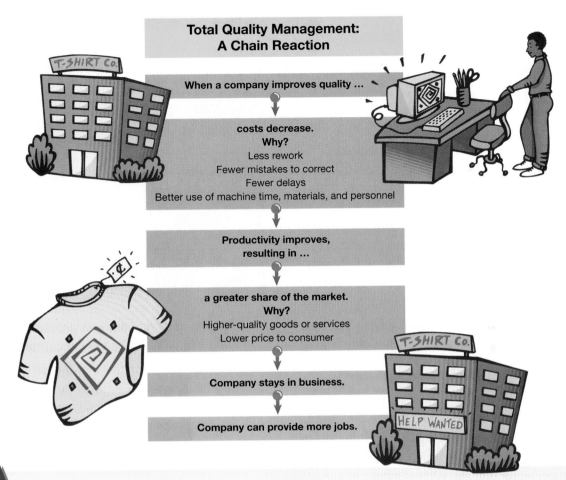

**Total Quality Management:
A Chain Reaction**

When a company improves quality ...

costs decrease.
Why?
Less rework
Fewer mistakes to correct
Fewer delays
Better use of machine time, materials, and personnel

Productivity improves,
resulting in ...

a greater share of the market.
Why?
Higher-quality goods or services
Lower price to consumer

Company stays in business.

Company can provide more jobs.

▲ **Figure 14-2** An important part of the TQM philosophy is that providing high-quality goods or services actually costs less than providing low-quality ones. Why do you suppose this is true?

SECTION 14-1 *Review*

Understanding Key Concepts

Using complete sentences, answer the following questions on a separate sheet of paper.

1. What might be the consequences of employees not working as a team?

2. The salespeople in an appliance store are planning a campaign to improve sales. Identify a short-, a medium-, and a long-range team goal.

3. Choose two obstacles to team success, and provide suggestions for dealing with them.

4. Your company has decided to change to a TQM style of management. Describe two ways that this might affect you as an employee.

Exploring Careers: Fine Arts and Humanities

Thomas R. McPhee
Sculptor

Q: Did you have formal fine arts training?

A: I went to art school for a while, but I never graduated. The instructors taught abstract art. I wanted to do small realistic stuff. Mostly I learned on my own. I drew for hours each day.

There's a lot of informal education possible. You can search out artists whose work you admire and see if you can study with them.

Q: Why do you specialize in gemstone sculpture?

A: Gemstone material fascinates me. It has everything I want in a medium. It holds any image I put into it. It has a hardness and a durability that no other medium has. I like that a lot. I like to think that some of my work will last a long time.

Q: Can someone make a living as a sculptor?

A: Anyone who wants to work with realistic, figurative sculpture, either of animals or humans, is practically guaranteed work, but the pieces have to be very accurate.

You can work for the film industry, design gift items, work in advertising, make architectural sculptures, or make models for the pewter, porcelain, or glass industries. There is no end of work you can get. The key is to work in whatever field interests you.

Thinking Critically

What problems or conflicts might an artist face while working in a mass-market business such as the manufacture of gift items?

CAREER FACTS

Nature of the Work:
Work in a variety of media to express an artistic idea.

Training or Education Needed:
Bachelor's degree in fine arts or independent art study.

Aptitudes, Abilities, and Skills:
Ability to work with tools and equipment; good hand-eye coordination; ability to concentrate for extended periods of time; an eye for color, form, and composition.

Salary Range:
$40,000 to $45,000 once established; much higher as reputation grows.

Career Path:
Work as an apprentice for a sculptor; work in a business using your specialty; work independently as a freelance artist.

Leadership

After studying this section, you will be able to:

- List the qualities of a good leader and compare leadership styles.
- Describe the characteristics of an effective supervisor.
- Describe procedures commonly used in leading formal meetings.

leadership style
parliamentary
procedure

What do your favorite teacher, a coach, and the president of the United States have in common? All are leaders. Consider what it takes to be a leader. Then write a list of qualities in your journal. As you read this section, revise and add to your list.

What Makes a Leader?

Whether you are a supervisor, a team facilitator, or simply the person in charge of training a new intern, you are a leader. Leaders are necessary if workers are to achieve their maximum potential. People have different ideas about what makes a good leader, but most agree on certain qualities.

Personal Qualities: A Leadership Checklist

Look back at the list you wrote in your journal. Now compare the items on your list to the leadership qualities defined in *Figure 14-3* on page 286.

Of course, no one is born with every quality. If you want to be a leader, you must work at developing those qualities that are most useful to you. How do you know which ones those are? Both your career choices and your personal values will be a guide.

Leadership Styles

How you behave when you are in charge of other employees is called your **leadership style.** Here are the four basic styles:

1. *directing,* or giving others specific instructions and closely supervising tasks;

2. *coaching,* or closely supervising but also explaining decisions and asking for suggestions;

3. *supporting,* or sharing decision-making responsibility and encouraging independent completion of tasks; and

4. *delegating,* or turning over responsibility for decision making and completion of tasks.

The most effective leaders combine these styles. The challenge is to decide which style will work best in a given situation. Whatever style you use, your

Leadership Qualities

Quality	Definition
Accountability	Willingness to take both the credit and the blame for one's actions
Anticipation	Ability to predict, on the basis of experience, what is likely to happen
Competitiveness	Drive to succeed or to be the best
Courage	Ability and willingness to face difficulties and take risks
Credibility	Trustworthiness
Decisiveness	Clarity of purpose, determination
Dependability	Stability, constancy
Emotional strength	Mental alertness, evenness of temper, ability to recover from disappointment
Empathy	Identification with and understanding of others
Enthusiasm	Eagerness, passion, excitement
Honesty	Truthfulness, sincerity
Imagination	Creativity, ingenuity, resourcefulness
Integrity	Soundness of moral character, sticking to one's values
Loyalty	Faithful commitment, fidelity
Physical strength	Good health, vigor, energy
Positive attitude	Optimistic outlook on life
Responsibility	Reliability, accountability
Self-confidence	Belief in oneself and one's ability to succeed
Sense of humor	Ability and readiness to see the comic side of things
Stewardship	Ability to take care of resources, including human resources
Tenacity	Unyielding drive to accomplish one's goals
Timing	Ability to judge the best moment for action
Vision	Clear idea of where one wants to go

Figure 14-3

No one could be expected to have <u>all</u> these leadership qualities! Which ones do you strive to develop? Why?

success as a leader will depend on your ability to communicate well.

Leading a Meeting: Parliamentary Procedure

As a team leader or supervisor, you will probably find yourself leading meetings. Most business meetings are casual. However, some are formal, especially when many people are involved. To keep meetings running smoothly, many companies follow a formal process with strict rules of order. It is known as **parliamentary procedure.** This way of running meetings was developed in 16th-century England to keep order in Parliament, England's governing body.

The best way to learn parliamentary procedure is to observe it in action. You might try, for example, sitting in on meetings of your school board or community government. **Figure 14-4** lists some of the parliamentary terminology that you'll hear

Parliamentary Terminology

adjourn motion to close a meeting	**majority** number greater than one-half of the voting members at a meeting
agenda list of items to be adressed at a meeting	**minority** number less than one-half of the voting members at a meeting
amend change a motion	**minutes** written record of what is said and done during a meeting; kept by the secretary
aye formal way of saying yes (pronounced *eye*)	
bylaws rules and regulations that govern an organization's operation, including such matters as the election of officers, membership qualifications, and meeting times	**motion** official request for a group to take action or reach a decision
	nay formal way of saying no
call to question statement made by a member when he or she believes it is time to vote on a motion	**new business** topic brought before the group for the first time
chair chairperson; one who is in charge of a meeting	**quorum** minimum number of members who must be present at a meeting for the group to conduct official business
constitution document stating an organization's official name, objectives, and purposes and describing how it is organized	**second** statement made to show approval of a motion made by another member of the group; at least one member must second a motion before it can be discussed
convene gather for a meeting; call a meeting to order	
	table postpone making a decision on an issue under discussion
gavel mallet used by the chair to bring a meeting to order	**unfinished business** topic brought before the members for at least the second time

▲ Figure 14-4 The terms used in parliamentary procedure have evolved over several centuries. How do you think formal terminology and an established procedure help large meetings?

used at such meetings. You can further develop your skills with the help of groups such as the Future Business Leaders of America, who hold conferences and competitions on a range of leadership skills.

When you attend a formal meeting, you'll find that it follows an *agenda*. This is a list of topics drawn up beforehand that will be discussed at the meeting. An agenda usually includes a reading of the minutes. The *minutes* are a written

 Figure 14-5

Parliamentary Procedure

Following parliamentary procedure can be an effective way for leaders to make sure meetings are orderly and productive. A quick formal meeting might look something like this. (Refer to Figure 14-4 for definitions of any terms you do not understand.)

A The chair taps her gavel to convene the meeting. She announces: "The meeting will now come to order." The first item on the agenda is for the secretary to read the minutes of the last meeting. Then two individuals give brief reports—the treasurer and the chair of the committee on business operations.

B Now the chair asks if there is any unfinished business. There is not, so topics in the category of new business may be introduced. A member makes a motion to create a trial cross-functional team. Another member seconds the motion.

summary of the last meeting. The agenda will usually include *unfinished business,* or topics from the last meeting that need more discussion. It will also include *new business.* **Figure 14-5** shows parliamentary procedure being followed in a sample meeting.

Parliamentary procedure may seem complicated. Remember, however, that it has a simple aim: to make sure that meetings are run efficiently and fairly. Using parliamentary procedure to run a meeting is a skill every business leader should master.

D Because there is no additional business, a member moves to adjourn. The motion is seconded, voted on, and passed. The meeting is now over.

C Discussion of the motion may now occur. The chair recognizes each member who wishes to comment on the trial team motion. After all have spoken, she calls for a vote: "All in favor of forming a trial cross-functional team signify by raising their hands and saying aye." In this case, a clear majority has voted aye, and the motion is carried, or approved.

Communicating as a Leader

You already know how important communication is for team members. It's twice as important for a team leader. No matter how clear your vision of a business goal, if you cannot communicate it, your team will never reach it. Effective communication requires the SCANS skills of speaking and writing. In Chapter 15, you'll read more about how to develop these skills.

Some Tips for Supervisors

In Chapter 13, you learned some tips for working with your supervisor. Now consider the other side of the coin. How can *you* be a good supervisor? Here are some do's and don'ts for being in charge:

- Provide enough training, and be a patient teacher.
- Give clear direction.
- Know when to intervene.

- Don't be afraid to admit when you have made a mistake.
- Be consistent in what you say and do.
- Treat workers fairly and equally.
- Be firm when necessary.

SECTION 14-2 *Review*

Understanding Key Concepts

Using complete sentences, answer the following questions on a separate sheet of paper.

1. Name a leadership quality that is important for each of the four leadership styles.

2. Which elements of a formal meeting might also help an informal meeting run more smoothly?

3. Why do supervisors need good communication skills?

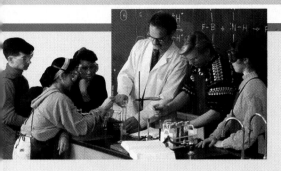

SECTION 14-1 Summary

- A team is a group of people who work together to reach a common goal. Businesses today rely more and more on teamwork.

- Teamwork benefits both team members and the companies they work for. Companies find that teams are more productive than individuals working alone. Team members experience greater job satisfaction and improved self-esteem.

- The two basic types of teams are cross-functional and functional.

- Team planning involves setting goals, assigning roles, and conducting regular assessment.

- Obstacles to teamwork include unclear goals, competitiveness among team members, and teams that are too large. Most obstacles can be overcome by clear goal definition, prompt action, and good communication.

- Total quality management (TQM) is a management process that tries to continually improve product quality and maximize customer satisfaction at every stage of the process.

Key Terms

self-directed *(p. 276)*
cross-functional team *(p. 278)*
functional team *(p. 278)*
team planning *(p. 278)*
facilitator *(p. 280)*
total quality management (TQM) *(p. 282)*

Key Terms

leadership style *(p. 286)*
parliamentary procedure *(p. 287)*

SECTION 14-2 Summary

- To act effectively as a leader, you must develop qualities such as decisiveness, enthusiasm, and vision.

- Leadership styles include directing, coaching, supporting, and delegating. Most leaders use a combination of these styles.

- Strong communication skills are essential for a leader.

- To lead or participate in a formal meeting, you need to know the basics of parliamentary procedure. This procedure is a process that helps meetings run smoothly.

- When following parliamentary procedure, a meeting begins with the reading of the minutes. It continues with unfinished business and then with new business. Motions are made, seconded, discussed, and then voted on. The meeting ends with adjournment.

Reviewing Key Terms

On separate paper, write several paragraphs telling what you might learn at a teamwork and leadership seminar. Use the following key terms in your description.

self-directed
cross-functional team
functional team
team planning
facilitator

total quality management (TQM)
leadership style
parliamentary procedure

Recalling Key Concepts

Choose the correct answer for each item below. Write your answers on a separate sheet of paper.

1. Which of the following is *not* a benefit of teamwork?

    (a) improved worker self-esteem

    (b) TQM (c) improved productivity

2. Potential obstacles to team success include ____.

    (a) unclear goals (b) regular assessment

    (c) conflict resolution

3. Maximizing customer satisfaction through constant quality improvement is the goal of ____.

    (a) every leadership style (b) TQM

    (c) parliamentary procedure

4. The four leadership styles are directing, coaching, supporting, and ____.

    (a) convening (b) tracking

    (c) delegating

5. A(n) ____ is a request at a formal meeting.

    (a) motion (b) agenda (c) gavel

Thinking Critically

Using complete sentences, answer each of the questions below on a separate sheet of paper.

1. Why do you think teams that are too large run into problems?

2. You've been asked to train a new intern in sales at your office. Which leadership style will you use? Why?

3. Imagine that you are running a company according to the principles of total quality management. Will you use teams? Why or why not?

 ## SCANS Foundation Skills and Workplace Competencies

Basic Skills: *Writing*

1. Write a paper that compares the four leadership styles. Discuss at least two advantages and two disadvantages of each style.

Interpersonal Skills: *Exercising Leadership*

2. Valia is a department manager. She is concerned about the attitude of her staff. Employees are often late, show little enthusiasm, and rarely make suggestions or show initiative. What questions should she ask herself as a leader about her own role in her department's problems?

Connecting Academics to the Workplace

Math

1. Imagine that you are the coordinating supervisor for the delivery team at a dairy. The dairy owns two trucks and employs two drivers. Each truck can deliver up to 45 crates of milk a day. Right now, the dairy delivers 80 crates a day. As the result of a successful advertising campaign, however, orders for the next month are 275 percent of what they were before. How many trucks (and drivers) will you need to make your new deliveries? How many additional crates will you then be able to carry before needing another new truck?

Social Studies

2. Your company is preparing a report on total quality management throughout the world. Your assignment is to research Japan's use of TQM. Use the library or Internet to learn how TQM has been applied in Japan.

Human Relations

3. Suppose you are on a personnel development team at a computer software company. Your company wants to increase its staff. It plans to hire 20 men and women with programming skills. You have been given the job of creating a list of five schools or training programs that could be sources of new talent. Make up such a list for your own community or region.

Developing Teamwork and Leadership Skills

With a team of five to seven students, plan an end-of-semester party for the class. Begin by choosing a facilitator and assigning roles. Then decide what tasks need to be completed and by what dates. Draw up a tracking schedule to lay out the entire project. Present your plan to the class, and compare it to those of the other teams. Which plan does the class think is the most workable? Why?

Real-World Workshop

Hold a class meeting to decide on and to arrange a field trip. Start by creating an agenda and selecting a chairperson. Run the meeting according to parliamentary procedure. (You may want to do additional reading on parliamentary procedure.) Final decisions should be reached by a majority vote.

School-to-Work Connection

Identify local groups that use parliamentary procedure. Arrange to sit in on a meeting either individually, in small groups, or as a class. Take notes, then prepare a brief report on the meeting.

Individual Career Plan

Research the use of teams in the career you have chosen to pursue. This may involve library and Internet research, letters of inquiry, or direct interviews either in person or by telephone. Write an article of no more than a page analyzing your findings.

Chapter 15

Professional Communication Skills

Section 15-1
Speaking and Listening

Section 15-2
Writing and Reading

In this video segment, find out why effective communication skills are vital to your job success.

Journal
Personal Career Plan

At a large state convention, your vocational education club is unexpectedly invited to present a five-minute speech. You and the other club members will have only half an hour to prepare. Which do you choose to do—write the speech, deliver the speech, or both write and deliver it? Why? Write a journal entry describing your responses.

Speaking and Listening

OBJECTIVES

After studying this section, you will be able to:

- Explain the importance of knowing purpose, audience, and subject before speaking.
- Identify ways of planning and organizing oral messages.
- Describe and demonstrate active listening, including taking notes.
- Describe the importance of effective speaking and listening skills in customer relations.

KEY TERMS

communication
customer relations
purpose
audience
subject
inflection
pronunciation
enunciation
active listening

If a tree falls in a forest and no one is there, does it make a sound? If you have a great idea at work but don't share it with others, does it have an effect? What's missing in both cases?

For a sound or an idea to have an effect, it needs a receiver as well as a sender. The exchange of information between senders and receivers is called **communication.** Regardless of your task at work, you'll spend much of your time communicating: speaking, listening, writing, and reading. *Figure 15-1* shows percentages of time spent speaking and listening on the job.

Speaking, listening, writing, and reading are important basic SCANS skills. You'll use them as tools to gain information, solve problems, and share ideas. Most important of all, you'll use them in customer relations. **Customer relations** is the use of communication skills to meet the needs of customers.

Consumers are more sophisticated and demanding than ever. Your success on the job will depend a great deal upon your ability to communicate effectively with customers.

Speaking: What's Your Point?

Whether you're speaking to an audience of one or one hundred, you'll want to make sure that your listeners get your point. This means that you'll need to be clear about your purpose, your audience, and your subject.

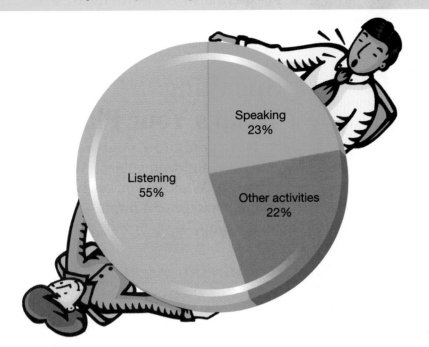

Time Spent Speaking and Listening on the Job

Speaking 23%

Listening 55%

Other activities 22%

Figure 15-1

Statistics show that the average employee spends more than half the workday listening. Why do you think this is so?

Know Your Purpose

Who was the last person you spoke to? What was your reason for speaking? A speaker's **purpose** is his or her overall goal or reason for speaking. Purposes for speaking may include the following:

- greeting clients or customers,
- informing employees of a new policy,
- giving directions to a coworker,
- requesting help or information,
- persuading a supervisor to make a change, and
- proposing a new idea.

Sometimes you may have overlapping purposes. What examples can you give?

Know Your Audience

When you think of an audience, do you imagine people seated at a theater or a stadium? In fact, an **audience** is anyone who receives information. Once you know your purpose in speaking, you need to know your audience. You might ask yourself questions such as these:

- Who are my listeners? What are their beliefs, values, and interests?
- What do they already know about my subject? What do they need to know?
- What do they expect to learn from me? Do they expect to be entertained, informed, or persuaded?

Elicia is explaining a new company insurance program to her coworkers. **Why is it important for her to know her audience?**

Your answers to these questions can help you develop a clear idea of your subject and purpose. In addition, when you know your listeners, you're better able to reach them with your words and ideas.

Know Your Subject

The **subject** in speaking is the main topic or key idea. Which of these statements makes you stop and think: "Rain forests are important," or "Rain forests house three-fourths of the plant and animal species found on Earth"? The first statement is a *generality*, or broad statement. The second is a specific fact. Generalities are easy to make, but most people are convinced by hard facts.

Knowing your subject may require research. It's well worth the time, though. Using specific facts and examples will give "muscle" to what you say.

Speaking: What's Your Plan?

Now you know your purpose, your audience, and your subject. What more do you need? Whether you're giving a simple phone message or a formal speech, you'll need a plan.

Organizing What You Want to Say

As you plan your message, ask yourself questions such as these:

- How does my subject relate to my listeners' needs?
- What's my most important point?
- How can I make this point clearly?
- What facts and examples can I use?

No matter what technique you use, the best approach is to be clear, brief, and direct.

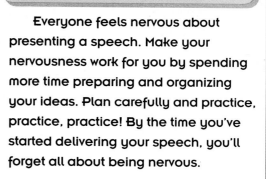

Attitude Counts ✔

Everyone feels nervous about presenting a speech. Make your nervousness work for you by spending more time preparing and organizing your ideas. Plan carefully and practice, practice, practice! By the time you've started delivering your speech, you'll forget all about being nervous.

Move logically from point to point as you speak. Reinforce main ideas. Look for signs from your listeners that your message is getting through. *Figure 15-2* shows various techniques for organizing your message.

Using Good Speaking Habits

Which is more important: *what* you say or *how* you say it? Your delivery, style, and attitude are as important as your message.

Say this sentence aloud: "I didn't say you were late for work." Now say it a different way, emphasizing a different word.

How many different messages can you send by changing the **inflection**, or the pitch or loudness of your voice?

Keep these suggestions in mind as you think about your spoken messages:

- Make emotional contact with listeners. "Communicating is a contact sport," advises communications consultant Bert Decker. Address people by name. Make eye contact with your listeners.

- Use posture and body language that match your message.

- Avoid nonwords such as *uh* and *um* and "empty" words such as *sort of,*

Technique	Description	Example
Enumeration	Listing key points	"As part of our lawn service contract, we'll cut your grass, weed your flower beds, and trim your shrubs once every week."
Generalization, followed by examples	Stating a general law, condition, or principle, backed up by specific facts or examples	"The parking situation at work is getting worse. Last week, my car was blocked by another car in the parking lot. Yesterday, I couldn't even find a parking space."
Cause and Effect	Telling what happened and why it happened	"Ladies and gentlemen, Flight 473 will be delayed. The airport in Chicago is experiencing ice on the runways, and planes are unable to leave the ground.
Comparison and Contrast	Pointing out similarities and differences	"Our cheesecakes contain fresh ingredients, as do our competitor's. However, ours are much lower in fat."

Figure 15-2 Successful speaking means being organized. Could you use more than one of these organizing techniques in the same message? If so, give an example.

well, and *OK* that clutter your message and make you seem uncertain.

- Use inflection to stress key ideas.
- Pay attention to volume and speed.
- Pronounce words correctly and enunciate clearly. **Pronunciation** is how you say the sounds and stresses of a word. **Enunciation** is the speaking of each syllable clearly and separately.
- Project enthusiasm and a positive attitude, or outlook. Be courteous and attentive when speaking to customers. If you show that you really care, customers are more likely to do business with your company. When speaking in a group, be responsive to others and avoid interrupting them.

Telephone Tips

When you place calls in today's world, you may find yourself speaking to machines as often as to people. Either way, good speaking habits still apply. Keep these additional tips in mind when placing calls and leaving voice mail or answering machine messages:

- Be aware of differences in time zones when placing calls.
- Always identify yourself. Give your first and last name.
- Speak clearly and directly into the mouthpiece.
- "Smile" with your voice by using a pleasant tone.

Sometimes you'll need to take or leave a message. If you answer a call for another person, ask, "May I take a message?" Then write a brief, clear message with the date

Michael answers the phone for his department. *Why is effective speaking especially important when answering the phone?*

and time, the full name of the caller, his or her phone number, and the purpose of the call. When you leave a message, the same rules apply. Briefly and clearly state the key information as to why you are calling.

Active Listening

Is there a difference between hearing and listening? Suppose a friend is talking to you in a noisy hallway. You may hear the noise, but you're listening to your friend. Hearing is an automatic response. Listening is a conscious action. You use your brain to *interpret*, or make sense of, what you hear.

Active listening is listening and responding with full attention to what's being said.

In the world of work, active listening can be your most powerful communication tool. It involves the following steps:

- identifying the speaker's purpose;
- listening for main ideas;
- distinguishing between fact and opinion;
- noting the speaker's inflection, speed, and volume, as well as body language;
- using your own body language and facial expressions to respond to the speaker—for example, sitting up straight or leaning toward the speaker to show that you're interested; and
- reacting to the speaker with comments or questions.

Active listening can help others communicate better. "As you learn to listen," says management consultant Nancy Austin, "people will get better at telling you things."

Career Do's & Don'ts

To Be a Professional...
Do:
- listen attentively.
- treat coworkers as skilled, competent associates.
- exude confidence.
- make decisions.

Don't:
- expect that someone understands you without asking for feedback.
- fail to deliver what you promise.
- be afraid of admitting mistakes.
- blame someone else.

Taking Notes

What are some ways that taking notes in class helps you succeed in school? Note taking can help you succeed in the world of work too. It helps you remember facts and keeps your attention focused. When you take notes, both your mind and your hands are involved in listening.

"I always take notes when a client makes a special request," says caterer Janna Hyde. "That way, I always get the order right." Practice these skills as you take notes in class or on the job:

- Don't try to write down everything a speaker says. Instead, focus on key words and main ideas. Jot down summaries in your own words.

▶ Sonia takes notes on the teacher's main points. Later she'll review her notes before the weekly quiz. *Why is taking notes in your own words better than copying someone else's words?*

Figure 15-3

Handling Customer Complaints

Handling customer complaints skillfully is important to a company's success. People don't always remember when things go right, but they do remember when things go wrong. Make sure to follow your company's established policies and procedures for handling customer complaints.

- Note actions you need to take.
- Use bulleted lists, asterisks, and arrows to show relationships among ideas.
- Review your notes to make sure you understand concepts and instructions.
- If you can't take written notes, make mental notes of main points.

Figure 15-3 shows how speaking and listening skills can be used when you handle customer complaints.

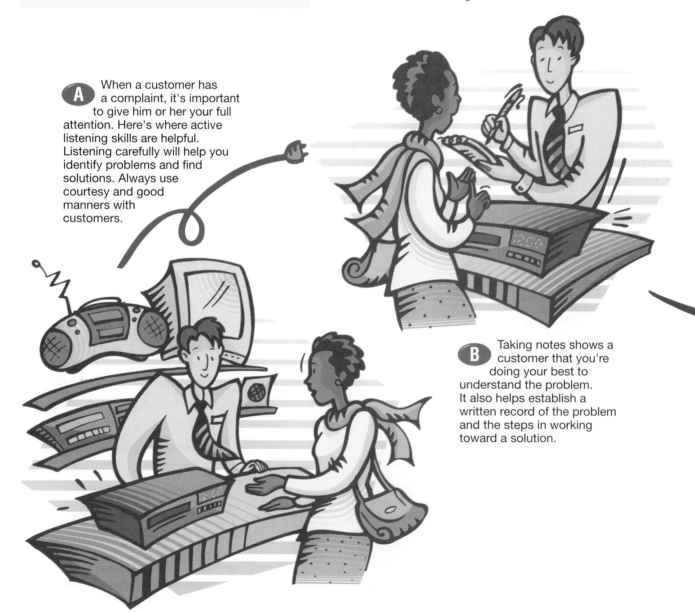

A When a customer has a complaint, it's important to give him or her your full attention. Here's where active listening skills are helpful. Listening carefully will help you identify problems and find solutions. Always use courtesy and good manners with customers.

B Taking notes shows a customer that you're doing your best to understand the problem. It also helps establish a written record of the problem and the steps in working toward a solution.

C When speaking to a customer who has a complaint, be polite, clear, and brief. Let the customer know that you understand the problem and will do all you can to solve it.

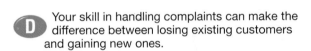

D Your skill in handling complaints can make the difference between losing existing customers and gaining new ones.

SECTION 15-1 *Review*

Understanding Key Concepts

Using complete sentences, answer the following questions on a separate sheet of paper.

1. Your supervisor wants you to give your division's progress report to company executives at their fall meeting. Should you use the opportunity to complain about the company vacation policy? Explain.

2. Why might you choose to vary your speed when making a long speech?

3. Why do people "get better at telling you things" when you listen well?

4. Why is note taking a good idea when a customer is making a complaint?

Exploring Careers: Public Service

Helen Jun
Elementary Schoolteacher

Q: How did you choose teaching?

A: I wanted to do something that involved working with people. I couldn't handle working in an office. I have always loved kids and worked with kids, tutoring and camp counseling. I like the feeling that I'm making a difference somehow.

Q: What is teaching like?

A: It's so much hard work. I tell friends who are thinking about teaching, "Don't think teaching is easy. You need determination and perseverance, or you're not going to make it."

Everything in the lower grades now is hands-on. This approach requires a lot more preparation for the teacher than does a traditional teaching method. The paperwork is overwhelming. There are always surveys to fill out, and grading papers takes up more hours.

Q: What sort of working relationship do you have with other teachers?

A: I really enjoy the camaraderie with the other teachers. I would never have gotten through my first year if another teacher, acting as my mentor, hadn't guided me step by step.

Thinking Critically

In your working career, you will teach and be taught. What are the attributes of a skilled teacher?

CAREER FACTS

Nature of the Work:
Prepare lessons; work with students, teachers, and parents.

Training or Education Needed:
Bachelor's degree; may require teaching credentials.

Aptitudes, Abilities, and Skills:
Math, listening, speaking, and interpersonal skills; problem-solving skills, self-management skills; reading and writing skills; ability to instruct and motivate people; patience; the flexibility to adapt to students' levels of learning.

Salary Range:
Depends on the state or district and the college degree; average starting salary—$27,000 to $31,000.

Career Path:
Most teachers continue as classroom teachers; may move into administration.

Writing and Reading

Can you name a job that doesn't involve writing and reading? Vast amounts of written information are exchanged every business day. Increasingly, a company's success depends on employees who have strong skills in writing and reading.

Basic Writing Skills

Suppose you receive a customer bulletin from a local company. The bulletin begins: "Companies are increasingly turning to capacity planning techniques to determine when future processing loads will exceed processing capabilities." What does this sentence mean? It might as well be written in an unfamiliar foreign language. No customer wants to work this hard to understand a company's message.

Much of the advice for speaking well applies to writing well: define your audience, purpose, and subject; be clear, direct, and organized. Here are some additional tips to keep in mind:

- Organize your writing. Use a logical order, such as chronological, or time order, or order of importance. Use headings and subheadings when writing reports.

- Pay close attention to spelling and grammar. Use a dictionary and style book to check words and rules you are unsure of.

- Be aware of your *tone*, or manner, when you write. In a letter responding to a customer's request, you would write in a tone that is respectful and polite.

Style Do's and Don'ts

Do...	Don't...	Examples
use language everyone can understand.	use *jargon,* or vocabulary specific to your area of work.	Instead of "Let's interface on that," write: "Let's meet to talk about that."
use your own language	use clichés, or overused phrases and expressions.	Instead of "It's raining cats and dogs," write: "It's raining hard."
use gender-neutral language.	use sexist language.	Instead of "Each man will make his own choice," write: "Each person will make his or her own choice."
use the active voice.	use the passive voice.	Instead of "The report was written by Zach," write: "Zach wrote the report."
use simple, natural words and phrases.	use complicated words or phrases.	Instead of "My home is in proximity to hers," write: "My home is near hers."
use short, simple sentences.	use long, complicated sentences.	Instead of "I am requesting that you write to the client, after which you should contact her by telephone," write: "Please write to the client. Then call her."

▲ **Figure 15-4** This chart shows ways to develop your own style. Why is developing your own style important in writing?

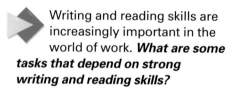

Writing and reading skills are increasingly important in the world of work. **What are some tasks that depend on strong writing and reading skills?**

- When you think you are done, go back one more time and edit your work. Keep revising until your message is clear.

- Carefully proofread your work before sending it out.

Writing Style

Writer E. B. White defined *style* as "the sound [a writer's] words make on paper." Style isn't something you "add" to your writing, as a top hat or glittery necklace; it's what shines through when you write in a clear and straightforward way. See ***Figure 15-4*** for some basics on developing style.

Common Forms of Business Writing

At some point in your job, you may need to write a memo, a business letter, or a report. *Figures 15-5* below and *15-6* on page 308 show standard forms for business memos and letters. *Figure 15-7* on the next page compares the purposes of memos, letters, and reports.

Using E-Mail and Fax Machines

E-mail, or electronic mail, is a fast, efficient way to communicate. E-mail is sent by modem. A **modem** translates signals from your computer into sounds that travel over an ordinary telephone line. With the push of a button or the click of a mouse, you can send a message from one computer to another in seconds.

Many companies communicate by *fax*, short for *facsimile*, which means a copy or a replica. A fax machine is much like a copy machine. It is also like a computer in that it can send written messages via telephone lines.

When sending business E-mail and faxes, many of the same tips apply: keep messages short, make sure the recipient's name is clearly stated, and don't use E-mail or faxes for personal messages at work.

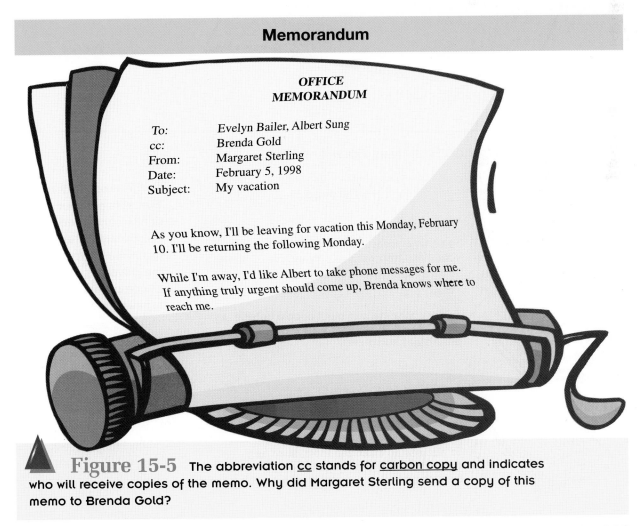

Memorandum

OFFICE MEMORANDUM

To: Evelyn Bailer, Albert Sung
cc: Brenda Gold
From: Margaret Sterling
Date: February 5, 1998
Subject: My vacation

As you know, I'll be leaving for vacation this Monday, February 10. I'll be returning the following Monday.

While I'm away, I'd like Albert to take phone messages for me. If anything truly urgent should come up, Brenda knows where to reach me.

Figure 15-5 The abbreviation <u>cc</u> stands for <u>carbon copy</u> and indicates who will receive copies of the memo. Why did Margaret Sterling send a copy of this memo to Brenda Gold?

Letter

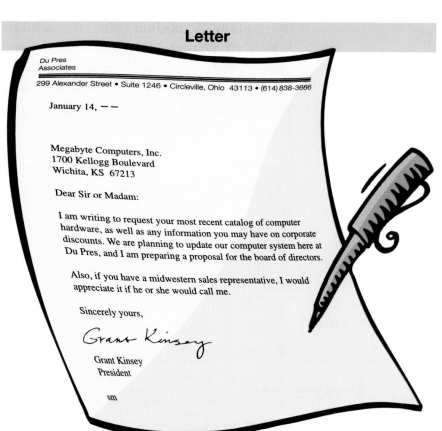

Du Pres
Associates

299 Alexander Street • Suite 1246 • Circleville, Ohio 43113 • (614) 838-3666

January 14, — —

Megabyte Computers, Inc.
1700 Kellogg Boulevard
Wichita, KS 67213

Dear Sir or Madam:

I am writing to request your most recent catalog of computer hardware, as well as any information you may have on corporate discounts. We are planning to update our computer system here at Du Pres, and I am preparing a proposal for the board of directors.

Also, if you have a midwestern sales representative, I would appreciate it if he or she would call me.

Sincerely yours,

Grant Kinsey

Grant Kinsey
President

sm

Figure 15-6

This letter was printed in <u>block style,</u> which means that all lines begin at the left margin and a line of space separates paragraphs. How would you respond to this letter if you were an employee of Megabyte Computers?

Common Business Forms

Form	Purpose
Memo	• To communicate with others in your office • To communicate informally with people outside your office who work closely with your business • To address a limited topic
Letter	• To communicate with most people outside your office, including representatives of other businesses and clients
Report	• To communicate with people, both within and outside your office, who need extensive information about your business • To address an extended topic, such as a proposal for a new project, the progress of an existing project, or the results of research

Figure 15-7

Today, most written business communication is composed on computers instead of typewriters. What are the advantages of computers over typewriters?

Reading Skills

You're likely to spend as much time reading as writing on the job. Name or list in your journal some of the reading skills you've used in social studies, science, and English classes. You'll find yourself using many of these skills in your job as you acquire, evaluate, and interpret information, all of which are important SCANS skills.

You'll use them to get a job: reading help-wanted ads and job applications. You'll use them on the job: reading memos, bulletins, letters, directions, and reports. You may need them to find information or to do research for a project. Sometimes you'll want to read quickly for general information. At other times, you'll want to read carefully for specific facts.

Previewing

Do you enjoy movie previews? What information can you get from them? When you're **previewing**, you read only those parts of a written work that outline or summarize its content. These parts may include book titles, chapter titles, or headings. Previewing saves time when you need a general idea of what is in a work.

EXCELLENT BUSINESS PRACTICES

Working with Visual Impairments

Telesensory Inc., of Mountain View, California, designs, develops, and manufactures high-tech devices to serve the needs of visually impaired individuals. These devices give employers the equipment they need to set up workstations that accommodate special needs. Such devices can also help students at school and at work.

The company's products for computers include hardware and software applications that magnify images on a computer screen. The company also offers software that converts text into synthesized speech.

One innovative product is a small portable electronic device for the visually impaired to use to take notes in braille and to calculate numbers. It can also be used as an address and appointment book. The device converts the braille input to standard text for speech or print.

Through these devices, individuals gain access to and interact with print and electronic information. Employees with visual impairments can be given the same opportunities as sighted workers.

Thinking Critically

Name three types of technology equipment commonly used to communicate on the job. How could these forms of technology be modified to accommodate people with hearing and visual impairments?

Skimming can be very helpful, especially when you're researching a great deal of material. **How do you decide when to skim a book or document and when to read it more carefully?**

Skimming

Another timesaving reading skill is skimming. In **skimming**, you read through a book or a document quickly, picking out key points. To skim, you look at the first sentences of paragraphs, as well as key words and phrases.

Taking Notes

Taking notes is important as a reading skill as well as a listening skill. Jotting down main ideas, useful quotes, new vocabulary, and your own summaries of information helps you understand and recall what you read. Note taking can be especially helpful when you're reading technical information.

SECTION 15-2 *Review*

Understanding Key Concepts

Using complete sentences, answer the following questions on a separate sheet of paper.

1. What are some ways in which you might organize the information in a report that describes your company's activities this past year?

2. Which of these business forms would you use to respond to a customer complaint: memo, business letter, E-mail, fax? Explain why.

3. Which skill—previewing or skimming—would you use to find your weekly schedule in a company memo that shows all employee schedules? Explain your answer.

4. Give a specific example of the usefulness of good reading skills in customer relations.

Key Terms

communication *(p. 296)*
customer relations *(p. 296)*
purpose *(p. 297)*
audience *(p. 297)*
subject *(p. 298)*
inflection *(p. 299)*
pronunciation *(p. 300)*
enunciation *(p. 300)*
active listening *(p. 300)*

SECTION 15-1 Summary

- Communication is the process of exchanging information.
- Communication skills include speaking, listening, writing, and reading.
- Before you speak, you need to consider your purpose, audience, and subject. You also need to organize what you plan to say.
- There is more to speaking than what you say. How you say things matters too, whether in person or on the telephone.
- Active listening is especially important in customer relations. It involves body language and verbal responses.
- Taking notes can help you remember what you hear.

Key Terms

E-mail *(p. 307)*
modem *(p. 307)*
previewing *(p. 309)*
skimming *(p. 310)*

SECTION 15-2 Summary

- Writing requires some of the same skills as speaking. You need to know your audience, purpose, and subject. You must also be clear, direct, and organized.
- When you write, you must consider your style, tone, spelling, and grammar. You must also remember to revise and proofread.
- The most common business forms are messages, memos, letters, and reports.
- In today's business world, E-mail and faxes are important communication tools.
- Good reading skills, including previewing, skimming, and note taking, are necessary for any type of job.

Reviewing Key Terms

On a separate sheet of paper, write one or two paragraphs about the importance of communication skills in the world of work. Use the terms below.

communication	enunciation
customer relations	active listening
purpose	E-mail
audience	modem
subject	previewing
inflection	skimming
pronunciation	

Recalling Key Concepts

Choose the correct answer for each item below. Write your answers on a separate sheet of paper.

1. Before speaking to an audience, you should ____.

   (a) speak clearly

   (b) know who your audience is

   (c) use eye contact

2. "Our cleaning service costs less than others in town" is an example of ____.

   (a) enumeration

   (b) cause and effect

   (c) comparison and contrast

3. Taking notes when customers place orders is a type of ____ skill.

   (a) speaking (b) reading (c) listening

4. After writing a business letter to a customer, you should ____.

   (a) proofread it for errors

   (b) send it via E-mail

   (c) send it as a fax

5. To determine whether or not to buy a book for one of your projects, you should ____.

   (a) read the book carefully

   (b) skim it for the main ideas

   (c) preview it by looking at the table of contents, headings, and illustrations

Thinking Critically

Using complete sentences, answer each of the questions below on a separate sheet of paper.

1. Why is knowing your audience's values and expectations important in speaking?

2. When listening to a customer, what are some ways to show that your attention is focused on the customer?

3. Why would you want to avoid jargon when talking to people outside your department or company?

4. As an employer, how would you help employees strengthen communication skills in the workplace?

SCANS Foundation Skills and Workplace Competencies

Basic Skills: *Writing*

1. As the office manager of an accounting firm, you need to inform staff members that the office will close at 2:00 P.M. on the Wednesday before Thanksgiving. You also need to remind supervisors to submit weekly reports before the holiday closing. Use the form you learned in this chapter to write a memo that provides this information.

Interpersonal Skills: *Teaching Others*

2. Using only your voice, explain to classmates how to fold a letter on paper that measures 8½ x 11 inches so that it will fit into an envelope that measures 4¼ x 9½ inches. Use the speaking skills you learned in this chapter.

Connecting Academics to the Workplace

Social Studies

1. Aaron is a truck driver for a moving company in your state. As Aaron's supervisor, you need to give him written directions for his next assignment. Using your state map, plan a route that begins at one point in the state and ends at another point. Write the directions on a sheet of paper. Provide at least three steps in the directions. Then exchange your written directions with another student. Use a pencil to map Aaron's route on a road map of your state.

Language Arts

2. Toni is checking her supervisor's voice-mail messages. There is one call, recorded at 2:10 P.M. on February 7: "Hi, John. Sam Jennings here. I need to know if you want me to order that special card stock we talked about. If you let me know by the end of the day, I can still get you the discount rate. I'll be here till six o'clock. I'm at 555-6636. Thanks. So long." Using this information, write a professional phone message for Toni's supervisor.

Developing Teamwork and Leadership Skills

Collaborate with five or six other students to prepare a newscast. Cover recent events, including sports and weather in your community and school. Choose a director, writers, researchers, reporters, and an anchorperson. Take some time to rehearse. Then present your newscast to the class.

Real-World Workshop

Prepare a brief speech on an issue in the world of work that interests you. Issues might include women in the workplace, the effects of new technology, or using the Internet at work. Present your speech to the class. You may want to have a classmate videotape your speech so that you can review and evaluate it.

School-to-Work Connection

Arrange to spend a day observing a job that interests you. For example, if you are interested in the visual arts, you might "shadow" a museum curator. Throughout the day, take notes on aspects of the job that most interest you and aspects you would like to learn more about. Save time at the end of the day to ask questions of the person you observed. Record his or her answers.

Individual Career Plan

Using the answers to your questions in the School-to-Work Connection, write a brief report about the job you observed.

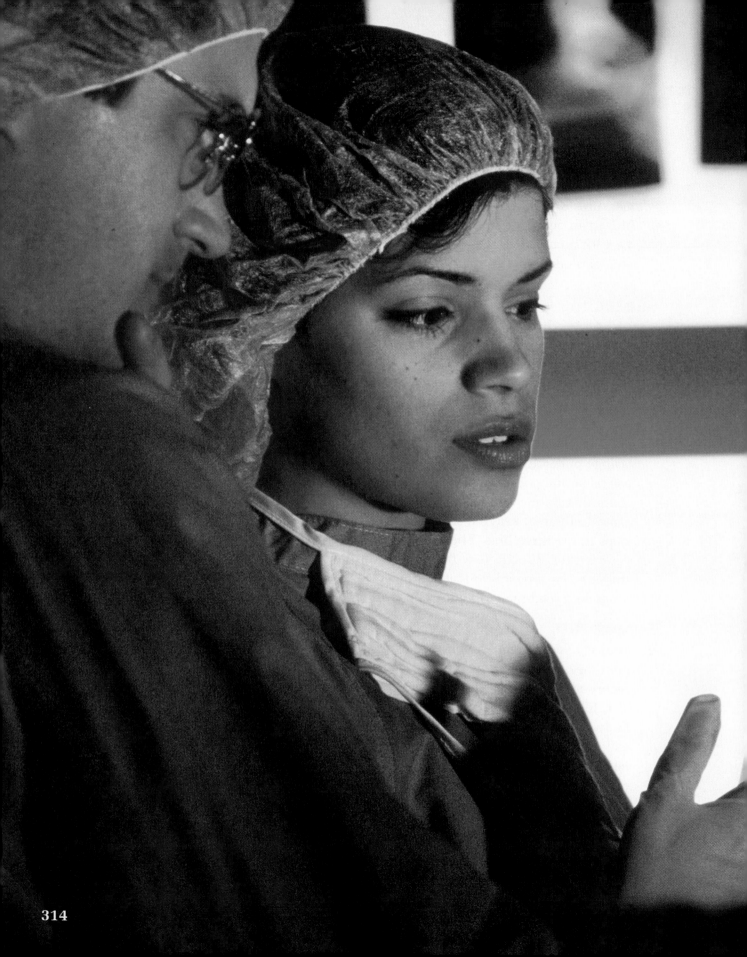

Chapter 16

Thinking Skills on the Job

Section 16-1
Making Decisions on the Job

Section 16-2
Solving Workplace Problems

In this video segment, learn how to use thinking skills to make decisions and solve workplace problems.

Journal
Personal Career Plan

Think of a difficult situation you faced recently, either at school or at work. What was the problem? How did you try to solve it? If you could go back now and deal with the situation again, what would you do this time? Why? Discuss your experiences and ideas by writing them down in a journal.

Making Decisions on the Job

You make hundreds of decisions every day, some trivial, some important. Do you turn left here? What do you want for lunch? What career do you choose? In the world of work, you will want to make the best decisions possible, both everyday decisions and significant long-term ones.

Reviewing the Decision-Making Process

As you learned in Chapter 2, decision making is following a logical series of steps to identify and evaluate possibilities and arrive at a workable choice. Whether you're buying new shoes or facing a big on-the-job decision, the steps are basically the same. What decisions have you made lately that followed this process?

1. Define your needs or wants.
2. Analyze your resources.
3. Identify your choices.
4. Gather information.
5. Evaluate your choices.
6. Make a decision.
7. Plan how to reach your goal.

 The second step of the decision-making process involves analyzing your resources. *What resources are being used here to make a decision?*

Step 1. Figuring Out What You Need and Want

Once you know what you need or want in order to meet your job responsibilities, you have completed the first step of the decision-making process. Having a strong grasp of your purpose will help you clarify the decision you need to make.

When Maria Delfino starts her new job at SuperSounds, a large music store, her duties include making sure that the display racks are kept filled with the latest CDs. When she discovers an empty rack,

she faces a decision. She needs to keep the rack filled, and she needs a new supply of CDs. She wants to fulfill her responsibility and to do a good job too.

Step 2. Checking Out Resources

Can you make something out of nothing? Of course not—you need resources. In the world of work, the most basic **resources** are time, money, material, information, facilities, and people.

At SuperSounds, Maria moves to the second step of the decision-making process by finding out what resources she has. She checks back in the stockroom, and she finds that the CD she needs is out of stock. She knows, however, that new supplies—additional resources—are available from a distributor.

Step 3. Identifying the Best and the Rest

What do you do when different choices all seem like good ones? Smart decision makers use **criteria**—standards of judgment—for comparing and evaluating choices.

Criteria for decision making will often be provided by your employer or other experienced coworkers. As you learn more about a workplace, you'll learn not only *how* but also *why* certain decisions are made—in other words, what criteria are important, including product quality, customer satisfaction, safety, efficiency, and economic factors known as "the bottom line."

Maria knows that SuperSounds values keeping its display racks filled. However, another criterion—the chain of command—is also important. Maria identifies her three choices. She can (a) order the CDs immediately, (b) inform her supervisor of the situation, or (c) do nothing about the CDs and wait for someone else to notice the situation.

EXCELLENT BUSINESS PRACTICES

Total Quality Management

L.L. Bean, a catalog clothing company located in Freeport, Maine, has developed programs designed to increase the effectiveness of the entire organization. L.L. Bean developed a process in which managers were rated by those in lower-level positions. The manufacturing division asked employees to identify cost-saving methods of operation and made changes. Workers in the retail store traded jobs with workers in the distribution centers. As a result of the job-swap experience, workers simplified processes that previously had not been questioned.

The various programs put people before processes. The programs saved the company money, and solved potential problems at early stages.

Thinking Critically

What would be the benefit of a job-swap experience?

No one knows everything. If you have a question, ask it. *What might a supervisor think of a worker who never asks questions?*

Step 4. Collecting More Info

Sometimes you simply don't have enough information to make a good decision. What's the solution? Don't act in the dark—ask questions. Get the information you need. If you don't ask, no one will know you need information.

Maria has taken a SuperSounds training program in how to place orders. However, she does not have the authority to do so or even know the number of new CDs to order. Her next move is to ask a coworker for more *information*. Steven, an assistant who has been on the job for about six months, recommends that Maria inform the supervisor of the situation.

Step 5. Assuming the Role of Judge

Every decision you make will have a **consequence**—an effect or outcome. Evaluating alternatives usually means understanding and predicting possible consequences. These questions may help as you consider an on-the-job decision:

• What are the risks involved in this decision? Are the rewards worth it?

Prioritizing

On any job, a worker must often decide what to do first, second, third, and so on. For example, a housepainter must decide in what order to paint the surfaces of a room so as to avoid doing extra work. Various factors may influence prioritizing a sequence of decisions or actions.

- How does this decision directly affect me? How will I be judged?

- What effect will this decision have on my team or department?

- What effect will this decision have on my company?

Maria thinks about the consequences of the three choices she faces. If she orders the CDs herself, she may be praised for her initiative. However, she may also be

A Since the moldings are to remain a natural wood color, the painter has decided to place tape over them before painting the other surfaces.

B Since the floor is not going to be refinished, the painter has decided to cover it.

reprimanded for breaking the chain of command. If she informs the supervisor, she will be following the store's standard procedure. If she waits and does nothing, she may be accused of not doing her job properly.

Step 6. Making Up Your Mind

After you've considered your options and evaluated the possible consequences, there's no need to **procrastinate,** or put off deciding, unless you still need more information. Have you ever decided not to decide? That's a decision too. Just don't procrastinate out of fear.

Maria doesn't procrastinate. She decides to follow the store's standard procedure—to inform her supervisor.

Step 7. Drawing Up Your Plan of Action

Once you've made a decision, put it into action. **Prioritize** the tasks to be done; that is, order them from first to last or from most to least important. *Figure 16-1* shows how a worker prioritizes his tasks.

C The painter has decided to start with the ceiling because any paint splatters that get on the walls will be covered when the walls are painted.

D The painter paints the walls last, covering up any splattering.

Maria prioritizes her tasks. She first informs her supervisor, who praises her attentiveness and places the order. Second, she rearranges the display to make it look appealing until the new supply arrives. Third, she checks the other new titles to make sure the situation doesn't happen again. Maria will reach both her short-term goal (to fill the display) and her long-term goal (to be responsible).

Maria completes her work by prioritizing. **Why is it important to prioritize tasks?**

SECTION 16-1 *Review*

Understanding Key Concepts

Using complete sentences, answer the following questions on a separate sheet of paper.

1. In your own words, describe the seven steps of the decision-making process.

2. Why do you think having a clear purpose can make a decision easier?

3. What do you predict will happen to a business that does not have a strong chain of command?

4. In what way is customer satisfaction a criterion for decision making?

5. What do you think is the value of prioritizing your job responsibilities?

Exploring Careers: Transportation

Ricky Bachan
Driver

Q: What do you do for the transit company?

A: I drive a small bus for Dial-a-Ride, a service that takes the elderly, people in wheelchairs, or people who have medical problems to the hospital or to the doctors' offices. It's a curb-to-curb service. I pick the passengers up, help them into the bus, and make sure they're seated or that their wheelchairs are secure.

Q: How did you get your job?

A: I started doing this kind of work in New York. I think my driving experience is why the company here hired me so quickly. After driving in New York, driving in Santa Clarita Valley is a cinch.

Q: What skills did you need?

A: In California, you have to have a Class B driver's license, a commercial license that allows you to carry passengers. The company trains you in assisting passengers, including how to strap down the wheelchairs. We also learn CPR and other emergency procedures.

Q: What are your days like?

A: I spend about eight hours a day on the road and cover more than a hundred miles a day. I get to meet a lot of people and I like that. I like driving, too, although sometimes it can get to you.

Thinking Critically

Why do you think there will be a growing need for drivers who provide transportation services to the elderly?

CAREER FACTS

Nature of the Work:
Pick up clients at home; take them to appointments; return to pick them up.

Training or Education Needed:
Strong driving experience; appropriate driver's license.

Aptitudes, Abilities, and Skills:
Listening, speaking, and interpersonal skills; reading and writing skills; ability to use maps; physical stamina; safe driving skills; decision-making skills.

Salary Range:
Depends on location and experience; average starting wage—$8.00 an hour.

Career Path:
Start by driving small buses or vans; qualify for the appropriate driver's license; work for a large or private transportation company.

Solving Workplace Problems

OBJECTIVES

After studying this section, you will be able to:

- Describe the six basic steps in the problem-solving process.
- Identify and clarify workplace problems.
- Generate alternative solutions to problems and compare their consequences.
- Implement solutions and evaluate results.

KEY TERMS

brainstorm
analogy
assumptions

"Houston, we have a problem," crackled the voice of astronaut Jim Lovell as the damaged *Apollo 13* capsule hurtled through space. That statement set in motion a heroic group effort in problem solving—resolving a difficulty through creative thinking and reasoning.

Understanding the Problem-Solving Process

Your workplace problems may not be as dramatic as those of *Apollo 13,* but your approach to solving them should be the same. Follow these six steps:

1. Identify and clarify the problem.
2. Generate alternative solutions, using creative thinking and logical reasoning.
3. Evaluate the probable consequences of the solutions.
4. Decide on the best solution.
5. Implement the solution.
6. Evaluate the results.

Step 1. Identify and Clarify the Problem

When an obstacle stands between you and something you need or want, you've got a problem. You

 Whether problems are simple or complex, they can usually be solved with creative thinking and logical reasoning. *What kinds of problems have you already solved during your life as a student?*

could try the ostrich approach: Stick your head in the sand and hope the problem goes away. Chances are, it won't. The wise move is to see the problem clearly for what it is—not a mystery, not a catastrophe, but just a situation that needs a solution.

First things first. Gather the facts— assemble all the information you can about the problem. Ask specific questions, and stay as objective as possible. Think about your sources too. Are they reliable? Are they giving you facts or opinions?

Lewis Iverson is a part-time assistant at Avery's, a small local hardware store. One day, Mr. Avery, the owner, tells Lewis that business has been very slow lately. He asks Lewis to think about possible solutions to the problem of the sales slump. To clarify the problem, Lewis makes this list of questions:

- Are fewer people coming in?

- Are customers spending less money?

- Do people want a different selection of goods?

- Do people expect lower prices?
- What products do other local hardware stores offer?

By asking their regular customers these questions, Lewis and Mr. Avery clarify the problem: People are buying less of certain kinds of items, especially tools, because the selection is better at a big new home supply store.

Step 2. Generate Alternative Solutions

One of the world's great problem solvers, physicist Albert Einstein, once said, "Imagination is more important than knowledge." Do you agree? Think of the problems you've solved by changing your way of thinking, by looking at something from a new angle, by being creative.

 Group brainstorming can result in a variety of creative solutions to a problem. *Why do you think the word* brainstorm *is a good one to describe this problem-solving strategy?*

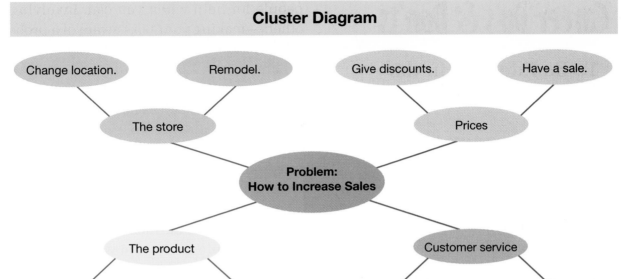

Cluster Diagram

Change location. — The store

Remodel. — The store

Give discounts. — Prices

Have a sale. — Prices

Problem: How to Increase Sales

The product

Customer service

Improve it.

Replace it.

Increase selection.

Speed it up.

?

Figure 16-2 A cluster diagram can help you associate a variety of ideas and see new connections. If you were using this cluster, what might you put in the oval with a question mark?

To attack a problem, come up with as many solutions as possible, no matter how "crazy" some of them might seem. **Brainstorm** alone or with a group, coming up with as many ideas as you can but not evaluating or judging those ideas right away. After all, multiple solutions increase your chances of success. Change your point of view. Putting yourself in someone else's shoes can make a problem look quite different.

Here are a few strategies for creative thinking that you can try:

- Use spider maps and clustering (techniques you've probably already used in school) to associate groups of ideas, such as the one shown in *Figure 16-2.*

- Invent a model, picture, or symbol to represent the problem. Revealing the "shape" of a problem can open a solution.

Career Do's & Don'ts

To Be Effective in the Workplace...

Do:
- carry out procedures and get things done.
- be innovative and creative.
- find out what you don't know.
- work with associates to solve problems together.

Don't:
- argue.
- overlook details.
- be secretive.
- try to do everything yourself.

- Use an **analogy**—a seeming similarity between one thing and another thing that are otherwise dissimilar— to suggest a solution. For example: This problem is like a game of basketball. We need to pass our product from one member of the team to another more quickly.

- Question **assumptions**—beliefs you take for granted—and beware of unspoken assumptions. For example: Are we assuming that all our customers are men? What about advertising aimed at women?

Remember that, in problem solving, more heads are often better than one simply because different people bring different experiences to the table. Participate as a team member to help identify alternative solutions (a SCANS skill), and ask other people for help when you can. Involving others—making your boss aware of a problem, for example—is often the right move.

Mr. Avery, Lewis, and Kim, another assistant, brainstorm one afternoon. Each proposes ideas, such as having a sale, lowering prices, putting up a new sign, and expanding the selection. In the spirit of imaginative brainstorming, Lewis says, "How about hiring someone to dress up in a huge hammer costume and stand outside the store?" Kim chimes in, "How about several people in costumes to show different kinds of hammers?"

Step 3. Evaluate the Probable Consequences of the Solutions

Not all solutions are created equal. After you've come up with some possible solutions, you need to evaluate how well each one will actually solve the problem.

List the specific consequences—both positive and negative—that may follow each possible solution. Which one best meets your short-term and long-term goals? What impact will the solutions have on you, on your team or department, and on your customers or clients? When you've answered these questions, you're ready to decide on one solution.

The problem-solving team at Avery's now looks at *consequences*. Mr. Avery can't afford to lower prices or to put up a big sign. Expanding the selection of all the items in the store is impractical because Avery's just doesn't have the space. The hammer-costume idea would get people's attention—a short-term goal—but it might also make people think the store was silly—missing a long-term goal of maintaining customers' respect.

Step 4. Decide on the Best Solution

When you choose a solution, remember that you're choosing the best one under the circumstances. Few solutions are perfect, and occasionally time forces you to choose when you're not quite ready. Time pressure is a reality that everyone has to deal with. Just stay calm, focus on the problem, and decide.

Lewis, Kim, and Mr. Avery decide that the best solution is a variation of what Kim said about "different kinds of hammers." They'll increase the selection of certain items—such as hammers—and specialize in tools.

Step 5. Implement the Solution

You may need to explain your solution to coworkers in order to put it into action. Identify the exact steps you need to follow and prioritize them. Following the chain of command, obtain the necessary permission and move ahead.

Mr. Avery takes action. He stops carrying certain items, such as house paint, to

 Prioritizing your steps and communicating your plan to others are keys to making a solution work. *What do you think are the advantages of presenting all the steps of a plan at a group meeting?*

make room for a greater selection of tools. He orders and stocks the new items, sets up new displays, and advertises in the local newspaper.

Step 6. Evaluate the Results

To evaluate a solution, look at both its benefits and its drawbacks. Be as objective in evaluating a solution as you were in identifying the problem. If your solution is working, you should be able to cite benefits for yourself, your team or department, and your customers or clients.

If the solution has drawbacks or if it creates new problems, identify them and correct them as well. On-the-job problem solving is a continuous process.

Finally, ask yourself what you learned. An old saying holds true: "The only really bad decisions are the ones you don't learn from." Apply what you learn to new situations to prevent similar problems from happening again.

YOU'RE THE BOSS!

Solving Workplace Problems

You ask a cashier/clerk in your hardware store to organize a display of tools. Half an hour later, you see long lines of customers waiting for cashier service. You point the customers out to this employee, who says, "I know, but you told me to work on the display." How will you respond?

At Avery's, the greatest drawback is eliminating house paint—a moneymaker—to make room for new tools. However, tool sales are increasing dramatically, so the benefits outweigh the drawbacks, as customers are impressed with the new selection and spend more money.

SECTION 16-2 *Review*

Understanding Key Concepts

Using complete sentences, answer the following questions on a separate sheet of paper.

1. In your own words, describe the six basic steps of problem solving.

2. In an on-the-job situation, how can you identify good sources of information?

3. Why is creating alternative solutions better than relying on only one solution?

4. What do you think are the advantages of group problem solving?

5. Describe how you and another person solved a similar problem, and compare the consequences of each solution.

Key Terms

resources *(p. 317)*
criteria *(p. 318)*
consequence *(p. 319)*
procrastinate *(p. 321)*
prioritize *(p. 321)*

SECTION 16-1 Summary

- The seven steps in the decision-making process are to define your needs or wants, analyze your resources, identify your choices, gather information, evaluate your choices, make a decision, and plan how to reach your goal.

- To determine which decisions are yours to make, follow the chain of command, and know your responsibilities.

- Use criteria for comparing and evaluating possible choices.

- If you need additional information, be sure to get it.

- Evaluate the possible consequences of alternative decisions.

- When you're ready to decide, don't procrastinate.

- Prioritize tasks to be performed in order to create a plan of action.

Key Terms

brainstorm *(p. 327)*
analogy *(p. 328)*
assumptions *(p. 328)*

SECTION 16-2 Summary

- The six basic steps in problem solving are to identify and clarify the problem, generate alternative solutions, evaluate probable consequences, decide on the best solution, implement the solution, and evaluate the results.

- Gather and evaluate information, distinguishing between reliable and unreliable sources.

- Generate alternative solutions with creative thinking strategies such as brainstorming, clustering, modeling, and using analogies.

- Evaluate consequences of solutions by judging how well they meet long-term and short-term goals.

- Choose the best solution under the circumstances, and prioritize the steps needed to implement it.

- Be objective in evaluating benefits and drawbacks of a solution.

Reviewing Key Terms

On a separate sheet of paper, write a description of one typical day at a job of your choice. Use the following key terms in your description.

resources   brainstorm
criteria   analogy
consequence   assumptions
procrastinate   prioritize

Recalling Key Concepts

On a separate sheet of paper, tell whether each statement is true or false. Rewrite any false statements to make them true.

1. The final step in the decision-making process is to evaluate your choices.

2. A criterion is a standard of judgment.

3. The first step to solving a problem is to consider analogies.

4. Brainstorming to generate alternative solutions can only be done alone.

5. Evaluating a solution objectively means taking your personal feelings into consideration.

Thinking Critically

Using complete sentences, answer each of the questions below on a separate sheet of paper.

1. Most organizations have a chain of command—a system of authority and responsibility. Describe the chain of command in one of the following: your school system, a professional sports team, your state government.

2. Explain in your own words what the following saying tells about procrastination: Don't put off until tomorrow what you can do today.

3. Identify a job or work-related goal, such as repairing a bicycle, or building a house. Prioritize at least five tasks that would lead to that goal.

4. If you were trying to solve a problem, how would you separate useful, relevant information from distracting, irrelevant information?

5. Identify a serious world problem, such as poverty or war. Brainstorm at least three creative solutions to the problem —no matter how unusual or "crazy."

 ## SCANS Foundation Skills and Workplace Competencies

Basic Skills: *Writing/Speaking*

1. Choose a problem facing your school or community, and present a solution to the class. Use a written form—such as an advertisement, poster, or song lyric—to accompany your spoken presentation.

Information: *Acquire and Evaluate Information*

2. Imagine that you plan to open an ice-cream shop, video arcade, or other business in your community. Create a questionnaire designed to gather the information you need about the qualities and features that would attract your classmates. Make your questions as specific as possible, and distribute the questionnaire to as many students

as you can. Evaluate the responses, and write a report describing how your shop will meet customers' demands.

Connecting Academics to the Workplace

Human Relations

1. In most jobs, productivity increases when morale is high. Workers who feel good about themselves and their work usually perform well. In a group of three, choose a type of company, identify a morale problem, and brainstorm at least five possible solutions to present to management. Then evaluate the possible solutions by asking yourself what their practical consequences are. Finally, decide on one solution, and create a presentation in which you cite the benefits of that solution.

Language Arts

2. Choose a short story or novel that you have read or a movie or television show that you have seen in which a character makes a job-related decision or solves a problem at work. Apply the steps of decision making or problem solving to the character's actions. Then explain whether you think the character should have arrived at a different decision or solution and why you think so.

Developing Teamwork and Leadership Skills

In a team of five or six, brainstorm a solution to the following problem: You are the owners and employees of a small successful restaurant; however, a large national chain is opening a fast-food restaurant next door. Conduct a meeting at which you explore multiple solutions to the situation. Listen to everyone's suggestions, and question everyone's assumptions. Then, as a group, decide on the best strategy for continuing success.

Real-World Workshop

With a partner, present a mock telephone conversation in which an employee who is a service worker (plumber, appliance repairer, delivery person) faces a problem in the field and calls the supervisor in the office. The employee may face lack of materials, lack of time, or lack of information. What questions does the employee ask? What advice does the supervisor give? What decisions are reached?

School-to-Work Connection

Interview someone who works in a career area that interests you. Ask about the usual methods for solving problems in that career area. If possible, obtain a specific example of a successful solution to a problem. Present your findings to the class.

Individual Career Plan

Different careers present different decisions to be made and different problems to be solved. For the career area that is most appealing to you, list the kinds of decisions you think you would have to make and the kinds of problems you would have to solve on a daily basis.

Chapter 17

Technology in the Workplace

Section 17-1
Changing Technology in Everyday Living

Section 17-2
Computer Software and Its Applications

In this video segment, learn how to use thinking skills to make decisions and solve workplace problems.

Journal
Personal Career Plan

Talk with an older adult about how computers and their uses have changed during that person's lifetime. Then think about further changes that may occur during your lifetime. Write a journal entry discussing your findings and ideas.

Changing Technology in Everyday Living

OBJECTIVES

After studying this section, you will be able to:

- Explain how changing technology affects the workplace.
- Describe ways workers can become technologically literate.

KEY TERMS

globalization
teleconferencing
laptop

Can you imagine a world not linked by telephone lines and satellite communications? Can you picture schools without computers or business offices without fax machines? You probably can't. Computer technology has become a part of everyday life.

People use a computer when they get money from an automated teller machine (ATM). At the supermarket and the department store, bar codes on purchases are computer-scanned. At school, you may use computers for doing research or writing and revising paragraphs. You can count on the fact that no matter where you choose to work, you will use some type of computer technology in your job.

Technological Change and the Workplace

Technological change isn't new. Technology has been advancing for thousands of years, from simple stone tools to the waterwheel, to the printing press, and to the automobile. The difference today is in the pace of change. Technology seems to be advancing at ever greater speed.

In just a couple of decades, businesses, large and small, have come to depend on computers and fax machines. Today more and more companies are using devices such as cellular phones, voice mail, electronic schedules, and document scanners. Many experts

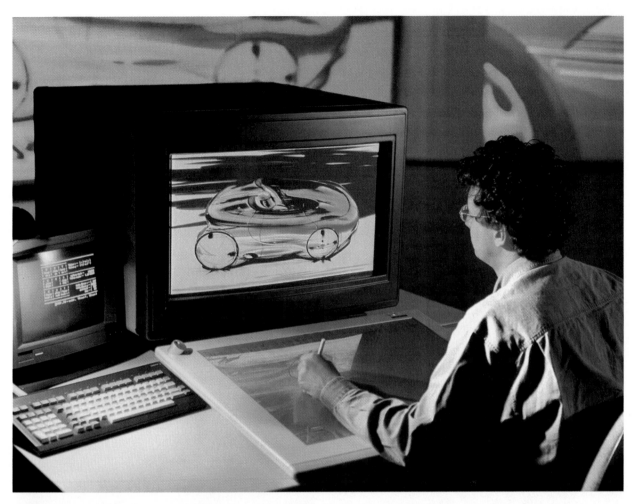

 Computers are used extensively in engineering. *How might computer simulations be used in designing new automobiles or aircraft?*

expect this trend toward greater use of technology to continue into the foreseeable future. How will this trend affect the workplace—and you?

A High-Tech Global Village

One effect of changing technology is the globalization of the workplace. **Globalization** refers to the establishment of worldwide communication links between people and groups. These links are made possible through modern technology.

Globalization is at work when a business owner in Chicago, Illinois, instantly communicates an investment decision to her partner in Sydney, Australia.

Globalization is at work when the two individuals meet through teleconferencing to discuss that decision. **Teleconferencing** involves simultaneous discussion among people in different locations, using electronic means. Teleconferencing is faster and less expensive than setting up a face-to-face meeting.

Do you find that some tasks make you feel uncertain or even nervous? Those aren't the jobs to avoid—they're the ones to tackle right away. Putting a difficult task off will only make you feel less confident. So, get that difficult job out of the way. You'll boost your confidence and make time for the tasks you find more enjoyable.

Through technology, the world becomes smaller—a global village. In the workplace, globalization means that you will have contact with people who are living in other cultures. You will need to know and understand what happens in other parts of the world. Those events may directly affect you and your workplace.

New Ways to Work

Technology has also brought about other types of changes in the workplace. Some examples follow.

 Business travelers often use laptop computers to make the most of their travel time. *How else might laptops be used in today's workplace?*

- *Businesses are moving toward a "distributed" workforce.* In other words, employees no longer work just at a company's place of business. Instead, they are distributed, or spread about, in many places. Many employees, for example, work at home.

  Chapter 1 introduced you to the concept of telecommuting. Thanks to personal computers, an employee can be on the job without leaving home. The New York-based research firm Link Resources, Inc., predicts that as many as 13 million people will soon be telecommuting.

  Another device that is distributing the workforce is the laptop computer. **Laptop** computers are small, portable computers with a screen and a keyboard. They make working outside the office easier. Many businesspeople travel. By taking their laptop computer along, their office goes with them.

- *Companies will need more "knowledge workers."* In the next decade, an emerging group of workers will be "knowledge workers." These workers will not produce products but will manage information. They will be responsible for finding, organizing, and delivering data. Today's medical technologists and computer installers are knowledge workers.

Laboratory technicians are knowledge workers. *What SCANS skills and competencies would be especially valuable for someone who wants to be a lab technician?*

What about tomorrow's knowledge workers? Consider a job in which a person navigates through the Internet, locates and packages valuable information, and delivers it to subscribers. This position, called "Internet surfer," has been predicted as one of the "hot" jobs of the 21st century.

Technological Literacy

How can you prepare for the technological workplace? First, you need to be comfortable with computer technology. Important SCANS skills to master include the following:

- using computers to process information,
- selecting technology,
- applying technology to task, and
- maintaining and troubleshooting technology.

 Figure 17-1

Skills for a Technological Workplace

Changes in technology often require new workplace skills. The following skills will be especially valuable in the workplace of the future.

A All workers, but especially managers, will need specialized communication skills. Communicating by electronic means does not provide the same type of feedback that is available in face-to-face meetings. New skills will be needed to make communication effective.

All of these skills are a part of *technological literacy*, which is knowing about and being able to use technology effectively. What else will you need in a high-tech workplace? **Figure 17-1** gives a few suggestions.

Tech for Success

Technological literacy is basic to workplace success. Fortunately, you probably already know quite a lot about computers. Continue to build your skills, however. At your job, don't just learn enough of a

B Because electronic communication is so rapid, people may need to respond more swiftly to decisions and events. The SCANS skills of reasoning and creative thinking will be increasingly important.

C The 21st century workplace may require new decision-making skills as well. The good news is that more people will be able to participate in decision making through such devices as electronic bulletin boards and E-mail. Decision makers, however, will need to discover ways to control the process and make it work smoothly.

program to get by. Read books or take courses. Ask questions to learn more about equipment you are using. Keep up-to-date with the latest workplace technology. The more you know, the more valuable you will be to your company.

Marissa Kovak, an office manager for a construction company, was asked to provide monthly project status reports in memo form. She took the assignment a step further and learned how to link her memos to detailed budget tables kept for all projects. Her method saved a time-consuming updating step. When Marissa showed her discovery to her boss, he was grateful enough to offer Marissa a bonus—and eventually a promotion.

New Skills for a New Workplace

What's the bottom line? Stay alert, be flexible, and sharpen your information-handling skills. Workers who can locate information quickly and present it in a clear and logical way will be valuable in tomorrow's workforce.

Career Do's & Don'ts

When Using Technology...

Do:
- stay current with the latest technological equipment in your workplace.
- ask for training and help when needed.
- constantly improve your technology skills.
- share your knowledge.

Don't:
- be resistant to learning new technology skills.
- try to learn everything by yourself.
- make changes without appropriate approvals.
- try to fix equipment with which you are not familiar.

SECTION 17-1 *Review*

Understanding Key Concepts

Using complete sentences, answer the following questions on a separate sheet of paper.

1. How could globalization create a more diverse workplace?

2. What can you do now while in school to increase your technological literacy?

Exploring Careers: Business and Office

Karlene Westerlund
Certified Insurance Claims Assistant

Q: How did you become a claims assistant?

A: I did a lot of career exploration at the community college and found I liked office work. I took office administration at the college which gave me the basics of working on the computer and an overview of all other office skills. The last six months, I worked in a cooperative work experience program with a large insurance company. That was the best hands-on experience.

Q: Why did you stay with the insurance company?

A: I had a friend there who had moved up quickly. It's such a large corporation, so it has many different departments: legal, claims, and medical. It seemed like the company had a lot to offer.

I was also attracted by the ongoing education programs. Some people don't think of training as a benefit. However, education is so expensive that if you have to take money out of your own pocket to pay for skills required to advance in your job, it could be hard.

Q: What would you tell people who are just entering the workforce?

A: When I went for my interview, my attitude was that the company needed me. I let the interviewer know that by the way I responded to questions. Treat yourself as the best product on the market.

Thinking Critically

Why is the ability to work with people necessary for an insurance claims assistant?

CAREER FACTS

Nature of the Work:
Provide support for insurance claims adjusters; make phone calls and appointments for clients and adjusters; write letters; work with attorneys.

Training or Education Needed:
Strong office experience or training in office administration; may require state certification.

Aptitudes, Abilities, and Skills:
Math, listening, speaking, and interpersonal skills; reading and writing skills.

Salary Range:
Average salary—$1,600 to $2,200 a month.

Career Path:
Work in other offices; train on the job; move into other insurance specialties.

Computer Software and Its Applications

Computers sometimes seem to have minds of their own, especially when errors crop up or viruses creep in. *Viruses* are programs that can damage computer files and even hard drives. Basically, however, computers do what they are instructed to do by their software. Selecting technology such as the most appropriate software and applying it to your task are valuable SCANS skills.

Using Computer Software

There are many different types of business software. Some of the simplest programs allow workers to produce text documents efficiently. More complex software, on the other hand, may permit architects to plan "virtual buildings" that can be navigated electronically. The types of software used most commonly in business include word-processing programs, databases, spreadsheets, and desktop publishing.

Word Processing

Using any software program that creates text-based documents is called **word processing**. Word processing allows you to create, edit, and format text. The difference between word processing and typing is that word processing allows you to add, move, and delete material (from letters to whole paragraphs or series of pages) with a couple of keyboard strokes. Most word-processing programs also include additional aids that check spelling and provide definitions and synonyms for words.

Spreadsheets are useful for accounting, budgeting, and scheduling. Each box on the spreadsheet is called a cell. Changing a number in one cell automatically causes adjustments in all the other cells. *How might this be used for making up or changing a schedule?*

Database Programs

Organizing business records is made easy with database programs. In a **database**, information is stored in a number of different formats, or tables. The program allows you to search through, sort, and recombine the stored data. A retail store owner, for example, may use a database program to record day-to-day inventory and sales information. Data can be recombined, however, to produce a sales report. Data might also be sorted to show fastest- or slowest-selling items.

Spreadsheet Programs

Data can be viewed and manipulated with a **spreadsheet**. This is a computer program that arranges or "spreads" data, usually numbers, into rows and columns. Spreadsheet programs also perform calculations. Businesspeople can try various calculations to see what would happen if different business decisions were made. These calculations help them make decisions. Spreadsheets are popular for such tasks as keeping accounts payable records and projecting sales and expenses.

Desktop Publishing

Many people now have their own publishing facilities—on their desks. This is the origin of the term *desktop publishing*. **Desktop publishing** involves using computers and special software to create documents that look as if they were printed by professional printers. You can produce just about anything this way, including reports, brochures, newsletters, invitations, greeting cards, and calendars. Desktop-publishing methods save businesses and individuals both time and money. They also provide greater control over the printed product.

Maintenance and Troubleshooting

Have you ever heard of Murphy's Law? Basically, it says that if something can go wrong, it will go wrong.

Here's a positive twist to Murphy's Law: If you are prepared for something to go wrong, you may be able to prevent it. Fortunately, you won't have to be a technical wizard to help prevent software problems. The following

 Desktop publishing is especially useful for people who are in business for themselves. *Why do you think this is true?*

tips will help you maintain and troubleshoot software at work.

- Attend training sessions and workshops whenever possible.

- Read operating manuals. Use your SCANS reading skills to improve your ability to understand technical material.

- Use the program's "Help" feature.

- Pay attention to what the machine is telling you. Copiers and fax machines, for example, often have a display that flashes a numerical code to indicate a specific problem.

- Know whom to call for help. Most commercial software programs have 800 or 888 help lines.

- Save your work frequently. Use the computer's autosave features, but don't rely on them. Save every half hour or so. At the end of the day, make disk copies and keep hard copy if you need to do so.

The Internet

You can hardly turn on the television set or look through a magazine today without encountering a reference to the Internet. The Internet, which millions of people navigate, is a vast network of computer

EXCELLENT BUSINESS PRACTICES

Preparing Students for Working with Technology

Intel Corporation, a semiconductor manufacturer, has responded to the need to help prepare students for the workplace. The company has created partnerships with schools and colleges to enhance their math, science, and technology programs.

Intel has developed a curriculum and donated millions of dollars to educational institutions in New Mexico and Arizona, where it has large manufacturing plants. The company encourages schools to teach students about skills needed in the business environment, such as technology. Instructors of community colleges are invited to Intel for the summer and paid salaries. There they gain valuable experience for themselves and bring the practical applications back to the classroom.

Intel also supports the future technology workforce by establishing a variety of work-study programs, by offering scholarships, and by donating equipment. The more education and training employees bring into the company, the less on-the-job training the company needs to provide.

Thinking Critically

Why is it important for companies, like Intel, to create technology partnerships with schools?

Internet Terminology

Term	Definition
Browser	A program you can use to visit sites on the Internet
Download	Transfer a file from an Internet site to your computer's hard drive
E-mail	A message composed on one computer to be received by another computer
FAQ	Abbreviation for frequently asked questions; a document that displays answers to common questions about particular sites on the internet
Freeware	Software provided by its creator at no charge
Home page	The name for the screen you see when you go to a site on the World Wide Web; also refers to the site itself
Hyperlink	A highlighted word, phrase, or image in a Web document; by clicking on it you can jump to a document about that subject
Log in, log on	Terms used to describe the process of connecting with a remote computer
Net	Nickname for the Internet
Search engine	Software that finds and retrieves data on the Internet
Shareware	Software you may download free to test; if you decide to use it, you should send the requested payment to the creator
Site	A location on the Internet
URL	Abbreviation for uniform resource locator; an Internet address
Web browser	See **browser**
Web site	See **site**

Figure 17-2 This Internet terminology is important for a "newbie" (newcomer) to know. Why would it be a good idea to look over FAQ files before you visit a site?

networks. In plain language, however, the Internet is people, their computers, the connections between them, and the software used to run the computers.

Figure 17-2 provides a list of Internet terms and their definitions. Look through the list. How many terms do you already know?

Uses of the Internet

Through the Internet, you can communicate with people all over the world. You also have access to vast amounts of information, including text, graphics, sound, and video. Businesses use the Internet in a variety of ways, some of which are indicated here:

- for low-cost, speedy communication and as an alternative to faxing for long documents;
- to advertise and sell products;
- to provide consumer information and assistance;
- to find information; and
- to advertise job openings and locate potential applicants.

Netiquette

Netiquette is a term referring to accepted rules of conduct when using the Internet. When you use the Internet at work, you need to be especially careful to use good manners. The following list gives a summary of netiquette principles.

- When sending a message, always include a clear subject line to help readers identify your subject.
- When responding, state to what you are responding. Never just say yes or no.
- Don't type in all caps.
- Don't ramble. Internet users appreciate specific, focused communications.
- Use a definite closing. Sign your name or write "the end."
- Don't publish other people's messages without their permission.
- Avoid personal or sensitive issues. Never use obscenity or make racial or ethnic slurs.
- Use *emoticons*, groups of keyboard symbols designed to show the writer's feelings. See *Figure 17-3* for examples.

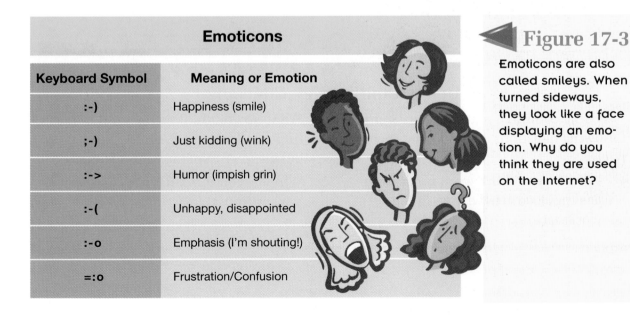

Emoticons	
Keyboard Symbol	**Meaning or Emotion**
:-)	Happiness (smile)
;-)	Just kidding (wink)
:->	Humor (impish grin)
:-(	Unhappy, disappointed
:-o	Emphasis (I'm shouting!)
=:o	Frustration/Confusion

Figure 17-3

Emoticons are also called smileys. When turned sideways, they look like a face displaying an emotion. Why do you think they are used on the Internet?

Legal and Ethical Technology Issues

In earlier chapters, you learned about ethical issues such as honesty and confidentiality. In business, one form of honesty involves giving credit to others when you make use of something they have created. This applies whether you are using an article from a magazine or a file you've downloaded from the Internet. Newer forms of technology don't change basic ethics.

Copyright law has been developed to help people protect what they create. **Copyright** is the legal right of authors or other creators of works to control the reproduction and use of their works. Permission is usually required to use copyrighted material. Works covered by copyright law include the following types:

- literary and dramatic works, such as poetry;
- computer software and databases;
- photographs, videos, and film;
- musical and artistic works; and
- recordings.

Copyright protection means that the copyright owner has the sole right to do the following, or to authorize others to do so:

- make copies,
- distribute copies for sale or lease,
- perform (play) or display (movie, photo), and
- prepare translations or adaptations.

Copyright law protects all written works, whether or not they have been formally published. A file from the Internet and even information you've created on your computer is protected. It is ethical to give credit to the source of any facts you use.

Get to know enough about copyright laws to protect yourself. There are many books and courses available on copyright protection. If you are not sure whether or not you need to ask permission, always do so—just to be safe.

SECTION 17-2 *Review*

Understanding Key Concepts

Using complete sentences, answer the following questions on a separate sheet of paper.

1. Why do you think word processing has replaced typewriting in the workplace?

2. What do you think is one of the most important uses of the Internet for businesses? Explain your answer.

3. Why do you think having copyright laws is important?

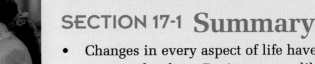

Key Terms

globalization *(p. 337)*
teleconferencing *(p. 337)*
laptop *(p. 339)*

SECTION 17-1 Summary

- Changes in every aspect of life have resulted from computer technology. Businesses are likely to continue to increase their use of technology.

- New technology has helped bring about globalization, or worldwide communication links. Teleconferencing is one example of globalization.

- Computers and telecommuting technology are making today's workforce more distributed (rather than centralized). Knowledge workers, who find and process information, are becoming increasingly important.

- Technological literacy involves knowing about and being able to use technology effectively.

- Workers should learn as much as they can about the technology they are using. Technology requires new communication and decision-making skills as well as quicker response times.

Key Terms

word processing *(p. 344)*
database *(p. 345)*
spreadsheet *(p. 345)*
desktop publishing *(p. 346)*
copyright *(p. 350)*

SECTION 17-2 Summary

- There are many different types of business software. Word processing is used for creating, editing, and formatting documents.

- Database programs store data and allow workers to sort and combine them in various forms.

- Spreadsheet programs allow data to be viewed and manipulated in a table format.

- Desktop publishing, which is the use of computers and special software for creating professional-looking documents, saves businesses and individuals time and money.

- Ways to prevent software problems include attending training sessions and workshops, reading operating manuals, and saving work frequently.

- The Internet is a network of computer networks. For business, it offers low-cost, speedy communication and access to information.

Reviewing Key Terms

On a separate sheet of paper, write a dialogue between two friends talking about technology in the workplace. Use the terms below.

globalization   spreadsheet
teleconferencing   desktop
laptop   publishing
word processing   copyright
database

Recalling Key Concepts

On a separate sheet of paper, tell whether each item below is true or false. Rewrite any false statements to make them true.

1. Teleconferencing is not an example of globalization.

2. Technological literacy involves knowing about and using technology effectively.

3. Spreadsheet programs are designed to create, edit, and format text.

4. The Internet has very few business uses.

5. Permission is usually required to use copyrighted material.

Thinking Critically

Using complete sentences, answer each of the questions below on a separate sheet of paper.

1. Why would it be wise for you to learn computer skills before entering the workforce?

2. Does technology always make life easier and draw people together? Explain your answer.

3. What might be one advantage and one disadvantage of a distributed workforce?

4. Discuss at least two ways that using the Internet to locate information could save time and money.

SCANS Foundation Skills and Workplace Competencies

Personal Qualities: *Integrity/Honesty*

1. A friend and coworker in your office is preparing to use her desktop-publishing capabilities to publish and distribute an essay about environmental hazards in industry. She plans to state that the work is her own. You know, however, that the essay appeared recently in a magazine. What should you say to your friend about copyright violation? Write a paragraph explaining and justifying your advice.

Technology: *Selecting Technology*

2. Purchasing a computer can be challenging. How do you know you are buying the right model? How do you decide which features you want and need? How do you know if the price is fair? What resources would you use to answer these questions?

Connecting Academics to the Workplace

Computer Science

1. Charles has just begun working for a public relations company that does a lot of desktop publishing.

His supervisor tells him that he will be expected to use a document scanner in his work. Do research to find out what a document scanner is and how it is used. Write a short report that would help Charles use this device.

Business and Office Education

2. You are employed by an advertising agency. Your firm needs to hire five temporary workers, but no office space is available. Your supervisor has asked you to research the advantages of having these workers telecommute. List the advantages to your company. Then suggest three ways to help the workers adjust to the agency.

Math

3. Ellen's supervisor is writing an article on the increased use of technology in everyday life. He has asked her to construct a graph that shows how the use of a particular type of technology, such as the personal computer, has increased. First, locate statistics about increased use of a particular type of technology. Then construct a graph. Finally, create a credit line that tells where you got the information.

Developing Teamwork and Leadership Skills

Working with a team of three people, create a chart that compares two brands of word-processing or spreadsheet software. Together, research the software by reading magazines, talking with store owners, and talking with users. Create a chart that compares the two products, showing strengths and weaknesses of each.

Real-World Workshop

Visit a company that employs telecommuters, and interview someone who works with them. Ask how the company communicates with these employees. What kind of work do they do? What are the advantages and disadvantages to the company? What is the future of telecommuting in the company? Share what you learn with your classmates.

School-to-Work Connection

Locate a business office or industry in your community that interests you. Meet with a representative to discuss the ways computers and other modern technology are used there. Ask the representative to indicate how the use of technology in that career field has changed over the last 10 years and how she or he expects it to change in the future. Prepare a brief report on your findings, identifying positive and negative effects of the changes.

Individual Career Plan

Select one work activity involving computers that appeals to you. In a career reference book, find a job related to this area of interest. Explain in a paragraph your interest and the job you have chosen, describing potential job opportunities.

Chapter 18

Time and Information Management

Section 18-1
Using Time Effectively

Section 18-2
Organizing Your Work

In this video segment, learn the importance of managing your time and organizing your work.

Journal
Personal Career Plan

Over the next two days, keep track of how you spend your time. Then consider your record. How much time—if any—is "wasted"? What do you think you should be doing with that time? Why? Write a journal entry detailing your time record and discussing your ideas.

Using Time Effectively

OBJECTIVES

After studying this section, you will be able to:

- **Prepare a schedule to accomplish your most important tasks.**
- **Employ common techniques to use time effectively.**

KEY TERMS

time line
schedule
downtime
delegating

Does time sometimes get away from you? Have you found yourself staying up late to finish a report or to prepare for an exam? When you move into the work world, time can get away just as fast. The consequences, however, can be even worse. In school, it's usually just you who suffers when you don't manage your time well. On the job, other people suffer as well—your coworkers, supervisor, and employer.

So what's the solution? Stay on top of your work by using your self-management skills and learning how to manage your time.

To Do or Not to Do

Think of time management as making choices. You can spend your time doing this task or that task. You've got to decide which one to do *now*. If you have just a few choices, the decision may be easy. If you have lots of tasks, though, you may need some tools to help you make the right decisions. The following process can help you manage your time.

1. List all your projects, appointments, and other tasks.

2. Rate the tasks by their importance.

3. Break large, complex projects into small steps.

4. Estimate the time needed to complete each task.

5. Set up a schedule for your tasks.

 In the business world, your work will always be connected to the work done by others. ***What would happen to your coworkers if your assignments were always late?***

Make a List

How can you make good choices? First, you have to know what your choices are, so make a task list. Write down every project, appointment, or meeting you have. List those you must do today plus all those you must complete in the days and weeks ahead. Include the meeting next Saturday, and the training session in December. Next to each task, write the date or time by which you must complete it.

What's Most Important?

If your task list is long, you may be thinking you'll never get it all done. It's okay if you don't. Successful time management doesn't mean always finding time to get *everything* done. It means getting the *most important things* done. You've got to prioritize, or decide the order of importance of completing all the different tasks.

Go back to your task list and analyze the tasks. Label them A, B, or C, according to order of importance. In deciding your priorities, consider the following:

- What were you hired to do? If you're a salesperson, your most important job is to sell. If you're a production worker, your most important job is to produce.

- Are you working alone or with others on a project? If you're working with others, you must coordinate your schedules to get the job done.

- What must you do to fulfill your obligations to the company? Are you expected to do paperwork or file reports? You must fulfill your obligations, even if they don't seem important to you.

Break Big Projects into Small Steps

Now take a second look at the major projects on your list. These large or long-term projects are often the most difficult to manage. People tend to focus on what has to be done today and tomorrow and to overlook things that are farther off. Moreover, long-term projects are often complex and require more work. It's hard to get a grip on what needs to be done today on a long-term project to ensure that it will be completed two months from now.

How can you deal with major projects? The best way is to break them into manageable steps. Then you can treat each part as a separate task.

When Walter Sanchez became assistant manager in an auto parts store, he was given several new responsibilities. One task was to find three new employees. Sanchez broke the job down into the following steps:

1. Compose and place a classified ad in the newspaper.

2. Review job applications and choose candidates for interviews.

3. Schedule and conduct interviews.

4. Select the best candidates and schedule them for interviews with the store manager.

5. Meet with the manager to make hiring decisions.

This process of identifying the steps in a project is essential. You have to know what you're facing so you can know

Walter Sanchez has three weeks to hire three new employees. *Why must Walter get started right away? What will happen if he puts the search off until the last week?*

how you're going to get it done. The SCANS skill of seeing things in the mind's eye will help you figure out the steps in a complex project. This is the skill of visualization. You'll use it to envision how to break down a project into manageable parts.

Estimate Time Needed to Do Tasks

You now know what jobs you have to do. How long will it take you to do each one?

- If you've done the job before, base your estimate on past experience.

- If the job is new to you, ask someone with experience how long it took him or her.

- If you've been assigned the job, ask your supervisor how long it should take.

- Be wary of underestimating how long a job will take.

- If a job depends on other people, allow for their time.

For large projects, such as Walter Sanchez's, you'll want to set deadlines for completing each step in the project. One way to figure out a timetable for long-term projects is to create a time line. A **time line** is a type of chart that shows the order in which events occur in time. It will help you visualize an entire project so that you can see when to work on each step.

Set Up a Schedule

Now it's time to pull all the steps in this process together. How? By making a schedule. A **schedule** is a list or chart showing when tasks must be completed. If

People choose different types of planners because they have different work needs, work habits, and lifestyles. ***Compare the advantages and disadvantages of the different planners shown here.***

a task must be completed today and you know that it will take an hour, write the time you'll start the task on your schedule. You will then know that an hour of time is set aside for one purpose, getting that task completed. Fill in your schedule hour by hour.

You now have a daily schedule that shows everything to be done today. Your daily schedule will be part of a long-term schedule that shows tasks well into the future. Many people use a calendar or day planner for scheduling. They can enter tasks on the schedule as soon as they know about them. That way, they always know what's coming up.

Here are some more suggestions for making up your schedule:

- Think about your work habits. Are you a morning person or an afternoon person? Schedule difficult tasks for times when you perform at your peak.

- Consider color coding your schedule. Use different colors for deadlines, meetings, travel, and so on.

- Transfer your priorities from your task list to your schedule. If you run out of time, you can see at a glance which tasks you can postpone.

- Check off tasks as you complete them. The accumulating check marks will give you a boost.

Building a schedule is an ongoing process. *Figure 18-1* shows the process Walter Sanchez might follow to put together his schedule. Look at his task list and time line. How do they appear on his schedule?

▶ **Figure 18-1**

Creating a Schedule

Managing time effectively is a process involving several steps.

A Making a task list is a first step in using time wisely. List everything that's coming up, such as meetings, projects, and luncheons. Include personal and business appointments. That way you won't mistakenly schedule two things for the same time. Prioritize tasks by labeling them A, B, or C.

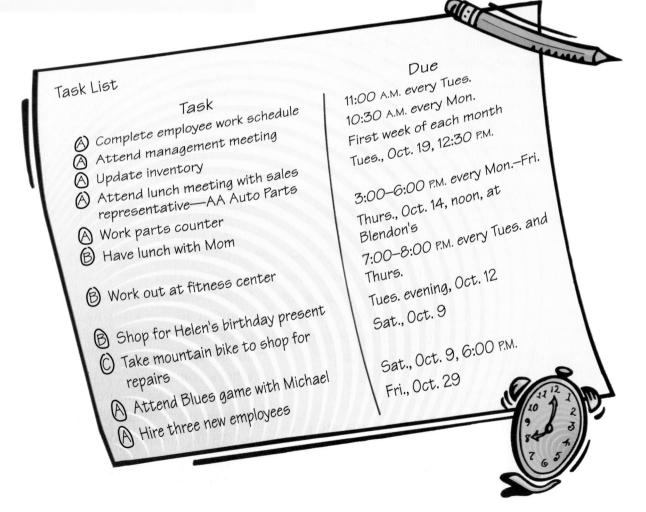

Task List	
Task	**Due**
Ⓐ Complete employee work schedule	11:00 A.M. every Tues.
Ⓐ Attend management meeting	10:30 A.M. every Mon.
Ⓐ Update inventory	First week of each month
Ⓐ Attend lunch meeting with sales representative—AA Auto Parts	Tues., Oct. 19, 12:30 P.M.
Ⓐ Work parts counter	3:00–6:00 P.M. every Mon.–Fri.
Ⓑ Have lunch with Mom	Thurs., Oct. 14, noon, at Blendon's
Ⓑ Work out at fitness center	7:00–8:00 P.M. every Tues. and Thurs.
Ⓑ Shop for Helen's birthday present	Tues. evening, Oct. 12
Ⓒ Take mountain bike to shop for repairs	Sat., Oct. 9
Ⓐ Attend Blues game with Michael	Sat., Oct. 9, 6:00 P.M.
Ⓐ Hire three new employees	Fri., Oct. 29

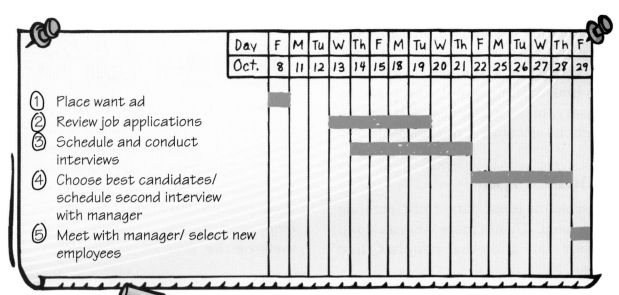

Day	F	M	Tu	W	Th	F	M	Tu	W	Th	F	M	Tu	W	Th	F
Oct.	8	11	12	13	14	15	18	19	20	21	22	25	26	27	28	29

1. Place want ad
2. Review job applications
3. Schedule and conduct interviews
4. Choose best candidates/ schedule second interview with manager
5. Meet with manager/ select new employees

B A time line can help you visualize the stages in a complex or long-term project. It will show how one stage must be completed before the next begins. This will give you a better grasp of when parts of the project have to be completed. The time line will also show when stages of the project overlap. Reviewing the time line during the project will help keep you aware of your progress and short-term deadlines.

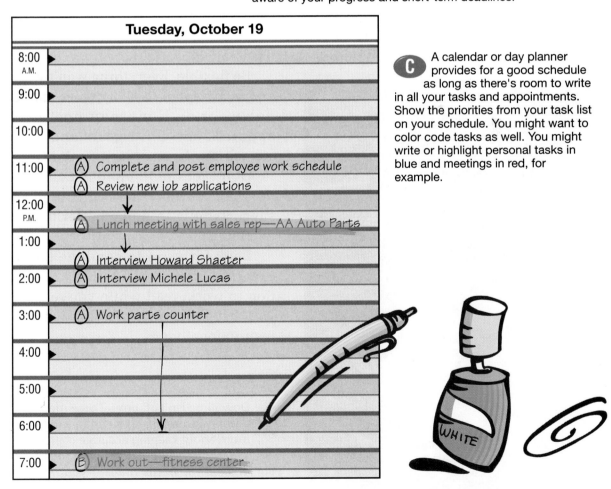

Tuesday, October 19

8:00 A.M.	
9:00	
10:00	
11:00	(A) Complete and post employee work schedule
	(A) Review new job applications
12:00 P.M.	(A) Lunch meeting with sales rep—AA Auto Parts
1:00	(A) Interview Howard Shaeter
2:00	(A) Interview Michele Lucas
3:00	(A) Work parts counter
4:00	
5:00	
6:00	
7:00	(B) Work out—fitness center

C A calendar or day planner provides for a good schedule as long as there's room to write in all your tasks and appointments. Show the priorities from your task list on your schedule. You might want to color code tasks as well. You might write or highlight personal tasks in blue and meetings in red, for example.

A schedule is a helpful tool for managing your time. You must keep it current, however. Take a few minutes every morning to look at it, update it, and plan. As necessary, make a new task list and go through the scheduling process again.

Timely Tips

A schedule is one part of efficient time management. There's more you can do to use your time and other people's time wisely.

Using Your Time Wisely

Everyone has occasional periods when nothing is on his or her schedule. This is called **downtime**. Don't waste it! Downtime is a good time to get ahead or to improve your skills. You might read an

equipment service manual or learn a new computer program.

Avoid procrastination. As you read in Chapter 16, procrastination is the putting off of work you should be doing. If a job has to be done, do it.

Be flexible. Everything won't work out just as you plan it. The copier may break down, or a client may postpone an appointment. Shift gears and go on to something else on your schedule.

Don't let the telephone control your time. The checklist shown in *Figure 18-2* suggests how to make better use of the telephone.

Look for ways to combine tasks. For example, if you take public transportation to work, read while you're riding. If you drive to work, consider listening to instructional tapes.

 Downtime isn't off time. These medical employees are using downtime to learn more about keeping accurate charts. *How will learning something new about your job help you better manage your time on the next project?*

Always be prepared to get work done. Carry a pen and paper with you all the time. You can write notes when stuck in traffic or waiting in line somewhere.

Using Other People's Time Wisely

When you work with other people, be aware of how you use their time. When people are busy, keep your conversations focused. Give them only the important information. Don't bother them with nonessential details.

When you are assigned a task, listen carefully to the details. Ask questions if you don't understand something. Then you won't have to go back later and interrupt your supervisor or coworker with more questions.

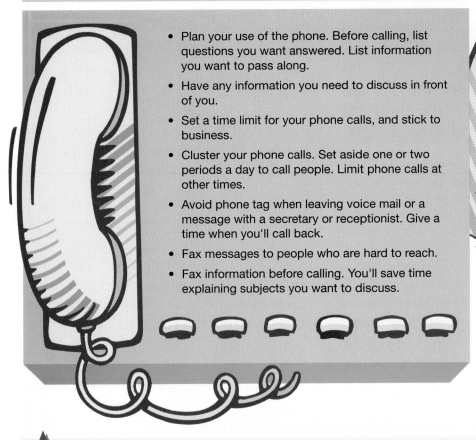

Getting the Most from Your Telephone

- Plan your use of the phone. Before calling, list questions you want answered. List information you want to pass along.
- Have any information you need to discuss in front of you.
- Set a time limit for your phone calls, and stick to business.
- Cluster your phone calls. Set aside one or two periods a day to call people. Limit phone calls at other times.
- Avoid phone tag when leaving voice mail or a message with a secretary or receptionist. Give a time when you'll call back.
- Fax messages to people who are hard to reach.
- Fax information before calling. You'll save time explaining subjects you want to discuss.

Figure 18-2   The telephone can take a great deal of your time. This checklist can help you use the phone more efficiently. How can you use the telephone to save time?

There's no reason to just sit and wait while waiting for the bus. Get something done. The work you do may give you more time later for an activity you enjoy. *What kinds of work might you do while riding a bus or waiting in traffic?*

Career Do's & Don'ts

When Managing Time Effectively...

Do:
- plan.
- focus on activities with long-term payoffs.
- complete the most important work first.
- tackle one task at a time.
- write down questions you have ahead of time, then plan a short meeting in which you can obtain answers to your questions.

Don't:
- procrastinate.
- spend your prime time cleaning your desk area or chatting with associates.
- get stuck on minor details to the extent it jeopardizes the bigger picture.

Give complete instructions when delegating work to others. **Delegating** means assigning tasks to other people. Make sure they understand what you're asking them to do. Take time to answer questions. How will spending more time answering questions initially save you time later?

SECTION 18-1 *Review*

Understanding Key Concepts

Using complete sentences, answer the following questions on a separate sheet of paper.

1. How can a schedule help you use your time more efficiently?

2. Why is it important to use your coworkers' time wisely?

Exploring Careers: Hospitality and Recreation

Ted Lai
School Food Service Manager

Q: **Do you have a background in food service?**

A: The first food service experience I had was helping feed the homeless when I was in high school. I worked in food service jobs to help put myself through college.

When I started in food service, I began by washing dishes. After a while, I began helping by making salads. Then I moved up to doing some cooking. Finally, I advanced to manager.

Q: **How is school food service different from work in a restaurant?**

A: The biggest difference is that schools have regular hours: 6 A.M. to 2:30 P.M., Monday through Friday, with the holidays and the weekends off. When you're working in schools, you usually have better health benefits than you do in when working in a restaurant. However, the financial reward is higher in restaurant work, and there is more chance for advancement.

Q: **What do you like about food service?**

A: It's not only a good industry but also one that will always be needed. I think the art of cooking at home is being lost. Instead, a lot of people are going out to dinner.

I like the cooking aspects of food service more than the management aspects. Cooking lets you explore the creativity of food. I like getting people to enjoy something I've made.

Thinking Critically

What skills do you have that would be useful in a food service career?

CAREER FACTS

Nature of the Work:
Make sure supplies are available; oversee work crew; keep records of compliance with government regulations.

Training or Education Needed:
Bachelor's degree in food service management; experience in the industry.

Aptitudes, Abilities, and Skills:
Reading and writing skills; knowledge of cooking; skill in menu planning, food purchasing, and presentation; organizational skills; management skills, including the ability to supervise others.

Salary Range:
$18,000 to $50,000.

Career Path:
Start in the restaurant kitchen; work through different jobs to a managerial position.

Organizing Your Work

After studying this section, you will be able to:

- **Organize yourself and your tasks.**
- **Develop and maintain a useful system for filing paperwork.**
- **Create and maintain computer files.**

access
directory
subdirectories

You've learned strategies for using your time more effectively. What else can you do to get your work done faster and better? First, you can organize the things around you in your work area. Second, you can organize the information you use to do your work.

Organizing Your Work Area

You may be very skilled at your job. However, if you can't quickly find the tools or materials you need to do your job, your skill won't matter. Think about your work area. Find a place for everything.

Everything in Its Place

The first rule for organizing a work area might be called the near-far rule. What things do you use most often? They should be near you. What things do you use less frequently? These things can be placed farther away.

Plumbers, for example, carry a toolbox with them when they make a house call. The toolbox contains the most frequently used tools of their trade. Plumbers keep these tools close at hand. Tools used less frequently are kept in the truck.

A second guideline is to put like things together. Files, supplies, and tools used for one project or type of job should be kept together. Those used for another project or job might be kept in a separate area.

- Avoid putting each document in a separate file. Group documents by type.
- Avoid massive files with many documents. Divide them by subtopics.
- Color-code folders or labels to help identify categories or subcategories. For example, green folders might indicate one project, blue another, and so on.
- File on a regular basis.

Filing systems should be organized in the most logical way possible. People using them should be able to locate needed information quickly. *How might you organize a filing system for your school classes?*

EXCELLENT BUSINESS PRACTICES

On-Site Child Care

PacifiCare Health Systems is one of the nation's largest managed health-care organizations. To help serve its employees better, it has built an on-site child-care center.

Company employees working 32 or more hours a week are eligible to enroll their dependents from six weeks old to kindergarten-entry age. For working parents, the child-care center offers the convenience of bringing their children to the workplace and the comfort of having their youngsters close enough to visit during lunch. For businesses, on-site child care is proving to be a cost-effective investment that results in more loyal and productive employees, reduced absenteeism due to child-care problems, and enhanced job satisfaction. PacifiCare Health

Systems also offers employees access to child- and elder-care counselors, child-care subsidies, and parenting and elder-care workshops.

Thinking Critically

If you were a working parent with a young child or children, why would you want to work at a company that had an on-site child-care facility?

Managing Computer Information

If you look around most offices, you'll see desks covered with paper. Despite appearances, more and more information is entering offices as computer files and E-mail. Managing electronic information has become as great a challenge as managing paper documents.

Many of the rules for managing paper documents also apply to managing electronic files. Don't clutter your files with information you don't need. Make a separate **directory**, or computer file, for each category of information. A directory is like a filing cabinet that contains many files on a large topic, such as a project.

Don't let directories get too full; create new **subdirectories**. These are smaller groupings of files. For example, you may have a directory for XYZ Company. As business improves, you might create subdirectories for invoices, orders, letters, and so on.

Choose names for computer files carefully. Select logical, descriptive names, ones you'll remember six months from now. It's also helpful to keep a written record of file names.

Directories and subdirectories should be given logical, brief names. Some software programs only record up to eight letters for a name. Use abbreviations that are easy to recognize. *What might you name a directory for* **Succeeding in the World of Work?**

SECTION 18-2 *Review*

Understanding Key Concepts

Using complete sentences, answer the following questions on a separate sheet of paper.

1. How can organizing your work space make you more efficient?

2. Why should you avoid creating very large files with many documents?

3. Why is it important to choose names for computer files carefully?

Key Terms

time line *(p. 359)*
schedule *(p. 359)*
downtime *(p. 362)*
delegating *(p. 364)*

SECTION 18-1 Summary

- The effective use of time requires knowledge of the SCANS skill of self-management and the SCANS competency in time management.

- Time management is a process of deciding how to use your time wisely. The first step is to identify all your tasks by making a task list. Then prioritize each task.

- Manage long-term projects best by breaking them into smaller, more manageable parts. Then treat the parts as separate tasks.

- Decide how long each task will take to complete. Make a time line to help you figure out how long larger projects will take.

- There are many forms for schedules. Choose the form that fits your style and individual needs.

- Keep your schedule current. Review it daily.

- Use your time wisely by making use of downtime, avoiding procrastination, and being flexible when plans don't work out. Use the telephone wisely, and combine tasks.

- Use other people's time wisely. Keep conversations brief, listen to assignments carefully, and give complete directions when delegating tasks.

Key Terms

access *(p. 367)*
directory *(p. 370)*
subdirectories *(p. 370)*

SECTION 18-2 Summary

- Organizing your work area helps you work efficiently.

- Keep your work area organized so that you can find tools and supplies when you need them.

- Organize information so that it is accessible. Discard information you do not and will not need.

- File paper documents in file folders. Place the folders in hanging files. Categorize information. Avoid creating files with either too many or too few documents. Label files, and consider using color coding to identify information.

- Many of the rules for managing paper documents also apply to managing computer information.

Reviewing Key Terms

On a separate sheet of paper, write one or two paragraphs explaining how you can better manage your time and information. Use each term below.

time line   access
schedule   directory
downtime   subdirectories
delegating

Recalling Key Concepts

On a separate sheet of paper, tell whether each statement is true or false. Rewrite any false statements to make them true.

1. A schedule should include only tasks of the highest priority.

2. A time line helps you visualize how the parts of a large project fit together.

3. If you organize your work space by the near-far rule, the materials you use most often will be within easy reach.

4. If you don't need the information in a document and are sure you won't need it in the future, you should file it.

5. When setting up computer files, you should create subdirectories to prevent directories from becoming too full.

Thinking Critically

Using complete sentences, answer each of the questions below on a separate sheet of paper.

1. In managing your time, why should your emphasis be on getting the most important things done rather than on getting everything done?

2. How does breaking a large task into smaller parts help you manage the work?

3. Should you make a time line for every task? Why or why not?

4. How does a disorganized work area waste your time?

5. Is managing information a greater challenge if the information is on paper or in electronic files? Explain your answer.

SCANS Foundation Skills and Workplace Competencies

Thinking Skills: *Seeing Things in the Mind's Eye*

1. You've been asked to plan your company's annual employee picnic. You must take care of all details. Break down the assignment into manageable parts. List the smaller tasks.

Information: *Organizing and Maintaining Information*

2. Documents on the following topics have arrived on your desk: revised employee insurance policy, company holidays for 1998, winter hours for the child-care facility, vacation policy, flu shots covered under health plan, how to file for health insurance coverage, New Year's Day work schedule, and child-care policy for children who are ill. Make a list to show how you would organize the topics in files and folders. Name each file and folder.

Connecting Academics to the Workplace

Social Studies

1. Jeffrey manages a small electronics store. He has three salespeople and an office assistant. The owner has come to town unexpectedly and has called an all-afternoon meeting. Jeffrey cannot finish the following tasks that remain on his schedule. What should he do about them?

   Meet with distributor of new products—2:00 P.M.

   Complete inventory of computer software.

   Select items for next week's sale.

   Read and deal with mail, E-mail, and faxes.

   Lunch with sister at noon.

   Train new salesperson in how to demonstrate camcorders.

Computer Science

2. Do research to learn about computer software that will create personal schedules. Compare and contrast the software available, and determine the pros and cons of each. Summarize your findings in a 250-word report.

Developing Teamwork and Leadership Skills

Work with a group of classmates. Together, choose a type of business. Imagine that you are designing the work space for a specific department in that business. Investigate the kinds of work done in that department. You may want to tour a similar business in your area and talk to employees to learn what goes on in the chosen department. Then design the department work space for your company. Make the space as efficient as possible.

Real-World Workshop

Think about one of the jobs you've had. It may have been either a volunteer or for-pay job. How well did you use your time on the job? List the ways that you used time well. List the ways in which you could have improved your use of time.

School-to-Work Connection

With a partner, select a local company. Then contact the personnel director or another supervisor at that firm. Make an appointment and interview the person about ways in which the company manages work areas and employee time to improve efficiency. Report your findings to the class.

Individual Career Plan

Write a self-evaluation of how you manage your time. Do you procrastinate? Are you a morning or afternoon person? Do you meet deadlines easily, or do you scramble to get them done on time? Are you always on time, or do you often show up late? List things you might do to improve your use of time.

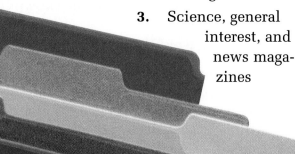

ASPECTS OF INDUSTRY
Underlying Principles of Technology

Overview

In Unit Five, you read about a variety of skills you'll use in your career. In this Unit Lab, you will put into practice what you have learned about using thinking skills and technology in the workplace while exploring another aspect of industry: **Underlying Principles of Technology.**

Technology is the way in which science is applied to the practical aspects of life—in this case, work. Understanding the Underlying Principles of Technology can be vital to your career. If you can't keep pace with technological changes, you may be out of a job. By understanding how technology can affect your career, you can plan for training or even a career change.

Tools

1. Internet
2. Trade and business magazines
3. Science, general interest, and news magazines

Procedures

STEP A

Choose three careers that interest you from the 15 job clusters shown in Figure 3-1 in Chapter 3. You may choose the careers from the same cluster, or from three different clusters. You may choose the same cluster you explored in the previous Lab, or a different one.

For each career, find at least three trade publications from 10 years ago. What technology was being used? What was new at the time? What scientific developments were affecting the career? What predictions were being made about the future of the career?

Next, find at least two science magazines (such as *Discover*), two general interest magazines (such as *Smithsonian*), and two news magazines (such as *Time*) from 10 years ago. Skim them for stories that relate to your chosen field. Note the technological, scientific, economic, and social trends of the time. What were the concerns of the public?

Keep copies of the articles you read or take notes. Refer to them when you do Step C and when you write your report.

STEP B

Fast forward to the present. Follow the procedure in Step A, using at least three current trade publications (or two publications and an Internet source) to find out what technology is being used today. What is new? What scientific discoveries are affecting the career? What predictions are being made about the future?

Next, skim magazines published within the last year for stories that relate to each field. Note the technological, scientific, economic, and social trends, and public concerns.

how it has been affected by scientific, technological, economic, and social changes. In your "trip to the future," you may discover that your chosen field has undergone considerable transformation. Show how that change took place, and why. Note the training that students of the future will need, or that your company may provide. What are the benefits of working in your career of the future?

STEP C

Flash 10 years into the future. You are recruiting high school and college students for a company or agency in one of the fields you previously researched. Working alone or with classmates, prepare a recruitment campaign.

In your campaign, show how the career has changed over the previous 20 years, and

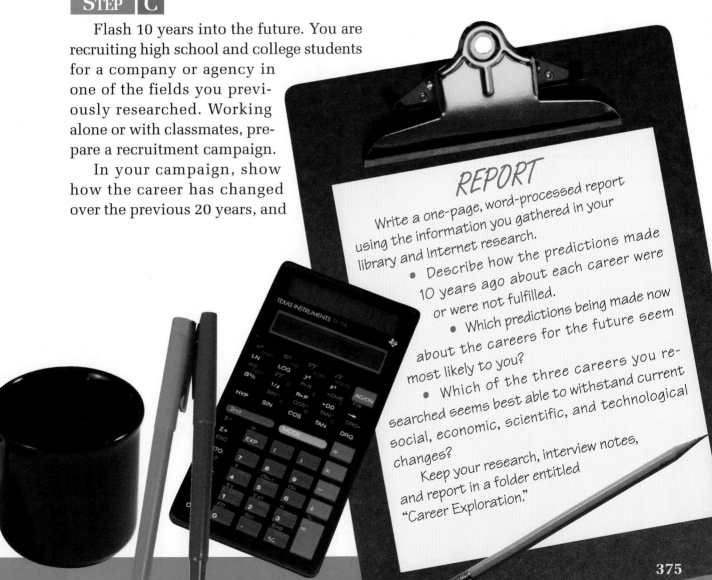

REPORT

Write a one-page, word-processed report using the information you gathered in your library and Internet research.

- Describe how the predictions made 10 years ago about each career were or were not fulfilled.
- Which predictions being made now about the careers for the future seem most likely to you?
- Which of the three careers you researched seems best able to withstand current social, economic, scientific, and technological changes?

Keep your research, interview notes, and report in a folder entitled "Career Exploration."

UNIT 6
Life Skills

UNIT 6 QUIZ:

What Do You Know About Life Skills?

- How does the economy affect your life?
- How can you effectively manage your money?
- Can you name three ways to save money?
- Why is insurance important?
- Why do we pay taxes?

Chapter 19

Economics and the Consumer

Section 19-1
Our Economic System

Section 19-2
You, the Consumer

In this video segment, find out how to become a wise consumer.

Journal
Personal Career Plan

In your journal, list the last five purchases you have made. For each purchase, record at least two factors that influenced you to buy that specific item at that specific time. On the basis of this list, how would you describe yourself as a consumer?

Our Economic System

OBJECTIVES

After studying this section, you will be able to:

- Define a free-enterprise system and identify producers and consumers.
- Describe the marketplace and explain why prices go up and down.
- Explain three ways that the health of the economy can be measured.

KEY TERMS

economics
economic system
free enterprise
consumers
producers
marketplace
gross domestic
    product (GDP)
inflation

You buy goods and services all the time. It may seem like a simple process, but is it? What do you know about why businesses make and sell the goods they do? How are prices set? What causes prices to drop, or rise? How does this system of buying and selling goods and services work? How does it affect you?

You'll find answers to these questions by studying **economics**, the field of study that tries to explain how people produce, distribute, and use goods and services. The way people participate in these activities depends on the economic system of the country where they live.

An **economic system** is a country's way of using resources to provide goods and services that its people want and need. *Producing* means creating goods or services. *Distributing* means making goods and services available—through selling or delivering, for example—to the people who need them. What kind of economic system does the United States have?

As you learn about how our economic system works, you will also learn why conditions change so rapidly. With a basic understanding of the system, you will be able to prepare yourself for the challenges such a system presents.

The Free-Enterprise System

The economic system used in the United States is known as the free-enterprise system. **Free enterprise** means that individuals or businesses may buy and sell and set prices with little government interference. The government does have a role in our economic system, however. Laws set safety standards, regulate some prices and wages, and protect **consumers**. These are the people who buy and use goods and services.

Producers and Consumers

The companies or individuals who make or provide goods and services are known as **producers.** If you make specialty T-shirts, you are a producer of goods. If you baby-sit, you are a producer of a service. Have you ever been a producer?

What happens once goods and services are produced? People or other businesses *consume,* or buy and use, them. The people who buy your T-shirts and the people for whom you baby-sit are consumers. You become a consumer when you buy lunch, have clothes cleaned, or ride the subway.

Most people are both consumers and producers, although usually not at the same time. *Who are the consumers in this photograph? Who are the producers? How do you know?*

Producers and consumers are like two sides of a coin. Although they're opposites, one can't exist without the other. *Figure 19-1* shows the flow of economic activity between producers and consumers. While you may be both a producer and a consumer, your goals are different in each role.

- Producers try to make goods or provide services that consumers will buy. A producer's main purpose is to make a net profit. As you know, net profit is the money left after operating costs and the cost of the goods or services have been paid.

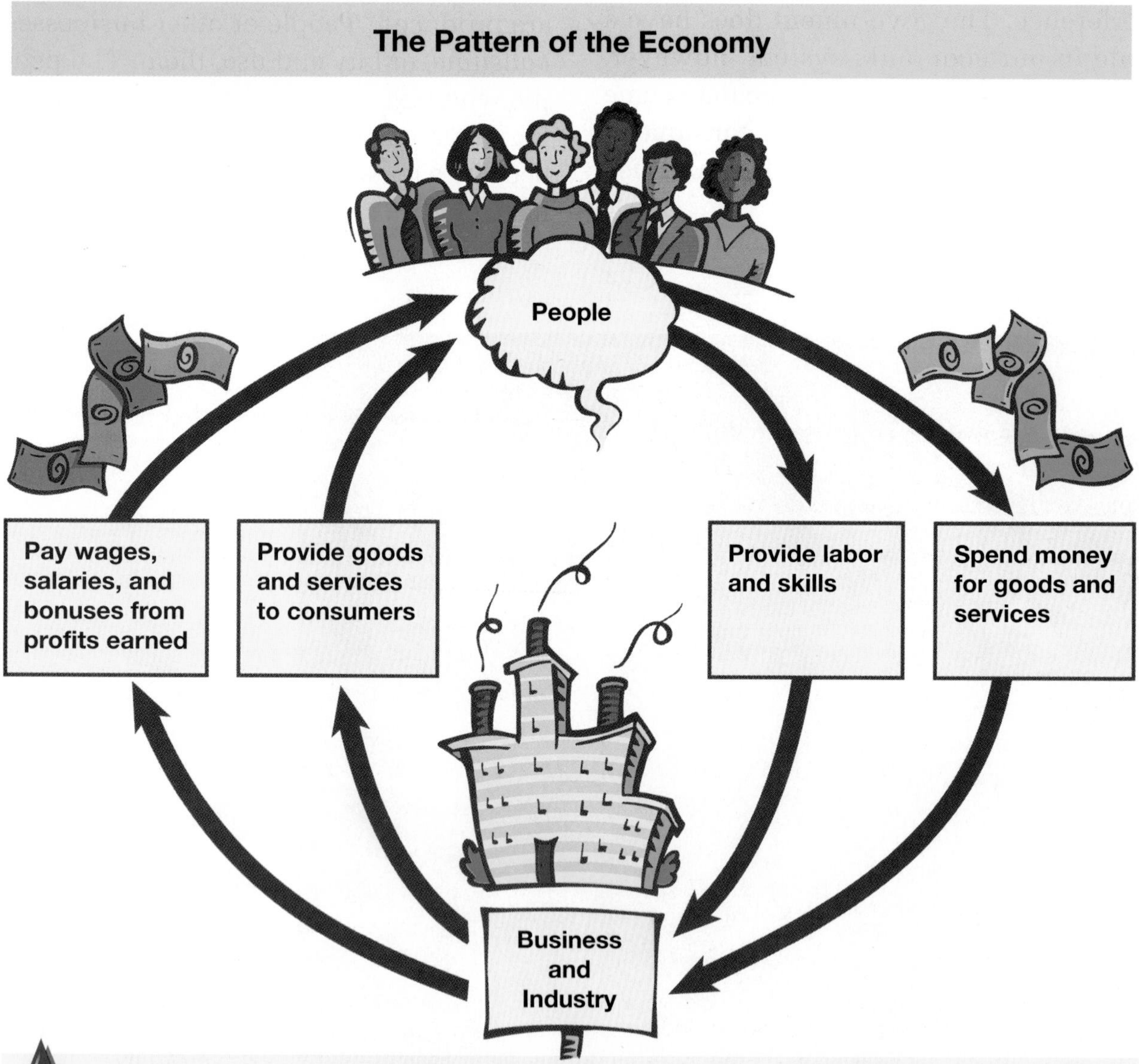

The Pattern of the Economy

People

Pay wages, salaries, and bonuses from profits earned

Provide goods and services to consumers

Provide labor and skills

Spend money for goods and services

Business and Industry

Figure 19-1 You are a participant in the free-enterprise system. You will work to help produce goods and services (if you don't already), and you consume goods and services. The outer circle of this illustration shows how consumer spending goes into businesses and comes back to you as a worker. The inner circle shows how your skills help produce goods and services, which consumers such as you need and want. How does the freedom of choice of a free-enterprise system affect these circles?

- Consumers try to get what they need and want within the limits of how much money they have. Consumers influence what is made by what they buy.

How do producers and consumers accomplish their aims? They go to the marketplace!

What Is the Marketplace?

The **marketplace** is where buying and selling occur. This term really covers the whole realm of trade and business. Sometimes the producer and consumer are actually in the same place, as when you get your hair cut. Producers and consumers can also be geographically far apart. For example, you might buy a computer that was produced in another country or buy a magazine that was published in another state.

To reach consumers and to promote buying, producers practice marketing. *Marketing* is the process of getting products to consumers. It includes packaging, shipping, advertising, and selling goods and services. Because our economy is based on buying and selling, our free-enterprise system is called a market system.

Price Fluctuations

Have you noticed how the prices of CDs, jeans, haircuts, and other goods and

▶ All of these "places" are part of the marketplace. *What are some examples of the marketplace you've "visited" recently?*

services keep changing? This is normal in a free-enterprise system. Why? Prices *fluctuate,* or go up and down, as a result of three main factors.

- *Supply and demand.* Supply is the amount of goods and services available for sale. Demand is the amount of goods and services that consumers want to buy. When supply is greater than demand, prices lower. When demand is greater than supply, prices rise.

- *Production costs.* The more it costs to make a good or provide a service, the higher its price will be. Because businesses must make a profit, they must sell their goods or services for more than it costs to produce them.

- *Competition.* When two similar products are offered for sale, they are in competition. When competition is great, prices tend to be lower. When there is little or no competition, prices are higher.

In addition to prices going up and down, the economy itself fluctuates. This movement from good times to bad and back to good is known as the *business cycle*. **Figure 19-2** illustrates the four parts of this cycle.

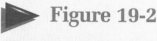

The Business Cycle

The economy normally goes up and down—somewhat like a roller coaster. However, no one can really be sure when each period of the business cycle will occur or how long it will last. For this reason, many economists prefer to talk about business fluctuations rather than the business cycle.

A **Peak or Boom.** The peak, or boom, is the high point of the business cycle. Leading up to this period is a time of prosperity marked by economic growth, low unemployment, and a general sense of well-being among most of the population.

D **Expansion.** Expansion is an increase in business activity after a depression or recession. The economy starts to recover. People begin to spend money and open new businesses again, and employment rises. The expansion continues until the economy reaches another peak, or boom. Then the cycle starts all over again.

B **Contraction.** Contraction occurs as the period of prosperity draws toward an end. Business activity slows down. If a contraction lasts long enough, it can lead to a *recession,* which is a six-month or longer period when the economy does not grow.

C **Depression.** If things continue to go poorly after the contraction, the economy can slide into a *depression,* which is a very serious recession. During a depression, many businesses fail, prices drop, and unemployment shoots up. Not every recession turns into a depression. In each cycle, the trough is the lowest point to which the economy falls.

Measuring the Economy

Does the condition of the economy affect you? Absolutely! It can determine how much you make at a job, what you can afford to buy, and whether you can save money. Economic indicators measure the performance of the economy each year.

Gross Domestic Product

The total dollar value of all goods and services produced in the United States during a year is known as the **gross domestic product,** or **GDP.** This is the main indicator of the condition of the economy.

It enables one to compare this year's economy with last year's.

Consumer Price Index

The consumer price index, or CPI, measures changes in the prices of consumer goods and services. It is based on a monthly survey conducted by the Bureau of Labor Statistics. The survey tracks prices for a specific group of household goods and services. Among these are the costs for food, clothing, shelter, fuel, and medical services.

By showing increases or decreases in the cost of living, the CPI also measures inflation. **Inflation** occurs when the average

EXCELLENT BUSINESS PRACTICES

Ribs 101

Gates Bar-B-Q, a fast-food chain in Kansas City, Missouri, sends all 300 of its employees to training school. The company created seven basic classes to teach employees how to serve quality products. Each course lasts about two hours and concludes with a written test. Depending on their job, employees might learn how to cut a sandwich without leaving fingerprints, how to cut ribs, or how to brush sauce on the ribs and create an appetizing platter. All employees must attend classes, and they receive a nominal hourly raise upon completion.

Training helps solve the challenge of maintaining consistent quality in a service business with multiple locations. It creates a pattern of teamwork and accountability and employees feel the company has a vested interest in their success.

Thinking Critically

How does consistency affect the consumer?

prices of goods and services rise sharply. If prices rise sharply but your wages don't, you cannot buy as much as you used to. Your *standard of living,* a measure of your quality of life based on the amount of goods and services you can buy, declines. Inflation affects the business cycle and can lead to higher unemployment.

Unemployment

A third economic indicator is the unemployment rate. The government figures this rate each month. It identifies the percentage of the labor force that is without work but is actively seeking employment. Low unemployment is a sign the economy is doing well because most people are working, earning wages, and consuming. High unemployment, on the other hand, indicates problems in the economy because many people are out of work. The result is a lower standard of living and personal difficulties for the families involved.

YOU'RE THE BOSS!

Solving Workplace Problems

At your busy coffee shop, the cashier usually asks customers how they enjoyed their meal. Today you hear a customer reply with complaints about both the food and the service. You are surprised when your cashier just smiles and says what she always says: "Come back soon!" What will you do?

SECTION 19-1 *Review*

Understanding Key Concepts

Using complete sentences, answer the following questions on a separate sheet of paper.

1. Why do you think the government exercises some control over producers in our free-enterprise system?

2. Why do you think the government keeps track of fluctuations in the economy?

3. What could you infer if the gross domestic product was higher each year for three years in a row?

Exploring Careers: Communications and Media

Valerie Zavala
Vice President, News
and Public Affairs, KCET

Q: **What are the most important skills for a television journalist?**

A: Being able to determine immediately the essence of the story is a vital skill. You must be able to make decisions about which questions are the most important to ask in a short interview. You must be able to write a news story under tight deadlines. You also have to be able to present the information with some sense of drama or story.

Q: **How does someone begin to get experience in television journalism?**

A: Internships are very important. There is nothing like an internship to give you hands-on experience. You can see what it really takes to put a program together. It puts you in contact with people who can give you a job or recommend you to someone if they recognize you as being reliable and bright.

Q: **What would you tell someone interested in television journalism?**

A: I would advise that person to minor in communications, with a major in another field. A lot of young people going through college are not learning something meaty enough, like the history of the world or our country, or science, or English. Communication is a skill, not a body of knowledge. Intellectual depth can only come when you understand a field of knowledge really well.

Thinking Critically

Would you make a good television journalist? Why or why not?

CAREER FACTS

Nature of the Work:
Oversee program planning, editing, and taping; meet with community leaders and freelancers; budget money and time.

Training or Education Needed:
Degree in journalism or communications; experience in reporting.

Aptitudes, Abilities, and Skills:
Creative-thinking, decision-making, and writing skills; responsibility.

Salary Range:
Starting salary in a small market, about $12,000 to $16,000 a year; anchoring in a small market, about $27,000 to $35,000; higher salary possible in large markets.

Career Path:
Start with an internship; become an assistant to others in the field; advance as a reporter from small, to medium, then to large markets; move into production or management.

You, the Consumer

In our free-enterprise system, individuals as well as businesses make choices about earning and spending money. These individual choices are not always easy to make. How can you know the right goods and services to buy? How can you get the best price? If you're like most people, you have only so much money to spend. This makes the right choices very important.

Smart Shopping

Making good choices takes SCANS competencies such as allocating time, allocating money, and acquiring and evaluating information. Consider how these competencies are used when you follow each of these practical tips:

- *Pay attention to quality.* You'll save money in the long run by buying well-made items, especially when you expect to keep your purchases for a long time. Does a high price mean an item has higher quality than a less costly one? Not necessarily. *Generic products*, or products without brand names, usually have plain packaging and are relatively inexpensive.

  Buying generic products can be a smart move. When the quality of such products is high, you save because you are not paying for fancy packaging or expensive advertising.

- *When possible, plan the timing of your purchases.* You will find more bargains at certain times of the year. January and August are good sale months because many stores try to sell as much as possible to make room for the next season's goods.

You can also use the law of supply and demand. Instead of rushing out to buy a new videotape or CD, wait a few months. By then, the price may have been marked down because demand has lessened.

- *Take advantage of discount stores.* Discount and "warehouse" stores can offer excellent buys. Do your homework, however, *before* you get to the store because customer service may not be a high priority.

- *Explore on-line options.* On-line prices can be surprisingly low, and

It's easy to be influenced by your friends when you are buying clothes. ***In what ways can your friends help you be a responsible consumer?***

When shopping for clothing, a smart shopping tip is to always make a list. ***Why do you think it might be a good idea to look through your wardrobe carefully before you shop for clothing?***

you may find electronic shopping very convenient. In addition, product information is often available on the Internet. To protect yourself, however, read about on-line shopping in consumer magazines first. You cannot assume that all the information you get and all the companies you encounter on-line will be trustworthy.

Buyer Beware!

Be a smart consumer. Learn to protect yourself from **consumer fraud,** or dishonest business practices used by people who are trying to trick or cheat you.

Kathleen Coventry of Illinois learned about fraud the hard way. She responded to a telephone work-at-home offer. She sent a salesperson a check for $153.95, trusting the salesperson's assurance that her money would be refunded if she were unhappy. Kathleen soon received a large envelope full of useless materials that provided only general suggestions such as "Start a home typing business." Kathleen said, "There was no way that any person could read this stuff and actually use the information [to start a home business]."

Kathleen promptly returned the envelope and requested a refund. More than a year later and after follow-up calls and letters, she still had gotten nothing back.

How can you avoid fraud? First, be aware that scams exist. Here are some common tricks of the fraud trade:

- *Fraudulent advertising.* Using a tactic known as **bait and switch,** a retailer advertises a bargain—the bait—to lure people into the store. When the

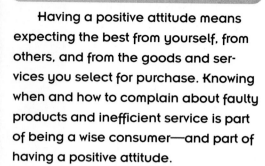

Attitude Counts ✔

Having a positive attitude means expecting the best from yourself, from others, and from the goods and services you select for purchase. Knowing when and how to complain about faulty products and inefficient service is part of being a wise consumer—and part of having a positive attitude.

customers arrive, the store is "out" of the item. A salesperson tries to sell a similar product at a much higher price. This is the switch.

- *Auto repair fraud.* Dishonest mechanics may try to charge you much more than the estimated cost of a repair. They may replace parts that are not defective. To protect yourself, ask for written estimates and request that mechanics keep the old parts and show them to you.

▶ Automobile repairs can be expensive. Make sure anyone working on your car explains the recommended repair to your satisfaction. *Why do you think some auto repair shops get away with fraudulent practices?*

- *Phony prize notifications.* "Congratulations! You've just won our grand prize!" This great news may come by mail or phone. To get your prize, all you have to do is send in some money or make a small purchase. Some companies ask you to provide a credit card or checking account number for identification. Beware. Even cautious consumers can fall for this scam.

Most consumer frauds succeed by taking advantage of the consumer's search for a good deal. If an offer sounds too good to be true, it probably is. These tips may save you from becoming a victim: First, *never* give your credit card number over the phone if you didn't place the call. Second, don't send money to any unknown business or organization without checking first to be sure it is legitimate. For information, check with your state or local consumer office or the Better Business Bureau.

Groups That Protect Consumers

Suppose you buy something that breaks the first time you use it. What should you do? First, try to solve the problem by visiting the store where you bought it or by calling the company that produced it. If this doesn't work, you might write a letter of complaint. In your letter, be polite but firm. Be sure to save store receipts, and keep records of your communications with the business. As a last resort, you may need to take legal action. However, help is also available from several other sources.

Government Agencies

Government agencies, specialized organizations within the government, enforce consumer protection laws. They act as watchdogs over certain areas of the marketplace.

- The Federal Trade Commission (FTC) enforces rules about labeling, advertising, and warranties. Thanks to the FTC, the labels in your clothes provide care instructions. This agency also regulates the descriptions of products in ads and commercials to

Career Do's & Don'ts

To Be an Informed Consumer...

Do:
- compare prices.
- plan for and save up for large purchases.
- ask questions about quality.
- find out the store's policy on returning goods.

Don't:
- buy any large purchases on impulse.
- buy anything you aren't sure you will use.
- give in to a good sales pitch—be sure you want the product or service.
- hesitate to point out your rights as a consumer if you are not satisfied with service.

make sure they are accurate.

A **warranty** is a guarantee that a product meets certain standards of quality. By FTC standards, a warranty must be clearly worded and conveniently placed.

- The Consumer Product Safety Commission (CPSC) helps protect the public against dangerous products. It sets safety standards for equipment and makes sure these standards are met.

- The Food and Drug Administration (FDA) enforces laws about the quality and labeling of food, drugs, and medical devices. It inspects workplaces that produce food and drugs.

Government agencies at the state and local levels also work to protect consumers.

Consumer Groups

Many private groups investigate consumer complaints, educate the public on consumer issues, and try to get consumer legislation passed. Examples of such groups are consumer action panels (CAPs) formed by trade associations, such as MACAP for major appliance manufacturers. A well-known consumer group is Consumers' Union, which publishes *Consumer Reports* and *Consumers' Research*.

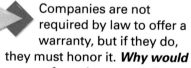
Companies are not required by law to offer a warranty, but if they do, they must honor it. ***Why would you prefer to buy an appliance that comes with a warranty?***

SECTION 19-2 *Review*

Understanding Key Concepts

Using complete sentences, answer the following questions on a separate sheet of paper.

1. What benefits will you obtain from being a wise shopper?

2. Where might you find information about new types of consumer fraud?

3. How does protecting yourself against consumer fraud help other consumers as well?

Key Terms

economics *(p. 380)*
economic system *(p. 380)*
free enterprise *(p. 381)*
consumers *(p. 381)*
producers *(p. 381)*
marketplace *(p. 383)*
gross domestic product
    (GDP) *(p. 385)*
inflation *(p. 385)*

SECTION 19-1 Summary

- The United States has a free-enterprise economic system, in which there is limited governmental intervention in the production, buying, and selling of goods and services.

- The marketplace is the arena where producers and consumers "meet" for buying and selling, even though producers and consumers may be geographically far apart.

- Prices may go up or down, depending on supply and demand, production costs, and competition.

- The economy moves from good times to bad and back to good again. These fluctuations are called the business cycle.

- The condition of the economy can be measured by the gross domestic product, the consumer price index, and the unemployment rate.

Key Terms

consumer fraud *(p. 389)*
bait and switch *(p. 390)*
warranty *(p. 392)*

SECTION 19-2 Summary

- Smart shopping involves paying attention to quality, timing purchases, taking advantage of discount stores, and exploring on-line options when possible.

- Consumers have both rights and responsibilities.

- There are a number of methods of consumer fraud, including fraudulent advertising and phony prize notifications. Consumers need to be aware of fraud schemes and to be on guard against getting cheated.

- Government agencies and private consumer groups protect and educate the consumer as well as handle consumer complaints.

Reviewing Key Terms

On a separate sheet of paper, write a series of questions and answers that use the following key terms.

economics
economic system
free enterprise
consumers
producers
marketplace

gross domestic
  product
inflation
consumer fraud
bait and switch
warranty

Recalling Key Concepts

On a separate sheet of paper, tell whether each of the following statements is true or false. Rewrite any false statements to make them true.

1. In a free-enterprise system, prices and wages are strictly controlled by government regulations.

2. The presence or absence of competition has no effect on prices.

3. The consumer price index and the unemployment rate are two yardsticks for measuring the economy.

4. Buying generic products when their quality is comparable to brand-name products is one way to save money.

5. The Consumer Product Safety Commission enforces rules about advertising, labeling, and warranties.

Thinking Critically

Using complete sentences, answer each of the following questions on a separate sheet of paper.

1. How would life in the United States be different if our economy had much stricter controls?

2. Describe a situation in which your friends might have a negative influence on your shopping choices.

3. How would you deal with a bait-and-switch scam?

4. List three features not mentioned in the text that you think would be important in an effective letter of complaint.

SCANS Foundation Skills and Workplace Competencies

Thinking Skills: *Creative Thinking*

1. You have taken a job with a consumer protection agency. Your first task is to create a poster that provides consumer tips expressed in eye-catching and imaginative ways. Conduct research to come up with 10 tips. Then illustrate each one with drawings or magazine photos. Present your poster to the class.

Information Skills: *Acquiring and Evaluating Information*

2. The Consumer Information Center of the U.S. General Services Administration publishes a booklet called the *Consumer Information Catalog.* Find out the number to call to obtain it, how much the booklet costs, and what information it provides. Prepare a report of your findings.

Connecting Academics to the Workplace

Language Arts

1. Adena recently bought an electronic pocket organizer to replace her address book. To her disappointment, the phone numbers keep getting lost. When she tries to recall a name, the number is garbled or has disappeared. Write a letter from Adena to the manufacturer explaining the defect. Tell the manufacturer what kind of action she would like it to take.

Math

2. Allen rents a cart in the business district to sell coffee to people on their way to work. In one week, he spends $17 on coffee, $7 on milk, and $3 on sugar. The rent for the cart is $105 per week. If each cup of coffee is 65¢, how many cups must Allen sell in a week before he begins to make a profit? What would his profit be if he sold 500 cups in one week?

Developing Teamwork and Leadership Skills

Working with a team of other students, find out about one consumer organization in your community. (Coordinate your efforts with other teams so that no two contact the same organization.) As a team, come up with 8 to 10 questions about the organization. Have one team member conduct a telephone or personal interview with a representative of the organization, being sure to get answers to the team's questions. Then write a report on the team's findings, and share it with the class. Divide tasks (such as conducting the interview, writing the report, and sharing the report with the class) equitably among team members.

Real-World Workshop

Select a local government agency that protects consumers. Examples include the health inspector's office and the office of the city building inspector. Interview an agency representative and learn what kinds of consumer protection are provided. Speculate on how you would be affected if the agency did not exist. Discuss your conclusions with the class.

School-to-Work Connection

Choose a consumer product that costs at least $200. Research three sources for the product, such as a department store, a discount warehouse, and the Internet. Write a report that compares prices, services, and other factors that would be involved in obtaining the item through each of the channels you have analyzed. At the end of the report, suggest which source you think would be the best choice.

Individual Career Plan

Write a journal entry describing how what you've learned about economics affects your view of the world of work. Would you like to find out more about starting your own business? Are you interested in fighting consumer fraud? Do you want to learn more about ways of measuring the economy?

Chapter 20

Managing Your Money

Section 20-1
Budgeting

Section 20-2
Coping with Financial Responsibility

In this video segment, learn why it's important to have a well-planned budget.

Journal
Personal Career Plan

In your journal, write your first responses to these questions:

- Do you think the government should stick to a budget? Why or why not?

- Do you think a small business should stick to a budget? Why or why not?

- Do you think you should stick to a budget? Why or why not?

Budgeting

After studying this section, you will be able to:

- **Identify the steps in planning a budget.**
- **Explain how to keep records effectively.**
- **Describe strategies for staying within your budget.**

KEY TERMS

budget
record keeping

Imagine driving a car with a broken fuel gauge. You wouldn't know how far you could go. You couldn't be sure when your car might sputter and roll to a stop. A fuel gauge enables you to operate for a planned distance. It allows you to balance what you have with how far you want to go. A fuel gauge is a kind of reality check.

Now think about your economic life. To act effectively, you need enough fuel (income) to get where you need to go (to cover your expenses). Your economic fuel gauge is your budget. A **budget** is a plan for saving and spending money based on your income and your expenses. A well-planned budget can give you the same feeling of confidence that a fuel gauge that shows full does. With careful budgeting, you'll be able to handle everyday needs as well as achieve your dreams for the future.

Planning Your Budget

Why take the time to plan a budget? There are many valid reasons. After all, the stakes are pretty high. When you work, you trade valuable assets—your time, knowledge, skills, and effort—for money. You'll want to spend this money on things that are worth the time and effort you've put into earning it.

Begin your planning by asking yourself a few questions.

Many young couples dream of owning their own home. *What types of costs, other than the actual cost of buying the home, will this couple have to think about as they consider purchasing it?*

- What are your lifestyle goals?
- What's really important to you?
- What do you have, and what do you need?

You'll use your answers to develop a budget plan. You'll also use the SCANS competencies of allocating time, money, material, and human resources.

Defining Goals

The first step in getting anywhere is to decide on your goals. To begin budget planning, make two lists. On one list, write the things you need or want to spend money on now or within the next six months. Perhaps you need new glasses or want to buy a new bicycle. On the other list, put the things you need or want to spend money on in the future. Paying for an education, buying a home, and saving for retirement might go on this list.

The lists identify your financial objectives—at least right now. You aren't locked in to them. You can add or cut out some at any time. Writing down your objectives, however, helps you make plans to achieve them.

ETHICS in Action

You are shopping in the jewelry department of a large department store. While you are discussing a possible purchase with the clerk, you see an older customer slip an expensive watch into her purse and start to walk away. What will you do? Why?

Making Choices

You probably have more items on the lists than you have money for. That's why the next step is to prioritize—that is, to put your goals in order of importance. Prioritizing helps you clarify what is most important to you and distinguish between your financial needs and your financial wants. As you prioritize, note a target date for each goal. This will help you keep track of how well you're doing.

Estimating Income and Expenses

The next step in planning your budget is to find out how much money you expect to have coming in *(income)* and how much you think will be going out *(expenses)*. Try to estimate these amounts as accurately as you can.

If you have a job, your main source of income is likely to be your earnings. When you are figuring your earnings income, count only *net earnings*, the amount left after taxes and other amounts are taken out. Income also, however, includes tips, gifts of money, and interest on bank accounts.

Your expenses include costs for food, housing, and so on. Sometimes people divide expenses into two types. One type is *fixed expenses*, expenses you have already agreed to pay and that must be paid by a particular date. Rent and car payments are examples of fixed expenses. *Flexible expenses* are the other type. These are expenses that come irregularly or that you may be able to adjust more easily. Medical costs and costs of clothing are examples of flexible expenses.

Funding your education is a valuable financial goal. *How is money that you put into education an investment?*

Estimating Income and Expenses

Average Monthly Income

Net earnings	$1,188
Interest on savings	5
Gifts	20
	$1,213

Average Monthly Expenses

Rent (my share)	$350
Car loan	220
Car insurance	70
Food	160
Medical and dental care	50
Clothing	80
Transportation	125
Entertainment	60
Gifts and contributions	40
Miscellaneous	40
	$1,195

Figure 20-1 Here is one person's estimate of her average monthly income and expenses. Which of the expenses listed here vary most from month to month?

Preparing and Following Your Budget

You've identified and prioritized your goals and estimated your income and expenses. Now it's time to get down to preparing your budget. Your budget will be your financial plan of action for the next month or year.

As you draw up your budget, remember to be realistic. Just like a diet that's too strict, a budget that's too strict will be impossible to fulfill. You'll end up feeling resentful. Having a budget doesn't mean doing without all the pleasures in your life. It may mean cutting back, however, and it always requires thinking before you spend.

Examine your income and expenses for at least a month at a time. Many expenses (such as car or insurance payments) are paid monthly. Some will be paid even less often. For planning purposes, divide these kinds of payments into monthly chunks. For example, if you pay a life insurance premium every three months, or quarterly, divide the payment amount by three and place that number in your expense record as a monthly expense. *Figure 20-1* shows a sample income and expenses worksheet for a single person in her twenties who has a full-time job and shares an apartment with a friend.

YOU'RE THE BOSS!

Solving Workplace Problems

Your dry-cleaning business has only two employees, both of whom are hard-working and loyal. One of them tells you she should earn more than her coworker. "He has a wife who works and no children," she explains. "I'm on my own with three children to support. It's only fair that you pay me more." How do you respond?

Career Do's & Don'ts

When Keeping Track of Your Money...

Do:
- make a budget and periodically update it.
- keep track of what you spend.
- pay bills when they are due.
- keep receipts of major purchases or anything you might return.

Don't:
- spend more than you make.
- make personal loans.
- put all your savings in long-term investments.
- let someone else be in charge of your money.

Keeping Effective Records

You'll need to get into the habit of **record keeping**, that is, organizing and maintaining records of your income and spending. Records will be useful in many different ways. To estimate income and expenses, for example, you would use records such as a check register, bank account statements, and bill receipts.

A handy and inexpensive way to organize your records is with an accordion folder. If you have a filing cabinet available, that's even better. Record-keeping software allows you to keep records on disk as well in hard copy. Even so, you'll need file folders or an accordion folder to keep your records. Remember, however, that records are useful only if they're kept up-to-date. Here are some tips for good record keeping:

- Keep files where you can get to them easily.

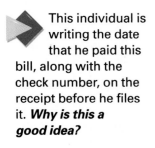

This individual is writing the date that he paid this bill, along with the check number, on the receipt before he files it. *Why is this a good idea?*

- File bills and records when you receive them.
- Keep a calendar where you can record when bills are due and when they were paid.
- Buy a fireproof box—or rent a safe-deposit box at a bank—to store important documents such as insurance papers, birth certificates, and car titles.

Getting Started

Use a standard form to plan your budget. The form shown in *Figure 20-2* is a good place to start. First, transfer the information from your income and expense estimate into your budget. Your income should be equal to or more than your total expenses. To make this happen, you may need to adjust various categories.

A Budget Form

Categories	Budgeted Monthly Expenses	Actual Monthly Expenses
Savings		
Emergency fund		
Savings account		
Fixed Expenses		
Rent or mortgage payment		
Installment payments		
Car loan		
Car insurance		
Health insurance		
Life insurance		
Credit card interest		
Flexible Expenses		
Food		
Utilities		
Household supplies		
Medical and dental care		
Clothing		
Transportation		
Entertainment		
Gifts and contributions		
Miscellaneous		
Total Spent		
Total Income		

Figure 20-2 This form is a typical one for planning a budget. How would you use the column at the far right?

Notice that there is a category for savings. This should *not* be an afterthought. Get in the habit of considering savings as a type of projected expense. If you establish a plan to save the same way you formulate a plan to pay your bills and make necessary purchases, you'll be more likely to do it. Chapter 21 will explain different savings options.

Your savings plan is your ticket to achieving your goals. There is also another reason to save regularly. Savings can help you create an emergency fund. An *emergency fund* is money you put aside for needs you can't anticipate. Everyone should have an emergency fund. A major illness or the loss of a job can be devastating if you do not have some money put away in an emergency fund.

Fine-Tuning Your Budget

You've prepared a budget, and you're using it as a guide. Is your job done? Of course it isn't. You will always need to make adjustments.

At the end of each month, check to see how you did at staying within your

EXCELLENT BUSINESS PRACTICES

Choose Your Own Benefits

Calvert Group, of Bethesda, Maryland, is a mutual funds company. It invests in companies that make safe products and have good environmental practices.

Calvert provides employees with core benefits that include life insurance, sick leave, disability benefits, holiday pay, and a retirement savings plan. Optional benefits, such as medical coverage and additional disability insurance, are paid for with pretax payroll deductions and with money Calvert gives employees each year for their benefits.

From their overall benefits dollars, employees can choose the level of insurance coverage and other programs. For example, the company gives employees who walk to work up to $120 per year for shoes. Those employees who bike to work are given up to $350 a year for a new bicycle. Employees can be reimbursed up to $3,000 a year for any classes they take. Calvert even allows up to 12 days off a year for community service and sponsors a wide variety of community activities. Since Calvert instituted its benefits plan, the turnover rate dropped from 30 percent to 5 percent.

Thinking Critically

What are the advantages and disadvantages of a flexible benefits program?

 Cooking meals at home rather than eating out is one way to cut your expenses. *What is another way you could cut expenses at this point in your life?*

budget. If your income doesn't cover your expenses or barely does, what can you do? You really have only two choices.

- *You can cut back on your expenses.* You may be able to fine-tune your budget by cutting flexible expenses. For example, pack your lunch every day instead of buying it. Save money on gas and parking by carpooling with a coworker.

- *You can increase your income.* You may be able to increase your income by working more hours or getting a better-paying job.

Keep fine-tuning your budget until it fits your needs. Your budget should serve as a guide, but it's not set in concrete. It can be adjusted as your income, expenses, needs, and wants change.

Following Your Budget

Your budget can help you only if you follow it. Use your SCANS self-management skills to keep spending within the limits you have set. You'll find some practical hints for staying within the limits of your budget in *Figure 20-3*.

▶ Figure 20-3

Staying Within Your Budget

Following a few simple spending rules can help you stay within your budget.

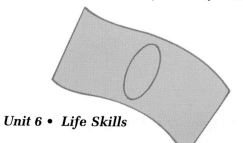

A Keep track of your spending. Carry a small notebook with you at all times. Get in the habit of making a note of every penny you spend. It will help your record keeping, and you will never have to ask yourself where your money went.

B Don't carry around a large amount of cash. You'll be too tempted to spend it on impulse. Just take what you'll need for your trip, along with a little extra for an emergency. Leave your ATM card at home too. This will force you to think before making a purchase.

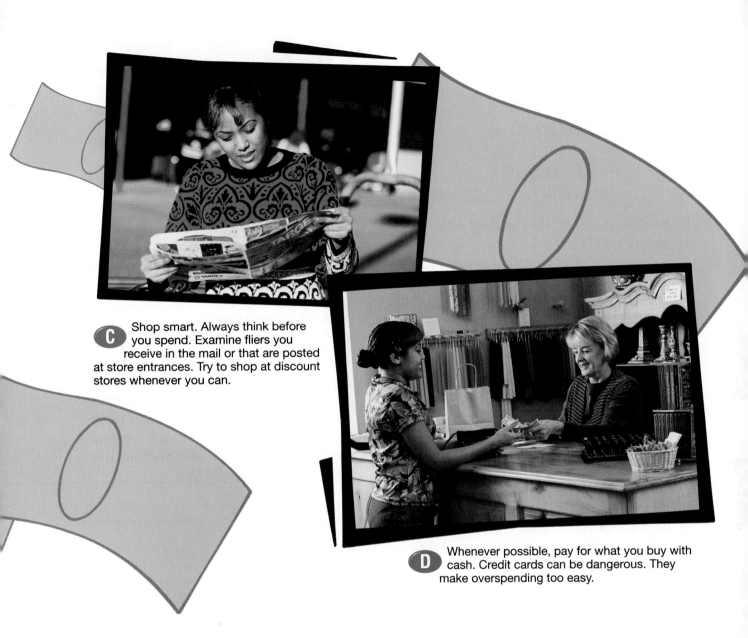

C Shop smart. Always think before you spend. Examine fliers you receive in the mail or that are posted at store entrances. Try to shop at discount stores whenever you can.

D Whenever possible, pay for what you buy with cash. Credit cards can be dangerous. They make overspending too easy.

SECTION 20-1 *Review*

Understanding Key Concepts

Using complete sentences, answer the following questions on a separate sheet of paper.

1. Why do you need to examine your financial goals before you create a budget?

2. How might accurate records be useful for tasks other than drawing up a budget?

3. How could you apply skills used in sticking to a budget in your workplace?

CASE STUDY

Exploring Careers: Communications and Media

Bob Hernandez
Photojournalist

Q: How long have you been involved with photography?

A: I was about 12 when I got interested in it through a youth club near my house. Both my older brother and my father were amateur photographers. I started shooting pictures for a community newspaper when I was 13. I got about $2.50 for my first picture and thought I could get rich doing this.

Q: What's the most important skill for a photojournalist?

A: Good storytelling ability. It doesn't make any difference whether you're shooting stills or video or film. You have to be able to tell a complete story with the camera, regardless of what the narration is going to be. Composition and the ability to use light will come. Those are skills you can learn.

Q: How does someone get started as a photojournalist?

A: A decent audition reel is the best thing you can have. It doesn't lie. It tells what you're capable of doing. You can't see that on a résumé.

Q: How did you get started?

A: I got an internship at the television station while I was still in school. I worked hard, won several awards, and made contacts. When the station expanded its programming, I applied for a full-time position. Because I had proved myself during my internship, I earned the support of the newsroom staff and was hired for the full-time position.

Thinking Critically

In what other careers might you be asked to provide more than a résumé as proof of your skills?

CAREER FACTS

Nature of the Work:
Hold meetings to plan stories; call to set up appointments; shoot the story; edit the film; sometimes, write stories.

Training or Education Needed:
Photography/video schools; internships; work at television stations

Aptitudes, Abilities, and Skills:
Listening, speaking, and interpersonal skills; ability to see images in the mind's eye; ability to work with your hands.

Salary Range:
Approximately $20,000 to $25,000 a year to start; higher salary possible with experience.

Career Path:
Start with an internship; work at a community television station or in small markets; work into the market you want.

Coping with Financial Responsibility

OBJECTIVES

After studying this section, you will be able to:

- **Identify personal changes that might affect your finances.**
- **Discuss ways to adjust to economic change.**
- **List several sources of help for financial problems.**

KEY TERM

financial
responsibility

Ellie was feeling good. She'd landed the job she wanted and her salary was fine. She'd had to move and to buy a car, but with her salary, she thought she'd have no trouble making the payments. Unfortunately, several months into her job, Ellie found out that her employers had overextended themselves. They couldn't afford all the new people they had taken on. Laid off, Ellie was faced with high monthly bills and no way to pay them.

What could she have done differently? After all, no one can be expected to see into the future. Should people go through life expecting the worst to happen? Neither option is a good one. There is a middle ground, however, in which you are willing to take some risks but are also prepared for unexpected problems. The key is responsible financial planning.

Adjusting to Personal Change

As you move toward adulthood, your **financial responsibility**, or accountability in money matters, increases. When you were a young child, someone else paid for your food and clothing as well as your wants. When you started getting an allowance or began a part-time job, your financial responsibility may have increased. Perhaps you were expected to pay for some family purchases. In the future, as you move out on your own, your level of financial responsibility will increase even more.

Personal Life Changes

Family	Occupation	Health
Marriage	Starting a career	Becoming disabled
Birth or adoption of children	Changing jobs	Growing older
Family member in need of financial help	Starting your own business	Experiencing chronic illness
Aging parents in need of care	Becoming unemployed	Being diagnosed with terminal illness
Death of a spouse or other close family member		
Receipt of an inheritance		
Separation or divorce		

Figure 20-4 This list shows life changes that might require you to alter your financial plans. Choose one item from the list and explain how you could prepare yourself for it ahead of time.

Increasing independence is one type of personal change that requires financial planning skills. You will experience other types as well. Take a look at *Figure 20-4.* It lists life events—some positive, some not—that will require changes in your financial plans. By recognizing these possibilities, you'll be better able to cope with the changes they will bring.

Adjusting to Economic Change

It's not just personal events that can change your financial outlook. Events throughout the nation and the world also can affect your finances.

Inflation and Recession

You may have to refigure your budget during a time of inflation, or a general increase in prices. As long as economic conditions are good, prices tend to edge upward over time, as do wages. What hurts is rapid inflation, when prices go up but wages don't.

During times of inflation, your dollars will buy less than they did before. Some tips for coping with inflation include:

- Cut back on unnecessary expenses.
- Look for a second job to increase income.
- Be a wise shopper. Take advantage of sales, for example, and buy food in bulk whenever possible.

During a recession, when the economy does not grow for six months or more, your finances may also be affected. Recessions may be local—as when a major employer in the area closes down or moves away—or national. During a recession, some employers lay off workers. Because of widespread unemployment, workers often find it difficult to land new jobs.

The tips you just read for times of inflation will also be helpful in a recession. In addition, you can do the following:

- Save as much money as possible.
- If you are laid off, accept job placement help if your former employer offers it.
- Talk to a loan officer at your bank to see whether you can refinance any debt to make lower payments.

If you've planned well before the period of inflation or recession, you'll have an emergency fund. That will be a source of help to you.

 Most banks are willing to help with financial planning when a job loss occurs. *How could a bank help you if you lost your job?*

Finding Help for Money Management Problems

If you run into trouble managing your finances, help is available. The list that follows highlights sources of help. Remember that many of these sources are good suppliers of financial information even if you aren't having problems.

- *Published sources.* Newspapers often have money management columns that offer timely advice. You can also examine magazines devoted to money matters, such as *Kiplinger's Personal Finance* and *Money*. In addition, most family magazines regularly provide useful tips on money issues. Bookstores carry a comprehensive selection of books on managing your money.
- *On-line sources.* Don't forget the Internet. Financial Web sites may provide informational articles, useful statistics, and practical advice.
- *Schools.* Many continuing education institutions and community colleges offer money management classes. Teachers and counselors may also be available to give you one-on-one advice.
- *Government agencies.* Free or inexpensive booklets providing consumer financial information are available from government agencies. You can find these at local libraries and at federal and county offices.
- *Banks.* Many banks offer free financial advice to their customers. Some even hold seminars on money management.
- *Professionals.* Lawyers, accountants, and financial planners will also provide financial advice. You will have to pay for their services, however.

SECTION 20-2 *Review*

Understanding Key Concepts

Using complete sentences, answer the following questions on a separate sheet of paper.

1. How will having a budget help you cope with personal changes?

2. What could you do to keep yourself informed about possible economic change?

3. Describe how you might use two of the sources listed in the text to help you manage your money now.

Key Terms

budget *(p. 398)*
record keeping *(p. 402)*

SECTION 20-1 Summary

- Begin planning your budget by defining your financial goals, prioritizing those goals, and estimating current income and expenses.

- Make your budget realistic. Otherwise, you probably won't follow it.

- Record keeping—organizing and maintaining records of all of your income and spending—is important. Your files should be up-to-date and accessible. Store important documents in a fireproof box or in a safe-deposit box at a bank.

- Your budget will be based on your estimated income and expenses. Be sure to include savings in your budget. You may need to fine-tune your plan by decreasing expenses or increasing income.

- Effective strategies for staying within your budget include paying cash for purchases, shopping wisely, and thinking before spending.

Key Term

financial responsibility
(p. 409)

SECTION 20-2 Summary

- Financial responsibility, or accountability in money matters, increases during a person's lifetime. Over time, personal changes also occur that require adjustments to budgets and goals.

- Economic changes such as price increases during times of inflation and economic downturns, or recessions, require effective money management skills. Economic changes also may mean cutting down on expenses, increasing income, and accepting help from others.

- Help for money management problems can come from publications, on-line sources, educational institutions, government agencies, banks, and various types of professionals.

Reviewing Key Terms

On a separate sheet of paper, write a paragraph about managing your own money. Use the terms below in your paragraph.

budget
record keeping
financial responsibility

Recalling Key Concepts

Choose the correct answer for each item below. Write your answers on a separate sheet of paper.

1. The first step in planning your budget is to ____.
   (a) cut expenses
   (b) obtain budget software
   (c) identify your financial goals

2. You should file your bills ____.
   (a) once a year
   (b) as you receive or pay them
   (c) only after you prepare your taxes

3. One way to help yourself stay within your budget is to ____.
   (a) track your spending
   (b) use credit cards for most purchases
   (c) carry your ATM card at all times

4. Personal changes that affect your finances include ____.
   (a) inflation (b) adopting a child
   (c) recession

5. Inflation, recession, and unemployment are all examples of ____.
   (a) economic change
   (b) flexible expenses
   (c) fixed expenses

6. You can usually receive free or low-cost help for financial problems from ____.
   (a) lawyers (b) accountants
   (c) government publications

Thinking Critically

Using complete sentences, answer each of the questions below on a separate sheet of paper.

1. When you are preparing a budget, why is honesty with yourself important in estimating income and expenses?

2. How are the effects of inflation and a recession similar, and how are they different?

3. Why do you think that many people avoid seeking help with financial problems until the problems become serious?

 SCANS Foundation Skills and Workplace Competencies

Thinking Skills: *Problem Solving*

1. Miranda hopes to have her own pottery shop someday. She currently makes and sells planters. This supplements her salary from the grocery store where she works full-time. She is having trouble staying within her budget. List at least three factors that Miranda will have to consider as she seeks to solve her budgeting problem.

Information: *Organizing and Maintaining Information*

2. Assume that you live at home and go to school, have a part-time job, make

payments on a car, pay for your own phone, and volunteer at a hospital. You want to set up a record-keeping system. How will you organize and label your files? Write an alphabetized list of the files you'll want to keep.

Connecting Academics to the Workplace

Math

1. Kim's net earnings are $640 a month. Kim lives at home, paying $100 a month for room and board. She also spends $3 a day on lunch at school, five days a week. She wants to be an electrician and needs to save $120 each month toward classes at a trade school. She's making payments of $220 a month on a used car she bought, and she pays her parents $25 a month toward the insurance. She spends an average of $7 a week on gas. How much does Kim have left over each month for other expenses?

Human Relations

2. Tim works for a large company that has recently experienced financial setbacks. The company plans to cut all salaries by 5 percent. To help employees adjust, the company wants to offer financial counseling. Research resources that could be used in such a program.

Developing Teamwork and Leadership Skills

Work with a team of three. First, agree on a realistic money management problem that might occur in an individual's or a family's life. Then assign each team member one of the sources of financial help listed in Section 20-2. Each team member should find out from the assigned source what help would be available for the problem. Finally, work together to prepare an oral report on the team's findings for presentation to the class.

Real-World Workshop

Describe a hypothetical family that might live in your region. Find out what income, living expenses, transportation costs, and other budget items there might be for this family. Create a monthly budget for the family (use a form similar to the one shown in Figure 20-2), and present it to the class.

School-to-Work Connection

Work with a group of three. Contact a bank, school, or professional organization that helps people with financial planning. Set up an interview to find out what five tips a representative would give to people graduating from high school to avoid financial problems. Within your group, decide how you will present the tips to the class. Possible formats include a skit or a poster.

Individual Career Plan

Choose a career in a business or industry that interests you. Create a list of ways that you think good management of your own finances could help you succeed in this career.

Chapter 21

Banking and Credit

Section 21-1
Saving Money

Section 21-2
Checking Accounts and Other Banking Services

Section 21-3
Using Credit Wisely

In this video segment, find out about the disadvantages of credit.

Journal
Personal Career Plan

Even though you don't yet have a full-time job, your first credit card—preapproved—has just arrived in the mail. Will you keep the card? Why or why not? If so, how will you use it? Record your responses in your journal.

Saving Money

After studying this section, you will be able to:

- **Compare common saving methods.**
- **Explain the characteristics of different retirement plans.**

KEY TERMS

**dividend
certificate of
    deposit (CD)
401(k) plan
individual
    retirement
    account (IRA)
Keogh plan
simplified employee
    pension (SEP)**

It's been termed *moolah, bread, dough, bucks,* and *greenbacks.* In plain language, it's money. Chapter 20 explained how a budget allows you to keep track of money you've worked for. This chapter will give you guidance on how your money can work for you.

Ways to Save

Saving and investing are the way to put your money to work. Most people begin by opening a savings account at a bank, savings and loan association, or credit union. A *credit union* is a not-for-profit financial institution similar to a bank. People who belong to a credit union, however, share a common bond, such as working at the same company.

There are two basic types of savings accounts. With a *passbook account,* you receive a booklet in which transactions are recorded. With a *statement account,* you receive a computerized statement, usually monthly, of transactions.

With either type of account, you deposit money and the institution pays interest. *Interest* is the money that banks pay depositors for the use of their money. Usually, interest is a percentage of the amount deposited.

Normally, interest paid on a savings account is *compounded.* That is, the interest is figured on the amount of money you have deposited *plus* the interest that has accrued on your initial deposit. The effects of compounding are shown in *Figure 21-1.*

How Compounding Makes $1,000 Grow

Month	Beginning Balance	Monthly Interest at 5%	Ending Balance
January	$ 1,000.00	$ 4.17	$ 1,004.17
February	$ 1,004.17	$ 4.18	$ 1,008.35
March	$ 1,008.35	$ 4.20	$ 1,012.55
April	$ 1,012.55	$ 4.22	$ 1,016.77
May	$ 1,016.77	$ 4.24	$ 1,021.01
June	$ 1,021.01	$ 4.25	$ 1,025.26

Figure 21-1 This table shows how much interest is paid on a $1,000 deposit when the interest rate is 5 percent, compounded monthly. The beginning balance is multiplied by 5 percent and then divided by 12 (because a month is ¹/₁₂ of a year). Why does the interest increase from month to month?

How else can you put your money to work? Following are a few other ways of putting your money to work for you. Use your SCANS decision-making skills to choose the best ones for you.

- *Savings bonds.*   When you buy a U.S. savings bond, you are lending money to the government. You buy a bond for half the "face value," which is the amount printed on the bond. Each year the bond grows in value until it has matured, or become payable. You can then *redeem*, or cash it in, for the full face value.

- *Money market deposit accounts or money market mutual funds.*   These are other savings options. With a money market account or fund, you deposit money that is pooled with money from other savers and then invested. You are paid a **dividend**, or share of the fund's profits.

- *Certificates of deposit.*   With a **certificate of deposit (CD),** you deposit an amount of money for a fixed amount of time at a stated interest rate. Choosing a longer investment period often ensures you a higher interest rate.

Look at *Figure 21-2* on page 420. It compares these different savings strategies.

Retirement Plans

When should you start putting aside money for your retirement? According to many experts, you should begin when you receive your first paycheck. You may be surprised to learn that Social Security, even combined with retirement plans offered by employers, rarely provides sufficient income for the retirement years. The following are some retirement plan options. Use your SCANS competency of acquiring and interpreting information as you examine them.

Pension Plans

A pension plan is a retirement plan funded, at least in part, by an employer

Comparing Ways to Save

Type of Savings	Characteristics	Advantages	Disadvantages
Savings **Passbook or Statement Account**	• Money deposited in a savings account at a bank, credit union, or savings and loan association • Interest paid on the money in the account	• Can open account with only a few dollars • Easy access • Savings of up to $100,000 often protected by Federal Deposit Insurance Corporation (FDIC)	• Low interest rate • Interest rate not fixed
Certificate of Deposit (CD)	• Purchased at banks and other financial institutions • Money invested for a fixed time, usually six months to several years • Interest paid on money in the account • Traditionally, the longer the term of investment, the higher the interest rate	• Fixed rate of interest guaranteed for term of the deposit • Better interest than regular savings account • Savings of up to $100,000 often protected by FDIC	• Money tied up for fixed period of time • Penalty for early withdrawal • Must invest larger amounts of money, usually $500 or more
Money Market Deposit Account/ Money Market Mutual Fund	• Money market deposit accounts purchased at banks; money market mutual funds sold by mutual funds or insurance companies (a fund is made up of many investors)	• Usually pays higher interest than regular savings account • Money can be withdrawn at any time • Checks usually can be written on account • Savings in money market accounts often insured by FDIC	• Interest rate varies • Requires minimum deposit, which varies with type of account • Bank may not pay interest if balance drops below a minimum amount
U.S. Savings Bond	• Purchased at banks or other financial institutions or directly from the government • Available in set amounts from $50 to $30,000 (face value) • Purchased for half the face value • Grows in value each year; worth face value at maturity	• Can be purchased for as little as $25 • Interest not subject to state or local taxes • Very safe; value guaranteed by the U.S. Treasury	• Money tied up for a period of time • If money is withdrawn early, owner gets less than face value

or union. The pension builds up throughout a worker's career. The amount of the pension is based on the employee's salary and the length of service with the company. Here are three common types of pension plans:

- In a *defined-benefit plan*, your company pays you a fixed amount at retirement. You know before you retire what amount you will receive.

- In a *defined-contribution plan*, sometimes called a profit-sharing plan, your employer contributes a set amount to the plan each year. The amount you receive at retirement depends on how much money has built up in the fund.

- In a **401(k) plan**, you put a specific portion of your salary into the plan. Employers often match this contribution, up to a specific amount or salary percentage.

 People today are living longer, healthier lives than past generations. *What does this mean for individuals just starting out in their career?*

Individual Retirement Accounts

Even if you have a pension plan, you can have an **individual retirement account (IRA)** as well. This is a personal retirement account into which you can put a limited amount of money yearly. The earnings are not taxed until you retire.

Depending on your annual earnings, you can invest up to $2,000 a year in an IRA. One disadvantage of an IRA is that you are charged a penalty if you withdraw the money before you reach the age of 59½.

Plans for the Self-Employed

Do you plan to work for yourself? If so, a Keogh plan or a simplified employee pension may be the right type of plan for you. Both have the tax-deferment advantage of an IRA.

- With a **Keogh plan** (pronounced KEE-oh), you can invest up to 15 percent of your yearly earnings (up to $150,000) each year for retirement. There are special rules for setting up a Keogh account, so you should check with an accountant before you create one.

YOU'RE THE BOSS!

✔ Solving Workplace Problems

The pastry chef in your restaurant is very talented and earns a good salary, but you realize she has trouble managing her money. She often asks you for an advance or wonders about getting a raise, and you've heard her asking the chef for loans. What will you do to help her solve these problems?

- A **simplified employee pension (SEP)** is a simpler tax-deferred retirement plan than the Keogh but one that also offers tax savings. It, too, is for the self-employed. Individuals can set aside as much as 15 percent of their yearly earnings, up to $150,000. (Owner-employees can set aside up to 13 percent.) A SEP account is easier to establish and maintain than a Keogh account, and some people prefer it for that reason.

SECTION 21-1 *Review*

Understanding Key Concepts

Using complete sentences, answer the following questions on a separate sheet of paper.

1. Why might someone who is just starting out prefer a regular savings account to a CD?

2. Explain why you should start contributing to a retirement plan as soon as you can.

Checking Accounts and Other Banking Services

OBJECTIVES

After studying this section, you will be able to:
- Shop wisely for a checking account.
- Write a check and fill out a check register.
- Reconcile a checking account.

KEY TERMS

endorse
check register
reconcile

"Will that be cash, check, or charge?" This question is asked countless times each day. Just what are checks, and how do they work?

Checking Accounts

A check is a written document that authorizes the transfer of money from a bank account to a person or business. Most businesses and individuals rely on checks. For paying bills, they are easier and safer than cash. They also simplify record keeping.

Types of Checking Accounts

You open a checking account at a bank or credit union by depositing money into the account. To make a deposit, you fill out a deposit slip. Deposit slips are available in all bank branch offices. You will also receive a supply of deposit slips with your checks.

You can write checks up to the amount of your balance. Whether you gain interest on your balance or have to pay fees depends on the bank and the type of account you have.

A *regular checking account* often requires no minimum balance. However, it rarely earns interest, and you are usually charged a monthly fee for maintaining it. This fee may be a flat monthly rate ($4 to $8

 Choices about where to bank depend on many different factors.
What factors do you think are most important in choosing a bank?

a month, for example) or a charge for each check you write. A *NOW account* (negotiable order of withdrawal) pays interest on your deposits. However, you must keep a minimum balance in the account, usually at least $500. A *Super-NOW account* is similar to a NOW account except that the interest rate and minimum balance required are both higher.

Managing Your Checking Account

Having a checking account allows you to write checks when you need to pay bills or buy groceries. When you write a check, you must fill it out completely and accurately. (*Figure 21-3* shows how to do this.)

Sometimes you will receive checks. Your employer, for example, will probably pay you with a check. Normally, you will take the check to your bank to deposit it or cash it. To complete either transaction, you must **endorse** the check—sign your name on the back.

Attitude Counts ✔

Who's in charge here? When it comes to managing your money, there should be only one answer: You're in charge! You may want to blame another person or an outside influence for some of your financial choices. However, you'll be successful in managing your money only when you accept full responsibility for your decisions.

Figure 21-3

Using a Checking Account

A checking account makes paying your bills convenient and safe. It also helps you track your expenses and manage your budget. A check authorizes your bank to take money from your account for payment to someone else. Be sure to write your checks clearly and completely.

Keeping Track of Your Account

If you write checks for more money than you have in your account, the account will be *overdrawn*. Banks charge a high fee for overdrawn checks. They may also send a check back to the business that

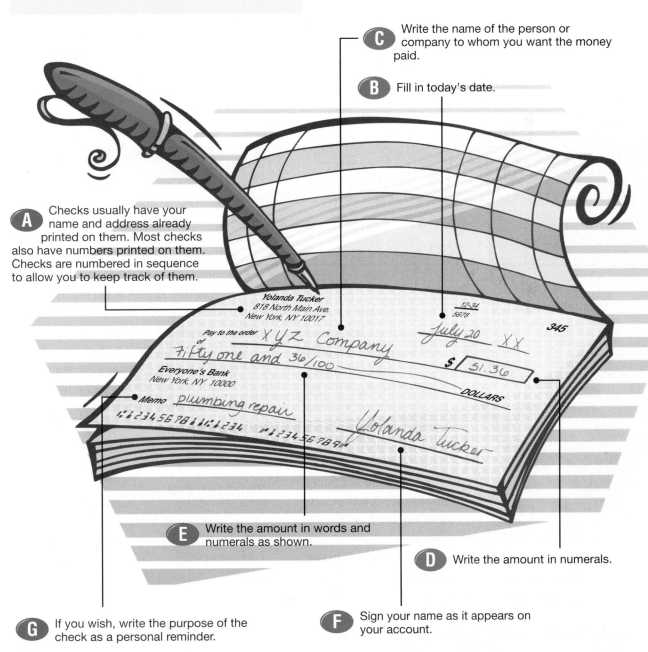

C Write the name of the person or company to whom you want the money paid.

B Fill in today's date.

A Checks usually have your name and address already printed on them. Most checks also have numbers printed on them. Checks are numbered in sequence to allow you to keep track of them.

E Write the amount in words and numerals as shown.

D Write the amount in numerals.

G If you wish, write the purpose of the check as a personal reminder.

F Sign your name as it appears on your account.

submitted it for payment, causing you embarrassment. For these reasons, keep track of your account.

When you purchase your checks, you will get a **check register**, a small booklet for tracking your account. (See *Figure 21-4.*) Record all checks, deposits, fees, interest charges, and other transactions in the check register. Add and subtract amounts immediately so that you know exactly how much is in your account at any time.

Each month, you will get a statement of your account. You will need to reconcile the statement with your check register. To **reconcile** two items means to make them agree.

Using Other Banking Services

Banks offer additional services to help you manage your money.

- *Electronic fund transfer.* Most banks offer electronic fund transfer (EFT). In most cases, this is accomplished with an ATM card. You'll get a card with a personal identification number (PIN) that will allow you to use an automated teller machine (ATM). This allows you to make deposits and withdrawals to your account electronically—any time of the day or night.

EXCELLENT BUSINESS PRACTICES

A Slice of the Pie

PepsiCo Inc. of Purchase, New York, created a basis for its 470,000 workers to own part of the business. PepsiCo owns such businesses as Pepsi-Cola, Frito-Lay, Taco Bell, Kentucky Fried Chicken, and Pizza Hut. To help employees have a vested interest in the quality of the products and the service, the company offered a stock-option program to workers.

Stock-option plans can help employees accumulate capital over time.

Eligible employees receive the equivalent of 10 percent of their previous year's salary in stock options.

To exercise the option, each year employees can "cash in" 20 percent of the options by buying the stock at the grant price and holding onto it. Or they can sell it at its current value.

Employees who have a monetary interest in the prosperity of a company are more likely to make efforts on a daily basis to serve a good product, treat customers well, identify potential workplace hazards, and make suggestions for improving efficiency.

Thinking Critically

Why do many companies tie in stock options with salaries for top executives' compensation?

Check Register

NUMBER	DATE	DESCRIPTION OF TRANSACTION	PAYMENT/DEBIT (-)		√ T	FEE (IF ANY) (-)	DEPOSIT/CREDIT (+)		BALANCE $ 172	16
343	7/15	Bob's Service Station	$ 24	36		$	$		24	36
		oil change							147	80
344	7/15	General Service Co.	72	14					72	14
		heater contract							75	66
	7/16	ATM transfer					200	00	200	00
		from savings							275	66
	7/17	Deposit					424	62	424	62
		paycheck							700	28
345	7/20	XYZ Company	51	36					51	36
		plumbing repair							648	92
	7/20	ATM withdrawal	40	00					40	00
		gift for James							608	92

▲ **Figure 21-4** Each time you make any transaction involving your checking account, immediately record it in your check register. Add or subtract the transaction from your previous balance in the final column. Why is it important to keep your balance current?

- *Banking on-line.* Another increasingly popular development is banking on-line. This service lets you manage your money from your home computer. Costs for on-line banking are becoming lower each year.

SECTION 21-2 *Review*

Understanding Key Concepts

Using complete sentences, answer the following questions on a separate sheet of paper.

1. Why might you choose a regular checking account instead of a NOW account?

2. Why must you write the amount of a check in both numerals and words?

3. Why is it important to reconcile your check register and bank statement?

Exploring Careers: Manufacturing

Richard J. Kulp
Toolmaker

Q: **How did you get into toolmaking?**

A: I was a helicopter mechanic in the Army. When I got out, I didn't feel I had enough knowledge to go into that field as a civilian. My military training was very specialized. I came to Hoover & Strong as a production worker. Then the company offered me the apprenticeship in toolmaking.

Q: **What does the apprenticeship consist of?**

A: It's different state by state. In Virginia, it's four years long. There are many different classes you have to take, including machining, welding, metalworking and heat treating, hydraulics and pneumatics, and math. Math skills are very important in toolmaking. You have to be very precise.

Q: **What is your job like?**

A: We're designing and making tools for the production of gold jewelry and similar items.

We do everything from designing the tools from scratch to maintaining, sharpening, and cleaning them to keep them in working condition.

Q: **Do you like it?**

A: I like making things. I like taking a chunk of steel and turning it into something that can actually be used for a specific purpose.

Thinking Critically

What skills does a toolmaker have that might transfer into the field of engineering?

CAREER FACTS

Nature of the Work:
Design and make tools from steel for specific uses; use large machinery and small hand tools.

Training or Education Needed:
Apprenticeship program through state, union, or private sources; journeyman certificate.

Aptitudes, Abilities, and Skills:
Very strong math skills; listening skills; problem-solving skills; ability to see things in the mind's eye; self-management skills; ability to use large machinery; ability to work with tools; attention to detail.

Salary Range:
Approximately $12 to $13 an hour in nonunion shops; rates are higher in union shops.

Career Path:
Most journeymen toolmakers usually stay on as toolmakers; other options include becoming a toolroom manager or going into engineering.

Using Credit Wisely

Now and then, life has a way of demanding more money than you have on hand. One way to obtain that money is through credit. **Credit** is a sum of money a person can use before having to reimburse the credit lender. It allows the person to receive a good or service now but to pay for it later. When you use credit, you are really taking out a loan.

Understanding Credit

Most businesses that sell a good or service offer credit. Car dealers, department stores, appliance dealers, and even some doctors offer credit. In fact, some companies (such as VISA and MasterCard) are in business just to extend credit.

Types of Credit

The most common type of credit is that offered through a credit card. A *credit card*, issued by a bank or other financial institution, allows the cardholder to charge amounts in many different places. The lender issues you a plastic card stamped with your name and account number. Usually, you are given a *credit limit*. This is the maximum amount you can charge against your account.

Many businesses offer consumers charge accounts. A charge account is similar to a credit card account. In this case, the business issues the credit and often a credit card that can be used only at the company, or store, that issued it. When you buy an item, you charge it to your account. Each business sets the terms for its charge accounts.

Loans are another type of credit. People get loans from banks, credit unions, and other financial institutions to make large purchases. Car loans and mortgages are typical consumer loans.

Most loans are *installment loans*, in which you receive the money as a lump sum and pay it back in regular (usually monthly) payments called installments. You may have to pay an **application fee**, an amount of money charged to apply for the loan. Usually, you also have to make a **down payment**, a sum (usually a percentage of the total payment) paid at the time of the purchase.

Secured loans are guaranteed by *collateral*, an asset such as the borrower's home or car. If the borrower defaults on the loan—that is, fails to pay it—the lender can take the collateral. Unsecured loans do not require collateral.

Disadvantages of Credit

While the advantages of credit are clear to most people, credit also has at least two disadvantages. First, lenders charge a **finance charge**, which is a fee based on the amount of money you owe. Finance charges are based on a particular interest rate and can be figured in a number of ways. (The cost of credit is described in the next section.)

The second disadvantage of credit is the risk of overusing it. If you accumulate too much debt, you may not be able to make timely payments. You may lose your collateral on secured loans. Your financial reputation will also suffer.

Use credit when you need to, but avoid overusing it. People with credit problems can find help through organizations such as American Consumer Credit Counseling and the Consumer Credit Counseling Service.

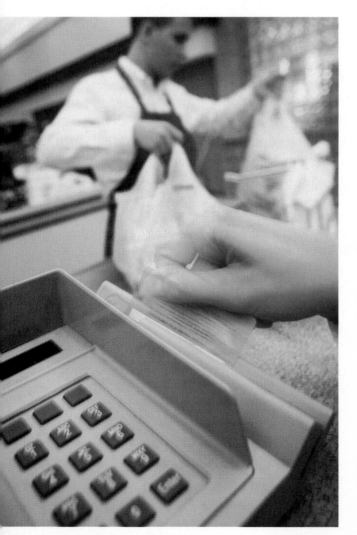

Many stores will be able to process your credit card electronically by passing it through a special machine. *What tasks do you think this machine performs?*

Talking with someone from a credit counseling service can help you work out credit problems effectively. *What might be the consequences of ignoring credit problems?*

Career Do's & Don'ts

When Working with Checks and Balances...

Do:
- keep your checking account balanced.
- set up a savings plan for special goals.
- keep charge card receipts and compare them to the bills.
- investigate tax-free savings and retirement plans.

Don't:
- open more than one or two charge cards.
- charge more than you can quickly pay off.
- invest money in any scheme that is not documented as legitimate and sound.
- sign any credit documents that don't clearly state the amount loaned, the length of the loan, and the interest rate.

The Cost of Credit

Credit costs vary widely. Your best bet is to shop around. Not all companies compute costs in the same way or charge the same amounts.

- *Annual fees.* Many credit card companies charge an annual fee or a membership fee. The amount is fixed and is charged to your account no matter how often you use the card.

- *Finance charges.* If you pay off your entire balance every month, you will not incur finance charges, which are interest on your unpaid balance. Finance charges commonly amount to 1.5 percent of your balance per month, or 18 percent per year. The Federal Truth in Lending Act requires lenders to state the cost of the interest as an **annual percentage rate (APR)**. This is the yearly cost of the loan, expressed as a percentage. An APR allows you to compare the costs of credit from different lenders.

Most credit cards have a *grace period*. This is a time during which interest is not charged. With most credit cards, if you pay the entire amount by the due date stated on your first bill, you are not charged interest or any other finance charges.

Credit Agreements and Reports

When you apply for credit, you must complete a *credit application*. This form asks for details about your salary, bank accounts, and credit history. Before your application is approved, the lender will usually check with a credit bureau. A **credit bureau** is an agency that collects information on how promptly people and businesses pay their bills. The credit bureau provides this information, in the form of a credit report, to businesses that request it.

The credit bureau gives you a *credit rating*, a numerical rating that indicates how likely you are to pay your bills. If you have a poor credit rating, you may be denied a car loan or a mortgage. Make a habit of checking your credit rating regularly. You can do this by contacting a credit reporting agency such as Equifax, Trans

It can be tempting to use a credit card to buy items on the spur of the moment. *How could you prevent yourself from overusing credit?*

Union, or TRW and paying a fee. Errors sometimes occur, and you will want to see that the credit bureau corrects them as soon as possible.

SECTION 21-3 *Review*

Understanding Key Concepts

Using complete sentences, answer the following questions on a separate sheet of paper.

1. Why is a credit card more convenient for everyday purchases than a loan?

2. Why is it easy for some people to get into financial trouble when they have credit cards?

3. Why do businesses check with credit bureaus before extending credit to individuals?

Key Terms

dividend *(p. 419)*
certificate of deposit (CD)
   (p. 419)
401(k) plan *(p. 421)*
individual retirement
   account (IRA) *(p. 422)*
Keogh plan *(p. 422)*
simplified employee
   pension (SEP) *(p. 422)*

SECTION 21-1 Summary

- Saving your money in an interest-bearing account puts it to work for you. When interest is compounded, your savings will grow even more quickly.

- You can save money by depositing it in a savings account or money market account or fund. You can also buy savings bonds and certificates of deposit.

- You should start saving for your retirement as soon as possible. Participating in a pension plan is a good way to begin. In addition, you will probably want to contribute to an individual retirement account (IRA) or a 401(k) plan. For self-employed people, Keogh plans and simplified employee pension (SEP) plans allow tax-deferred savings.

Key Terms

endorse *(p. 424)*
check register *(p. 426)*
reconcile *(p. 426)*

SECTION 21-2 Summary

- With a checking account, you deposit money and then write checks on your balance.

- Keep track of your checking account with a check register. Reconcile it monthly against your bank statement.

- Electronic fund transfer and banking on-line make banking more convenient.

Key Terms

credit *(p. 429)*
application fee *(p. 430)*
down payment *(p. 430)*
finance charge *(p. 430)*
annual percentage rate
   (APR) *(p. 431)*
credit bureau *(p. 432)*

SECTION 21-3 Summary

- Credit allows you to buy something now and pay for it later. Credit may be obtained through the use of credit cards, charge accounts, and loans.

- Disadvantages of credit include finance charges and the possibility of taking on too much debt.

- The costs of credit include annual fees and finance charges.

- A credit bureau keeps track of how timely debts are paid.

Reviewing Key Terms

On a separate sheet of paper, write a brief speech giving advice on banking and credit to a person your age. Use each of the following terms.

dividend	endorse
certificate of deposit (CD)	check register
	reconcile
401(k) plan	credit
individual retirement account (IRA)	application fee
	down payment
	finance charge
Keogh plan	annual percentage rate (APR)
simplified employee pension (SEP)	credit bureau

Recalling Key Concepts

Choose the correct answer for each item below. Write your answers on a separate sheet of paper.

1. You agree to keep your money deposited for a specific length of time in a ____.

    (a) certificate of deposit

    (b) money market mutual fund

    (c) checking account

2. Only self-employed workers can open a ____.

    (a) money market deposit account

    (b) CD (c) Keogh plan

3. When you compare a checking account statement with your check register to make sure they agree, you are ____ your checking account.

    (a) reconciling (b) overdrawing

    (c) transferring

4. The most common type of credit vehicle is a ____.

    (a) SEP (b) charge account

    (c) credit card

5. Credit can be costly because of ____.

    (a) credit bureaus

    (b) high interest rates

    (c) credit ratings

Thinking Critically

Using complete sentences, answer each of the questions below on a separate sheet of paper.

1. What factors might help you choose between a very safe investment with a low interest rate and a riskier investment with a higher interest rate?

2. How can you use your checking account to keep track of your spending habits?

3. Why do you think most businesses offer credit to their customers?

4. Explain which is the wiser strategy: to save $100 a month in a savings account or to repay $100 a month toward a credit card debt of $1,200.

 ## SCANS Foundation Skills and Workplace Competencies

Thinking Skills: *Problem Solving*

1. Imagine that you earn a good salary but have allowed the balances on several credit cards to get too high. Suggest two actions you might take to begin solving your problem.

Interpersonal Skills: *Negotiating to Arrive at a Decision*

2. Your sister has asked you to cosign a loan to help her buy a car. By cosigning, you are stating that if she can't repay the loan, you will. You don't think your sister can repay the loan. How do you handle this situation without harming your relationship with your sister?

Connecting Academics to the Workplace

Math

1. Steve's bank pays an annual interest rate of 2.8 percent on savings accounts of less than $5,000. The interest is compounded monthly. If Steve deposits $1,000 in a savings account, how much interest will he earn if he leaves his money in this account for three months?

Family and Consumer Science

2. A credit card company has refused to issue Howard a credit card, claiming that he has a bad credit rating. Howard is sure that the credit card company made a mistake about his credit history. What documentation should Howard have in front of him when he makes a call to the credit bureau to check his credit report?

Developing Teamwork and Leadership Skills

Working on a team with three classmates, imagine that you work for a company that does not provide a retirement plan. Your team has been asked to explain to the employees the importance of setting up their own retirement plans. As a team, gather data to show why retirement income in addition to Social Security is needed, and find out what options are available. Then write a presentation to convince other employees to set up their own retirement plans now. Deliver your presentation to the class.

Real-World Workshop

Assume you have $5,000 to invest for one year. Where can you put the money so it will earn the best return? Investigate savings accounts, CDs, money market funds and deposit accounts, and savings bonds. You might check newspaper ads and visit banks and other financial institutions. Choose one or more places to invest the money. Write an explanation of your choice.

School-to-Work Connection

Visit a local bank, credit union, or other financial institution. Interview an employee to learn what advice he or she would give to someone your age about saving money, planning for retirement, and obtaining credit. Ask about special plans that the institution offers for beginning savers, retirement savings, and credit management. Prepare a brief written report on your findings.

Individual Career Plan

Select a career in the banking and credit industry that interests you, such as loan officer or investment counselor. In a paragraph, describe qualities you think would be important for a person in this position.

Buying Insurance

Section 22-1
Insurance Basics

Section 22-2
Home and Automobile Insurance

Section 22-3
Health and Life Insurance

In this video segment, discover why you should budget for insurance.

Journal
Personal Career Plan

Write a short journal entry, identifying the kinds of insurance you now have, and your reasons for having no other kinds of insurance. After you have studied this chapter, reread your journal entry and add a follow-up, explaining the kinds of insurance you expect to buy in the next few years.

Insurance Basics

When was the last time you made plans, only to have them changed by an unexpected event? One thing is certain in life: No matter how carefully we plan, some things go wrong. A driver backs into your new car. While you are at work, your television set is stolen. You break an arm and need emergency surgery.

How can you plan for life's unexpected events? One way is to buy insurance. When you purchase insurance, you pay an agreed-upon amount of money to an insurance company. The company in turn agrees to pay for losses caused by such events as automobile accidents, theft, or injuries that might otherwise ruin you financially.

The Language of Insurance

Remember when you first used a computer? You had to learn "computerese"—the language of computers. The same is true of insurance. The terms below are part of the language of insurance.

Insurance Policy

When you buy insurance, you'll receive an insurance policy. An **insurance policy** is a legal contract between a person buying insurance (a *policyholder*) and an insurance company. The policy explains:

- who is covered,
- types of losses for which the company will pay,
- amounts the company will pay, and
- the cost of the insurance.

An insurance policy is long and technical. In spite of this, you should read it carefully and ask questions about any unclear parts before you sign it.

Insurance Coverage

An insurance policy describes a policyholder's coverage. Insurance *coverage* refers to losses that an insurance company agrees to cover. The amount of coverage is the actual dollar amount that will be paid by the company in case of a loss.

All insurance policies have a list of *exclusions*. These are losses or risks that are not covered.

Benefit and Beneficiary

Money paid by an insurance company for a loss is called the *benefit*. In most cases the benefit is paid to the *beneficiary*, who is usually the policyholder.

Premiums

The amount a policyholder pays an insurance company is known as the **premium**. You can usually pay premiums in installments rather than all at once.

Deductibles

When you buy most types of coverage, you agree to pay a deductible. A **deductible** is the portion of a loss that you pay before the insurance company pays the remaining cost. The higher the deductible that you pay, the lower the cost of your premiums.

Claim

How does an insurance company know to pay you for a loss? You file a **claim**, an oral or written notice to the insurance company.

Even though it takes time to read an insurance policy, you should understand its terms fully before you buy the coverage it provides. *Why do you think it is as important to understand what a policy does* not *cover as what it does cover?*

Kinds of Insurance

You can buy insurance for almost anything. It's possible to purchase marine insurance, space flight insurance, and dread-disease insurance. Professional dancers can have their legs insured. Concert pianists can have their hands insured.

Government Insurance Programs

These programs provide coverage if you lose your job (unemployment insurance), are injured on the job (workers' compensation), or qualify for health coverage (Medicare, Medicaid). See Chapter 23, Types of Benefits.

Holding Down Insurance Costs

How do you shop for big items such as a car or stereo system? Taking time to shop around can save you money when buying insurance. This is where SCANS workplace skills such as reading, math, decision making, problem solving, and reasoning are especially helpful. Here are several tips for controlling insurance costs:

Knowing what type of insurance you want can help you control insurance costs. *What other tips can help you hold down insurance costs?*

- Know what type of insurance you want.

- Call several insurance agencies in your area to ask about coverages and costs.

- Ask about differences in premium costs with different deductibles. Consider paying higher deductibles in order to lower your premium costs.

- Don't buy more coverage than you need or less coverage than you need.

SECTION 22-1 *Review*

Understanding Key Concepts

Using complete sentences, answer the following questions on a separate sheet of paper.

1. Explain the difference between a premium and a deductible.

2. Imagine that you are drawing up a new budget for the coming year. Describe three ways to save money on your insurance costs.

Home and Automobile Insurance

After studying this section, you will be able to:

- **Describe the importance of owning home insurance.**
- **Describe five types of auto insurance coverage.**
- **Explain the factors that influence auto insurance premiums.**

KEY TERMS

liability insurance
collision insurance
comprehensive
    insurance

What are your insurance needs? If you're like most people, you'll need only the basics: home, automobile, health, and perhaps life insurance.

You will want to be sure you have the right protection and that you do everything necessary to keep your coverage up-to-date. It is important to understand how insurance works because a great deal of money will be at stake.

Home Insurance

If you decide to rent an apartment, you'll need renter's insurance. This type of insurance covers your belongings up to a set amount, minus your deductible. *Figure 22-1* on page 442 shows one way to keep track of your belongings in case you need to file a claim.

If you decide to buy a house or condominium, you'll purchase homeowner's insurance. This type of coverage protects your house and its contents.

Automobile Insurance

Many states require by law that drivers have insurance. You can find out about a state's requirements from the insurance commissioner or motor vehicle division.

Inventory of Personal Property

Item	Purchase Price	Date of Purchase	Item	Purchase Price	Date of Purchase
Electronic items:			Collections:		
TV	_____	_____	_____	_____	_____
CD player	_____	_____	_____	_____	_____
Radio	_____	_____			
Stereo	_____	_____	Other valuables:		
Camera	_____	_____	_____	_____	_____
Computer	_____	_____	_____	_____	_____
_____	_____	_____	_____	_____	_____
_____	_____	_____	_____	_____	_____
Jewelry:			Furniture:		
Watch	_____	_____	_____	_____	_____
Ring	_____	_____	_____	_____	_____
			_____	_____	_____
Sports equipment:					
_____	_____	_____	Silverware, dishes, glassware:		
_____	_____	_____	_____	_____	_____
_____	_____	_____	_____	_____	_____
Musical instruments:			_____	_____	_____
_____	_____	_____	Electrical appliances:		
_____	_____	_____	_____	_____	_____
Clothing:			_____	_____	_____
_____	_____	_____	_____	_____	_____
_____	_____	_____	Linens:		
Tools:			_____	_____	_____
_____	_____	_____	_____	_____	_____
_____	_____	_____			

Figure 22-1   When you buy renter's or homeowner's insurance, make an inventory of your possessions and keep receipts for items of value. Update your records annually. What other kinds of items would you include on a list such as this? Why is it also a good idea to photograph or videotape your possessions?

Types of Coverage

When you buy a standard automobile insurance policy, you usually buy several different kinds of coverage. Each type of coverage insures your car and you for a different kind of loss, damage, or injury.

Liability Insurance. What if you're involved in an accident that's your fault? **Liability insurance** covers damage or injury for which you're responsible. This includes injuries suffered by the driver and passengers in the other car and by passengers in your car. It also covers property damage to the other car. Liability insurance doesn't cover your injuries or property damage to your car.

Medical Payments Insurance. If you suffer injuries in an auto accident, whether or not it's your fault, *medical payments insurance* will cover your medical expenses. Medical payments insurance also covers medical expenses of your passengers. This insurance is more limited than liability insurance, though. For example, many policies cover only up to $5,000 in medical expenses per person. Liability insurance will cover expenses beyond the maximum amount per person of medical payments coverage.

Liability insurance protects you against claims or lawsuits by people whose cars are damaged and who are injured in an accident that is your responsibility. *Why is it important to have as much auto liability insurance as you can afford?*

Collision Insurance. In an accident that's your fault, **collision insurance** covers the cost of repairs to your car. It also covers damage to your car if you're in an accident caused by a driver who is not insured. *Figure 22-2* provides advice on what to do in case you're involved in an auto accident.

Comprehensive Insurance. What if your car is stolen? **Comprehensive insurance** covers your car for reasons other than a collision. These reasons include theft, fire, and vandalism.

Uninsured Motorist Insurance. You can buy *uninsured motorist coverage* to

▶ Figure 22-2

Handling Auto Accidents

Sooner or later, you may be involved in an automobile accident. If and when this happens, what should you do?

A When you're involved in an auto accident, try to stay calm so that you can think clearly. Move your car to the side of the road, if possible, away from traffic.

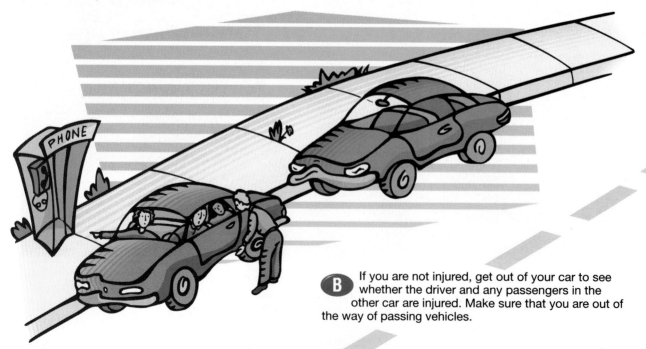

B If you are not injured, get out of your car to see whether the driver and any passengers in the other car are injured. Make sure that you are out of the way of passing vehicles.

C Call the police to report the accident. Request an ambulance if someone is injured.

D When the police arrive, be prepared to show your driver's license, auto registration, and proof of insurance. As clearly as possible, explain to the police officer the facts as you saw them. If you and the other driver disagree over the incident, avoid arguing. Exchange driver's license numbers and names of auto insurers with the other driver.

E As soon as possible, call your insurance company to report the accident and file a claim.

protect yourself against drivers who do not have liability insurance. This coverage is optional. You may not need it if you have medical payments or health coverage.

Systems of Automobile Insurance

When people are in automobile accidents, they sometimes disagree about who is at fault. To limit delays and disagreements, some states have passed laws establishing a *no-fault system*. This means that policyholders have their claims paid by their own insurance companies, no matter who is at fault.

Buying Automobile Insurance

Automobile insurance can be costly. You will want to get the best possible buy

Example Auto Insurance Discounts	
Defensive driving courses	10% discount on liability, collision, medical payments, and personal injury protection*
Airbags and other passive restraints	15% discount on medical payments and personal injury protection (driver's side); 30% off medical payments and personal injury protection (both sides)
Drug/alcohol education	5% discount on liability, collision, medical payments, and personal injury protection
Antitheft devices	Reduces comprehensive premium; amount varies by device and county
Two or more cars on a policy	15% discount on liability, collision, medical payments, and personal injury protection

* Personal injury protection pays the same as medical payments, plus 80 percent of lost income and the cost of hiring someone to take on household and caregiver responsibilities of an injured person. The coverage is the same as with medical payments insurance.

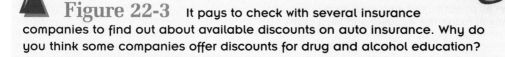

▲ **Figure 22-3** It pays to check with several insurance companies to find out about available discounts on auto insurance. Why do you think some companies offer discounts for drug and alcohol education?

for the right amount of coverage. There are several ways to control or lower the cost of your auto insurance premiums. They include the following:

- *Shop around.* Try to get prices from at least three different companies.

- *Drive carefully.* Some companies offer safe-driver discounts to policy-holders with good driving records.

- *Take driver education classes.* Some companies give discounts to drivers who take driver education courses.

- *Buy only the coverage you need.* If you have health insurance coverage, you may not need medical payments coverage or uninsured motorist protection. Also, if the premium is more than 10 percent of your car's value, think twice about buying collision coverage.

- *Raise your deductibles.* If you have a good driving record and can afford higher deductibles, this will save you money.

- *Take advantage of insurance discounts.* Some insurance discounts are required by state law; others are optional. **Figure 22-3** provides examples of auto insurance discounts.

Career Do's & Don'ts

To Get Value from Insurance...

Do:
- get comparable quotes from several insurers bidding on the same amount of insurance.
- keep all documents and receipts relating to insurance policies and claims.
- carry proof of health and car insurance with you.
- follow up on claims.

Don't:
- buy more or less insurance than you need.
- hesitate to contact your health insurance provider to find out specifically what is covered.
- allow health-care providers or car repair shops to directly bill your insurer without reviewing what they are billing.
- let your insurance coverage lapse.

SECTION 22-2 *Review*

Understanding Key Concepts

Using complete sentences, answer the following questions on a separate sheet of paper.

1. Why is it important to purchase home insurance?

2. Which of the five types of auto insurance coverage would you most likely select if you were buying a new car? Explain your reasoning.

3. How might you influence the cost of your auto insurance premiums even before you buy a car?

Exploring Careers: Office and Business

Sylvia Ramirez
Corporate Software Sales

Q: Have you always been in corporate sales?

A: I never thought of myself as a salesperson. I started out in human resources. Part of my job was to recruit people at job fairs. My company's booth was always next to Xerox's booth. Their recruiter recruited me.

Q: What kind of training did you have?

A: I was trained by Xerox. They have an intense sales-training program that is well known throughout the industry. It gave me a solid base to start with. After four years, there was an opening selling software for another company. I worked there selling to large corporate accounts before coming to Microsoft.

Q: What skills are important in sales?

A: Communication skills are the most important. They give you the ability to get your ideas across. You also have to be able to stand up in front of an audience of high-level executives and make your presentation. You have to be able to manage problems tactfully and professionally—and to the customer's satisfaction.

Q: Do you like what you do?

A: I love what I do. When I'm in front of customers and selling, it's exciting and it's fun. I can listen to customer's needs and match them with what my company has to offer.

Thinking Critically

What personal traits should a good salesperson have?

CAREER FACTS

Nature of the Work:
Meet clients; present products; deal with problems in customer satisfaction.

Training or Education Needed:
Bachelor's degree, preferably in business; experience in sales.

Aptitudes, Abilities, and Skills:
Math, listening, speaking, and interpersonal skills; creative-thinking, decision-making, and problem-solving skills; responsibility; self-management skills.

Salary Range:
Salary plus commission; starting level about $20,000; much higher with experience.

Career Path:
Start in an internship or an entry-level position as an account representative; move up through higher-level sales positions.

Health and Life Insurance

OBJECTIVES

After studying this section, you will be able to:

- Compare and contrast basic types of health insurance coverage.
- Distinguish between group and individual health insurance plans.
- Explain the basic types of life insurance.

KEY TERMS

major medical coverage
coinsurance
term life insurance
face value
cash-value life insurance
whole life insurance

So far, you've thought about planning for unexpected events involving your belongings and your car. Now you'll consider coverage for your most basic possessions: your health and your life.

Health Insurance

The cost of health care in the United States is rising. How can you ensure that your medical costs stay within your budget? You may be able to participate in a health insurance plan provided by your employer. You can also learn about types of coverage and the advantages and disadvantages of each.

Types of Coverage

As with auto insurance, health insurance coverage varies. Types of health coverage fall within three major categories.

Major Medical Coverage. As with other types of health insurance, **major medical coverage** includes hospital and surgical expenses, doctor visits, prescription drugs, and medical tests. It differs from other types because it requires you to pay a deductible and **coinsurance,** which is a percentage of your medical expenses. An advantage of major medical coverage, though, is that you're able to choose any hospitals and physicians you prefer.

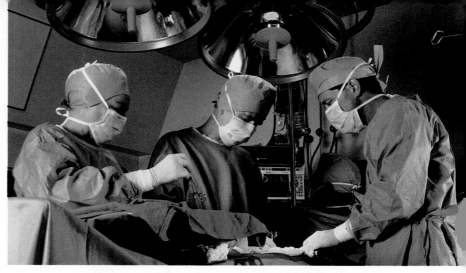

Health Maintenance Organizations. Unlike major medical coverage, a *health maintenance organization (HMO)* is a type of health coverage with no deductibles. Members usually pay a small *copayment* for doctor visits. In an HMO, checkups and well-baby care are covered, but your choice of physicians is limited.

Preferred Provider Organizations. Do you prefer a wider choice of doctors than you would have with an HMO? Then a *preferred provider organization (PPO)* may be for you. PPOs offer some of the low-cost advantages of HMOs while allowing more freedom of choice of doctors. With a PPO you often pay higher premiums and higher copayments than you would with HMO coverage.

 Health-care costs are rising. ***What can you do to keep such costs within your budget?***

Types of Plans

You can buy health insurance through a group plan or an individual plan. Most people in the United States belong to group plans, either through their employers or through associations such as trade or alumni associations.

Group Plans. Most group plans are offered through employers. Group plans

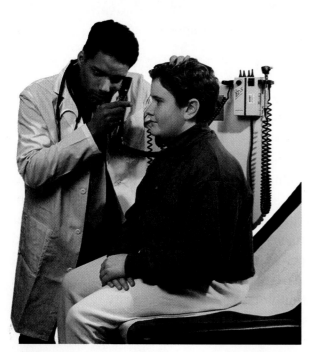

If your health-care insurance pays for annual checkups, take advantage of this coverage. ***How can regular checkups help keep you healthy?***

keep premium costs down by spreading the risk over a large number of people. These plans usually have a deductible, coinsurance, and major medical coverage.

Individual Plans. People not enrolled in a group plan can buy insurance coverage through an individual plan. This may include students living on their own, self-employed workers, or retirees. Such coverage can be expensive.

Disability Coverage

Suppose that you become ill and can't return to work for a month or two. How would you pay your bills? Disability insurance pays you a percentage of your salary.

Short-term disability insurance usually covers you for only a few months.

Long-term disability insurance can pay for a lifetime of missed work.

Life Insurance

If others in your household, such as a spouse and children, count on your salary, life insurance will provide money to them in case you die. Some employers offer life insurance as a company benefit.

Types of Life Insurance

There's a wide and confusing array of life insurance choices. It's important to understand each type. The two basic types of life insurance are term life insurance and cash-value life insurance.

EXCELLENT BUSINESS PRACTICES

Reducing Injury on the Job

Kennebec Health Systems of Augusta, Maine, operates a hospital and two nursing homes. The company was experiencing a high injury rate. The injury rate affected the company's bottom line through lost workdays, employee turnover, and expensive premiums for workers' compensation insurance.

Most of the injuries were back injuries sustained when workers were lifting patients. Employees got together to investigate a number of new lifting machines. Kennebec bought the machines the employees liked best. All employees were trained on their proper use and continue to encourage each other to use them.

In a five-year period, the number of days lost because of injury dropped to less than 30 days a year. Annual workers' compensation costs dropped from $1.55 million to $770,000.

Thinking Critically

How does a lower rate of injury and illness affect insurance rates?

Term Life Insurance. Of the two types of life insurance, term is less costly. **Term life insurance** simply protects your dependents if you die. It has no cash value and provides coverage for a set number of years. If you should die, the beneficiary receives an amount of money known as the **face value** of the policy.

Cash-Value Life Insurance. The second basic type of life insurance, **cash-value life insurance**, is part insurance and part investment. You can borrow money against the total amount of premiums paid on a cash-value policy. One kind of cash-value life insurance is whole life insurance. **Whole life insurance** works in part like term life insurance but has a savings component. With whole life insurance, you can build a reserve of money that you can borrow against or collect when you retire.

Buying Life Insurance

As with other types of insurance, when you buy life insurance, you'll purchase a policy and pay premiums to an insurance company. The company agrees to pay a benefit to your beneficiary if you die. The premium amount will depend on factors such as your age, your health, and the type of policy you buy. Here are some questions to consider before buying life insurance:

- *Should you buy life insurance?* If someone depends on you for your earning power, you should have life insurance. If you have no dependents, you may not need the insurance.

- *How much life insurance do you need?* This depends on how old you are, whether you have dependents, how much your family will need if you die, and how much insurance you can afford.

- *What are some tips on buying life insurance?* Take the time to shop around for life insurance, just as you would when buying a car. Life insurance prices vary widely. Don't make your decision solely on an agent's advice. Talk to others and take advantage of consumer guides.

SECTION 22-3 *Review*

Understanding Key Concepts

Using complete sentences, answer the following questions on a separate sheet of paper.

1. What are the advantages and disadvantages of major medical coverage, HMO coverage, and PPO coverage?

2. If your employer doesn't offer health insurance, what choices do you have in buying health insurance?

3. Explain the difference between term life insurance and whole life insurance.

Highlights

Key Terms

insurance policy *(p. 438)*
premium *(p. 439)*
deductible *(p. 439)*
claim *(p. 439)*

SECTION 22-1 Summary

- Although insurance policies are long and complex, it pays to learn the language of insurance.

- Most people purchase homeowner's or renter's, auto, health, and life coverage.

- You can hold down your insurance costs by shopping around, buying only the coverage you need, and seeking discounts.

Key Terms

liability insurance *(p. 443)*
collision insurance *(p. 444)*
comprehensive
    insurance *(p. 444)*

SECTION 22-2 Summary

- The five major types of auto insurance are liability, medical expenses, collision, comprehensive, and uninsured motorist coverage.

- Premium costs for auto insurance are influenced by a driver's age, driving record, location, and type of car, among other factors.

- You can lower your auto insurance premiums by shopping around, maintaining a good driving record, taking driver education courses, buying only the coverage you need, raising your deductibles, and buying a less expensive car.

Key Terms

major medical
    coverage *(p. 449)*
coinsurance *(p. 449)*
term life insurance *(p. 452)*
face value *(p. 452)*
cash-value life
    insurance *(p. 452)*
whole life insurance *(p. 452)*

SECTION 22-3 Summary

- The cost of health care is rising, but you have choices in limiting what you pay for coverage.

- Three basic types of health-care coverage are major medical coverage, HMO coverage, and PPO coverage.

- Types of health insurance plans are group and individual plans.

- Life insurance provides for the protection of your dependents.

- Two broad categories of life insurance are cash-value and term life insurance.

Reviewing Key Terms

On separate paper, write one paragraph each about insurance basics, auto insurance, health insurance, and life insurance. Use the terms below in your paragraphs.

insurance policy
premium
deductible
claim
liability
    insurance
collision
    insurance
comprehensive
    insurance

major medical
    coverage
coinsurance
term life
    insurance
face value
cash-value life
    insurance
whole life
    insurance

Recalling Key Concepts

Choose the correct answer for each item below. Write your answers on a separate sheet of paper.

1. Insurance premiums are paid by ____.

    (a) an insurance company

    (b) a policyholder to an insurance company

    (c) an insurance company to a beneficiary

2. One way to lower your insurance costs is to ____.

    (a) raise your risk

    (b) lower your deductibles

    (c) raise your deductibles

3. The type of automobile insurance that covers the cost of repairs to a car that you run into in an accident is ____.

    (a) comprehensive (b) collision

    (c) liability

4. You are likely to pay lower auto insurance premiums if you ____.

    (a) buy a less expensive car

    (b) buy more coverage than required by law

    (c) lower your deductibles

5. Which type of health insurance requires policyholders to pay coinsurance? ____.

    (a) an HMO (b) a PPO

    (c) major medical coverage

6. Whole life is a type of ____ life insurance.

    (a) face value (b) cash-value (c) term

Thinking Critically

Using complete sentences, answer each of the questions below on a separate sheet of paper.

1. Why do you think most insurance policies provide for a deductible?

2. Which type of auto insurance coverage do you think is most important?

3. Why should you buy health insurance even if you're well and practice a healthy lifestyle?

 SCANS Foundation Skills and Workplace Competencies

Basic Skills: *Writing*

As a writer for a consumer magazine, you are preparing an article on the relationship between lower auto insurance rates and automobile safety features. Research existing safety features on a variety of cars. Include information on the development of future auto safety features. Prepare a list of these, with a brief description of their functions.

Connecting Academics to the Workplace

Social Studies

1. Kai is a supervisor for an electronics company. The company wants him to spend a year training new supervisors in its plant in Monterey, Mexico. Kai will use his own car while he lives in Mexico. Use the Internet and sources such as *Birnbaum's Mexico* to research insurance requirements for using your own car in Mexico.

Math

2. On her way to work one morning, Carla slipped on an icy sidewalk and broke her arm. The total cost for medical treatment was $1,000. Carla has major medical coverage through her employer. Her deductible is $500, and coinsurance is 20 percent. Of the medical costs for her broken arm, how much will Carla have to pay?

Developing Teamwork and Leadership Skills

Form groups of four or five. Work as a team to plan a full range of insurance coverage needed by a family of two adults and two young children. You can choose to have the family rent or own their home. Assume that they own at least one automobile. One or both adults can be wage earners for the family. List each type of insurance recommended. Briefly describe the coverage and tell why you recommend it. Choose a leader to share your recommendations with the class.

Real-World Workshop

Working in the same teams as in the previous activity, contact a local insurance company representative. Share your recommendations for the family of four. Ask if there is additional coverage needed by the family. Then find out what the approximate annual cost of complete coverage would be for the family.

School-to-Work Connection

Contact people in charge of employee benefits for three local companies, and discuss with them insurance benefits provided to employees of each company. Ask how the company chooses insurers and provides information on insurance benefits to employees. Then prepare a brief report on your findings.

Individual Career Plan

Research insurance-related careers. Find an area that interests you, and use the Internet to find out more about it. If possible, arrange an interview with a person in your town who works in this career area. Write a paragraph or two about this aspect of the insurance industry.

Chapter 23

Taxes and Social Security

Section 23-1
All About Taxes

Section 23-2
All About Social Security

In this video segment, find out how the government uses your tax dollars.

Journal
Personal Career Plan

Who pays taxes? Why? Who benefits from taxes? How? Record your responses in a journal entry.

All About Taxes

OBJECTIVES

After studying this section, you will be able to:

- **Identify five characteristics of a good tax system.**
- **Determine whether you owe income tax.**
- **Complete a federal tax return.**

KEY TERMS

Internal Revenue Service (IRS)
withhold
income tax return
exemption
deduction

What do you think of when you hear the word *taxes*? The extra charge that's added to your bill when you buy a CD? The money your employer takes out of your paycheck each week? It's all money that comes out of your pocket and goes to the government, and it really adds up. You do get a great deal out of the taxes you pay, though. Think about it. What benefits from paying taxes can you name? How many have you enjoyed today?

Understanding Taxes

You may think that the whole topic of taxes is confusing. Actually, the general structure and workings of our tax system are easy to understand.

First of all, *taxes* are payments that you make to support the government and to pay for government services. There are three levels of government: federal, state, and local. The federal government runs the country as a whole. State governments manage the 50 states. Local governments govern counties, cities, and towns. All three levels of government need money to operate, so you must pay taxes to all three.

The **Internal Revenue Service**, or **IRS**, is the agency that collects federal taxes and oversees the federal tax system. Taxes paid to the IRS go into the U.S. Treasury.

The federal government has spent billions of tax dollars on space exploration. *Do you think this is a wise use of funds? Why or why not?*

profit you make on selling real estate. Income taxes are the federal government's main source of money.

Income tax is calculated as a percentage of the taxable income you earn. (*Taxable income* is your income after you subtract certain permitted amounts.) At the present time, the federal income tax ranges from 15 to 39.6 percent. In general, the greater your taxable income, the higher the rate of income tax you must pay. Your employer will **withhold**, or take out, money from your paychecks to pay income tax due on your wages.

In most states, people also pay state income tax. Many cities also have income taxes. State and local income tax rates vary, but they're generally much lower than federal rates.

Types of Taxes

There are many kinds of taxes. The following are common ones.

- *Income taxes.* You pay income tax on your income, or the money you make. This income may come from working or from other sources, such as the interest your bank pays you on your savings, or it may come from

- *Social Security taxes.* Workers pay Social Security taxes so that they can receive benefits when they retire. (You'll read more about Social Security on pages 471–474.) Like income taxes, Social Security taxes are figured as a percentage of the money you earn.

Employers withhold money from paychecks to pay Social Security taxes, just as they do for

| | | | MICHAELS, LISA N | | |
| | | | 0987426143 | | |

(STATEMENT OF EARNINGS AND DEDUCTIONS. DETACH AND RETAIN FOR YOUR RECORDS. NON-NEGOTIABLE)

DESCRIPTION	RATE	HOURS	EARNINGS	YEAR TO DATE
REGULAR EARNING		54:00	380:50	2:280:05

	TAXES / DEDUCTIONS	YEAR TO DATE
FEDERAL	23:03	138:18
STATE	4:29	25:74
SOCIAL SECURITY	7:20	43:20
MEDICARE	5:45	32:70

NOT ELIGIBLE FOR LEAVE ACCRUALS

	EARNINGS	TAXES	DEDUCTIONS	NET PAY	PAY PERIOD	WARRANT NO	AMT OF WARRANT
CURRENT	380:50	39:97	0	338:65	BEGIN 03-19	22072196	338:90
YEAR TO DATE	2:280:05	239:82	0	2:040:23	END 04-02		

▲ **Figure 23-1** <u>Gross pay</u> is the total amount you earn. <u>Net pay</u>, sometimes called take-home pay, is the amount that remains after money has been deducted for various taxes. How much money did the employer withhold from this paycheck? If you are preparing a monthly budget, should you plan on using your gross pay or your net pay? Why?

YOU'RE THE BOSS!

Solving Workplace Problems

Your gardening service is doing well, and you're ready to hire an assistant. The most promising applicant says, "I'd love to have this job, but I don't really need any benefits, and I certainly don't need to pay any taxes. Can't you just pay me in cash every week? Then we won't need to worry about all those forms." How do you respond?

income taxes. Your paycheck stub shows the money withheld in a box labeled "FICA." This stands for Federal Insurance Contribution Act. See **Figure 23-1.**

- *Sales taxes.* When you buy something, the salesperson may add sales tax to the price. This tax goes to the state or local government. Almost every state has a sales tax.

  Sales tax is calculated as a percentage of the price of an item. The tax rate varies from state to state. See **Figure 23-2,** which shows the various state sales tax rates. In addition to state taxes, local sales taxes may be added to the cost of items you purchase.

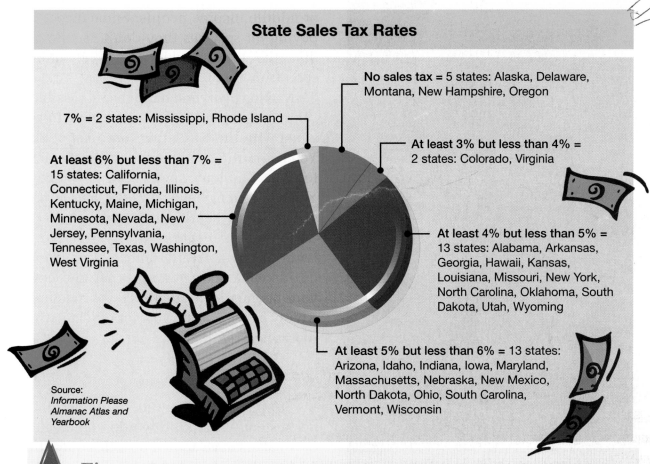

State Sales Tax Rates

No sales tax = 5 states: Alaska, Delaware, Montana, New Hampshire, Oregon

7% = 2 states: Mississippi, Rhode Island

At least 6% but less than 7% = 15 states: California, Connecticut, Florida, Illinois, Kentucky, Maine, Michigan, Minnesota, Nevada, New Jersey, Pennsylvania, Tennessee, Texas, Washington, West Virginia

At least 3% but less than 4% = 2 states: Colorado, Virginia

At least 4% but less than 5% = 13 states: Alabama, Arkansas, Georgia, Hawaii, Kansas, Louisiana, Missouri, New York, North Carolina, Oklahoma, South Dakota, Utah, Wyoming

At least 5% but less than 6% = 13 states: Arizona, Idaho, Indiana, Iowa, Maryland, Massachusetts, Nebraska, New Mexico, North Dakota, Ohio, South Carolina, Vermont, Wisconsin

Source: *Information Please Almanac Atlas and Yearbook*

Figure 23-2 Sales tax is the chief source of revenue for most state governments. Sales tax is calculated on purchase price. For example, if you buy a $10.00 book and the sales tax rate is 5 percent, you'll pay $10.00 plus 50¢ (5% $\times$ $10 = 0.50), or $10.50. In some states, some items (for example, clothing or other necessities) are free from sales tax. What's the tax rate in your state?

- *Property taxes.* The main source of money for local governments is property taxes. These taxes are based on the value of property—generally land and buildings.

Where Do Your Tax Dollars Go?

Each year, federal, state, and local governments take in billions of dollars in taxes. Where does this money go? Here's just a partial list of services paid for in full, or in part, by your tax dollars:

- *education*, including public schools and libraries;
- *transportation*, ranging from roadways and mass transit to dams and airports;
- *safety*, including law enforcement and fire protection;
- *health*, ranging from hospitals to medical research studies;
- *military services*; and
- *postal services*.

Local services, such as fire and police protection, are paid for primarily through local taxes. **What other services does your community provide?**

It's Your Responsibility

When you go out to eat with friends, you split the bill. As a citizen, you also have to split the bill for the services the government provides.

Since we all share in the benefits, we should all contribute our fair share of taxes. That seems reasonable. The problem is that people disagree on what's fair. Some taxpayers think that rich people should pay a larger share of their income than low

or middle income people. Some object to paying for services they don't use. Some disagree with the way the government spends money.

Making everyone happy is impossible. Does that mean that you just have to go along with the way things are? Not at all. You can influence how federal, state, and local governments spend your tax money. You can also influence the tax laws themselves. How? That's easy: vote.

Voters elect representatives at every level of government. These lawmakers decide what taxes you must pay and how your tax money is spent. It's your responsibility as a citizen to vote for officials who represent your beliefs.

A Good Tax System

Suppose it were up to you to design a tax system. What kind would you create? Lawmakers have argued over this question for decades, and the debate goes on. Still, most people agree that a good tax system has certain features.

- A tax system should be fair. Everyone who is able to pay should pay his or her fair share.

- Tax laws should be clear and simple. Many people think that the present system is too complicated. There are too many rules and tax forms.

- Taxes should be collected at a convenient time when most people are able to pay.

- A tax system should be stable. Taxpayers should know in advance how much they'll owe. If tax laws are always changing, people can't predict how much money to budget for taxes.

- A tax system should be flexible. When necessary, the government should be able to adjust the tax system to bring in more or less income. For example, during a war, the government may need to raise more money.

Understanding Federal Income Tax Returns

You've probably heard stories about people who got in trouble over their taxes. Maybe they didn't file their tax return on time. Maybe an audit, or review of their taxes by the IRS, revealed that they had failed to report some of their income. These kinds of mistakes can lead to hefty fines. So should you worry about your taxes? No, but you should understand that the IRS takes tax paying seriously. You've got to do it, and you need to do it right. If you make an honest effort, though, you have little to worry about.

To pay federal income tax, you must complete and file an income tax return each year. An **income tax return** is a form that shows how much you earned from working and made from other sources. It also shows how much tax you owe. If your employer withheld more money from your paychecks than you owe, you'll get a tax refund. If your employer didn't withhold enough, you'll have to pay the difference.

EXCELLENT BUSINESS PRACTICES

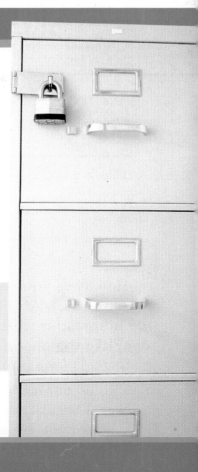

Protecting Your Privacy

Atmel Corporation is a San Jose, California, company that manufactures specialized semiconductors. The company has established procedures to ensure that human resources data doesn't fall into the wrong hands.

Records of Atmel's 3,000 employees are stored in locked file cabinets. They can't be looked at by anyone other than an approved clerk. Medical records are kept in separate locked cabinets to keep sensitive medical information from becoming public.

On all employee files, the company uses an employee number rather than the Social Security number, which could be used for financial fraud and other invasions of privacy. Prospective employees are briefed on security and privacy issues concerning their coworkers and on the confidentiality of information pertaining to the company.

Thinking Critically

How can private information be used against a person?

Personal Allowances Worksheet

A Enter "1" for **yourself** if no one else can claim you as a dependent . . . . **A** _____

B Enter "1" if:
- You are single and have only one job; or
- You are married, have only one job, and your spouse does not work; or
- Your wages from a second job or your spouse's wages (or the total of both) are $1,000 or less. . . **B** _____

C Enter "1" for your **spouse**. But, you may choose to enter -0- if you are married and have either a working spouse or more than one job (this may help you avoid having too little tax withheld) . . . . **C** _____

D Enter number of **dependents** (other than your spouse or yourself) you will claim on your tax return . . . . . **D** _____

E Enter "1" if you will file as **head of household** on your tax return (see conditions under **Head of Household** above) . **E** _____

F Enter "1" if you have at least $1,500 of **child or dependent care expenses** for which you plan to claim a credit . . **F** _____

G Add lines A through F and enter total here. **Note:** This amount may be different from the number of exemptions you claim on your return ▶ **G** _____

For accuracy, do all worksheets that apply.
- If you plan to **itemize or claim adjustments to income** and want to reduce your withholding, see the Deductions and Adjustments Worksheet on page 2.
- If you are **single** and have **more than one job** and your combined earnings from all jobs exceed $30,000 OR if you are **married** and have a **working spouse or more than one job,** and the combined earnings from all jobs exceed $50,000, see the Two-Earner/Two-Job Worksheet on page 2 if you want to avoid having too little tax withheld.
- If **neither** of the above situations applies, **stop here** and enter the number from line G on line 5 of Form W-4 below.

---------- **Cut here and give the certificate to your employer. Keep the top portion for your records.** ----------

Form **W-4** Department of the Treasury Internal Revenue Service	**Employee's Withholding Allowance Certificate** ▶ **For Privacy Act and Paperwork Reduction Act Notice, see reverse.**	OMB No. 1545-0010

1 Type or print your first name and middle initial Lisa N.   Last name Michaels   **2** Your social security number 123 : 45 : 6789

Home address (number and street or rural route) 33 Clark Lane

3 ☒ Single ☐ Married ☐ Married, but withhold at higher Single rate.
Note: If married, but legally separated, or spouse is a nonresident alien, check the Single box.

City or town, state, and ZIP code Greenville, MA 01234

4 If your last name differs from that on your social security card, check here and call 1-800-772-1213 for a new card . . . . . ▶ ☐

5 Total number of allowances you are claiming (from line G above or from the worksheets on page 2 if they apply) . **5** 0

6 Additional amount, if any, you want withheld from each paycheck . . . . **6** $ _____

7 I claim exemption from withholding for 1996 and I certify that I meet **BOTH** of the following conditions for exemption:
- Last year I had a right to a refund of **ALL** Federal income tax withheld because I had **NO** tax liability; **AND**
- This year I expect a refund of **ALL** Federal income tax withheld because I expect to have **NO** tax liability.
If you meet both conditions, enter "EXEMPT" here . . . . ▶ **7** _____

Under penalties of perjury, I certify that I am entitled to the number of withholding allowances claimed on this certificate or entitled to claim exempt status.

Employee's signature ▶ *Lisa N. Michaels*   Date ▶ 8/10/

8 Employer's name and address (Employer: Complete 8 and 10 only if sending to the IRS)   **9** Office code (optional)   **10** Employer identification number

Cat. No. 10220Q

Figure 23-3 All employees must fill out a Form W-4. Why is it important to complete this form accurately?

How does your employer know how much to withhold? Simple: by looking at the information you provide on a Form W-4, like the one in *Figure 23-3.* Completing this form is easy.

- Fill in your name, address, and Social Security number. Indicate whether you are married or single.

- Write the number of *allowances*, or deductions, you are allowed to claim. The higher the number, the less tax withheld. Use the "Personal Allowances Worksheet" on the Form W-4 .

- Indicate whether you are *exempt*—excused—from having to pay tax.

- Sign and date the form.

How Do You File a Return?

In general, if you're single and earn at least $6,400 in a calendar year, you must file an income tax return. This figure changes from time to time, however. Check with the IRS for the current figure. You have to mail your tax return to the IRS by April 15.

To prepare your return, you'll need Form W-2. See *Figure 23-4.* Your employer will send this form to you. It shows how much money you earned and how much your employer withheld for taxes.

There are three basic federal income tax forms: 1040EZ, 1040A, and 1040. Form 1040EZ is the simplest one to fill out. It will probably work for you. These key terms will help you understand the tax forms:

- An **exemption** is a fixed amount of money that is excused from taxes. For example, in one recent year the IRS let each taxpayer claim a $2,500 personal exemption.

- A *dependent* is someone whom you support, such as a child.

a Control number	22222	Void ☐	For Official Use Only ▶ OMB No. 1545-0008		
b Employer's identification number 08-XIXOXIX			1 Wages, tips, other compensation 9175	2 Federal income tax withheld 701.42	
c Employer's name, address, and ZIP code ABC Painting Co., Inc. 432 Lomard Avenue Greenville, MA 01234			3 Social security wages 9175	4 Social security tax withheld 228.06	
			5 Medicare wages and tips 9175	6 Medicare tax withheld 63.93	
			7 Social security tips	8 Allocated tips	
d Employee's social security number 0X1·XX·1X00			9 Advance EIC payment	10 Dependent care benefits	
e Employee's name (first, middle initial, last) Lisa N. Michaels 33 Clark Lane Greenville, MA 01234			11 Nonqualified plans	12 Benefits included in box 1	
			13 See Instrs. for box 13 D1000	14 Other	
			15 Statutory employee ☐ Deceased ☐ Pension plan ☐ Legal rep. ☐ Hshld. emp. ☐ Subtotal ☐ Deferred compensation ☐		
f Employee's address and ZIP code					
16 State MA	Employer's state I.D. No. 11-XIXOXIX	17 State wages, tips, etc. 9175	18 State income tax 402	19 Locality name Greenville	20 Local wages, tips, etc. 9175	21 Local income tax 215

Cat. No. 10134D   Department of the Treasury—Internal Revenue Service

Form **W-2** Wage and Tax Statement

For Paperwork Reduction Act Notice, see separate instructions.

Copy A For Social Security Administration

Figure 23-4 Your employer will send you a Form W-2 in January. What information on this form will help you prepare your income tax return?

Department of the Treasury—Internal Revenue Service

Form 1040EZ

Income Tax Return for Single and Joint Filers With No Dependents (U)

OMB No. 1545-0675

Use the IRS label here

Your first name and initial — Last name
LISA N MICHAELS

If a joint return, spouse's first name and initial — Last name

Home address (number and street). If you have a P.O. box, see page 7. — Apt. no.
33 CLARK LANE

City, town or post office, state, and ZIP code. If you have a foreign address, see page 7.
GREENVILLE MA 01234

Your social security number
123 45 6789

Spouse's social security number

Presidential Election Campaign (See page 7.)

Note: Checking "Yes" will not change your tax or reduce your refund.

Do you want $3 to go to this fund? ▶ Yes ☐ No ☐

If a joint return, does your spouse want $3 to go to this fund? ▶ Yes ☐ No ☐

Dollars | Cents

Income

Attach Copy B of Form(s) W-2 here. Enclose, but do not attach, any payment with your return.

1 Total wages, salaries, and tips. This should be shown in box 1 of your W-2 form(s). Attach your W-2 form(s). 1 9,175

2 Taxable interest income of $400 or less. If the total is over $400, you cannot use Form 1040EZ. 2 63

3 Unemployment compensation (see page 9). 3

4 Add lines 1, 2, and 3. This is your **adjusted gross income.** If under $9,500, see page 9 to find out if you can claim the earned income credit on line 8. 4 9,238

Note: You must check Yes or No.

5 Can your parents (or someone else) claim you on their return?
Yes. ✓ Enter amount from worksheet on back. **No.** If **single,** enter 6,550.00. If **married,** enter 11,800.00. See back for explanation. 5 3,900

6 Subtract line 5 from line 4. If line 5 is larger than line 4, enter 0. This is your **taxable income.** ▶ 6 5,338

Payments and tax

7 Enter your Federal income tax withheld from box 2 of your W-2 form(s). 7 701

8 **Earned income credit** (see page 9). Enter type and amount of nontaxable earned income below.
Type — $ 8

9 Add lines 7 and 8 (do not include nontaxable earned income). These are your **total payments.** 9 701

10 **Tax.** Use the amount on **line 6** to find your tax in the tax table on pages 20–24 of the booklet. Then, enter the tax from the table on this line. 10 799

Refund

Have it sent directly to your bank account! See page 13 and fill in 11b, c, and d.

11a If line 9 is larger than line 10, subtract line 10 from line 9. This is your **refund.** 11a

b Routing number

c Type   Checking   Savings   d Account number

Amount you owe

12 If line 10 is larger than line 9, subtract line 9 from line 10. This is the **amount you owe.** See page 13 for details on how to pay and what to write on your payment. 12 98

I have read this return. Under penalties of perjury, I declare that to the best of my knowledge and belief, the return is true, correct, and accurately lists all amounts and sources of income I received during the tax year.

Sign here

Keep copy for your records.

Your signature
Lisa V. Michals

Date
1/10/

Your occupation
PROGRAMMER

Spouse's signature if joint return

Date

Spouse's occupation

For Official Use Only

For Privacy Act and Paperwork Reduction Act Notice, see page 5.

Cat. No. 14090A

Form 1040EZ

▲ **Figure 23-5** Most young taxpayers can use Form 1040EZ for at least the first few years they file tax returns. What form do you need to attach to Form 1040EZ?

1040EZ Tax Table—

If Form 1040EZ, line 6, is—		And you are—	
At least	But less than	Single	Married filing jointly
		Your tax is—	

11,000

At least	But less than	Single	Married filing jointly
11,000	11,050	1,654	1,654
11,050	11,100	1,661	1,661
11,100	11,150	1,669	1,669
11,150	11,200	1,676	1,676
11,200	11,250	1,684	1,684
11,250	11,300	1,691	1,691
11,300	11,350	1,699	1,699
11,350	11,400	1,706	1,706
11,400	11,450	1,714	1,714
11,450	11,500	1,721	1,721
11,500	11,550	1,729	1,729
11,550	11,600	1,736	1,736
11,600	11,650	1,744	1,744
11,650	11,700	1,751	1,751
11,700	11,750	1,759	1,759
11,750	11,800	1,766	1,766
11,800	11,850	1,774	1,774
11,850	11,900	1,781	1,781
11,900	11,950	1,789	1,789
11,950	12,000	1,796	1,796

▲ **Figure 23-6** Using a tax table is easy. First, find the line that corresponds to your taxable income. Then find the column that corresponds to your status— single or married, for example. Your tax is the amount shown where the income line and status column meet. If you're single and your taxable income was $11,200, how much tax would you owe?

- A **deduction** is an expense that you are allowed to subtract from your income. Examples may include medical or business expenses. The less taxable income you have, the less tax you'll have to pay. The *standard deduction* is an amount set by the IRS.

You can probably file Form 1040EZ if you meet the following qualifications.

- You're single and earned less than $50,000 during the year. (Check each year with the IRS about the current figure.)

- You had no other income, such as taxable interest or dividends totaling more than $400 each.

- You are not claiming an exemption for being over 65 or for being blind.

- You have no dependents.

There are some additional requirements for using Form 1040EZ but they will probably not apply to you. Check with the IRS to be sure.

Figure 23-5 shows Form 1040EZ. Completing this form involves several basic steps.

- Add up your total income from working and from other sources.

- Subtract your standard deduction and personal exemption.

- Use the tax table to find out how much tax is due on your income. *Figure 23-6* shows a portion of the table. By comparing this amount with the taxes withheld on your Form W-2, you'll see whether you owe more taxes or will get a refund.

Figure 23-7

Filing a Federal Tax Return

Filing a federal tax return is not difficult if you organize your information and follow instructions.

As **Figure 23-7** shows, figuring your taxes isn't hard if you're organized. Need help? Don't worry. The IRS provides free publications that will help. You can also get help over the phone, via the Internet, and from tax-help books at the library. If you have a computer, you might try tax-preparation software. Alternatively, you can pay a tax-preparation service to prepare your forms for you.

A Gather the necessary information. For example, you'll need Form W-2 and records of any other earnings, such as a statement of interest from your bank. If you've filed a tax return before, have a copy of your previous return on hand for reference.

B Obtain the tax form you'll need, such as a Form 1040EZ or 1040A, and the corresponding IRS instruction booklet. You can find forms and booklets at post offices, libraries, and most banks. You can also get them from the IRS. (The IRS even has a site on the World Wide Web from which you can download forms.) If you use a tax-preparation computer program, the software will probably include the forms you need.

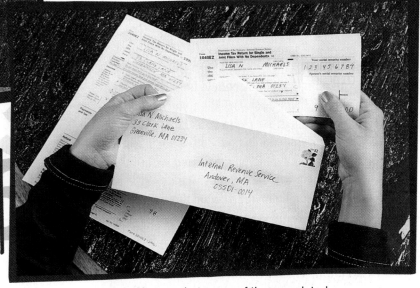

C Take your time completing the forms. Read instructions carefully. Get help if you need it. Be sure to provide all the required information. Double-check your math.

D Keep a photocopy of the completed tax return for your records. Attach any necessary forms (such as the W-2) to the original return, and send it to the IRS by April 15.

SECTION 23-1 *Review*

Understanding Key Concepts

Using complete sentences, answer the following questions on a separate sheet of paper.

1. List five characteristics of a good tax system. Why are these desirable features?

2. How does the amount of money you earn and the amount withheld determine whether you owe income tax?

3. How will understanding such terms as *exemption, dependent,* and *deduction* help you complete a tax return?

Exploring Careers: Manufacturing

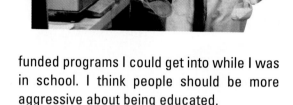

Joshua Boughton
Production/Administrative Lead
Bullseye Glass

Q: How did you start at Bullseye Glass?

A: I started pulling glass out of bins, packing it into crates that we built ourselves, and shipping it out. Later I worked in quality control. Now I'm in an administrative position and training to be a glass technologist.

Q: Is starting at the bottom best?

A: I don't think anybody should be afraid to take an entry-level position. Then you should try to see if this is the place you want to work. A lot of people don't take into consideration what I call psychic pay: enjoying where they work, liking the people they work with, liking the product, believing in what they are doing.

Q: What's your educational background?

A: I come from a single-parent family of seven children. We didn't have money for schooling. I found out what kind of government-funded programs I could get into while I was in school. I think people should be more aggressive about being educated.

Q: What do you advise students starting out?

A: Don't do only what you're required to do. Look at how your job could be done better. Try to find out where the firm is going, how it has performed in the past. Find out what training your company will fund. Keep yourself "market-ready".

Thinking Critically

Bullseye makes glass for artists. What skills learned in glass production might transfer to other manufacturing fields?

CAREER FACTS

Nature of the Work:
Control quality of glass by analysis, process tracking, and testing; collect and disseminate information to staff.

Training or Education Needed:
Art training in any medium; knowledge of chemistry; glass-working experience.

Aptitudes, Abilities, and Skills:
Math skills; listening, speaking, and interpersonal skills; problem-solving and decision-making skills; computer skills; ability to see things in the mind's eye; ability to work with your hands; ability to learn.

Salary Range:
Approximately $7 to $8 an hour to start; higher as experience increases.

Career Path:
Start in an entry-level position and work your way up; obtain glass technology training; move into an administrative position.

All About Social Security

OBJECTIVES

After studying this section, you will be able to:

- **Describe how the Social Security system works.**
- **Identify four Social Security program benefits and two state social insurance benefits.**
- **Explain the main problem that is facing the Social Security system today.**

KEY TERMS

work credits
disabled worker
Medicare
unemployment insurance
workers' compensation

What does the term *Social Security* mean to you? Do you think of retired workers who depend on their Social Security checks to live? That's part of it, but there's more to Social Security than that. It's a program that provides benefits for people of all ages. For example, if a worker becomes disabled, Social Security will help his or her family cope with the loss of income.

How the Social Security Program Works

Where does the money that pays for Social Security benefits come from? Most of it comes from Social Security taxes. Both workers and employers pay these taxes. As you read earlier, employers deduct Social Security tax from your paycheck. Your employer matches your contribution. If you're self-employed, you must pay both the employee's and employer's share of the tax. (Currently, however, self-employed workers may deduct half of their Social Security tax from their federal income tax.)

Your Social Security Number

Do you know your Social Security number? Your parent or guardian probably got one for you when you were little. This is your permanent identification number. The government uses it to keep track of your contributions and work history. Your employer will ask you for this number. You'll also need to put it on tax forms.

Many people lost their jobs during the Great Depression of the 1930s. Families suffered severe hardship. Congress passed the Social Security Act of 1935 to aid families whose members lost their jobs, were unable to work, or were retired. ***Whom do you know who receives Social Security benefits?***

Becoming Eligible for Benefits

Once you begin working, you start to earn work credits. **Work credits** are measurements of how long you've worked. You must earn a certain number of credits to get Social Security benefits. You earn work credits for each year you work and pay Social Security taxes.

Types of Benefits

There are many different kinds of Social Security benefits. Some are for eligible people of any age.

- *Disability benefits* are paid to disabled workers. A **disabled worker** is someone who cannot work because of a physical or mental condition.

The amount of the benefit is based on the worker's average earnings.

- *Survivors' benefits* are paid to the family of a worker who dies.

- *Retirement benefits* are paid to workers who retire. Up to a certain amount, the higher your average yearly earnings, the higher your benefits. The retirement age for reduced benefits is now 62. The retirement age for full benefits is now 65. That age will gradually rise to 67 by 2027.

- *Health insurance benefits* are paid to people who need hospitalization or other medical care. These benefits, called **Medicare**, cover nearly everyone who is 65 or older.

Social Security is a federal program. As a worker, you're also entitled to benefits from two state-run social insurance programs. These are similar to Social Security. Their rules vary from state to state, however.

- **Unemployment insurance** provides temporary income to workers who have lost their jobs. To be eligible, you generally must have worked for a certain length of time and not have lost your job through your fault. Unemployment insurance is funded by taxes both the employer and employee pay.

Career Do's & Don'ts

When Paying Taxes...
Do:
- be sure the right amount of taxes are being taken out of your paycheck.
- use professional help if tax forms are too complicated for you or if you are eligible for deductions.
- keep copies of tax returns and other related documents.

Don't:
- freely give out your social security number.
- wait until the last moment to file your tax returns.
- allow an employer to pay you without withholding taxes and paying the appropriate share.

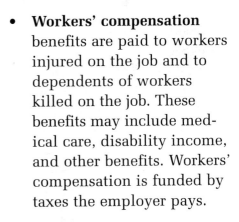

- **Workers' compensation** benefits are paid to workers injured on the job and to dependents of workers killed on the job. These benefits may include medical care, disability income, and other benefits. Workers' compensation is funded by taxes the employer pays.

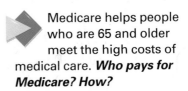

Medicare helps people who are 65 and older meet the high costs of medical care. *Who pays for Medicare? How?*

 It is the U.S. Congress's responsibility to solve the problem with Social Security. *What can you do to influence the decisions that are made?*

The Future of Social Security

If you follow the news, you know that Social Security is a "hot issue" these days. That's because the system has a big problem: it's going broke.

The Social Security taxes you pay provide benefits for workers who have already retired. When it's your turn to retire, younger workers will pay the taxes to fund *your* retirement.

Well, maybe. Here's the problem: People are living longer, and many are retiring earlier. As a result, more workers will collect more years of benefits. At the same time, the U.S. birthrate is declining. This means that there will be fewer young workers around to support retired people in the future. The situation will worsen as the large number of workers now in their 40s and 50s reach retirement age. Before long, the money being paid out will exceed the amount coming in.

There are many proposed solutions to this problem. Some would increase taxes. Others would cut benefits. One way or another, the system needs changes. You can play a part in making these changes by staying informed and voting.

SECTION 23-2 *Review*

Understanding Key Concepts

Using complete sentences, answer the following questions on a separate sheet of paper.

1. Why is it important to build up work credits?

2. Why is the program of benefits discussed in this section called Social Security?

3. What may happen to Social Security by the time you retire if the system isn't changed soon?

Key Terms

**Internal Revenue
   Service (IRS)** *(p. 458)*
withhold *(p. 459)*
income tax return *(p. 463)*
exemption *(p. 465)*
deduction *(p. 467)*

SECTION 23-1 Summary

- Taxes are payments that people must make to support federal, state, and local governments. Common taxes include income taxes, Social Security taxes, sales taxes, and property taxes.

- Tax dollars pay for a wide range of services, such as education, transportation, and military services.

- You can influence the way that tax dollars are spent by voting for officials who represent your views.

- A good tax system should be fair, simple, convenient, stable, and flexible.

- Your income tax return shows how much income you received and how much tax you owe. If your employer withholds more money than you owe, you'll get a tax refund. If your employer withholds too little, you'll have to pay the difference.

Key Terms

work credits *(p. 472)*
disabled worker *(p. 472)*
Medicare *(p. 472)*
**unemployment
   insurance** *(p. 473)*
workers' compensation
   (p. 473)

SECTION 23-2 Summary

- The money for Social Security benefits comes chiefly from Social Security taxes paid by workers and employers.

- The government uses your Social Security number to keep track of your contributions and work history.

- You earn work credits each year that you work and pay Social Security taxes. You must earn a certain number of credits to become eligible for Social Security benefits.

- Social Security benefits include disability benefits, survivors' benefits, retirement benefits, and health insurance benefits.

- Two state-run programs that provide benefits for workers are unemployment insurance and workers' compensation.

- The Social Security system must be changed to keep the amount of money being paid out from exceeding the amount coming in.

Reviewing Key Terms

Write one paragraph about taxes and one paragraph about Social Security. Use the terms below.

Internal Revenue Service (IRS)	work credits
	disabled worker
withhold	Medicare
income tax return	unemployment insurance
exemption	workers' compensation
deduction	

Recalling Key Concepts

Choose the correct answer for each item below. Write your answers on a separate sheet of paper.

1. Which of the following is *not* a characteristic of a good tax system?

   (a) Everyone pays his or her fair share.

   (b) Tax rules are clear and simple.

   (c) Taxes are collected at the beginning of each year.

2. You'll have to pay additional income tax if ____.

   (a) your employer withholds too little tax

   (b) your employer withholds too much tax

   (c) you don't receive a Form W-2

3. Social Security taxes are paid by ____.

   (a) workers (b) employers

   (c) both workers and employers

4. Which one of the following benefits is *not* part of the Social Security program?

   (a) workers' compensation

   (b) survivors' benefits (c) Medicare

5. One reason why the Social Security system is in trouble is that ____.

   (a) fewer people are retiring

   (b) the birthrate is declining

   (c) the birthrate is increasing

Thinking Critically

Using complete sentences, answer each of the questions below on a separate sheet of paper.

1. Do you agree that because everyone shares the benefits of tax dollars, everyone should pay a fair share of taxes? Explain.

2. How does voting give all citizens an equal voice in deciding how their government spends tax dollars?

3. Suppose you discover that your employer has recorded the wrong Social Security number for you. Why is it important to correct the error?

4. What is the drawback of having the Social Security taxes of younger workers pay for the benefits that go to older workers?

SCANS Foundation Skills and Workplace Competencies

Basic Skills: *Math*

1. Suppose you bought an exercise machine for $161, books for $36, CDs for $32, and a watch for $45. If the state sales tax is 4 percent, how much did you spend? Suppose the sales tax had been 6 percent. How much more would you have spent?

Information: *Acquiring and Evaluating Information*

2. Over the past year, you held several different part-time jobs. Now it's time to file an income tax return. However, you're not sure which form to complete or how to complete it. Describe two ways in which you could get answers to your questions. Which way would probably be better? Explain.

Connecting Academics to the Workplace

Computer Science

1. Amy works in the human resources department of a large corporation. Her supervisor has asked her to help run a workshop for new employees. Part of the workshop will focus on taxes. Amy wants to include information about tax-preparation software. Research tax-preparation programs in the library, via the Internet, or by speaking to taxpayers who have used such programs. Are there any that you think Amy should recommend? Why or why not?

Math

2. In 1995, Daniel earned $22,490 as a paralegal aide. He got paid every two weeks. His employer withheld Social Security tax at a rate of 7.65 percent. How much Social Security tax did Daniel's employer withhold from each paycheck?

Developing Teamwork and Leadership Skills

Divide into teams of four. Assume that you all work in the human resources department of a major company. You've been asked to make a wall chart briefly summarizing the six kinds of benefits workers are generally eligible for: disability benefits, survivors' benefits, retirement benefits, health benefits, unemployment benefits, and workers' compensation. Work together to make the chart. You may use pictures as well as words.

Real-World Workshop

Obtain a paycheck stub. List the categories for which money was deducted. Which deduction was the largest? Which was the smallest?

School-to-Work Connection

Accountants and bookkeepers handle many financial duties, including tax-related matters. Identify a worker in the accounting department of a company. Discuss with the person the challenges of his or her work. Ask how the person uses computer technology. Summarize your discussion in a brief report.

Individual Career Plan

Look into the future. Imagine that you have pursued your career for about 45 years. You're thinking about retiring. However, you enjoy your work and don't want to stop working entirely. List your options for remaining active in your field. You may want to talk with several adults to hear their ideas.

ASPECTS OF INDUSTRY:
Finance

Overview

In Unit Six, you learned about making wise consumer decisions, managing your money through savings and budgeting, and using credit carefully. Businesses, too, must use money responsibly. In this Unit Lab, you will use what you have learned about budgeting, buying, paying taxes, and banking while exploring another aspect of industry: **Finance.**

Business finance involves keeping track of sales and expenditures, planning for future purchases, deciding when a product is not profitable, and raising money to start or expand a business. Even if you are not making financial decisions for your company, you should understand what underlies those decisions.

Tools

1. Internet
2. Trade and business magazines
3. Books on starting a business

Procedures

STEP A

Choose two careers that interest you from the 15 job clusters outlined in Figure 3-1 in Chapter 3.

Using trade publications, books on business, and the Internet, research the kinds of financing available to a corporation that wants to expand. Then look at the kind of money available to an entrepreneur who wants to start a business.

Keep copies of what you read or take careful notes. You will need this information for your report and for the interviews in Steps B and C.

STEP B

Make an appointment to interview a loan officer at a local bank. You may want to do this in teams of two or three. Explain to the loan officer that you are working on a class project and would like information on business loans.

Some of the questions you might ask are:

1. What criteria does a bank use to determine whether or not a business is loan worthy?
2. How do these criteria differ if the request is for a new business or for expansion of an existing business?

3. Does it make a difference whether the business is a sole proprietorship or a corporation? Why?

4. What is the most common reason a bank refuses a business loan?

STEP C

For each job you chose in Step A, find two businesses that employ people in that job. One should be a large company or corporation, the other a small business.

Make an appointment with a financial officer from the larger company and with the owner of the small business. Explain that you would like to ask a few questions on business finance for a class project.

Some of the questions you might ask are:

1. When does each company seek credit?

2. How does each determine the financial impact on its business when expanding the product line or eliminating a product?

3. What is the company's most common source of funding?

4. What is the most common reason for being turned down for a loan?

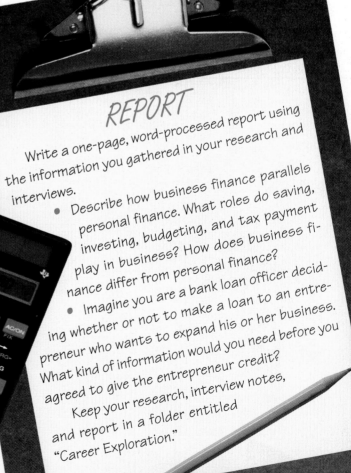

REPORT

Write a one-page, word-processed report using the information you gathered in your research and interviews.

- Describe how business finance parallels personal finance. What roles do saving, investing, budgeting, and tax payment play in business? How does business finance differ from personal finance?

- Imagine you are a bank loan officer deciding whether or not to make a loan to an entrepreneur who wants to expand his or her business. What kind of information would you need before you agreed to give the entrepreneur credit?

Keep your research, interview notes, and report in a folder entitled "Career Exploration."

Lifelong
Learning

UNIT 7 QUIZ:

What Do You Know About Lifelong Learning?

- What does it take to earn a promotion?
- When should you change jobs?
- How would you go about finding your own place to live?
- What steps can you take to balance your work and your personal life?
- What are your responsibilities as a citizen?

481

Chapter 24

Adapting to Change

Section 24-1
Managing Your Career

Section 24-2
Changing Jobs or Careers

In this video segment, explore ways to prepare for your changing role.

Journal
Personal Career Plan

Imagine that you have had the same job for four years. This job is an important step—but only a step—toward your career goal. Now you've been offered a promotion that will take you away from your familiar responsibilities and friendly colleagues. In your journal, list the advantages and disadvantages of this job change.

Managing Your Career

After studying this section, you will be able to:

- Identify ways to prepare yourself for the future.
- Describe actions and behaviors that lead to promotions.

KEY TERMS

downsizing
promotion
seniority
perseverance

Think back over your high school years. How have you changed? In the years ahead, changes will continue to occur. Your skills and interests will keep expanding in new directions. New career possibilities will emerge. The world of work will change, too. Changes at work may open even more doors. Can you predict these changes? No. You *can*, however, prepare yourself to respond to them.

Preparing for the Future

Today's workplace offers challenges that earlier generations of workers did not face. First of all, the job market changes quickly. Jobs that once employed a majority of the population have become much less significant. *Figure 24-1* shows the 12 jobs that experts predict will grow fastest through the year 2005.

Tracking employment trends is one way to prepare for the future. What else can you do?

Thinking in New Ways

You may know people who took jobs when they were young and stayed with the same company for their entire working lives. Forty years ago, that was typical. Today it is not. As you learned in the first chapter of this book, the average American has at least seven jobs before he or she reaches age 30. People can expect to change employers several—perhaps many—more times before they retire. What does this mean?

It means that your career and your job security are in your own hands. That can be to your advantage—if you use your SCANS self-management skills.

The new world of work is a leaner place than ever before. Many companies have gone through **downsizing**, the elimination of jobs in a company to promote efficiency or to cut costs. Some people end up losing their jobs from downsizing. Everyone, however, is affected. When, for example, management jobs are cut, individual workers acquire additional responsibilities. That can mean more job satisfaction. Yet it can also mean more work and greater demands on those workers.

Keeping Up

Luckily, the company you work for wants you to meet these demands at least as much as you do. To help workers, many of today's companies invest heavily in employee training and education. AT&T, for example, spends about $1 billion annually on training. The average AT&T employee receives a little more than a week of training every year. At your job, make use of all opportunities to keep your skills and knowledge up-to-date. In other words, become a *lifelong learner*.

The competitive global market puts added demands on workers. Businesses want to maintain the state of the art. These

The 12 Fastest Growing Occupations: 1992–2005

Occupation	Employment in 1992	Projected Employment in 2005	Percentage Change 1992–2005
Home health aides	347,000	827,000	138.1
Human services workers	189,000	445,000	135.9
Personal and home-care aides	127,000	293,000	129.8
Computer engineers and scientists	211,000	447,000	111.9
Systems analysts	455,000	956,000	110.1
Physical and corrective therapy assistants and aides	61,000	118,000	92.7
Physical therapists	90,000	170,000	88.0
Paralegals	95,000	176,000	86.1
Occupational therapy assistants and aides	12,000	21,000	78.1
Electronic pagination systems workers	18,000	32,000	77.9
Special education teachers	358,000	625,000	74.4
Medical assistants	181,000	308,000	70.5

Source: U. S. Bureau of Labor Statistics, *Monthly Labor Review,* November 1993.

Figure 24-1 This table shows the 12 jobs that experts believe will grow fastest through the year 2005. Which job is expected to grow at the highest rate? Even if the prediction is accurate, why can't a person count on a job in this field?

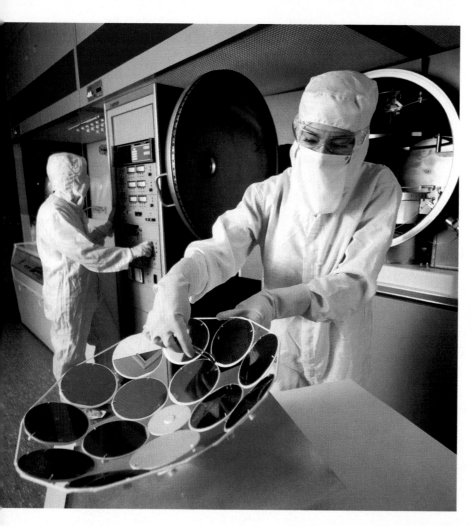

In the past, little was expected of factory employees. They were taught one simple step in a complex process. They repeated that step countless times each day without thinking much about it. Today, employees perform complicated tasks requiring advanced skills. *How has this change benefited workers?*

companies require workers with state-of-the-art knowledge and skills.

Since no one can predict with certainty what new technology will appear, master the SCANS skills in reading, writing, math, speaking, and listening. These skills will give you the basic tools for absorbing new technology.

When new technology appears in your workplace, get involved right away. Volunteer for training sessions or tasks that will give you hands-on training. Take technology courses at community colleges and vocational and technical centers. Many companies offer paid tuition for employees who want to take courses in areas related to their jobs.

Growing in Your Job

Continuing to update and improve your skills and knowledge will make you valuable to your employer. It may also help you earn a promotion. A **promotion** is a job advancement to a position of greater responsibility and authority. Promotions will offer new challenges. Usually promotions also bring increased income.

Who Gets Promoted?

The people who earn promotions are the people who have shown their supervisors that they can handle additional responsibility and authority. What qualities and behaviors do employers look for?

- *Seniority.* **Seniority** is the position or prestige you achieve by working for an employer for a sustained length of time. Greater seniority is usually thought of as indicating greater experience and dependability.

- *Knowledge and competence.* Employers want workers who know how to do their jobs, even if the new job requires different skills. Employers also look for workers who go a step beyond this—workers who excel. These employees are likely to do well in jobs with more responsibility.

- *Willingness to learn.* Employers promote workers who show they want to increase their knowledge and skills.

- *Initiative.* You'll probably advance in your career if you make it clear to your supervisor that advancement is an important goal for you. A good time to talk about career goals is during your performance evaluation. Avoid giving the impression that you want to get out of your current job, however. Emphasize that you want more responsibility and challenge.

EXCELLENT BUSINESS PRACTICES

Environmental Concerns

Pitney Bowes Inc. of Stamford, Connecticut, provides mailing, messaging, and document-handling products; software; and business and financial services.

To better serve the environment, Pitney Bowes has maximized energy conservation at its facilities and has eliminated or drastically reduced chemicals that produce hazardous waste, with a goal of completely eliminating the use of hazardous waste. All suppliers must comply with environmental requirements before Pitney Bowes purchases from them.

Pitney Bowes also keeps the environment in mind while designing products. Such factors as energy consumption, ease of disassembly, recycled and recyclable content, and the use of hazardous materials are considered in manufacturing.

A Pitney Bowes fax machine, for example, powers down when not in use and every piece of the machine can be recycled. The company also set up a program to help keep toner cartridges out of landfills. For every cartridge returned, the company makes a financial donation to the United Way.

Thinking Critically

How has environmental awareness caused companies to change?

- *Perseverance.* **Perseverance** is the quality of finishing what you start. Employers want to know that you will see a job through to completion.

- *Cooperativeness.* When you have more responsibility, you'll have to cooperate with more people. Employers want people who can get along well with others.

- *Thinking skills.* When considering whom to promote, employers look for people who can think through situations and solve problems.

- *Adaptability.* Business is constantly changing. Employers want workers who can adapt to new situations and get a job done.

- *Education and training.* Employers promote people who have the skills and education needed for the new job.

Handling Your New Responsibilities

Getting a promotion may change your work life in many ways. Often it means you'll become a supervisor. Then you will be responsible for both your own work and the work of others. Look back at Chapter 14 to remind yourself of the qualities of a good supervisor.

Be aware that as a supervisor your relationships with your former coworkers will change. You'll be the boss. You must oversee their work and give direction. You will review their performance. It may be difficult to have close friendships with people you supervise. Be sure you are prepared for these changes.

 Learning should not end with high school or even college. Workers must keep up-to-date on the latest information in their fields. *How can further education give you greater confidence?*

 If you want to decline a promotion, talk to your supervisor face-to-face.
Why do you think this is important?

Declining a Promotion

Being offered a promotion is always a good thing. It shows you've earned your employer's trust and appreciation. Not every promotion, however, is right for you. Perhaps the promotion requires too many personal sacrifices. For example, you might be asked to travel more than you want or to take on responsibilities you don't feel ready for.

It's OK to decline a promotion. Avoid closing the door on future offers, however. Even if this promotion is not right, the next one might be. Let your supervisor know your specific reasons for declining a promotion. Leave your supervisor with the impression that you like your work and want to be considered for future promotions.

SECTION 24-1 *Review*

Understanding Key Concepts

Using complete sentences, answer the following questions on a separate sheet of paper.

1. How will continuing your education help you be prepared for changes in the workplace?

2. Why is it important to let your supervisor know you're interested in a promotion?

Exploring Careers: Environment

**Brad Nanke
Corporate Environmental
Manager**

Q: What does your job involve?

A: I have the responsibility for seeing that my company complies with all environmental regulations. I take care of permits pertaining to water and air quality, hazardous waste handling, and waste-water discharge. I also take care of all the reports that go with the regulations. I report to the state fire marshal on the chemicals we use and on our emergency response procedures. I work with the city on water quality.

Q: Do you have environmental training?

A: I've learned along the way. I've never gotten a degree. Even if you have a degree in environmental science or engineering, you don't necessarily become a regulations expert.

I'm a certified hazardous materials manager. The certification was developed for people like me, who have come up through the field. We are recognized for what we know.

Q: Will there be a demand for environmental managers in the future?

A: Yes, especially among small companies that don't have a health or environmental staff.

Q: Is there anything you don't like about your job?

A: I don't like the legal liability. Because I sign the permits, I could go to jail if someone else does something wrong. You have to make sure that people know what the permits actually mean and that they don't operate outside the limits of those permits.

Thinking Critically

Would you be interested in an environmental career? Why or why not?

CAREER FACTS

Nature of the Work:
Oversee issuing of permits, environmental impact, and compliance with state, local, and federal environmental regulations.

Training or Education Needed:
Bachelor's degree in chemistry, chemical or civil engineering, or environmental science; experience in the field.

Aptitudes, Abilities, and Skills:
Computer skills; ability to learn; read blueprints; self-management skills; detail orientation.

Salary Range:
Approximately $30,000 with bachelor's degree and one year of experience.

Career Path:
Start in an entry-level position; move up to a position with more responsibility.

Changing Jobs or Careers

OBJECTIVES

After studying this section, you will be able to:

- Explain why workers may want to change jobs.
- Describe strategies for seeking a new job or career.
- Describe steps to take if you lose your job.

KEY TERM

notice

As you know, you are likely to change employers several times during your work career. Sometimes you may choose the change because you want to seek new opportunities. At other times, the change may be forced on you by events beyond your control.

Why Change Jobs?

Changing your job should never be a snap decision. Before making a change, you should analyze what is missing from your current job and what you want from a new one. Always make sure you have thought through the change carefully. This section will help you clarify possible reasons for a job change. The next sections will help you make the transition.

Because You're Not Happy

When you are unhappy at work, a job change may be one solution. *Figure 24-2* on page 492 is a checklist of danger signs. Use it to evaluate your situation.

Before giving up on your job, however, consider whether there might be a way to stay and solve the problem. Ask advice from an experienced coworker or friend. If you decide to stay, set work goals for yourself. What do you want to achieve in your job—a pay raise, a promotion, new responsibilities or challenges? How long will you give yourself to reach your goals?

Signs of Trouble Checklist

- ☐ Do my coworkers ignore me or leave me out?
- ☐ Do I feel that I'm wasting my time?
- ☐ Do I find myself daydreaming what my life would be like without this job?
- ☐ Is being sick a relief to me because I don't have to go to work?
- ☐ Do I seem to be always making someone at work angry or upset?
- ☐ Do I feel as if I don't have a future with the company or a chance for advancement?
- ☐ Do I have trouble sleeping because I'm worrying about my job?

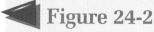

Use this checklist to evaluate your level of job satisfaction. Answering yes to any of these questions indicates that you should reassess your situation.

Changing your job isn't necessarily the answer, however. How might you solve a work problem if you plan to stay?

Because You Want to Grow

Is there a good time to change jobs? Yes! It is possible to outgrow your job. Perhaps you feel unfulfilled and unchallenged. Perhaps you have discovered that what you are doing isn't really what you want to do. In these cases, a job change may be what you need.

Because Your Job Is Terminated

There are times, of course, when a job change is forced on you. People can no longer count on keeping their jobs until retirement. Downsizing, corporate restructuring, and global economic factors have created a working world in which little is constant except change.

As illogical as it sounds, you *can* prepare for an unexpected job loss. How is this possible? Stay alert. Keep your ears open at work for signs of trouble. These include signals that your supervisor is displeased with your work or that the company is not doing well. Read newspaper articles and magazines about your industry to detect trends. Read the front page of the newspaper, too. Is there anything happening in the world that might affect the industry in which you work?

ETHICS in Action

You've been offered a new job that doesn't begin for another two months. You plan to keep working at your old job until your new job begins. Your best friend tells you that you should plan to tell your employer you will be leaving two weeks before you actually leave. Your coworker says you should give your employer more notice since you know what you are going to do so far in advance. What will you do?

Making the Change

When you decide to make a career or job change, put your SCANS decision-making skills to work. First you have to define your needs or wants.

Focusing Your Search

Consider where you want to look for a new job. Here are three possible ways to focus your search.

- *Same job, new company.* If you like what you're doing, explore similar positions with other companies. You already know you have the right skills for the job. A different company, however, may offer better opportunities.

- *New job, new company.* What if you have the right skills for your job but you really don't like it? That happened to Lisa Von Drasek. She was working in book sales when a layoff forced her to do some rethinking. She suddenly realized she didn't feel fulfilled in her career. She wanted a job that would allow her to make a difference in the world. When a friend suggested library school, Von Drasek was skeptical. After talking with several librarians, however, she signed up for a master's program.

Today she's a children's librarian at the Brooklyn Public Library. Every day, she sees young teen mothers, recent immigrants, and others discover the world of books. She has even developed her own children's

Keeping up with business news can bring early warnings of trouble in your industry or company. It can also bring news of better times to come. *What are some examples of business news that could affect employment in your area?*

writing program. "The kids run up to my desk and say, 'When are we going to write?'" she says. "I make a difference."

- *Starting over.* A third possibility is to turn a hobby or interest into a career. Geoffrey Macon had spent 17 years in the banking industry. When a combination of health problems and corporate restructuring cost him his job, he turned his career in a different direction. Macon had always

had a passionate interest in ethnic art. He became an entrepreneur designing, manufacturing, and selling plates and other tableware based on ethnic designs.

What's Different This Time Around?

In this book, you have been introduced to many job search strategies. Chapter 2, for example, talked about career decision making. Chapter 3 gave tips on researching careers. Chapter 6 provided basic

These entrepreneurs have turned a personal interest into a way of making a living. **What interest of yours might you turn into a business?**

information on finding and applying for a job. Chapter 7 covered interview techniques. The main focus in these chapters was on choosing your career and landing your first job. The advice is just as useful when you are finding a new job or changing your career. In addition, consider the following points:

- Because you've been out in the world of work, you have much more data available to you. What are your work skills? Which tasks have you enjoyed most? Which have you enjoyed least?

- Consider how you can use proven skills in new ways. Suppose you have been a receptionist. Your telephone skills could be used in marketing. Your ability to remain in control when all the lines are flashing could be valuable in retail sales.

- List jobs or careers that you might like. Then analyze them. What are the pros and cons of each? How can your current skills and interests be applied to them?

- Research jobs in which you are interested. You have probably built up a network of people at your current job. Use these contacts to explore new directions.

- Try to arrange your interviews so that you don't miss work.

- Don't burn your bridges with your present employer. You don't want to lose your current job until you've landed a new one. Besides, you never know when your old contacts will once again be valuable to you.

Career Do's & Don'ts

When Preparing for Change...

Do:
- take initiative.
- be flexible.
- keep physically active.
- maintain your sense of humor.

Don't:
- focus on the negative aspects of change.
- overlook your strengths and long-term goals.
- make change too big in your mind.

- When you've found a new job, give proper notice to your current employer. **Notice** is an official written statement that you are leaving the company. Most people prepare a formal letter of resignation. Businesses usually have a policy stating how long they expect employees to work after giving notice. This period of time gives the employer time to find a replacement.

- Don't tell coworkers about your job hunt. They don't need to know. Always inform coworkers about the new job *after* you've given notice.

- Don't lose steam at work. Perhaps you've worked long hours for five years. Unfortunately, people will remember if you slack off during your last two weeks. Leave a good impression.

- Let people outside the company know what's happening. Tell clients or other business contacts that you are leaving. Don't criticize the

► Figure 24-3

Losing a Job

If you lose your job, you may think you have nothing to do. That's not true! You'll be working full-time getting a new job.

A Your first response to the news of the job loss may be a powerful negative emotion such as anger or sadness. As soon as you have your emotions under control, talk with your supervisor. Ask about job-search services available through your employer, severance pay (money that may be offered to employees who are dismissed), funds from profit-sharing or pension plans, payment for unused vacation time, and terms for extension of your health insurance coverage.

B Next review your financial situation. Figure out how much money you have to live on. Then prepare a budget so you know you can pay for the things you must have. Find ways to cut back on your expenses.

No . 1004882

Benefits from Department of Unemployment

August 13

Pay to the order of Susan D. Smith 430.00

Four Hundred Thirty and no/100 DOLLARS

Dept. of Economic Security

J Jones OFFICER

C In most cases, workers who lose their jobs can get unemployment benefits. These checks will help you get by until you find your next job. Every state has its own guidelines for applying for unemployment compensation. Make your application as soon as possible.

company, however, no matter how disappointed or angry you feel. Doing so will only make you seem petty, and it could lose you a future job.

Dealing with a Job Loss

Most people are laid off or have their jobs terminated at least once during their working careers (See **Figure 24-3**). It is always a painful experience. If it happens to you, you may feel depressed, embarrassed, resentful, angry, afraid, or discouraged.

These are valid emotions, and you shouldn't be ashamed of feeling them. However, don't let them overwhelm you.

D Update and improve your résumé. Remember that it should be brief and to the point. Ask several people to read it over, and consider having it printed professionally. Use every strategy you can think of in your job search. These include networking, contacting employment agencies, and reading the classified ads.

E Stay positive as you go for interviews. Remember that a job loss can be a good opportunity to find a better job or to follow your dreams.

Try to remain positive. Look on the event as an opportunity to start over. Perhaps, like Lisa Von Drasek or Geoffrey Macon, you may be able to do what you've always wanted. You may even be able to earn a better income than you did before.

▶ Try to be open-minded when you are looking for a new job. You might find that your skills apply to some very interesting jobs. **What kinds of skills would be important in the job pictured here?**

SECTION 24-2 *Review*

Understanding Key Concepts

Using complete sentences, answer the following questions on a separate sheet of paper.

1. Why is the desire for personal growth a good reason to change jobs?

2. What are some of the unique aspects of looking for a job when you already have one?

3. Why is it important to keep a positive attitude when you have lost your job?

Key Terms

downsizing *(p. 485)*
promotion *(p. 486)*
seniority *(p. 487)*
perseverance *(p. 488)*

SECTION 24-1 Summary

- You can prepare for the future by tracking employment trends and managing your own career.

- Many businesses are downsizing, or eliminating jobs to cut costs. Some employees lose their jobs, and others gain new responsibilities.

- Businesses help employees meet the demands of the workplace by offering training and paying for education.

- Continuing to update your skills and knowledge may also help you get a promotion.

- Employers look for many different qualities and behaviors when selecting employees to promote, including competence, willingness to learn, initiative, and adaptability.

- Getting a promotion may change your relationships with coworkers. Be prepared for this change.

- If a promotion is not right for you, decline it. Keep your options open, however. Let your employer know you are open to future offers.

Key Term

notice *(p. 495)*

SECTION 24-2 Summary

- You may choose to change jobs for a number of reasons, including unhappiness in your job, the desire to grow, or termination of your job.

- Focus your job search. You might look for a job like the one you have but with a different company. You might look for a job that will use your current skills but in a different field. You might look for a job that involves a hobby or personal interest that you have.

- You will use many of the job search strategies that you learned in previous chapters. This time, however, you have more information about yourself and your skills.

- If you lose your job, first find out what your former employer is offering to you at termination. Then assess your financial situation, and arrange for unemployment benefits. Update and improve your résumé. Stay positive as you go for interviews.

Reviewing Key Terms

On a separate sheet of paper, write a checklist of ways to manage your own career. Use each of the following terms.

downsizing   perseverance
promotion   notice
seniority

Recalling Key Concepts

On a piece of paper, tell whether each statement is true or false. Rewrite any false statements to make them true.

1. In today's workplace, your career and your job security are mainly in your own hands.

2. Businesses do little to help employees keep their job skills current.

3. When promoting workers, employers consider such factors as seniority, initiative, and perseverance.

4. If you have problems with your coworkers or supervisor, the only thing you can do is find a new job.

5. Emotions such as fear or sadness are normal when you lose your job.

Thinking Critically

Using complete sentences, answer each of the questions below on a separate sheet of paper.

1. How can tracking employment trends help you manage your own career?

2. How can the SCANS skills in reading, writing, math, speaking, and listening help you keep up with new technology?

3. You have learned that you can either adjust to a negative work situation or decide to make a job change. List two possible benefits and two drawbacks to each choice.

4. Suppose you find a new job, and you know that you will never want to work for your former employer again. Why is it still a good policy not to criticize your former employer?

5. Why should you examine your financial situation soon after finding out about a job loss?

 ## SCANS Foundation Skills and Workplace Competencies

Basic Skills: *Writing*

1. Write a letter of resignation that includes a gracious opening, a body stating the reason for leaving and notification of the last day you plan to be on the job, and a cordial closing.

Interpersonal Skills: *Exercising Leadership*

2. You have received a promotion, and you now supervise Carrie, a coworker who is also a good friend. Carrie has begun coming in to work late, leaving early, and not performing as well on the job as before. When you talk with her, she says: "What's the big deal? I thought you were my friend. You sure have changed since you became a boss." What should you say?

Connecting Academics to the Workplace

Human Relations

1. Margo is an admissions clerk in a health-care center. She has held the job for three years. A better position in the department has become available, and Margo thinks she is qualified for the promotion. Her supervisor, however, has not offered the position to her. Margo feels overlooked and also a little angry. What should she do?

Computer Science

2. Miguel is an equipment specialist for a construction firm. His supervisor has asked him to recommend a laptop computer that engineers can take with them to the work site. Create a list of features Miguel might look for in a laptop that would make it suitable.

Developing Teamwork and Leadership Skills

Work with a group of three or four classmates. Together, decide on one technological device or a group of technological devices that are currently being developed and marketed for business or industrial use. Do research to learn about the technology and how it may be used in the next 5 or 10 years. Present your findings to the class.

Real-World Workshop

Work with a classmate. First choose a type of company that you might work for and a job that you might have in the company. Then role-play the following situation. An employee has been offered a promotion but does not want to accept it. (You and your partner must decide what the employee's reasons are.) Perform two role-plays. In one, you should be the employee and your partner should be the supervisor; in the other, your roles should be switched. Show through the role-plays either two good ways to decline a promotion or a good way and a poor way to decline a promotion. Present your role-plays to the class.

School-to-Work Connection

Select a local company for which you might like to work. Interview the human resources manager or a department supervisor. Ask what qualities or behaviors this individual looks for when considering employees for promotions. Ask also what training opportunities the company provides to help employees develop the skills needed for promotion. Prepare a brief report on your findings.

Individual Career Plan

Choose a job or career you wish to pursue. Do research to learn about trends in that field. Find answers to questions such as the following: How will the field be affected by new technology? What kind of an impact will globalization have? What are the predictions for future employment growth (or decline) in the field? Outline a plan for keeping your knowledge and skills current. Include formal training and education as well as individual efforts you might make, such as reading specialized magazines or volunteering for jobs using new technology.

Chapter 25

Balancing Work and Personal Life

Section 25-1
Setting Up Your Own Household

Section 25-2
Managing Work, Family, and Community Life

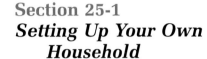

In this video segment, see why it's important to plan for the future.

Journal
Personal Career Plan

After years of living with parents or other adults who have taken responsibility for you, you will soon be living on your own. What are the most exciting and interesting aspects of this change? Which aspects do you expect to find most difficult? Why? Write a journal entry describing your ideas and your feelings.

Setting Up Your Own Household

OBJECTIVES

After studying this section, you will be able to:

- **Decide on a place to live.**
- **Organize your living space.**
- **Establish good housekeeping habits.**

KEY TERMS

commute
utilities
security deposit

You've planned your career, you've landed your first job, you've drawn your first paycheck. What's the next step? For many people, it's finding their own place to live. One of the most exciting decisions you'll ever make is choosing where you'll live.

To Move or Not to Move

Depending on your personal situation, you may be ready to move into a place of your own. Before settling on this plan, though, weigh the pros and cons of living at home.

As you may have guessed, living at home is much less expensive. Even if your parent(s), relative(s), or guardian(s) charge you room and board, you'll still probably be paying less than you would to rent an apartment. In addition, you won't have to buy your own furniture, and you can probably save money on food and laundry as well. On the negative side, living at home means you won't be able to make all your own decisions, and privacy may become a serious issue.

Now consider the pros and cons of having your own place. For most people, being more independent is the number one factor. The challenge of being on your own, the enjoyment of fixing up your own place, your sense of individual pride and responsibility—these are part of the joy of drawing a paycheck!

When you move into a place of your own, you accept new responsibilities and face new problems. It can be a stressful time. *How can your parents and friends help you through such a time?*

On the other hand, you'll have to pay the monthly rent, although you might reduce the expense by having roommates who will split the cost. Even good roommates, though, will complicate your life. The dwelling won't be yours alone. You'll have to adapt to other people's personalities and habits. *Figure 25-1* provides a questionnaire you might use to assess a potential roommate.

If you decide to move, choose the location carefully. These questions may help you evaluate possible areas:

- How far will I have to **commute,** or travel, to get to my job?

- Is the area safe?

- Is it close to public transportation?

Roommate Questionnaire

- Do you have a regular income?
- What hours do you work?
- When do you go to bed? Wake up?
- Do you drink alcohol?
- Do you smoke?
- Will you ever have friends or family staying with you? If so, who?
- Do you like to cook?
- Do you watch a lot of television? What programs? What hours?
- Do you listen to music much? If so, what kind(s) of music?

- Do you play a musical instrument? What kind(s) of music? Do you practice at home? If so, when?
- Do you have a pet or want one? If so, what kind?
- Do you enjoy time alone? If so, how much time and when?
- What kind of parties do you like to have and how often?
- What kind of housekeeper are you?
- How long do you think you'll want to share a place?

Figure 25-1 Learning details about a potential roommate before sharing an apartment is essential. Why would it be helpful to ask these questions even of someone you know?

- Is it close to my friends and family?
- Is it near places I go to for recreation and entertainment?

Money Matters

After you find a place you like, prepare a budget. Estimate how much you will have to spend each month to live on your own. You may want to review budgeting in Chapter 20.

Remember that the amount you budget needs to include more than the monthly rent. You may have to pay a monthly maintenance fee. You'll also have to pay for **utilities**—services for your dwelling, including the cost of electricity, gas or oil heat, and perhaps water. In addition, you will have telephone costs and probably cable TV costs.

You can't predict exactly how much your utility costs will be. Some may be included in your monthly rent, and heating and electricity costs can vary widely.

However, most utility companies can provide you with estimates based on other households in your neighborhood. Talk to your friends and neighbors, too, so that your monthly bills don't turn out to be an unpleasant surprise. Use your estimated monthly expenses as a guide to identify places you can afford.

Remember one of the most important elements you've learned about decision making—gather all the information you can. Before deciding on a place to live, inspect it thoroughly. *Figure 25-2* presents a useful checklist of things to look for.

When young people move into their first apartment, they often don't have a lot of money. *What can you do if you can't afford a place where you would feel comfortable and safe?*

Rental Property Checklist

Inside Areas

- Halls and stairways
  - _____ What condition are they in?
  - _____ Can you use them safely and conveniently when your arms are loaded with groceries?
  - _____ Does someone clean them regularly?
  - _____ Are there at least two exits?
- Cleanliness
  - _____ Is the apartment clean?
  - _____ Is the rental property clean?
- Room configuration
  - _____ Do you like the floor plan?
  - _____ Will there be enough privacy if you have a roommate?
- Storage
  - _____ Is there enough storage space?
  - _____ How many closets are there?
- Kitchen
  - _____ Do all appliances work?
  - _____ Do cabinet doors and drawers work?
  - _____ Is there enough space in the cabinets?
  - _____ Are the faucets and sink in good condition?
- Bathroom
  - _____ Is there a shower?
  - _____ Is there a bath?
  - _____ Are the faucets, sink, shower/bath in good condition?

- _____ Is there good water pressure?
- _____ Will there be plenty of hot water?
- Windows and screens
  - _____ Do the windows fit snugly and work smoothly?
  - _____ Do the windows have locks?
  - _____ Are there screens?
- Doors
  - _____ Are the doors sturdy and secure?
  - _____ Do they have deadbolts?
- Laundry facilities
  - _____ Are there washers and dryers in the building or in the complex?

Outside Areas

- Neighborhood
  - _____ Is it safe?
  - _____ Is it quiet?
  - _____ Is it clean?
- Parking
  - _____ Is there enough parking?
  - _____ Is parking convenient?
  - _____ Is the parking area safe?
- Safety
  - _____ Is the area around your building or complex well lighted?
  - _____ Is the general area safe at night?

Figure 25-2 Make copies of this checklist, and complete them as you visit different rental properties. Use the checklist to compare places that interest you. Which items are most important to you? Why?

Use it to compare places and to choose the one that's best for you.

When you're ready to sign on the dotted line, be sure you understand the following items:

- _Lease._ Usually, owners will ask you to sign a lease. This written agreement spells out the responsibilities

of the owner and _tenant_, or the person renting the property.

- _Rent and due date._ How much is the rent? When is it due? Is there a penalty for late payment?

- _Security deposit._ How much is the security deposit? A **security deposit** is money you pay the owner before you move in; often, it's equal to one or two months' rent. The deposit is held to cover potential damage while you live in the dwelling. If no damage occurs, the security deposit should be returned to you when you move out.

- *Landlord's responsibilities.* Which repairs and maintenance jobs (such as cleaning hallways) are the landlord's responsibility? Which are your responsibility?

- *Utilities.* Are any of the utilities included in the monthly rent?

Settling In and Getting Connected

As soon as possible after signing your lease, measure the rooms and begin deciding where your furniture will go.

On graph paper, draw a floor plan to scale of an apartment you'd like. Draw your pieces of furniture on separate sheets of paper so that you can move them around on the floor plan. *How will creating a scale model drawing of your apartment help save you time and trouble on moving day?*

Although moving is hard work, it can be fun. *What are some advantages in getting friends to help with the move?*

You might try drawing the rooms to scale on paper. For example, an inch on paper might equal a foot of floor space. By measuring your furniture and drawing it to scale, you can plan where the largest pieces will fit and decide on new items you'll need to buy.

You'll also have to make arrangements with your utility companies, telephone company, cable TV company, and so on to have services turned on. Call each company as soon as you sign your lease. Tell their representatives when you want service to begin and schedule appointments so that you can be present when the service people arrive.

Don't forget to report your new address to the post office. Your mail will be forwarded to your new address, beginning on the date you specify. You might also want to get a stack of postcards from the post office and send your new address to family, friends, and business acquaintances.

Housekeeping Habits

What makes a household work on an everyday basis? Routines are a large part of the answer. One of the biggest favors you can do for yourself is to establish a few basic housekeeping habits.

At the top of the list—pay your bills on time. Most bills arrive with a due date, the date by which the payment must be received. Don't bury your bills under piles of other mail. Consider buying a file or bill holder so that envelopes don't get lost or forgotten. Paying your monthly bills on time not only gives you a good credit record (valuable when you need a loan), but it will also undoubtedly save

you money on late fees and credit card finance charges.

Set aside a small amount of time on a regular basis for housecleaning. If you wait until you need a bulldozer to straighten up your rooms, the job will seem much harder than it really is. You can raise the quality of your life a great deal by regularly seeing to such simple jobs as washing the dishes and sweeping the floor.

The same basic rule applies to doing the laundry. Don't wait until the pile looks like Mt. Everest. Doing a load of laundry every few days will not only keep your living space looking better, you'll actually have more choices of clothes to wear!

Cook healthful meals and try to eat at regular times. A steady diet of fast food will not only rob you of energy, but it will also cost much more than cooking for yourself. Keep a list handy of groceries and other household items you need to buy. Jot things down when you notice you need them. That way, you won't run out of necessary items, and when you shop for groceries, you'll know what you need and won't buy items you already have. You'll be surprised at how these few housekeeping routines can actually save you time and money.

SECTION 25-1 *Review*

Understanding Key Concepts

Using complete sentences, answer the following questions on a separate sheet of paper.

1. Which items on the checklist used to compare places to live are most important to you? Why?

2. Why should you call the utility, telephone, and cable TV companies as soon as you sign your lease?

3. Which housekeeping habits do you think are the easiest to maintain? Which ones may be more difficult?

Exploring Careers: Public Service

Raymond C. Byrd
Police Officer

Q: **How did you become a police officer?**

A: When I went into the military, one of the choices the recruiter gave me was the opportunity to become a military police officer.

Q: **Was the training for military police different from that for civilian police?**

A: In the military, we spent more time on our combat role. In civilian training, we learned more about the law. We have to work within state, local, and federal laws, so we dealt more with that aspect of police work.

Q: **What is your work like?**

A: I'm assigned to the detective section of the department. I'm also the liaison officer for all the schools. I handle criminal calls in the schools, such as thefts or fights, but I'm also the school resource officer. I try to open myself up so the students know that they can talk to me and that I will do everything I can to protect them. I surprised them one day when

I was asked if I would give my life for them and I said I would.

Q: **That's a pretty strong commitment to service.**

A: I really do feel that value. It's a personal thing with me. I come from a military family. I wanted to be a soldier since I was five years old. There has never been a question that my life was for service. I think it's a mind-set you have to have to do this job.

Thinking Critically

Why are communication skills important to a police officer?

CAREER FACTS

Nature of the Work:
Answer phone calls about crime and accidents; take care of the paperwork related to those calls; work with the community.

Training or Education Needed:
Police academy training; ongoing training to update techniques; a bachelor's degree is often required in order to receive promotions.

Aptitudes, Abilities, and Skills:
Self-management skills; ability to learn; good judgment, honesty, and integrity.

Salary Range:
Approximately $1,500 to $3,000 a month to start; more with experience.

Career Path:
Start as a patrol officer; seek promotion through the ranks; may become a detective.

Managing Work, Family, and Community Life

OBJECTIVES

After studying this section, you will be able to:

- Describe ways of balancing your work life and your personal life.
- Identify some strategies for meeting family responsibilities.
- Identify some family-friendly employment practices.
- Participate in your community as a voter and as a volunteer.

KEY TERM

register

A job can take up a good deal of your time and energy. However, just as you wouldn't eat only one kind of food, you shouldn't let one aspect of your life dominate all the others. Balance is as essential to your personal life as it is to your diet. Knowing how to balance your work and your personal life is key to successfully managing your career.

Enriching Your Personal Life

You have a responsibility to yourself as well as to your job. Fulfilling that personal responsibility can bring about the feeling of life success that you value most of all. Here's a good rule of thumb: No matter what happens at work, don't forget what you're working for.

Strive to balance your work life and your commitments to yourself, your family, friends, and the community. By doing so, you will be successful in reaching your career goals as well as your personal goals in life. The pressures of a job can sometimes seem to overshadow the other aspects of your life, but in the long run, the time you spend outside of work will prove at least as valuable as the time you spend on the job. The right balance will make you happier, healthier, and probably even more satisfied with your work.

People must have time to play in order to remain mentally and physically healthy. *Why is it important to make time for physical activities such as soccer or dancing?*

Expand Your Circle of Friends

Since you spend so much time at work, you'll form friendships with coworkers. That's good, but you should also focus on developing friendships outside of work. This is a key to avoid keeping work at the center of your life. How can you expand your circle of friends?

Join a group. Get involved with an organization that interests you, such as an environmental association, arts group, or charity. Sign up for a sports league. Join a book group at a local bookstore. Take up a hobby or enroll in evening classes at a local community college.

Family Responsibilities

The biggest challenge for working parents is finding time for both work and home. They're torn between job responsibilities and the needs of their children. Life often becomes a delicate balancing act, and every hour can seem accounted for. When anything happens to upset the balance, there's a scramble to pick up the pieces. It can be tough on the parents and on the children. Magda Cosner knows about these difficulties.

Cosner is a Miami police officer. After returning to work from maternity leave, her schedule worked well—for a while. Now her department is going to change her schedule. "I'm going to have to start coming in at 6:30 in the morning instead of 8:30," Cosner explains. "That's going to cause a problem with the kids—they'll have to be up at 5:30. My husband's very helpful with the kids ... but he's a police officer, too, and with my new schedule, we're not going to have a day off together anymore."

There are no easy solutions to problems such as these. However, careful planning and communication are a start. They can enable families to build on the love for one another that is the foundation of their relationship.

People Need People

Everyone needs to share thoughts and feelings. The very act of talking and listening creates a bond between people and makes it easier to deal with problems. Make listening to the needs of your spouse or roommate a major priority. Communication is the key. Listen to what others have to say, what problems they're facing, what interests them. When work and other obligations present problems, keep the lines of communication open.

Be considerate of each other. Pay attention to the little things that can make life more pleasant for everyone in your household. This can mean anything from turning off lights to adjusting mealtimes. If you know that someone has a pet peeve, do what you can to avoid it.

Don't forget how good it feels to receive praise and encouragement. An enthusiastic word goes a long way toward keeping a relationship strong.

Children have many needs. They need to be fed, clothed, bathed, taken to activities, and helped with homework. That's just part of it. They need to be loved, and love takes time and energy. Make time for talking, playing, and being together.

Caring for children's emotional needs is as important as caring for their physical needs. *Why is it important for parents to play with their children every day, not just on weekends?*

Figure 25-3

Balancing Your Job and Family Responsibilities

Putting extra effort into balancing work and family responsibilities will undoubtedly lead to greater personal satisfaction.

A Balancing Act

There are no easy rules for balancing your responsibilities to your job and to your family. Everyone's situation is different. However, *Figure 25-3* provides a few hints that you can apply in your own way.

A Be realistic. Accept the fact that you will have to make compromises in your job and in your family life in order to make time for both.

B Share family duties and household chores so that no one person has to do them all.

C Don't overschedule your nonwork time. Allow for free time to spend doing something you enjoy with your family.

Help from Employers

You might think your company is the last place to look for help in managing your family life. In fact, employers are realizing that it is to their benefit to help families. Studies show that employees who are under less family stress are more loyal and more productive. What kind of help do employers offer? Benefits vary from company to company, but here are a few:

- *Flextime.* You can work the schedule that's best for you and your family.

- *On-site day care.* It's sometimes easier to bring children to work with

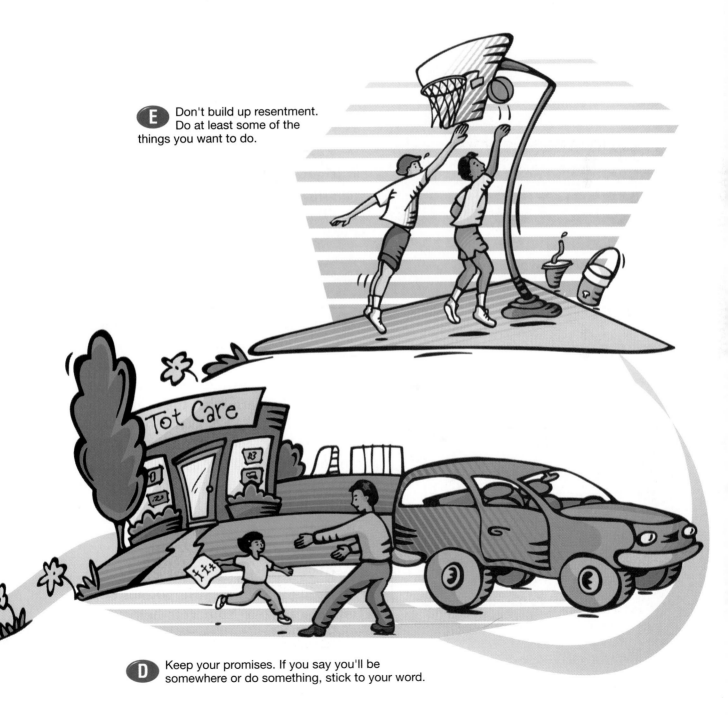

E Don't build up resentment. Do at least some of the things you want to do.

D Keep your promises. If you say you'll be somewhere or do something, stick to your word.

On-site day care centers are one of the most popular employee benefits for working parents. *How do such day care centers help parents concentrate on their jobs?*

YOU'RE THE BOSS!

✓ Solving Workplace Problems

You want to promote an employee to manage your plumbing business. You've narrowed your choice to two good workers: one is an older man with years of experience but only moderate people skills; the other is a young, less-experienced plumber who's unusually good at dealing with people. Which employee will you choose? Why?

you than to take them elsewhere. You can also visit them during your breaks or at lunchtimes.

- *Family-friendly training for managers.* Many companies train their managers to be sensitive to the family needs of their staff. As a result, you may find it easier to make special arrangements to balance your job responsibilities and your family's needs.

Your Responsibilities as a Citizen

As you move into the world of work and get your own place to live, your responsibilities as a citizen will grow. You'll be a working adult, a taxpayer, and a voter.

Being Informed

As a citizen, your community is your responsibility. You need to stay informed on issues and events.

Read the newspaper. Listen to radio and television news reports. Talk to your neighbors to learn what they think about issues. The SCANS skills of reading, listening, and speaking and the SCANS competencies of acquiring and using information will help you as a citizen. Then you can put your knowledge to work by voting.

Voting

Voting is your most important obligation as a citizen. Your vote helps decide who our leaders will be and what laws we will live by. Don't let other people make these decisions for you.

Before you can vote, you must be at least 18 years old and **register,** or officially sign up as a qualified voter. Methods for registering vary from place to place. To find out how it is done in your area, call the League of Women Voters, your county election commission, or the county registrar's office. Any of these sources can tell

▶ To cast an informed vote, you have to prepare for an election by learning about the candidates and issues. *How important is your vote? Will it matter in an election in which thousands or millions of people vote? Explain.*

EXCELLENT BUSINESS PRACTICES

Career Management

To help its 40,000 employees maintain a high level of skill awareness, Chicago-based Amoco Corporation has a career management program.

Employees go through a self-assessment process to identify their skills, establish goals, and add competencies. They work with team leaders to focus on career planning and to create an individual development plan.

The company has an interactive database that lists jobs available in the worldwide organization. Employees can review and apply for jobs electronically from their own computers. The database also provides information about emerging skills and competencies.

The program allows individuals to align their abilities and aspirations with company requirements and strategic planning. Together, employees and management share the responsibility of preparing for the future.

Thinking Critically

What are the advantages of a career management program?

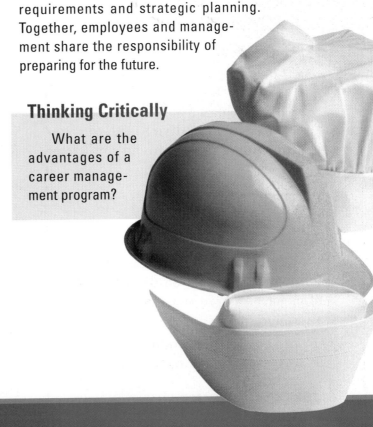

you how, when, and where you can go to register and what documents you'll need to take along.

Doing Your Part

Actively participating in your community is not only a responsibility, it's also a way to genuinely enrich your life. By engaging in volunteer work, you'll widen your circle of friends, learn new skills, and make your community a better place in which to live.

How can you get involved? Think of the activities you enjoy and the concerns that are important to you. Call the organizations that promote those activities and ask if they offer volunteer opportunities. Talk to people, ask questions, attend some meetings. Just remember that whether you're interested in restoring old buildings, reading to the blind, or coaching basketball, you've got a lot to give.

One Final Word: Give It All You've Got!

Whatever career you follow, whatever your family situation, live as fully as you can. Your job and your loved ones may

Career Do's & Don'ts

When Designing Your Life's Path...

Do:
- take charge of your life.
- ask for more responsibilities in your current position and seek ways to change your role in the organization.
- Volunteer to participate in team projects or short-term tasks.
- regularly update your goals.

Don't:
- be afraid to take a lower level job at another company or in another industry if you're unhappy with your present position.
- be satisfied with your work because it's easy for you to do.
- doubt yourself.
- stop challenging yourself.

take you to places you can't even imagine now. Above all, enjoy what you do. At work and at home, you get out of life as much as you put into it.

SECTION 25-2 *Review*

Understanding Key Concepts

Using complete sentences, answer the following questions on a separate sheet of paper.

1. How can making time for yourself make you more productive at work?
2. Why should you treat time scheduled

with your family with the same importance as you treat work?

3. Why are people frequently more productive when they work for a family-friendly company?

Key Terms

commute *(p. 505)*
utilities *(p. 506)*
security deposit *(p. 507)*

SECTION 25-1 Summary

- Setting up your own household is a major life change. Before moving out, be sure that staying at home for a while isn't better for you.

- Staying home will cost less, but in your own place, you'll have more independence and pride of ownership.

- If you have roommates, you'll have lower rent payments, but you'll have to adapt to other people.

- Prepare a budget to estimate how much you'll have to spend on your own place.

- Choose a location that fits your needs, values, and budget.

- Make your life easier by establishing some good house-keeping habits.

Key Term

register *(p. 517)*

SECTION 25-2 Summary

- Balance your work time and your personal time.

- Develop friends outside of work by joining groups.

- Fulfilling responsibilities to both your job and your family can be difficult. Communication is the key. A few rules of thumb include being realistic, sharing family duties, and keeping your promises.

- Employers sometimes help people manage their family lives by offering flexible work schedules and on-site day care centers.

- Voting is a citizen's most important duty. Before you can vote, you must register.

- Participate in your community by joining volunteer organizations.

Reviewing Key Terms

On a separate sheet of paper, write a paragraph describing how you will handle finding and living in your own place. Use the terms below in your paragraph.

commute   security deposit

utilities   register

Recalling Key Concepts

On a separate sheet of paper, tell whether each statement is true or false. Rewrite any false statements to make them true.

1. There are some advantages to living at home for a while after graduating from high school.

2. It's wiser to leave all housekeeping chores for the weekend.

3. Your responsibilities at work are the most important ones you have.

4. Having coworkers as friends is good, but you should try to have friends outside of work too.

5. Your only responsibility as a citizen is to vote.

Thinking Critically

Using complete sentences, answer each of the questions below on a separate sheet of paper.

1. Why should you carefully evaluate anyone whom you are considering as a roommate?

2. Which is most important to you when choosing a place to live—being close to work, the amount of the rent, or living in a safe neighborhood? Why?

3. What's wrong with making friends from work the center of your social life?

4. When a job takes up a good deal of your time, why is it especially important to schedule time with your family and friends?

5. Why do you need to be well informed to fulfill your responsibility as a voter?

SCANS Foundation Skills and Workplace Competencies

Basic Skills: *Knowing How to Learn*

1. Imagine that a proposition is on the ballot for the next election. The proposition calls for a special tax to support state parks. What are three sources of information you might use to form your decision about how to vote on this issue?

Resources: *Allocating Money*

2. You have take-home pay of $1,600 per month. You have a monthly car payment of $150. Your car insurance is $650 every six months. Estimate additional expenses for food, entertainment, clothes, gas and repairs for your car, laundry, and so on. (Refer to Figure 20-2 for any expense categories you may have forgotten.) Base your estimates on your actual spending habits. Use these figures to create a personal budget. Use the budget to figure out how much you can afford to spend on rent and utilities each month.

Connecting Academics to the Workplace

Math

1. You and your roommate have just rented an apartment together. The only furniture you have is bedroom furniture, which you each brought from home. You each have $500 to contribute toward furnishing the new apartment. What should you buy? Make a list of items you need. Then go shopping to find the best prices on those items. Finally, select the items you need most and can afford to buy right now.

Social Studies

2. Sandra has recently taken a job that requires her to move to your city. Except for her new coworkers, she doesn't know anyone there. She has decided she will join an organization or club in order to make new friends. Sandra enjoys dancing, photography, and art. What organizations might she join? Do research to find those related to her interests.

Developing Teamwork and Leadership Skills

Work as a team with three or four classmates. Individually, choose a firm in your area where you might like to work. Then imagine that you and the members of your team have decided to become roommates. Divide up responsibilities and search for a place to live. Estimate your income.

Determine a location and the cost of an actual place. Find out how much it will cost to move in. Interview the landlord to obtain realistic estimates on utility costs.

Real-World Workshop

Imagine that you and a classmate have decided to become roommates. Role-play an interview with each other. Use the checklist shown in Figure 25-1 as a basis for the interview. Then decide if you would get along as roommates.

School-to-Work Connection

Make a list of your interests and hobbies. Then identify a local organization or club that reflects your interests. Visit the organization and talk with some members. Then write your reaction to the group. Tell whether this is a group that you would be interested in joining. Could it be a source of new friendships?

Individual Career Plan

How ready are you to move into an apartment of your own? First, make a list of the furnishings you now have that you could take with you. Then make a second list of all the things you would need to get to move into an unfurnished apartment. Assume that the apartment has a stove and refrigerator. Don't forget items such as pots and pans, dinnerware, silverware, towels, sheets, and so on.

ASPECTS OF INDUSTRY:
Community Issues

Overview

In Unit Seven, you learned about how changes may affect your work life, and about balancing your work and personal lives. In this Unit Lab, you will use what you have learned about change and balance while exploring another aspect of industry: **Community Issues.**

Like people, businesses interact with the communities around them. Their factories may be eyesores to the people living near them, their wastes may pollute the air and water. If a company is a major employer in a community, the community may be crippled if the company closes. On the other hand, industries may contribute to the health of a community through fund-raising, donations, or education programs. Conversely, the community— people who live near the business, other businesses, community organizations, and government—also affects industries.

Tools

1. Internet
2. Trade and business magazines
3. News magazine
4. Newspapers

Procedures

STEP A

Choose a career that interests you from the 15 job clusters outlined in Figure 3-1 in Chapter 3. Working with two or more classmates who have chosen careers in your job cluster or have chosen related jobs in other clusters, brainstorm positive and negative ways industries and communities interact. For example: pollution, poor employee benefits, or financial help following natural disasters.

Using the Internet and trade, business, and news publications, examine how your chosen industry could affect the community. How do decisions made by government, social and environmental organizations, and other businesses affect your industry?

STEP B

As a team, interview a community leader such as a city councilperson, an environmental affairs expert, or social services specialist.

Using the information you obtained from your library research, develop questions to get the person's perspective on how your chosen industry affects the community, both positively and negatively. Also ask how the larger community—government, other industries, and organizations—affects the industry.

Try to balance your questions so that you see both positive and negative sides to the industry. The responses will probably vary according to whom you interview.

Based on your library research and previous interviews, develop questions that address both the positive and negative influences of the industry on the community.

Businesspeople may be sensitive to questions about the negative impact of their industry on the community. Be sure you ask about the positive impacts as well.

As always, dress appropriately, be prompt and courteous, and follow up the appointment with a thank-you note.

STEP C

Next, as a team interview a business person in your chosen industry. You should not choose someone you have already interviewed. Explain that you are doing a class project and want to ask how the particular business deals with environmental, cultural, and social concerns in the community.

REPORT

Write a one-page, word-processed report using the information you gathered in your research and interviews.

● First, look at how your chosen industry affects the community—its health, environment, crime level, social programs, and employment. Is the industry's effect on the community compatible with your values?

● Second, look at how changes in the community affect the industry. Are there changes you can imagine in the future that might affect your job? How can you prepare for those changes?

Keep your research, interview notes, and report in a folder titled "Career Exploration."

Glossary

A

ability A skill a person has already developed. (p. 36)

access To find and use information. (p. 367)

active listening Listening with full attention. (p. 300)

addiction The physical or psychological need for a substance. (p. 217)

affirmative action Action to give those who have suffered discrimination a fair chance. (p. 238)

agenda A list of items to be addressed at a meeting. (p. 288)

allowances Deductions. (p. 464)

analogy A problem-solving strategy in which a person says one thing is like another in order to suggest a solution. (p. 328)

annual percentage rate (APR) The amount of interest for one year, expressed as a percentage. (p. 431)

application fee An amount of money charged to apply for a loan. (p. 430)

application letter A cover letter that accompanies a résumé. (p. 125)

apprentice Someone who learns how to do a job through hands-on experience under the guidance of a skilled worker. (p. 99)

aptitude One's potential for learning a certain skill. (p. 36)

arbitration A hearing at which both sides present evidence and witnesses to an arbitrator, who issues a written decision, just as a judge or jury would do. (p. 245)

arrogance An excessive display of self-regard. (p. 201)

assertiveness The confident presentation of oneself and one's abilities. (p. 200)

assumptions Beliefs a person takes for granted. (p. 328)

attitude A person's basic outlook on life. (p. 194)

audience One or more persons who receive information. (p. 297)

B

bait and switch The fraudulent practice of advertising a bargain item that is not available for sale in the advertiser's store; when customers arrive, a salesperson tries to talk them into a more expensive item. (p. 390)

beneficiary The person who receives a benefit from an insurance company. (p. 439)

benefit Money paid by an insurance company for a loss or some occurrence. (p. 439)

block style A style of written communication in which all lines begin at the left margin. (p. 308)

body language The posture, gestures, and eye contact people use to express themselves nonverbally. (p. 136)

brainstorm To think creatively without evaluating ideas until later. (p. 327)

budget A plan for saving and spending money based on one's income and expenses. (p. 398)

business cycle The movement of the economy from good times to bad and back to good; includes a peak or boom, a contraction, a trough, and an expansion. (p. 384)

business description Specific information about a business's product(s), location, employees, and competitors. (p. 80)

C

cafeteria plan   A plan that allows employees to choose the benefits they want. (p. 167)

career   A series of related jobs built on a foundation of interest, knowledge, training, and experience. (p. 5)

cash-value life insurance   Part insurance and part investment, in which you can borrow money against the total amount of premiums paid on a cash-value life insurance policy. (p. 452)

cause and effect   What happened and what made it happen. (p. 299)

certificate of deposit (CD)   A type of investment in which a person deposits a specific amount of money for a fixed amount of time at a stated interest rate. (p. 419)

check register   A small booklet that allows one to keep track of the money in one's checking account. (p. 426)

chronological résumé   A résumé organized in reverse time order. (p. 122)

civil law   The type of law that pertains to arguments in which one person (or company) claims that another person (or company) has violated rights or neglected responsibilities. (p. 242)

claim   An oral or written notice given to an insurance company to collect for a loss or a certain occurrence. (p. 439)

coinsurance   The percentage of major medical expenses that a policyholder is required to pay. (p. 449)

cold call   A blind telephone call, or a call that is not the result of a lead or a referral, that is made to discover whether there is a job opening or to gain a contact. (p. 116)

collateral   An asset such as a house or a car that could be taken by the lender if a loan is not repaid as promised. (p. 430)

collective bargaining   Using the power of numbers (the workers in a union) to negotiate for better wages, increased benefits, better safety rules, and other job improvements. (p. 236)

collision insurance   Insurance that covers damage to a policyholder's car caused by an accident. (p. 444)

commission   Earnings based on how much a worker sells. (p. 165)

communication   The exchange of information between senders and receivers. (p. 296)

commute   To travel to and from one's job. (p. 505)

company culture   The behavior, attitudes, values, and habits of the employees and owners of a company that are unique to that particular company. (p. 156)

comparison and contrast   The pointing out of similarities and differences. (p. 299)

compensatory time   Paid time off from work, instead of cash, in exchange for working overtime. (p. 235)

compounded   Paid interest on money originally invested and also on any interest that has already been added. (p. 418)

comprehensive insurance   Insurance that covers damage to a policyholder's car for reasons other than a collision. (p. 444)

compromise   To settle a dispute by having each party give up something. (p. 268)

Glossary

confidentiality The keeping of secrets from people who are not supposed to know them. (p. 185)

conflict resolution A problem-solving strategy for settling disputes. (p. 268)

consequence An effect or outcome. (p. 319)

constructive criticism Criticism presented in a way that can lead to learning and growth. (p. 204)

consume To buy and use goods and services. (p. 381)

consumer fraud Dishonest business practices used by people trying to trick or cheat consumers. (p. 389)

consumers Individuals who buy and use goods and services. (p. 381)

contact list A list of people one knows and will contact to build a network. (p. 113)

contingency fee A lawyer's fee based on a percentage of the amount of money that a client wins in a court case. (p. 248)

continuing education Programs offered by high schools, colleges, and universities that are geared toward adult students. (p. 101)

convenience benefits Fringe benefits that make workers' lives easier. (p. 167)

cooperativeness A willingness to work well with everyone on the job to reach a common goal. (p. 174)

cooperative program A program combining school and work in which a local employer teams with a school, hiring students to perform jobs that are taught in school classes. (p. 54)

copayment The amount of money an HMO member pays for each service from a health-care provider. (p. 450)

copyright The legal right of authors or other creators of works to control the reproduction and use of their works. (p. 350)

corporation A business owned by people who buy part of, or shares in, the company. (p. 79)

coverage Losses or events that an insurance company will insure against. (p. 439)

cover letter A letter a job seeker sends along with a résumé to introduce the job seeker to an employer. (p. 125)

credit A sum of money a person can use before having to reimburse the credit lender. (p. 429)

credit application A form that a person must complete when seeking credit; it asks for details about the person's job, salary, bank account(s), and credit history. (p. 432)

credit bureau An agency that collects information on how promptly people and businesses pay their bills. (p. 432)

credit card A card usually issued by a bank or other financial institution that allows the holder to charge amounts of purchases in many different places. (p. 429)

credit limit The maximum amount of money a person can charge against an account. (p. 429)

credit rating An estimate made by a credit bureau that tells how likely an individual is to pay his or her bills. (p. 432)

credit union A not-for-profit financial institution similar to a bank; people who belong share a common bond. (p. 418)

criminal law The type of law under which the government charges an individual or organization with committing a crime. (p. 246)

criteria Standards of judgment. (p. 318)

cross-functional team   A group of people from two or more departments or areas of expertise who work together toward a common business goal. (p. 278)

customer relations   The use of communication skills to meet the needs of business customers or clients. (p. 296)

D

data   Information, knowledge, ideas, facts, words, symbols, figures, statistics. (p. 34)

database   A software program in which information is stored in tables and can be sorted and combined in different ways. (p. 345)

decision-making process   A logical series of steps used to identify and evaluate possibilities and arrive at a workable choice. (p. 24)

deductible   The portion of the cost of a loss that an insurance policyholder pays before the insurance company pays the remaining cost. (p. 439)

deduction   An expense, such as certain medical or business costs, that taxpayers are allowed to subtract from their income when figuring the amount of tax they must pay. (p. 467)

defensiveness   The guarding of oneself emotionally against negative opinions. (p. 205)

defined-benefit plan   A type of pension plan that provides a fixed amount of money at a person's retirement. (p. 421)

defined-contribution plan   A type of pension plan in which the employer contributes a set amount of money to the plan each year. (p. 421)

delegating   Assigning tasks to other people. (p. 364)

deliberate   Purposeful. (p. 243)

dependent   Someone, such as a child, who relies on another person for support. (p. 465)

depression   A very serious recession, or downturn in the economy. (p. 384)

desktop publishing   The use of computers and special software to create professional-looking printouts; uses include reports, brochures, newsletters, invitations, and greeting cards. (p. 346)

directory   A special computer file that contains the names of a group of files on a broad topic; also called a folder. (p. 370)

disabilities   Conditions that include visual or hearing impairment, mental illness, or paralysis. (p. 238)

disabled worker   Someone who cannot work because of a physical or mental condition. (p. 472)

discrimination   Unequal treatment based on such factors as race, religion, nationality, gender, age, or physical appearance. (p. 237)

disputes   Disagreements. (p. 242)

distributing   Making goods and services available, such as by selling or delivering, to the people who need or want them. (p. 380)

diversity   Variety. (p. 269)

dividend   A portion of a fund or an organization's profits. (p. 419)

down payment   The amount of money paid at the time something is purchased through an installment loan. (p. 430)

downsizing   The elimination of jobs in a company to promote efficiency or to cut costs. (p. 485)

downtime   Periods of time when nothing is scheduled. (p. 362)

drug-testing programs   Programs designed to detect illegal drug use. (p. 218)

Glossary

E

economics   The study of how a group produces, distributes, and uses its goods and services. (p. 380)

economic system   A country's way of using resources to provide the goods and services people want and need. (p. 380)

economy   The ways in which a group produces, distributes, and consumes its goods and services. (p. 11)

E-mail   Electronic mail; messages sent from computer to computer. (p. 307)

emergency fund   Money people put aside for needs they cannot anticipate. (p. 404)

emoticons   Groups of keyboard symbols designed to show Internet users' feelings. (p. 349)

empathize   To see someone else's point of view and to imagine oneself in his or her situation. (p. 263)

endorse   To sign one's name on the back of a check before depositing or cashing it. (p. 424)

enthusiasm   Lively interest or eagerness. (p. 198)

entrepreneur   Someone who starts and then runs a business. (p. 68)

enumeration   The listing or citing of key points when speaking or writing. (p. 299)

enunciation   The clear and separate vocalization of each sound in a word. (p. 300)

ergonomics   The applied science that attempts to design work areas that are safe, comfortable, and efficient. (p. 223)

ethics   The moral rules of society; the values that help people decide what is right and what is wrong. (p. 181)

etiquette   Good manners; the rules of polite behavior in dealing with other people. (p. 266)

evaluation   The comparison and contrast of data or possible outcomes to decide which is the best choice. (p. 88)

exclusions   Losses or risks not covered by an insurance company. (p. 439)

exempt   Excused from something, such as having to pay taxes. (p. 464)

exempt employees   Workers who are not eligible to earn overtime pay; generally, those who earn salaries. (p. 165)

exemption   A fixed amount of money that is excused from taxes. (p. 465)

expenses   Money that must be paid out. (p. 400)

exploratory interview   A short, informal talk with someone who works in a career one finds appealing. (p. 54)

F

face value   The amount of a death benefit that an insurance company pays. (p. 452)

facilitator   A leader who helps a team work more smoothly by coordinating its tasks. (p. 280)

fax   Facsimile; a copy or replica of a message received over telephone lines. (p. 307)

felony   A serious crime, such as murder or rape. (p. 246)

finance charges   Fees that lenders charge that are usually based on the amount of money owed. (p. 430)

financial plan   A description of a business's start-up costs, operating expenses, and other costs for its first few months of operation. (p. 81)

financial responsibility   Accountability in money matters. (p. 409)

first aid   Actions taken in a physical emergency before help arrives. (p. 224)

fixed expenses   Expenses that people have already agreed to pay and that must be paid by a particular date. (p. 400)

flexible expenses   Expenses that come irregularly or that people can adjust more easily than fixed expenses. (p. 400)

flextime   An arrangement in which workers construct their own work schedules. (p. 59)

fluctuate   To go up or down, as prices do in a free-enterprise system. (p. 383)

Food Guide Pyramid   A guideline created by the U.S. Department of Health and Human Services to show people the nutrients they need each day. (p. 215)

401(k) plan   A type of pension plan in which an employee contributes a specific portion of his or her salary to the plan each year; employers may match the contribution. (p. 421)

franchise   The legal right to sell a company's goods or services in a particular area. (p. 75)

free enterprise   A type of economic system in which individuals or individual businesses buy and sell and set prices with little intervention by the government. (p. 381)

fringe benefits   Forms of reward for employment beyond salary, including health insurance, vacation and holiday time, and retirement plans. (p. 61)

functional team   A group of people from one company department or area of expertise who work together toward a common business goal. (p. 278)

G

gender   Sex, either male or female. (p. 237)

generality   A broad or indefinite statement. (p. 298)

generalization   A broad law, statement, or principle. (p. 299)

generic products   Products without brand names that usually have plain packaging and are not advertised as brand-name products are. (p. 388)

global economy   The worldwide linkage of national economies. (p. 11)

globalization   The establishment of worldwide communication links between people and groups. (p. 337)

goods   Items that people buy. (p. 11)

goods-producing industries   Industries that provide goods, such as stereo systems, cars, and buildings. (p. 17)

goodwill   The loyalty of existing customers. (p. 75)

gossip   Idle talk or rumor, especially about the personal affairs of others. (p. 207)

grace period   A time during which interest is not charged on a loan. (p. 432)

gross domestic product (GDP)   The total dollar value of all goods and services produced in a country during one year. (p. 385)

gross pay   The total amount of money a person earns. (p. 460)

gross profit   The difference between the cost of a good or service and its selling price. (p. 82)

Glossary

H

health maintenance organization (HMO) A health-care plan that has no deductibles but that usually requires a copayment and offers limited physician choice. (p. 450)

hot call A telephone call made to a referral or to follow up on a lead. (p. 115)

hourly wages Pay that is based on a fixed rate for each hour worked. (p. 164)

I

income Money one receives. (p. 400)

income statement A document showing how much money a business earned or lost during a specified period of time. (p. 82)

income tax return A form that shows how much income a person received from working and other sources and how much tax that person must pay. (p. 463)

indictment Under criminal law, a list of charges the government brings against an individual or organization. (p. 246)

individual career plan The final step in the decision-making process leading to a career. (p. 93)

individual retirement account (IRA) A personal retirement account into which a working person can put a limited amount of money each year; a portion or all of this money may be tax deferred until the person retires, depending on his or her annual earnings. (p. 422)

inflation A sharp increase in the average price of goods and services. (p. 385)

inflection A change in the pitch or loudness of one's voice, often used for emphasis. (p. 299)

initiative A willingness to do what is necessary without having to be told to do it. (p. 176)

installment loans Loans in which people receive money in a lump sum and pay it back in installments, or regularly scheduled payments. (p. 430)

insurance policy A legal contract between a person buying insurance and an insurance company. (p. 438)

interest The money that banks pay depositors for the use of their money. (p. 418)

interests Favorite activities. (p. 4)

Internal Revenue Service (IRS) The government agency that collects federal taxes and oversees the federal tax system. (p. 458)

Internet A worldwide electronic community in which millions of computers and computer users are linked. (p. 117)

Internet job services Web sites, newsgroups, and bulletin boards created by trade organizations, companies, and individuals specifically for job recruitment and career research. (p. 53)

internship A formally defined temporary position, usually unpaid, that often requires a longer-term commitment than volunteering. (p. 55)

interpret To make sense of; to translate. (p. 300)

interview A formal meeting in which a job seeker and an employer meet face-to-face to discuss possible employment. (p. 132)

J

jargon The vocabulary of a particular trade, profession, or group. (p. 306)

job Work that a person does for pay. (p. 5)

job application A document that job seekers fill out so that employers can use it to screen applicants. (p. 120)

job lead Information about a job opening. (p. 112)

job market The demand for particular jobs. (p. 11)

job shadowing Following a worker on the job for a few days to learn the routine. (p. 55)

K

Keogh plan A retirement plan for self-employed people in which a certain percentage of one's earnings can be invested and is tax deferred until one retires. (p. 422)

keywords Descriptive words that tell a computer what to search for. (p. 117)

L

laptop A small, portable computer with a screen and a keyboard. (p. 339)

layoff Job termination that results when a company's business becomes slow. (p. 168)

leadership style How a person behaves when he or she is in charge of other people. (p. 286)

learning styles The different ways that people naturally think and learn. (p. 37)

lease A contract to use something for a specified period of time. (p. 74)

liability insurance Insurance that covers damage or injury for which a policyholder is responsible. (p. 443)

liable Responsible. (p. 243)

lifelong learner A person who makes use of all opportunities to keep his or her skills and knowledge up-to-date. (p. 485)

lifestyle The way a person uses his or her time, energy, and resources. (p. 6)

lifestyle goals The ways in which a person wants to spend his or her time, energy, and resources in the future. (p. 30)

M

major medical coverage Insurance that covers hospital and medical expenses, allowing for full choice of hospitals and doctors but requiring a deductible and coinsurance. (p. 449)

marketing The process of getting goods and services to consumers; includes the packaging, shipping, advertising, and selling of goods and services. (p. 383)

market outlook The potential for future sales. (p. 75)

marketplace The entire realm of trade and business; the "place" where buying and selling go on. (p. 383)

mediation A process in which two opposing people or organizations present their cases to a neutral panel or person who helps them reach a compromise or an agreement. (p. 245)

medical payments insurance Insurance that covers medical expenses of a policyholder and his or her passengers involved in an auto accident. (p. 443)

Medicare A part of the Social Security program that provides health insurance benefits to people who need hospitalization or other medical care. (p. 472)

mentors Experienced coworkers who act as guides or informal teachers for new employees. (p. 159)

minimum wage The lowest hourly wage that an employer can legally pay for a worker's services. (p. 234)

minutes The written record of what is said and done during a meeting, kept by the secretary. (p. 288)

misdemeanor A crime, such as shoplifting, that is less serious than a felony. (p. 246)

mission A company's overall goal. (p. 278)

modem A device that translates digital signals from a computer into sounds that can travel over telephone lines. (p. 307)

N

negligence Disregard. (p. 243)

net pay The amount of income left after taxes and other deductions are taken out. (p. 460)

netiquette Accepted rules of conduct when using the Internet. (p. 349)

net profit The amount of money left after operating costs are subtracted from the gross profit. (p. 82)

networking Communicating with people one knows or can get to know to share information and advice. (p. 112)

new business Any topic brought before the participants of a meeting for the first time. (p. 289)

no-fault system A system of insurance in which insurance companies pay for their policyholders' damage no matter who is at fault in an accident. (p. 446)

nonexempt employees Workers who are covered by a law that entitles them to earn overtime pay. (p. 165)

notice An official written statement that one is leaving a company. (p. 495)

NOW account A negotiable order of withdrawal; a type of checking account that pays interest on deposits but requires a minimum balance. (p. 424)

nutrients The substances in food that the body needs to produce energy and stay healthy. (p. 215)

O

Occupational Safety and Health Administration (OSHA) The branch of the Department of Labor that sets job safety standards and inspects job sites. (p. 222)

on-the-job training On-site instruction in how to perform a job. (p. 99)

operating expenses The costs of doing business. (p. 81)

orientation A program that introduces new employees to their new company and its policies, procedures, values, and benefits. (p. 158)

outsourcing A practice in which businesses hire other companies or individuals to produce their services or goods. (p. 15)

overdrawn An account in which checks have been written for more money than is in the account. (p. 425)

overtime Extra pay for each hour worked in excess of 40 hours per week. (p. 164)

P

parliamentary procedure Strict rules of order for conducting a meeting. (p. 287)

partnership A business arrangement in which two or more people share ownership. (p. 78)

passbook account A savings account with which one receives a booklet in which to record transactions. (p. 418)

pending Temporarily on hold. (p. 367)

pension plan A benefit that builds a retirement fund for each worker. (p. 167)

performance bonuses Rewards given to workers for high levels of performance. (p. 166)

performance reviews Meetings between an employee and his or her supervisor to evaluate how well the employee is doing his or her job. (p. 167)

perseverance The quality of finishing what one starts. (p. 488)

personal career profile form A chart in which one can arrange what one has learned about oneself and what one has learned about a possible career side by side, along with a number indicating how closely the two match. (p. 89)

personality The combination of an individual's attitudes, behaviors, and characteristics. (p. 37)

policyholder A person who buys insurance. (p. 438)

positive self-talk The use of positive statements to "outtalk" one's negative inner voice. (p. 197)

preferred provider organization (PPO) A health-care plan similar to an HMO, with more choice of physicians but with higher premium and copayment costs. (p. 450)

prejudice An unjustifiable negative attitude toward a person or group. (p. 187)

premium The amount of money a policyholder pays for insurance. (p. 439)

previewing Reading only the parts of a document that outline or summarize its contents. (p. 309)

prioritize To put in order from first to last or from most important to least important. (p. 321)

probation The period after an employee is first hired, when he or she is "on trial." (p. 168)

problem solving A technique involving the use of thinking skills to suggest solutions to problems or situations, such as theoretical ones posed by an interviewer. (p. 141)

procrastinate To put off deciding or acting. (p. 321)

producers Companies or individuals who make or provide goods and services. (p. 381)

producing Creating goods or services. (p. 380)

professionalism A mature approach and appropriate behavior in regard to one's job. (p. 203)

profit-sharing plan A program that gives workers a portion of their company's profits. (p. 166)

promotion A job advancement to a position of greater responsibility and authority. (p. 486)

pronunciation How the sounds and stresses of a word are voiced. (p. 300)

purpose An overall goal or aim. (p. 297)

Glossary

Glossary

R

recession   A six-month or longer period when the economy does not grow. (p. 384)

reconcile   To compare items and make them agree; used to refer to a checking account statement and check register. (p. 426)

record keeping   Organizing and maintaining records, often of one's income and spending. (p. 402)

redeem   To cash in. (p. 419)

references   People who will recommend applicants to an employer. (p. 121)

referral   Someone to whom one has been directed who may have information about a job or job opening. (p. 113)

register   To officially sign up as a qualified voter. (p. 517)

regular checking account   A type of checking account that usually does not require a minimum balance but generally charges service fees. (p. 423)

repetitive stress injuries   Injuries caused when the same motions are performed over and over. (p. 223)

resources   Time, money, material, information, facilities, and people needed to get a job done. (p. 317)

responsibility   A willingness to accept an obligation and to be accountable for an action or situation. (p. 177)

résumé   A brief summary of a job seeker's personal information, education, skills, work experience, activities, and interests. (p. 122)

revenue   Income from sales. (p. 82)

role-playing   Acting out a role in a make-believe situation, usually at the request of another person for the purpose of evaluation. (p. 140)

S

salary   A fixed amount of pay for a certain period of time, usually a month or a year. (p. 165)

scan   A method of electronically copying a document into a computer. (p. 124)

schedule   A list or chart showing when tasks must be completed. (p. 359)

school-to-work programs   Programs that bring local schools and businesses together so that students can gain work experience and training. (p. 115)

security deposit   Money a tenant pays a property owner before moving in, usually equal to one or two months' rent. (p. 507)

sedentary   A type of activity in which most of one's time is spent sitting. (p. 215)

self-concept   The way one sees oneself. (p. 37)

self-directed   Responsible for choosing one's own methods for reaching a goal. (p. 276)

self-esteem   Recognition and regard for oneself and one's abilities. (p. 197)

self-management   The act of making oneself do what is necessary to build a better career. (p. 178)

self-starters   Workers who do not always have to be told what to do. (p. 277)

seniority   A position or prestige achieved by working for an employer for a sustained length of time. (p. 487)

service learning   Programs in which students do community service—such as helping to clean up urban neighborhoods—as part of their schoolwork. (p. 55)

service-producing industries   Industries that provide services for a fee. (p. 17)

services   Activities done for others for a fee. (p. 11)

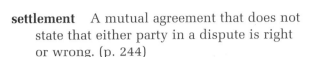
settlement   A mutual agreement that does not state that either party in a dispute is right or wrong. (p. 244)

sexual harassment   Any unwelcome behavior of a sexual nature. (p. 239)

shareholders   The owners of a company who buy shares, or parts, of the company and earn a profit based on the number of shares they own. (p. 79)

simplified employee pension (SEP)   A tax-deferred retirement plan for the self-employed that is simpler and easier to set up and maintain than a Keogh plan. (p. 422)

skills   Developed abilities. (p. 4)

skills résumé   A résumé organized around skills and accomplishments rather than time order. (p. 122)

skimming   Reading quickly for main ideas and key points. (p. 310)

small-claims court   A court that handles disputes over relatively small amounts of money and does not require lawyers. (p. 244)

Social Security   A government program that provides benefits for people of all ages. (p. 471)

Social Security number   A number issued by the federal government that one needs in order to get a job. (p. 120)

sole proprietorship   A business that is completely owned by one person. (p. 78)

spreadsheet   A software program that arranges data in rows and columns; often used for keeping accounts payable records and projecting expenses. (p. 345)

standard deduction   A set amount of money taxpayers may subtract from their income when figuring how much tax they must pay; amount is set by the IRS and based on itemized deductions claimed by thousands of "average" taxpayers. (p. 467)

standard English   The form of writing and speaking taught in school and used in newspapers and on television news programs. (p. 120)

standard of living   A measure of quality of life based on the amount of goods and services individuals can buy. (p. 386)

start-up costs   The expenses involved in beginning a business. (p. 73)

statement account   A savings account with which a person receives a computerized statement of transactions, usually monthly. (p. 418)

stereotype   An oversimplified and distorted belief about a person or group without attention to individual differences. (p. 269)

stress   Emotional and physical tension resulting from the body's natural response to conflict. (p. 142)

style   An individual way of expressing oneself. (p. 306)

subdirectories   Smaller groupings of files within a computer directory. (p. 370)

subject   A main topic or key idea. (p. 298)

summons   An order to appear in court. (p. 244)

Super-NOW account   An enhanced version of the NOW account; a checking account that pays a higher interest rate than a NOW account but also requires a higher minimum balance. (p. 424)

Glossary

Glossary

T

tact   The ability to say and do things in a way that will not offend other people. (p. 259)

taxable income   A person's income after he or she subtracts certain permitted amounts of money for tax-figuring purposes. (p. 459)

taxes   Payments made to support the government and to pay for government services. (p. 458)

team   An organized group that sets goals, makes decisions, and implements actions. (p. 15)

team planning   A process that involves setting goals, assigning roles, and communicating regularly. (p. 278)

technological literacy   Knowing about and being able to use technology effectively. (p. 341)

telecommuting   Using modern technology—especially computers, fax machines, and telephones—to perform a job at home. (p. 16)

teleconferencing   Holding discussions among people in different locations by electronic means. (p. 337)

tenant   A person renting a property. (p. 507)

terminate   To end a worker's employment. (p. 168)

term life insurance   Insurance that provides money to the policyholder's dependents or other beneficiaries if he or she dies. (p. 452)

time line   A type of chart that shows the order in which events occur in time. (p. 359)

tone   Manner or mood, as in writing. (p. 305)

total quality management (TQM)   A theory of management that carefully coordinates company efforts to achieve customer satisfaction and continuous product improvement. (p. 282)

tracking schedule   A chart that identifies the people who will be working on each part of a project and when they will start and finish. (p. 280)

trade school   A privately run institution that trains students for particular types of jobs. (p. 100)

U

unemployment insurance   A state-run social insurance program that provides some temporary income to workers who have lost their jobs. (p. 473)

unfinished business   Any topic brought before the participants of a meeting for at least the second time. (p. 289)

uninsured motorist coverage   Insurance that provides coverage for damage or injuries caused by a driver who is at fault in an auto accident and does not have liability insurance. (p. 444)

utilities   Services for one's dwelling, including electricity, heat, and water. (p. 506)

V

values   The principles a person wants to live by and the beliefs that are important to that person. (p. 31)

viruses   Programs that can damage computer files and even hard drives. (p. 344)

vocational-technical center   A school that offers a variety of skills-oriented programs. (p. 99)

W

warranty   A guarantee that a product meets certain standards of quality. (p. 392)

whole life insurance   A type of cash-value insurance with a savings component, which can build a reserve of money that a policyholder can borrow against or collect when he or she retires. (p. 452)

withhold   Deduct, as money from a paycheck. (p. 459)

word processing   Using any software program that creates text-based documents. (p. 344)

work credits   Measurements of how long a person has worked, a certain number of which the person must earn in order to become eligible for Social Security benefits. (p. 472)

work environment   The social and physical surroundings of a job, which can affect a worker's well-being. (p. 59)

workers' compensation   A state-run social insurance program that provides benefits to workers injured on the job and to dependents of workers killed on the job. (p. 222, p. 473)

work permit   A document needed by workers under 16 and sometimes by those under 18, showing that the young person knows about restrictions on the hours young people can work and the kinds of jobs they can hold. (p. 120)

Index A

Page numbers in *italics* refer to illustrations.

Index

Index

Index

Index

Index

Index

School-to-Work Applications and Connections

School-to-Work Applications and Connections Index

Acknowledgments

Chapter 4

Excerpt from "The Young and Entrepreneurial." From *Occupational Outlook Quarterly,* Fall 1994, a publication of the U.S. Department of Labor. Public Domain. Excerpt from "Overcoming Isolation" by Don Wallace. Reprinted with permission from *Home Office Computing Magazine.* Copyright ©1995.

Chapter 6

Excerpt from "Secrets of Highly Successful Job Hunters" by Annette Foglino. *Glamour,* October 1995. Reprinted by permission of Condé Nast. Excerpt from "How to Find a Job when 'There Aren't Any'" by E. Bingo Wyer, from *Cosmopolitan,* Spring 1992. Reprinted by permission of the author.

Chapter 7

Excerpt from "Into the Loop" by Charlie Drozdyk from *Rolling Stone,* March 23, 1995. Copyright © by Straight Arrow Publishers Company L.P., 1995. All Rights Reserved. Reprinted by Permission. Excerpt with permission from *Inc.* magazine, June 1996. Copyright ©1996 by Goldhirsh Group, Inc., 38 Commercial Wharf, Boston, MA 02110.

Chapter 9

Excerpt from *The 100 Best Jobs for the 1990s and Beyond* by Carol Kleiman. Copyright ©1992 by Carol Kleiman. Published by Dearborn Financial Publishing, Inc./ Chicago. Reprinted by permission. All rights reserved. Excerpt from "Finding, Training and Keeping the Best Service Workers" by Ronald Henkoff. *Fortune,* October 3, 1994. Reprinted by permission. Excerpt from "Office Ethics." First appeared in *Working Woman* in December 1991. Written by Catherine Fredman. Reprinted with the permission of *Working Woman* magazine. Copyright ©1991 by *Working Woman* magazine.

Chapter 10

Excerpt from "How to Get what You Want in '95" from Johnson Publishing Co. (Ebony).

Chapter 11

Excerpt from "Time Out" by John Marks. Copyright © December 11, 1995, *U.S. News & World Report.* Excerpt from *The American Red Cross First Aid & Safety Handbook.* Courtesy of the American Red Cross. All Rights Reserved in all Countries.

Chapter 12

Excerpt from *Sexual Harassment on the Job* by Attorneys William Petrocelli and Barbarea Kate Repa. Copyright ©1995 by William Petrocelli and Barbara Kate Repa, published by Nolo Press.

Chapter 14

Excerpt from *Taking the Mystery Out of TQM* by Peter Capezio and Debra Morehouse. Copyright ©1993. Reprinted by permission of The Career Press, Franklin Lakes, NJ.

Chapter 24

Excerpt from "What I Do for Love" first appeared in *Working Woman* in December 1995. Written by Katherine Griffin. Reprinted with permission of *Working Woman* magazine. Copyright ©1995 by MacDonald Communications Corporation. Excerpt from "Reinvent Yourself" by Caroline V. Clarke. *Black Enterprise,* February 1994. Reprinted by permission of Earl G. Graves Publishing Co., Inc.

Chapter 25

Excerpt from *Business Education Forum,* April 1996. Reprinted by permission. Excerpt from "How's the Job?" by Katie Monagle. *Ms. Magazine,* September/October 1995. Reprinted by permission.